CONTENTS

A LOOK AT PARIS

Writers and poets have extolled the charms of Paris for centuries, and for good reason: It's one of the most seductively beautiful cities in the world, with leafy boulevards stretching from one grand monument to another, magnificent churches, and graceful squares. The Seine River cuts a fetching swath between the city's Left and Right banks. Gardens like the Tuileries and Luxembourg are meticulously laid out, with spraying fountains and elegant statuary. But Paris is not just a pretty face; it's full of historical landmarks and world-class art. Cafe culture is state of the art here, and the local tribe is famously fashionable. The surrounding countryside is equally beautiful, home to storied châteaux like Versailles and Fontainebleau. It's all a feast for the eyes and senses—so here are a few reasons to visit Paris.

Enjoy the Seine in the sun at Paris Plage (p. 206), an annual summer fiesta where portions of the ancient riverbank become a thoroughly modern beach open to all.

The Louvre (p. 144) is one of the world's largest museums, with some 35,000 works of art and countless priceless masterpieces.

Look up: The Louvre was originally built as a palace, so even its ceilings are works of art.

You can explore Paris' St-Martin and de l'Ourcq canals in a self-drive electric boat from Marin d'Eau Douce (p. 199).

The shimmering, stainless steel–covered Géode in the Parc de la Villette holds an IMAX-style cinema (p. 178).

The banks of the Seine are a major gathering spot for Parisians when the weather turns warm.

The elegant Hôtel de Soubise (p. 280) holds the Musée des Archives Nationale.

Molière, Chopin, Jim Morrison, and other notables are buried in the Cimetière du Père-Lachaise (p. 175).

St-Eustache church (p. 151) has long evoked comparison to the Cathédrale de Notre-Dame—especially after the devastating fire to the latter in 2019.

Opened in 1846, the Hôtel Chopin (p. 65) has its entry in one of Paris' passages—covered arcades filled with shops.

The Philharmonie de Paris (p. 232) performs in this acoustically and visually rich space by French architect Jean Nouvel.

The grand foyer of the Opéra Garnier (p. 153).

The stunning Frank Gehry–designed art museum of the Louis Vuitton Foundation (p. 163).

Coco Chanel was one of the many famous people who sipped tea in the Belle Epoque interior of the Angelina tearoom (p. 131).

Stained glass and the beautiful vaulted ceiling of the Cathedral of Sainte-Chapelle (p. 150).

Jazz clubs abound in Paris, but few are as good as New Morning Theatre (p. 236).

The "inside-out" exterior of the Pompidou Centre (p. 155).

The Picasso Paris (p. 161) museum explores the master's vast oeuvre, from his earliest paintings to sculptures from his final years. Bathers at the beach, whether more realistic or somewhat surreal, were a popular subject for Picasso.

The BigLove Caffé (p. 99) in the hip Marais draws crowds for delicious pizza and more made with artisanal ingredients from Italy.

The gleaming white domes of the Basilique du Sacré-Coeur (p. 171) rise above the cafes and streets of Montmartre.

Some Métro stops are sights in themselves. With copper plates, portholes, and ceiling cogs, the steampunk-style Arts et Métiers station resembles a Jules Verne sci-fi submarine.

LEFT BANK

Ernest Hemingway was a regular at Les Deux Magots (p. 134) in St-Germain-des-Prés.

Children can rent vintage toy boats at the Jardin du Luxembourg (p. 186) and set them sailing for around 3€. Doing so in front of the Luxembourg Palace makes the experience even grander.

Many consider Le Bon Marché (p. 215), opened in 1852, the world's first department store. Even its escalators are elegant.

Brilliant stained-glass windows complete the collection of medieval art at the Musée de Cluny (p. 181).

The bones of Parisians line the tunnel walls of the underground cemetery known as Les Catacombes (p. 197).

The domed Panthéon (p. 185) is the final resting place of notable French citizens including Voltaire and Marie Curie.

The Musée d'Orsay, in the old Gare d'Orsay train station, holds one of the world's richest collections of Impressionist and Post-Impressionist art (p. 193).

Rodin sculpture in the formal gardens at the Musée Rodin (p. 195).

The church of St-Etienne-du-Mont (p. 185) embodies a striking mix of Gothic and Renaissance architecture.

Markets like the Marché Raspail (p. 217) tempt shoppers with fresh, beautifully displayed fruits and vegetables.

Venetian mirror makers were considered defectors when they came to France to create Versailles' Hall of Mirrors (p. 252). In fact, the Venetian government was so incensed that it hired assassins to try to kill the artisans.

One of three stained-glass rose windows in the Cathedral of Our Lady of Chartres (p. 255).

The most-visited theme park in Europe, Disneyland Paris has been a smash hit since it opened in 1992 (p. 265).

Generations of French kings, and Napoleon, used the Château de Fontainebleau (p. 262) as a residence.

Claude Monet famously painted his gardens at Giverny (p. 259); they look the same today as they did back then.

One of Fontainebleau's most dazzling spaces, the Salle de Bal is a royal ballroom with colorful frescoes and intricately carved woodwork (p. 264).

A foreword TO THIS EASY GUIDE TO PARIS

BY
ARTHUR FROMMER

It always happens. Toward the end of every TV, radio, or newspaper interview, I am asked, "If you could vacation in only one place in the world, where would it be?" And I disappoint the questioner by responding not with an exotic or colorful choice—such as New Guinea or Montevideo—but simply with the city of Paris. And while the deflated interviewer changes the subject, I go babbling on about how Paris never fails to enchant.

Let Me Count the Ways

It's true—I can never get enough of the City of Light. To me, Paris is on the frontier, the leading edge, of every touristic activity. It rules the roost not only in cuisine—who could deny that?—but also in art and museums; in concerts, dance, and opera; in political discourse and intellectual debate (scan the newspaper headlines if you doubt that); in monuments and history (from the Pantheon to the Tomb of Napoleon); in fashion and shopping; in its cafes and bars (where you can spend the entire afternoon sipping a single glass of wine and not be asked to move on); in the availability of its civic services (get sick and a roaming ambulance with a doctor on board will almost instantly be at your side); in its lusciouslooking open-air markets; in the excitement of its student life; in literature and economics (its resident novelists, philosophers, scientists, and scholars are legendary); and in every other field and endeavor I can name. Return to it for the second time or even the fiftieth—it still seems new.

So obviously, a guidebook series such as ours must have an important volume devoted to Paris. And this one, by Brit-turned-Parisienne Anna Brooke, is surely among the leading examples.

Anna came to Paris some 20 years ago and fell in love with it during a study abroad year. She moved straight back after her studies, thinking she'd stay a year or two, and here she still is! While enjoying the delights of her adopted city, she proceeded to carve out a career as a distinguished travel journalist, whose writings have appeared in numerous prestigious newspapers and magazines. Anna also composes music and lyrics for film and the stage and writes fiction for children.

Although her *Easy Guide to Paris* devotes more-than-sufficient space to organized commercial tours of Paris (including the fabled Bateaux Mouches riverboats), it's clear from the text that she primarily regards Paris as a walking city, to be explored on your own, often while wandering at random. Here, after all, is a metropolis so built to human scale, so lovely in its architectural design, so lined with small shops with their dynamic proprietors, that there is never an uninteresting block in it. Let me repeat: *You can walk its ancient streets for hours and you will never be uninterested.*

I hope that your decision to carry a light-and-manageable Easy Guide will greatly assist you in your enjoyment of Paris, and that Anna's own special perspectives will make your visit full of joy—and memorable.

Cordially,

Arthur Frommer

THE BEST OF PARIS

Paris is a magnificent city, worthy of all the superlatives that have been heaped upon it for centuries. Its graceful streets, soaked in history, really are as elegant as they say. Its monuments and museums really are extraordinary, and a slightly world-weary *fin-de-siècle* grandeur really is part of day-to-day existence. But Paris is so much more than a beautiful assemblage of buildings and monuments. It is the pulsing heart of the French nation.

When you look beyond its beautiful facade, however, you'll see that this is a city where flesh-and-blood people live and work and a place with a palpable urban buzz. Not only is Paris the nation's capital; if you include the suburbs, it is home to 20% of the country's population and is the source of most French jobs. For the best in art, culture, and business, all roads lead to Paris.

Not all that long ago, Paris was not only the navel of France but also the shining beacon of Europe. All the continent's greatest minds and talents clamored to come here: The city seduced Nietzsche, Chopin, Picasso, and Wilde, and then in the 1920s it drew Hemingway and the Lost Generation of American writers and artists. After World War II, it became the iconic backdrop of a new form of cinema: La Nouvelle Vague (the French New Wave), with many cineastes engaging with the political and social unrest of the time.

It is true: From before the French Revolution to the terrorist attacks of 2015, Paris has played center stage to turmoil—much of it romanticized (think "Les Misérables"), some of it too recent to properly put into perspective. But one thing is certain: Upheaval has always been as much a part of its urban makeup as the Seine—which is why Paris' coat of arms features a boat and the motto FLUCTUAT NEC MERGITUR ("She is tossed by the waves but does not sink"), a reminder that no matter what happens, Paris will prevail and protect those within her walls.

And it's true. Despite the heartache of recent years, the Covid-19 pandemic included, Paris is still a bastion of the best of French culture. The culinary legacy alone is enough to fill several books. You can eat your way to nirvana in the city's restaurants, gourmet food stores, and bakeries. The architecture ranges from the lavish opulence of **Place Vendôme** (p. 149) to the contemporary quirkiness of the **Fondation Louis Vuitton** (p. 163). The city is also home to some of the world's greatest museums, including the legendary **Louvre** (p. 144). And let's not even get into its concert halls, nightspots, parks, gardens, and cafes—at least not just yet. Even if you have time to see only a fraction of what you'd like to see, in the long run, it really won't matter. What counts is that you'll have been to Paris, sampled its wonders, and savored the experience—and that counts for a lot.

A view of the Alexandre III bridge and the Place de la Concorde.

THE best AUTHENTIC PARIS EXPERIENCES

○ **Seeing the city from above:** Whether it's from the top of the **Eiffel Tower** (p. 190) or in front of the **Sacré-Coeur** (p. 171), seeing the city from aloft will make your heart sing. Paris' only city-center skyscraper is the **Tour Montparnasse** (p. 196), but even that has a 56th-floor observation deck, from which you can scan the cityscape and see many of the most famous monuments poking out above Haussmann's elegant buildings.

○ **Strolling across the Pont Neuf:** The view from here is dramatic. To one side, you'll see the **Île de la Cité,** and to the other, the **Eiffel Tower** and the **Louvre.** It's a little like standing in the navel of the Parisian universe, and, in fact, you are: The island that this bridge straddles dates back to the city's earliest beginnings.

○ **Walking along the Seine at night:** Paris is beautiful in the daytime, but at night, when many of the monuments are lit up, it's positively bewitching. An evening stroll along the banks of the Seine is about as romantic as it gets. A **nighttime boat cruise** (p. 199) is another great way to enjoy the magic.

○ **Sipping an apéro at a sidewalk cafe at sunset:** After work or before play, Parisians love to meet up to have an *apéritif,* usually a light alcoholic drink like a glass of wine, a French beer, or—the latest trend—a Spritz (a sparkling wine cocktail made with Italian bitter orange Aperol) on a cafe terrace. Join the locals in this early evening ritual and feel like a real Parisian.

Riding a bike through Paris.

o **Soaking up the atmosphere at a street market:** All kinds of Parisians frequent the city's many **covered and open-air markets** (p. 216), which sell fresh fruits, vegetables, meats, cheeses, and other goodies. Don't be afraid to plunge into these noisy places; you'll be participating in a tradition that goes back centuries. Just ask before you touch the merchandise; the vendors do the selecting and the bagging here.

o **Riding a *trottinette* (scooter):** Ever since the advent of the **Vélib'** low-cost bike-rental program (p. 290) in 2007, Paris has been evolving into a two-wheeler city. Now you can try electric scooters (*trottinettes* in French) through rental schemes similar to Vélib'. Download one of the apps (p. 290) to buzz around like a local—the city is small enough and flat enough that riding is a snap.

PARIS' best ARCHITECTURAL LANDMARKS

o **Best monuments to La Gloire (the glory of France):** The **Arc de Triomphe**—the world's largest triumphal arch (p. 162)—is about as grandiose as it gets, at least until you arrive at the magnificent **Place de la Concorde** (p. 170), another flamboyant national gesture. If that's not enough, the church of **La Madeleine** (p. 164) was originally meant to be a temple to military glory, and the **Panthéon** (p. 185) is a church made into a crypt for the nation's intellectual heroes.

o **Best monuments to spiritual glory:** Despite the French obsession with keeping the Republic secular, the capital harbors some of the world's most exquisite churches. No matter what your views are on religion, you'll be bowled over by the soaring towers of the **Cathédrale de Notre-Dame,** even after the 2019 fire (p. 137), the stained glass of **Sainte-Chapelle** (p. 150), or the superb rood screen at **St-Etienne-du-Mont** (p. 185).

Arc de Triomphe on the Avenue des Champs-Élysées.

o **Best monuments to human ingenuity:** Extraordinary engineers and architects have spent time in this city, leaving behind some amazing buildings in their wake. Most famously, the **Eiffel Tower** (p. 190) gracefully reaches for the sky, while exerting minimal pressure on the ground. The land under the Belle Epoque wonder that is the **Palais Garnier** (p. 154) is stabilized by the man-made underground lake that inspired Gaston Leroux's "Phantom of the Opera" story. Modern architects also have made their mark, mostly on the city's museums, be it the inside-out structure of the **Centre Pompidou** (p. 155) or the spaceship-like aluminum shell of the **Philharmonie de Paris** (p. 232).

PARIS' best RESTAURANTS

o **Best for romance:** Thinking of popping the question? Reserve a table at **La Tour d'Argent** (p. 116) and go for it. With its panoramic views over the Seine, legendary kitchen (and wine cellar), and elegant decor, there's no better setting.

o **Best for families:** At **Rosa Bonheur** (p. 115), inside Buttes Chaumont park, parents can enjoy tapas on a large outdoor terrace while their kids play in the grass. French-fry freaks and their meat-eating parents will love **Le Relais de l'Entrecôte** (p. 124), where delicious steak frites with a special sauce is the only thing on the menu..

o **Best splurge:** The second floor of the Eiffel Tower has a restaurant where you can gorge on gastronomic French cuisine. After a refurb and a takeover by the talented chef, Frédéric Anton, the **Jules Verne** (p. 126) is a once-in-a-lifetime place to tuck into dishes like Breton lobster with black truffles, and absinthe and pistachio pavlova. Plus, there's the view: a magnificent bird's-eye sweep over the entire City of Light. Now sigh.

- **Best value:** In a hidden garden on the site of a former distillery, **Laïa** (p. 110) is an unpretentiously classy Mediterranean restaurant specializing in robata-grilled delights. Or try the affordable and ample Breton cooking at **Chez Michel** (p. 113) to satisfy any size appetite.
- **Best classic bistro:** Checkerboard tablecloths, art-clad walls, and a fabulous meat-centric menu? **La Tour de Montlhéry–Chez Denise** (p. 96) has got it all, with the bonus of being open until 5am.
- **Best seafood:** Next door to the much-hyped neo-bistro **Septime** (p. 109) is shellfish-centric **Clamato** (p. 109), an Eldorado for seafood lovers that serves plates of marinated sardines, fish *rillettes* (a sort of pâté), and smoked shrimp (not to mention excellent wine) in a beautifully toned-down dining room. Love oysters? Head to **Huîtrerie Régis** (p. 124); it serves the best in town, straight from Marennes-Oléron on France's west coast.
- **Best for gluten-free:** You don't need to suffer from gluten intolerance to appreciate the delicious home-cooked dishes at **Noglu** (p. 112), a snug little post in the trendy 11th arrondissement.
- **Best for wine enthusiasts:** If what's in your glass is just as important as what's on the plate, saunter over to **Frenchie Bar à Vins** (p. 105) in the Sentier district, where hand-picked wines by *petits producteurs* (small producers) are served alongside ultra-gourmet, tapas-size plates of mussels in artichoke and chorizo sauce, homemade pâté, and roasted cauliflower with smoked yogurt.

Reserve your table at the celebrated and historic La Tour d'Argent (p. 116) at least two weeks in advance.

PARIS' best HOTELS

- **Best view:** You won't want to get up in the morning at **Hôtel Brighton;** you'll be happy just staying in bed and gazing at the panorama, which, depending on the room you stay in, might include the Louvre, Tuileries gardens, or Eiffel Tower. See p. 190.

- **Best for families:** Right by the Bois de Vincennes (the city's eastern park, an ideal spot for a family picnic; p. 207), **Hôtel de la Porte Dorée** offers pretty rooms at very affordable rates and caters to kids with freebies like crayons, toys, and cots. See p. 70.

- **Best splurge:** It's hard to say whether the decor is modern or period at **Hôtel Relais Saint-Germain,** but it doesn't really matter, because it's simply beautiful. The coveted priority seating at **Le Comptoir** (p. 79) downstairs is all dark wood and plush fabrics. See p. 124.

- **Most charming period piece:** L'Hôtel re-creates the ambience of Belle Epoque Paris, when the hotel's most famous resident, Oscar Wilde, was cavorting in the neighborhood until he died here in 1900. It's a bit of Old France right in the middle of the trendy Saint Germain neighborhood. See p. 80.

- **Most eco-friendly:** Off the beaten track in the 11th arrondissement, **Eden Lodge Paris** uses solar panels for all its lighting, has high-tech self-cleaning floor tiles, and serves delicious organic breakfasts. It also overlooks one of the loveliest hidden residential gardens in town. See p. 70.

- **Best for a quirky honeymoon:** A location (quite literally) on the Seine; cool, cabinlike rooms; a hip cocktail bar; and a bijou outdoor pool—**OFF Paris Seine** is the city's first floating hotel and a wacky but romantic spot for couples with a sense of fun. See p. 74.

- **Best value:** Blessed with a prime location in the Marais next to a lovely and leafy square, **Hôtel Jeanne d'Arc Le Marais** is a terrific budget option. See p. 62.

- **Best for street cred:** With a hip brasserie, a cool cocktail bar, and rooms with a vintage-chic vibe, **Hôtel Bachaumont** is the place to be seen. See p. 65.

The classy Hotel Brighton offers a view of iconic Paris sites like the Eiffel Tower and the Louvre.

Contemplate *Mona Lisa's* smile with other admirers from around the world.

PARIS' best MUSEUMS

- **Musée d'Orsay:** A breathtaking collection of pre-, post-, and just plain old Impressionists deck the walls of this museum, including Renoir, Van Gogh, Manet, Degas, Gauguin, and a slew of other masters of 19th-century art. Not only is the artwork incredible, but the building itself, a transformed Belle Epoque train station, is a delight. See p. 193.
- **Musée du Louvre:** One of the world's largest and best museums, this colossus of culture has its share of masterpieces, including the *Mona Lisa,* the *Venus de Milo,* and *Winged Victory.* But aside from these three famous ladies are mountains of other incredible works to see, from ancient Egyptian sculptures to Renaissance masters to stunning gems and jewelry. See p. 144.
- **Musée du Quai Branly:** This ultramodern museum gives center stage to artworks that are often overlooked: those of traditional societies in Africa, Asia, and even North America. You'll find everything from a shaman's cloak from Papua New Guinea to Australian aboriginal art, as well as delicate carvings, intricate weavings, and other masterpieces. See p. 195.
- **Musée Jacquemart-André:** Set in a gorgeous 19th-century mansion, this small museum offers a chance to see exquisite art and also how the other half lived. Highlights include a beautiful winter garden, a collection of Italian Renaissance masters, and a magnificent tearoom with a Tiepolo on the ceiling. See p. 166.
- **Picasso Paris:** This magnificent museum offers a fantastic survey of all things Picasso. Housed in a grandiose 17th-century *hôtel particulier,* the gallery explores the artist's many periods in a beautiful Marais setting and holds ever-changing temporary exhibitions. See p. 161.

THE best FREE & DIRT-CHEAP PARIS

o **Attending a free concert:** Every summer, the Parc Floral (in the Bois de Vincennes) hosts a bevy of free concerts: first the Paris Jazz Festival in June and July, and then Classique au Vert in August. See p. 208.

o **Picnicking in the Jardin du Luxembourg:** You couldn't get richer surroundings if you were at a three-star restaurant, and yet you only pay a few euros for a sandwich. Sometimes being cheap is the best revenge. See p. 186.

o **Seeing Paris from a city bus:** Take your own tour of Paris by bus—for the price of a Métro ticket. Some of the municipal bus lines' routes would put a professional tour bus to shame, like route nos. 63 and 87, which hit many of the city's major sites. Visit www.ratp.fr for route maps. See p. 200.

o **Dawdling over a coffee in a cafe:** Okay, you might pay 2.50€ for a cup of coffee, but that means you can sit for hours watching the world go by in an atmospheric cafe and have an authentically Parisian experience to boot. See p. 135.

o **Discovering artworks for zip:** Hit one of the City of Paris museums, most of which offer free entry to their permanent collections all year round. This means you can see monumental sculpture at the **Musée Bourdelle** (p. 198), visit a stately mansion filled with 18th-century art at the **Musée Cognacq-Jay** (p. 158), and trace the history of Paris in the palatial **Musée Carnavalet** (p. 157) without ever having to open your wallet. See p. 141.

THE best NEIGHBORHOODS FOR GETTING LOST

o **Montmartre:** If you get away from the crowds at Sacré-Coeur, this mythic neighborhood is a great place to wander up and down winding lanes, tilt at windmills, admire the view, and cafe-hop. See our Montmartre walking tour on p. 268.

o **The Latin Quarter:** Once again, the trick here is to ditch the crowds on rue de la Huchette and take off for the less-trampled corners of this historic student quarter, such as near the universities on rue Erasme or down by the delightful **Jardin des Plantes.** See p. 184.

o **The Marais:** Get lost in style in this trendy neighborhood, known as much for its delightful boutiques and hip restaurants as for its magnificent 17th- and 18th-century *hôtels particuliers,* or aristocratic mansions, many of which have been turned into terrific museums. See our Marais walking tour on p. 275.

o **Belleville:** You'll see another side of Paris in this diverse working-class district, where a mix of artists and immigrants have made it into one of the city's most vibrant neighborhoods. **Parc de Belleville** offers wonderful views of Paris; around **rue de Menilmontant,** you'll find cool bars and vintage shops. Farther east is the romantic **Père-Lachaise** cemetery (p. 175).

THE best UNEXPECTED PLEASURES IN PARIS

o **Sipping cocktails on a rooftop:** Watch the sun set over Paris' chimney pots and the distant Byzantine Sacré-Coeur at **Le Perchoir** (p. 240), a hip rooftop cocktail bar and restaurant in the trendy 11th arrondissement.

o **Navigating a self-drive boat along Paris' canals:** You don't need a license to sail one of **Marin d'Eau Douce**'s electric boats, just a sense of adventure. From Bassin de la Villette in the 19th arrondissement, glide along the canals d'Ourcq and St-Martin, taking in the city from an unexpected angle (p. 179).

o **Drinking fizzy water from fountains in the street:** Paris has nine *fontaines pétillantes* dotted about the city, each spouting cold, sparkling tap water—a luxury on a sunny day. Try the fountain at **Parc André Citroën** in the 15th arrondissement.

o **Watching weavers make tapestries:** At the **Manufacture Nationale des Gobelins** (p. 181), you can take a tour and see skilled artists at their giant looms creating magnificent woven works.

o **Sipping mint tea in a Moroccan tearoom:** Dream you're in the Kasbah at the tearoom at the **Mosquée de Paris** (p. 132), which is covered in beautiful mosaic tiles.

Sip your mint tea at the Mosquée de Paris among vivid mosaics and splashing fountains.

PARIS' best OUTDOORS

o **The best gardens:** It's hard to choose between the grand geometry of the **Tuileries** (p. 142), the relaxed elegance of the **Jardin du Luxembourg** (p. 186), or the colorful palette of **Giverny** (p. 259).

o **The best parks:** The **Bois de Boulogne** (p. 205) has lakes, gardens, and even a small amusement park (the **Jardin d'Acclimatation;** p. 204) for your rambling pleasure. The Bois de Vincennes may not have an amusement park, but it does have a medieval castle, the **Château de Vincennes,** complete with ramparts and a keep (p. 208), as well as the **Parc Floral** (p. 208) and the **Parc Zoologique de Paris** (p. 174).

o **The best primrose promenade:** The **Promenade Plantée** (now called Coulée verte René-Dumont; p. 173) must be the world's skinniest garden: From this path atop a former train viaduct, you can stroll among the flowers and greenery from the Place de la Bastille all the way to the Bois de Vincennes.

THE best OF HIP PARIS

o **The coolest culture:** The **Musée Yves Saint Laurent** (p. 168) traces the fashion mogul's world-famous creations and his creative process in his former HQ, a sumptuous Belle Epoque mansion by the Champs-Élysées. The City of Lights wears its name well at the **Atelier des Lumières** (p. 173), a digital art museum in a former iron factory offering immersive light shows that walk you through famous artworks, blown up to smother all walls, floors, and ceilings.

o **The funkiest street food:** **Ground Control** (p. 111) in a gigantic former SNCF hangar has Mexican, Italian, and Central African Republic counters inside, and disused buses outside, hawking everything from ham 'n' cheese crepes to authentic British fish and chips.

o **The hippest bar:** Tucked behind a hidden door at the back of a taqueria, **Candelaria** (p. 243) opened in 2011 as the city's first speakeasy-style cocktail bar, and it's still the best.

o **The trendiest shop:** **Merci** (p. 224) is a fair-trade concept store, with everything from designer vintage clothes to funky household items, and three cozy cafes for a post-purchase respite.

SUGGESTED ITINERARIES & NEIGHBORHOODS

Paris is an embarrassment of riches—with so many wonderful things to see, it's hard to know where to begin. And while you are standing there thinking about it, the clock is ticking and your precious time is shrinking. In this chapter, we offer up detailed itineraries so you can see the city's highlights in a short time without wearing yourself to a frazzle. A couple of custom tours for particular interests provide other options. We also give you an overview of the city layout and break down the neighborhoods one by one, so you can design an itinerary of your own.

ICONIC PARIS IN 1 DAY

If you have just 1 day in Paris, your biggest challenge will be trying not to spend the whole day wishing you had more time. Here's an itinerary that will give you at least a taste of the city and ideas for your next trip. *Start: The Champs de Mars, 7th arrondissement, Métro: Ecole Militaire, RER: Champs de Mars–Tour Eiffel.*

---

1 The Eiffel Tower ★★★

Ideally you've booked an early-morning time slot online beforehand, and it won't take too long to go through security and up to the second or top floor to get a gander at the awe-inspiring view of the city. If you've not bought an advance ticket, try your luck or skip the climb and cross the bridge (Pont d'Iéna) to head up to the esplanade at the **Palais de Chaillot ★**, where you can admire the Iron Lady in all her splendor and take some iconic selfies. See p. 190.

If you haven't done so already, cross the bridge (Pont d'Iéna) and head up to the Palais de Chaillot and the Place du Trocadéro. Hop on the no. 63 bus (direction Gare de Lyon), which will cruise past Les Invalides and down boulevard St-Germain. Get off at stop St-Germain-des-Prés.

Paris Neighborhoods

RIGHT BANK

1 Louvre & Île de la Cité (1st)
2 Opéra & Grands Boulevards (2nd & 9th)
3 The Marais (3rd & 4th)
4 Champs-Élysées, Trocadéro & Western Paris (8th, 16th & 17th)
5 Montmartre (18th)
6 République, Bastille & Eastern Paris (11th & 12th)
7 Belleville, Canal St-Martin & La Villette (10th, 19th & 20th)

LEFT BANK

8 Latin Quarter (5th and 13th)
9 St-Germain-des-Prés & Luxembourg (6th)
10 Eiffel Tower & Les Invalides (7th)
11 Montparnasse (14th & 15th)

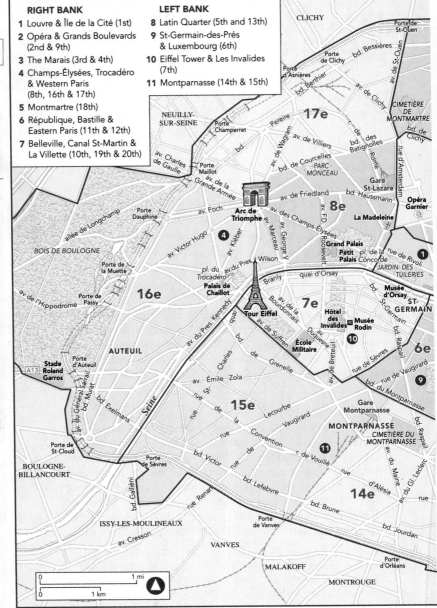

SUGGESTED ITINERARIES & NEIGHBORHOODS

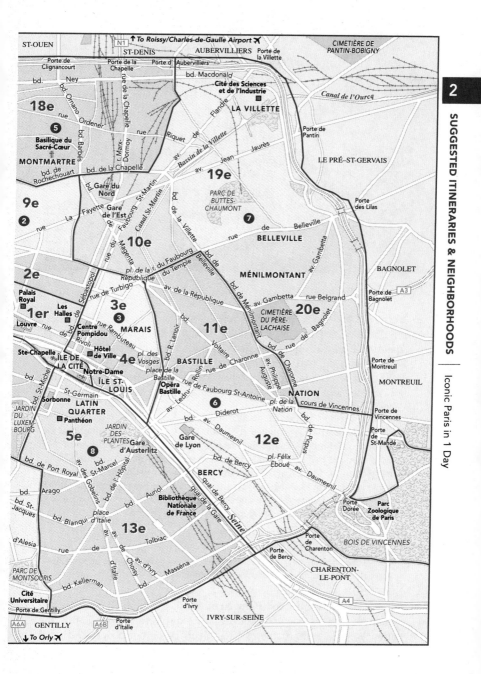

The Eiffel Tower.

2 St-Germain-des-Prés ★★★

First head to St-Germain-des-Prés church ★★ (p. 189), then cross the square to at least stroll by **Les Deux Magots** ★ (p. 134) and the **Café de Flore** ★ (p. 132), two legendary cafes that were the home base of Sartre and De Beauvoir and scores of other artists and intellectuals. The cafes are crowded and pricey for lunch, so here's another option:

Lunch at Marché St-Germain ▣

If you wander a little farther down boulevard St-Germain and take a right on rue Mabillon, you'll find yourself at the Marché St-Germain, a covered market that is half shops and half market stalls filled with delectable goodies (closed Mon). Either pick up the fixings for a picnic here or try one of the dozens of restaurants that surround the market. My personal favorite is **Chez Fernand** (p. 123), which looks the part in red-and-white checkered tablecloths; it serves lip-smacking French classics like beef bourguignon and chocolate soufflé.

Walk back out to boulevard St-Germain and turn right and continue to rue de l'Ancienne Comédie and turn left to Carrefour de Buci; then veer right on rue Dauphine and continue down to the Seine (admiring the galleries and antiques shops as you go). When you reach the river, cross the Pont Neuf.

3 Île de la Cité ★★

Admire the view from the **Pont Neuf** ★ (p. 158), which straddles the island. Wander around the pretty **Place Dauphine** ★ (you'll find the entrance opposite the statue of King Henri IV on horseback) and stroll along the quays of this island, where some of the first Parisians set up camp. Dominating its eastern edge is glorious **Notre-Dame cathedral,**

Please be aware that some places covered in this chapter may require advance booking with a time slot. As we went to press, visitors were also required to wear a mask and/or show proof of Covid vaccination (see box p. 285) or a negative PCR test in order to enter many indoor venues. Procedures and requirements can change regularly, so stay up-to-date by checking the official website for each place, along with the following websites (in English): the French government website (www.gouvernement.fr/en/coronavirus-covid-19) and the Paris Tourist Office (https://en.parisinfo.com/practical-paris/info/guides/info-disruption-paris).

probably still under mounds of scaffolding after the 2019 fire. If you opted for a picnic lunch, the tree-shaded **Square du Vert Gallant** (a park at the very tip of the island) is a lovely spot.

From Notre-Dame, cross over the Pont d'Arcole, turn left onto Quai de Gevres and walk to Place du Châtelet. If you are tired, you can take the no. 7 Métro from here to Palais-Royal–Musée du Louvre. Otherwise, you can walk another 10 minutes or so down the Quai de la Mégisserie and Quai du Louvre to the Louvre.

4 The Louvre ★★★

The sheer enormity of the former royal palace has to be seen to be believed. Turn right onto rue de l'Amiral de Coligny and admire its eastern facade, framed by Claude Perrault's 1660s Colonnade, a classical French facade of Corinthian columns. Below the columns is a passageway through to the Louvre's Cour Carrée, a sumptuous Renaissance-era courtyard. If the passage is open, enter here. If not, you'll have to turn left onto rue de Rivoli and walk to the main Cour Napoléon square (home to the museum's iconic glass pyramid) along the outside (entering at the first available passage). Save visiting the museum for the next trip and wander through to the **Tuileries Garden ★★★**. See p. 144.

5 Tuileries Garden ★★★

There are worse ways to spend a late afternoon than strolling through formal French gardens (p. 142) studded with statues by Rodin and Maillol. The Tuileries has play areas for children, cafes for grown-ups, and ponds that everyone can loll beside. And if you're desperate to see at least one famous artwork on your day, Monet's water lilies are housed at the **Musée de l'Orangerie ★★** in the gardens' southwest corner. You'll need to plan ahead and make an online reservation to get into the museum.

Stroll west through the gardens until you arrive at the Place de la Concorde.

6 Place de la Concorde ★★★

From this vantage point, you can not only take in the Place itself (p. 170) but also peer down the **Champs-Élysées ★★** and see the **Arc de Triomphe ★★★** (p. 162) in the distance.

The Jardin des Tuileries, near the Louvre.

If you still have energy in the evening, finish your visit with an **evening cruise** along the river (see "Boat Tours," p. 199), during which you can admire just about all of the above gussied up in elegant lighting effects.

ICONIC PARIS IN 2 DAYS

Now you have a little more space to breathe. This itinerary also starts at the Eiffel Tower, but then takes off in another direction. *Start: The Champs de Mars, 7th arrondissement, Métro: Ecole Militaire, RER: Champs de Mars– Tour Eiffel.*

Day 1

1 The Eiffel Tower ★★★

You could just turn up, but post-Covid it is likely that you won't be able to access the tower without reserving your ticket (which gives you a time slot for both the lifts and stairs) in advance, so be prepared for a little forward planning. Once you've seen the second and top floors, make sure you stop for coffee on the first-floor terrace, where you can sip with the monument's graceful girders towering above you. See p. 190.

Take the RER C to St-Michel–Notre-Dame.

2 The Latin Quarter ★★★

Admire the Place St-Michel and the Boul' Mich (boulevard St-Michel) and try to imagine it all filled with long-haired students throwing *pavés* (paving stones) during the heady days of May 1968, when protesters brought the country to a standstill. Then wander up the boulevard and consider stopping in at the **Musée de Cluny** ★★ (p. 181). After, continue up past the dome of **La Sorbonne** (one of France's oldest universities, founded in 1257) to the **Jardin du Luxembourg** ★★★ (p. 186). Either picnic here or settle down at a nearby table:

Lunch near the Jardin du Luxembourg 🍷
If it's a weekday and you are hungry, enjoy a terrific meal at **La Ferrandaise** (p.123), about a block away (closed Sun, also Mon lunch). If you just want something light, and/or La Ferrandaise is closed, stop in for a *croque-monsieur* (a French version of a grilled cheese sandwich) or a salad at **Le Rostand,** a Belle Epoque cafe with a lovely terrace just across the street from the gardens (6 pl. Edmond Rostand, 6th arrond.; https://lerostand.fr; ⓒ **01-43-54-61-58; RER: Luxembourg**).

Walk up rue Soufflot toward the stunning domed Panthéon at the top of the hill.

3 Le Panthéon ★★

Marvel at the neoclassical proportions of this national mausoleum's magnificent interior dome, home to a Foucault pendulum, the device that first proved the Earth's rotation. See p. 185.

Back on rue Soufflot, turn right down rue Saint-Jacques, the city's old Roman road, and cross the Seine to Île de la Cité.

4 Notre-Dame ★★★

Head to the cathedral to see (from the outside) how the renovation work is going: When a fire consumed its roof in 2019, threatening to engulf the entire structure, France received almost a billion euros in donations in just 24 hours. See p. 137.

Walk across the Pont d'Arcole to the Right Bank and the Place de l'Hôtel de Ville.

5 The Marais ★★★

By now you deserve a break from the city's icons and are ready to shop or just sit in a cafe in this trendy—and beautiful—neighborhood. If you are still hungry for culture, you could visit one of the many museums here, but if not, save them for another day/trip. Around sunset, stop by **Place des Vosges** ★★★ (p. 162) for a pre-dinner *apéritif* before you hunt down a restaurant (see p. 98).

Day 2

1 The Louvre ★★★

Reserve in advance to start your day as early as possible at this megamuseum (p. 144), which should keep you going until at least lunchtime, when you can either call it quits or simply take a nice long break and eat at one of the restaurants recommended on p. 91. If you are in a hurry to get back to the artwork, grab a sandwich from one of the lunch counters under the pyramid. After the Louvre, you can recover in the **Tuileries Garden** ★★★ (p. 142).

Le Nemours ☕

If you need refreshment after the Louvre (and who doesn't?), this slick cafe on the Place Colette (right next to the Palais Royal, p. 147) is an excellent choice. Great pastries, too.

Stroll west through the Tuileries Garden until you arrive at the Place de la Concorde.

2 Place de la Concorde ★★★

From this grandiose, traffic-clogged plaza (p. 170), you can look down the **Champs-Élysées** ★★ and see the **Arc de Triomphe** ★★★ (p. 162) in the distance.

Take the bus no. 84 or 94, or Métro line 12 (direction Mairie d'Issy) to the 6th arrondissement.

3 St-Germain-des-Prés ★★★

End your day in this delightful Left Bank neighborhood, where you can visit two of the city's loveliest churches (**St-Germain-des-Prés,** p. 189; **St-Sulpice,** p. 189), check out famous literary cafes (**Les Deux Magots,** p. 134; **Café de Flore,** p. 132), or shop 'til you drop. Then find a restaurant (p. 123), after which you can explore the nearby nightlife.

ICONIC PARIS IN 3 DAYS

Now that you've seen all the absolute must-sees, you have time to explore some of the great stuff you've missed. Here is a third day of discovery. *Start: Musée d'Orsay, Métro: Assemblée Nationale, RER: Musée d'Orsay.*

Day 3

1 Musée d'Orsay ★★★

Reserve ahead to spend the morning enjoying this incredible collection of Impressionist and 19th-century artworks (p. 193), and then break for lunch at one of the museum's three restaurants (light snacks, chic cafeteria, or full-on Belle Epoque restaurant). If Impressionists aren't your thing, you could start the day looking at non-Western tribal art at **Musée du Quai Branly** ★★★ (p. 195).

Leave the museum and take the steps down to the banks of the Seine. If you are starting from Musée d'Orsay, turn left (west); if you are coming from Musée du Quai Branly, turn right (east).

2 Les Berges ★★★

Weather willing, enjoy the restored riverbanks (p. 206), strolling westward. Once a busy roadway, this embankment is now a delight for pedestrians, with floating gardens, running lanes, and gourmet snack bars (May–Oct only).

At the Pont Alexandre III, go up the stairs and admire the winged horses hovering above before going down into the Métro Invalides and taking line 13 (direction Asnières or St-Denis) and changing to line 12 (direction Porte de la Chapelle) at Gare

Sacré-Coeur Basilica in Montmartre.

St-Lazare. Get off at Place des Abbesses. Take the elevator up (don't get smart and take the stairs; it's a looong way up).

3 Montmartre ★★★

While away the rest of the afternoon on top of this scenic hill ("La Butte"), clambering around the cobbled streets and perhaps taking a walking tour (p. 268). Visit the **Musée de Montmartre** (p. 172) to lounge in its garden cafe and find out more about the artists and poets who made this neighborhood famous, and **Dalí Paris** (p. 172) to see France's only museum dedicated to the surrealist master, Salvador Dalí. Around sunset, take in the panorama in front of **Sacré-Coeur** (p. 171), and bid adieu to Paris with a drink at one of the cafes on **Place des Abbesses** (p. 268).

AN ITINERARY FOR FAMILIES

Paris can be a challenge with kids, especially if they're in strollers (sidewalks are narrow and uneven, and the Métro is filled with stairs), and parents may grow frustrated because there are so many wonderful grown-up things to see and do. The trick is to admit to yourself that you just won't see as much as you'd like to, and to schedule lots of playtime. In the end, everyone will be less stressed out and happier, even if you didn't get to all 14 of those museums you had dreamed of visiting.

Spend the morning at the **Jardin du Luxembourg** (p. 186), where your offspring can go wild at the huge **playground, sail boats** in the fountain, **ride a pony** (weekends and Wed afternoons, weather permitting; daily during Paris school holidays; see www.animaponey.com), or just run around and have fun. Depending on your situation, parents can take turns sneaking off to visit nearby attractions, such as the **Panthéon** (p. 185), **Musée Zadkine** (p. 188), and **St-Etienne-du-Mont** (p. 185), or find peace and quiet in a **Latin Quarter** cafe (p. 116). Then walk down to **St-Germain-des-Prés** (p. 189) and peek into the church before lunching at **Le Relais de l'Entrecôte** (p. 124). After lunch, walk to boulevard St-Germain and catch the no. 86 bus to the **Champs de Mars,** where you will cross a playground-filled park to the **Eiffel Tower** (p. 190). After that, everyone will be pooped. Thankfully, the **boat ride on the Seine** leaves just down by the river.

Day 2

Start your day at the **Jardin des Plantes** (p. 180), where you can choose between the **Museum National d'Histoire Naturelle** (p. 184), the **Ménagerie** (a small zoo; p. 180), and the **playground.** There's also a fun boxwood **labyrinth** at the top of a little hill. Lunch at the nearby **Mosquée de Paris** (p. 132), a lovely tearoom attached to the Paris Mosque that has an outdoor enclosed patio. Then, if there are wannabe eggheads in your crew, hop on Métro line 5 to Jaurès and stroll along the Canal de l'Ourcq to the **Cité des Sciences et de l'Industrie** (p. 176), a hands-on science museum in **La Villette** (p. 178). The museum includes a section for young kids, and the vast canal-side park outside is filled with play areas and grassy expanses. If you're with older kids, you could even rent an electric self-hire boat from **Marin d'Eau Douce** from the Bassin de la Villette (p. 199; no license required; by Métro Jaurès) and watch the sunset as you sail along the Canal de l'Ourcq.

Day 3

Kids may not appreciate the view at **Sacré-Coeur** (p. 171), but they will enjoy the ride in the **funicular** that you take to get there (follow the signs from the Abbesses Métro stop). Once there, you'll find lots of buskers for entertainment. After toodling around Montmartre, grab a quick bite to eat at **Coquelicot** (24 rue des Abbesses, 18th arrond.; www.coquelicot-montmartre.com; ℂ **01-46-06-18-77**), a kid-friendly cafe-cum-bakery on rue des Abbesses. Or, if you're with a toddler, stop by the **Musée de Montmartre** (p. 172) and pay 5€ (or visit the museum) to enter its walled garden, where a basic cafe serves quiches and cakes, and you can let your little one run around without having to worry about passing cars (though there is a little pond). It's off the beaten tourist track too, thus offering a welcome respite from the clogged streets outside. After lunch, wander around the **covered passages** off the Grands Boulevards (see "Arcades," p. 211), where you can window shop to your heart's content and reward everyone's good behavior with a visit to **Grévin** (p. 153), a fun, and somewhat kitschy, wax museum just off the Passage Jouffroy.

PARIS FOR ROMANTICS

Paris must be the honeymoon capital of the world, and for good reason—it seems like every time you turn a corner you see something beautiful. Here is a 2-day itinerary for a romantic getaway, or just for hopeless romantics. *Start: Pont Neuf, in front of the statue of Henri IV.*

Day 1

This itinerary starts in front of a statue of one of France's great romantic kings, Henri IV, who was known for his good humor and love of wine, women, and song. Walk down the steps to the pretty **Square du Vert Galant,** a quiet garden at the very tip of the island where you can contemplate the fantastic view and/or make out without anyone bothering you (in general, make-out sessions are well-tolerated, and even applauded, in public parks here). From here, you can walk to the **Louvre** (p. 144) and take in endless representations of people in love, from all eras. If you're into wine, a *plat du jour* (daily special) at quaint, cozy **Juveniles** wine bar, washed down with a crisp chardonnay, will do the trick (p. 96).

Henri IV, also known by the epithet "Good King Henri."

After lunch, drift over to the **Palais Garnier,** also known as the Opéra Garnier (p. 153), the city's sumptuous opera house, where a true romantic will have bought tickets to an evening ballet. Or for some quirky romance, sign up for a virtual reality flight over Paris at **FlyView** (p. 152) to soar through the air in jetpacks and see the city's monuments close up, including Notre-Dame as it was before the fire. When it's time to think about dinner, you're right by the Japanese Quarter, which covers several streets around rue Ste-Anne. Grab a tasty *okonomiyaki*, a Japanese savory pancake topped with sauce, at **Aki** (p. 97), or head back toward the Louvre to **Le Fumoir** (p. 96) for Scandinavian-French fusion food. As night falls, the obligatory romantic stroll is along the pedestrian-only **Pont des Arts** (p. 158), where you can take in the gorgeously illuminated monuments lining the Seine.

Day 2

After sleeping in, start your day with a late breakfast at **Le Petit Cler** (p. 129), an adorable cafe on, that's right, rue Cler. After, mosey over to the **Musée Rodin** (p. 195), where you can contemplate, and even imitate, Rodin's famous marble sculpture *The Kiss*. When you are done inside, amble about the beautiful gardens and enjoy other legendary works, such as *The Thinker*. If it's nice out, grab a **Vélib'** (p. 290) and cycle down to the remodeled banks of the Seine, **Les Berges** (p. 206), where you can cycle or stroll free and easy by the river below the Quai d'Orsay. If the weather doesn't suit a bike ride, take the no. 13 Métro up to Miromesnil and have tea at the beautiful **tearoom** at the **Musée Jacquemart-André** (p. 132). Visiting the museum afterward is well worth an hour of your time (p. 166). Otherwise, it's time to start thinking about the evening's activities. Jazz lovers should head to **Duc des Lombards** (p. 236); others will be just fine with **La Bellevilloise** (p. 238) in trendy Ménilmontant, where you can eat, drink, and dance the night away. For late-night cocktails, hit the **Candelaria,** a speakeasy-like spot hidden at the back of a taqueria (p. 243).

CITY LAYOUT

One of the nice things about Paris is that it's relatively small. It's not a vast megalopolis like Tokyo or London. Paris *intramuros,* or inside the long-gone city walls, measures about 87 sq. km (34 sq. miles), excluding the parks of Bois de Vincennes and the Bois de Boulogne (which both lie just beyond the edge of the center), and the city counts a mere 2.2 million inhabitants. The suburbs, on the other hand, are sprawling.

Getting around is not difficult, provided you have a general sense of where things are. The city is vaguely egg shaped, with the Seine cutting a wide, upside-down U-shaped arc through the middle. The northern half is known as the **Right Bank,** and the southern, the **Left Bank.** To the uninitiated, the only way to remember is to face west, or downstream, so that the Right Bank will be to your right, and the Left to your left.

The city is neatly split up into 20 official *arrondissements,* or districts, which spiral out from the center of the city. The lower the number of the arrondissement, the closer you'll be to the center. As the numbers go up, you'll head toward the outer city limits. The lower-numbered arrondissements also correspond to some of the oldest parts of the city, like the Louvre and the Île de la Cité (1st arrond.) or the Marais (3rd and 4th arrond.). Note that the arrondissements don't always correspond to historical neighborhoods.

If you are in the city for more than a few days, download the app created by the city's transit authority, the RATP. Called "Next Stop Paris," this free app (available via www.ratp.fr as well as iTunes) will guide you around town on public transportation. You may also want to download such usable offline apps as CityMaps2Go, MAPS.ME, and Citymapper.

Paris is old, so the logic of its **streets and avenues** is often as contorted as the city's history. That said, some major boulevards function as reference points. On the Left Bank, boulevard St-Michel acts as a more or less north–south axis, with boulevard St-Germain cutting a vaguely east–west semicircle close to the city center and boulevard Montparnasse cutting a larger one farther out. On the Right Bank, boulevard de Sébastopol runs north–south, with rue de Rivoli crossing east–west near the river. As rue de Rivoli heads east, it turns into rue de St-Antoine; to the west, it jogs around the Place de la Concorde and becomes the Champs-Élysées. Farther north, a network of wide boulevards crisscrosses the area, including boulevards Haussmann, Capucines, and Lafayette.

Large avenues converge at several enormous star-shaped traffic round-abouts: On the Left Bank Place Denfert-Rochereau and Place d'Italie are major convergence points; on the Right Bank Place de la Bastille, Place de la Nation, and Place de la République reign to the east, and Place de Charles de Gaulle (also called Etoile), home of the Arc de Triomphe, commands to the west.

NEIGHBORHOODS IN BRIEF

Paris is a city for walkers. One lovely neighborhood after another unfolds along its sidewalks, punctuated by plazas and monuments that are best experienced at ground level. At every turn there seems to be an intriguing area that begs to be explored.

The Right Bank
LOUVRE & ÎLE DE LA CITÉ
Best for: *Museums, historic sights, architecture, transportation hubs*
What you won't find: *Evening entertainment, quiet streets*
Parameters of the neighborhood: *1st arrondissement & part of the 4th*

This is the heart of the city, and the oldest part of Paris, though you'd never know it to see it now. In the 19th century, Baron Haussmann, Napoleon's energetic urban planner, tore down almost all of the medieval houses that once

Rue Montorgueil in Les Halles district.

covered this area. The **Île de la Cité** is where the city first emerged after Gallic tribes started camping out here in the 3rd century B.C. By the 1st century A.D., the Romans were building temples, and by the Middle Ages, a mighty fortress sat across the river on the Right Bank. The fortress has long since been incorporated into the majestic buildings of the **Louvre** (p. 144), which along with the **Jardin des Tuileries** (p. 142) takes up a big chunk of the neighborhood. (You can see vestiges of it—the old stone foundations—in the **Carousel du Louvre,** an underground shopping mall set below the museum.) Today, the Île is mostly visited for the soaring **Cathédrale de Notre-Dame** (p. 137) and the gemlike **Sainte-Chapelle** (p. 150), along with the **Conciergerie,** a palace turned revolutionary prison (p. 140).

On the neighborhood's eastern edge, **Les Halles** (the city's former food market) is where Parisians go for shopping, particularly along the bustling **rue de Rivoli** and around the remodeled **Forum des Halles** mall and park (p. 142). When the covered food market was demolished and relocated to the suburban town of Rungis in the 1970s, Les Halles lost its charm—and unfortunately, despite its multimillion-euro refurbishment, it's still not particularly picturesque. It is, however, a hot spot for high-street boutiques and late-night bistros. And it's officially part of the "Golden Triangle of Les Halles," a vast, triangular-shaped area of gentrification that is home to three new hot spots:

the Pinault Collection, a contemporary art museum in the former Bourse de Commerce stock exchange (p. 137); the revamped La Samaritaine department store (p. 214); and the upmarket Poste du Louvre mall (opening early 2022; p. 214). During the day, the area's very safe—if overcrowded—but avoid its Châtelet-les-Halles RER station late at night, as troublemakers sometimes hang out. The same is true of the seedy rue St-Denis, just to the east, as this is one of Paris' red-light districts.

OPÉRA & GRANDS BOULEVARDS

Best for: *Good restaurants, covered shopping arcades, boutiques*
What you won't find: *Monuments (with the exception of the Opéra Garnier) and museums, green spaces*
Parameters of the neighborhood: *2nd & 9th arrondissements*

When the Grands Boulevards were plowed through the city in the 19th century (see box above), they created a new opportunity for stylish Parisians to stroll, see, and be seen, and theaters and cafes flourished. Times changed and so did fashion, and for decades this area was considered a has-been. In recent years, it's undergone a transformation, particularly in the 9th arrondissement, where cafes, boutiques, and restaurants have popped up in

---

Baron Haussmann: A Man with a Plan

The Paris you see before you was radically transformed in the late 19th century by a pugnacious urban planner named Georges-Eugène Haussmann. Before Haussmann got his hands on it, Paris was a mostly medieval city of tiny streets and narrow alleyways—and major sanitation problems. Everyone agreed that something needed to be done to facilitate traffic and clean up the city, but no one managed to come up with a solution.

Enter Baron Haussmann. Named prefect of the Seine by Napoleon III, Haussmann pushed through wide boulevards (Malsherbes, Haussmann, and Sébastopol, among others), demolished dozens of old neighborhoods, and encouraged promoters to build new buildings, following, of course, his strict rules on the style of the facades and the height of the structures. The result was the elegant Haussmannian architecture that lines most of the city's streets, as well as

the system of central arteries that collect in star-shaped intersections at various points. The boulevards were strategically placed—one of the reasons for their creation was to make it easier to crush rebellions in the workers' quarters, and garrisons were set up at crucial intersections. Streets were also now too wide in most areas to be easily barricaded. Haussmann also accessorized his new neighborhoods and streets; the famous kiosks, benches, and lampposts you see around the city today date from this epoch.

While there's no denying that his projects improved traffic, sanitation, and security and gave a pleasing architectural unity to the cityscape, Haussmann's take-no-prisoners approach has been criticized for having neutered the personality of entire neighborhoods (the Île de la Cité, for example, was almost entirely razed) and destroying important historical buildings.

between the church of St-Georges and Place de Clichy, in an area that used to be known as "New Athens." Many artists of the 19th-century Romantic movement, like George Sand and Eugène Delacroix, lived and worked here; the quaint **Musée de la Vie Romantique** (p. 152) is worth an hour's visit, with beautiful trinkets, letters, and drawings that once belonged to Sand. Today, those in the know call it SoPi (South of Pigalle), as entrepreneurial Parisians have begun opening trendy bakeries, shops, and restaurants.

The 9th is also the home of the **grands magasins** (big-name department stores), which are located on boulevard Haussmann near Gare St-Lazare, as well as the grandiose **Palais Garnier** (p. 153), home of the Opéra de Paris. An important monument in the 2nd arrondissement is the neoclassical **Palais Brogniart,** built between 1808 and 1813 on Place de la Bourse to house the city's former **Bourse,** the French stock exchange. To the east, the trendy set descends on **rue Montorgueil,** a picturesque, cobbled market street, and the pedestrian area around **rue Etienne Marcel,** which has gained a reputation as a hip fashion district. To the west, the city's restaurant-filled **Japanese Quarter** is found on and around rue Ste-Anne. This also is the arrondissement where you'll find **FlyView** (p. 152), Paris' quirky virtual reality tour, and the greatest concentration of *passages,* the **18th- and 19th-century covered shopping arcades** that were the forefathers of today's shopping malls (but much prettier; see "Arcades," p. 211).

THE MARAIS

Best for: Restaurants, nightlife, window-shopping, 17th-century mansions, museums
What you won't find: Bargain shopping, iconic sights, open spaces
Parameters of the neighborhood: 3rd & 4th arrondissements

What was once marshy farmland (*marais* means "marsh" or "swamp") quickly became a seat of power when the Knights Templar decided to build a fortress here in the Middle Ages. Other religious orders followed suit, and after King Charles V built a royal residence here in the 14th century, the ensuing real-estate boom produced a slew of mansions and palaces. In the 17th century, King Henri IV created a magnificent square bordered by Renaissance-style townhouses, today called the **Place des Vosges** (p. 162). If Marais real estate was in demand before, then after the Place des Vosges it was positively off the charts. Nobles and bourgeois pounced on the neighborhood, each one trying to outdo the other by constructing more and more resplendent *hôtels particuliers,* or private mansions.

By the time the Revolution flushed out all its aristocrats in the 18th century, the overstuffed quarter was already falling out of fashion. The magnificent dwellings were abandoned, pillaged, partitioned, and turned into stores, workshops, and even factories. The new residents were working class, with more immediate concerns than saving historic patrimony. The neighborhood fell into disrepair, and periodic attempts on the part of the city to "clean up" unfortunately resulted in the destruction of many architectural gems.

The area underwent a real renovation in the 1960s, and today several of the most **magnificent mansions** have been restored and are open to the public in the form of museums such as the **Carnavalet** (p. 157), **Musée Cognacq-Jay** (p. 158), and the **Picasso Paris** (p. 161). The architecturally odd **Centre Pompidou** (p. 155) is also located here.

Today the area is terribly *branché* (literally, "plugged in"), and you'll see some of the hippest styles in boutique windows here, as well as dozens of happening restaurants and bars lining the narrow streets. The neighborhood remains a mix, though—jewelry and clothing wholesalers bump up against stylish cafes and shops. The vibrant gay scene around rue Vielle du Temple intersects with what's left of the old Jewish quarter on **rue des Rosiers.**

CHAMPS-ÉLYSÉES, TROCADÉRO & WESTERN PARIS

Best for: Serious strolling (on the Champs-Élysées), museums, monuments, chic restaurants, and stores

What you won't find here: Affordable eateries or hotels, regular folk

Parameters of the neighborhood: 8th, 16th & 17th arrondissements

The **Champs-Élysées** cuts through this area like an asphalt river—it's the widest boulevard in Paris. Crossing the street here feels a bit like traversing a raging torrent (be sure to wait for the light). This epic roadway has its fans and foes. Some find its lights and sparkles good clean fun, while others dismiss it as crass and commercial. I find it lacks a soul. No matter how you may feel about the street itself, you're bound to be impressed by the **Arc de Triomphe** (p. 162), which lords over the boulevard from its western tip. To the south of the Champs are some of the most expensive stores, restaurants, and homes in the city, particularly around avenue Montaigne. This is also where you'll find the **Musée Yves Saint Laurent** (p. 168), dedicated to the couturier's life and career. To the north, a largely residential area extends up to the beautiful **Parc Monceau** (p. 169), which is surrounded by some equally delightful museums, such as the **Musée Jacquemart-André** (p. 166) and the **Musée Nissim de Camondo** (p. 168).

To the west, the illustrious Seizième (sez-ee-*em,* 16th arrond.) is the most exclusive arrondissement of the city. Lying on the outer western edge of the city, this residential area is packed with magnificent 19th-century residences and apartment houses, as well as many fine parks and gardens. In fact, the arrondissement shares its western border with the **Bois de Boulogne** (p. 205), one of the city's two huge, wooded parks. While the 16th is not known for its liveliness, it is graced with a terrific array of museums. The **Palais de Chaillot** shelters the **Cité de l'Architecture** (p. 164) and the **Musée de l'Homme** (p. 166), and just down the street is the vast **Musée National des Arts Asiatiques Guimet** (p. 167). A little farther on are two modern art museums in the **Palais de Tokyo** (p. 169), not to mention a half-dozen others, like the **Marmottan** (p. 167), sprinkled around the arrondissement. And a stop at the esplanade on the **Place du Trocadéro** is a must. Between the two wings of the Palais de Chaillot is a superb view of the Eiffel Tower, which you can walk to by strolling down the hill through the **Jardins du Trocadéro.**

MONTMARTRE

Best for: *Restaurants, nightlife, atmosphere*
What you won't find here: *Monuments (with the exception of Sacré-Coeur), major museums, grand architecture*
Parameters of the neighborhood: *18th arrondissement*

Once a village overlooking the distant city, Montmartre is now as inseparable from Paris as the Eiffel Tower, which means it's a major target for the tour-bus crowd. And crowded it is, especially in the area immediately around the **Basilique du Sacré-Coeur** (p. 171) and the overdone **Place du Tertre.** Yet, if you wander around the cobbled streets that surround **Place des Abbesses,** you'll find plenty of hip boutiques and cute restaurants frequented by an upwardly arty crowd, who have also staked out territory in the working-class neighborhoods immediately east and north of the basilica. Two small museums are worth your time here: **Musée de Montmartre** (p. 172), which traces the area's artistic history and has a peaceful garden; and **Dalí Paris** (p. 172), a must for fans of surrealism, with over 300 pieces of the artist's work.

RÉPUBLIQUE, BASTILLE & EASTERN PARIS

Best for: *Nightlife, good restaurants, Revolutionary history, arty boutiques*
What you won't find here: *Major monuments and museums, high-end shops*
Parameters of the neighborhood: *11th & 12th arrondissements*

These two arrondissements were pretty much off the tourist radar until 1989, when the new **Bastille opera house** provoked an explosion of bars and restaurants in the surrounding streets. Though the shine has already worn off the **nightspots** of rue de Lappe and rue de la Roquette (just off the Place de la Bastille), the nocturnal life of the 11th arrondissement is far from dull, as new clubs and cafes have opened farther north on rue de Charonne and **rue Oberkampf.**

Place de la Bastille, once the site of its namesake prison, has had a recent face-lift to make it pedestrian friendly and provide access to its centerpiece, the **Colonne de Juillet** (p. 175), a 50m (164-ft.) column with a crypt, which at time of writing was set to open to the public in 2022. North of the **Place de la Bastille** is the vast, pedestrian-friendly **Place de la République.** To the east is the Faubourg St-Antoine, a historic workers' quarter inhabited by woodworkers and furniture makers since the 13th century. After a few centuries, the density of underpaid, overburdened workers made St-Antoine a breeding ground for revolutionaries. The raging mob that stormed the Bastille prison in 1789 originated here, as did those of the subsequent uprisings of 1830, 1848, and the Paris commune.

In recent years, the area has become a magnet for foodies, as young chefs have opened some of the city's most exciting restaurants, like **Septime** (p. 109) on rue de Charonne. While the architecture here is nowhere near as grand as elsewhere in Paris, the neighborhood has retained an authenticity that's rarely found in the more popular parts of the city. A substantial number of furniture stores and ébénistes (woodworkers) are tucked into large interior courtyards accessible by covered passages off rue du Faubourg St-Antoine. Make a point of wandering down one of these; you'll be rewarded with a look at a way of life that has survived the centuries. This quarter extends all the way past the **Viaduc des Arts** (p. 212) and the **Gare de Lyon** train station (a magnificent example of Belle Epoque architecture) to **Bercy**, an area of former wine warehouses that is now home to the **Cinémathèque Française, Musée des Arts Forains** (p. 173), and the sprawling **Parc de Bercy** (p. 174). At the western end is the **Bois de Vincennes,** one of the city's two wooded parks.

BELLEVILLE, CANAL ST-MARTIN & NORTHEAST PARIS

Best for: Nightlife, restaurants, strolling (along the canal), arty boutiques
What you won't find here: Major monuments, museums, and architectural wonders
Parameters of the neighborhood: 10th, 19th & 20th arrondissements

For a long time, no one seemed to care about these arrondissements. They were too far from the center of the city, too working-class to be of interest to the trendy set, and too monument-less to appeal to tourists. Then, around 2000, with real estate skyrocketing, young professionals and artists began to move in. Suddenly, the forgotten **Canal St-Martin** was blooming with cafes and restaurants, and the streets around it were full of trendy shops. Then a handful of up-and-coming chefs arrived north of Bonne Nouvelle Métro station, kick-starting an exciting food scene. Artists looking for studio space discovered multi-ethnic **Belleville,** a cultural melting pot of immigrants from North Africa (both Jewish and Muslim), Asia (this is Paris' second-biggest Chinatown), and other parts of the world. The vast park and cultural venues of **La Villette** (p. 178) have also attracted new interest away from the center. Happily, these areas aren't really gentrified (yet), and parts are infused with a certain youthful energy that's hard to come by in other areas. Relatively tourist-free, these districts offer an opportunity to see a more local side of the city.

Aside from the **Parc de la Villette,** three other green havens are here: the **Parc de Belleville,** the **Parc des Buttes Chaumont** (p. 179), and the **Père-Lachaise cemetery** (p. 175), where the likes of Jim Morrison, Edith Piaf, and Chopin are buried. Several good bars and music venues are around **Ménilmontant** to the north of the cemetery.

The Left Bank
LATIN QUARTER & THE 13TH ARRONDISSEMENT
Best for: Affordable dining, student bars, art-house movie theaters, museums, botanical gardens
What you won't find here: Good shopping, quiet (at least not in the environs of Place St-Michel)
Parameters of the neighborhood: 5th & 13th arrondissements

Since the Middle Ages, when the **Sorbonne** and other academic institutions were founded, this has been a student neighborhood. (It earned its name as the "Latin" Quarter because back in the old days, all classes were taught in Latin.) Today the area still harbors the highest number of colleges and universities in the city, and you'll certainly see plenty of students and professors hanging around the restaurants and cafes here. You'll also see lots of tourists, who tend to swarm the warren of tiny streets that lead off the Place St-Michel. Avoid rue de la Huchette (except for the great swing-dancing club, **Le Caveau de la Huchette;** p. 235), which is lined with garish restaurants of questionable quality. **Boulevard St-Michel,** a legendary artery once lined with smoky cafes filled with thinkers and rabble-rousers, has now fallen prey to chain stores. The boulevard also harbors the **Musée de Cluny** (p. 181), a terrific collection of medieval art and Roman ruins.

The Panthéon.

For a more authentic taste of this neighborhood, wander east and upward, around the windy streets on the hill that leads to the **Panthéon** (p. 185), the church of **St-Etienne-du-Mont** (p. 185), and around rue Monge, toward the lovely **Jardin des Plantes** (p. 180). Surrounded by the city's **natural history museum,** this botanical garden is a wonderful place to relax. Down by the Seine, the museum of the **Institut du Monde Arabe** (p. 181) is housed in a spectacular building by architect Jean Nouvel.

South of here, in the 13th arrondissement, is Paris' main **Chinatown** (p. 122). Below rue de Tolbiac, high-rise apartment blocks house Chinese, Vietnamese and Laotian restaurants and shops, lending a distinctly Asian vibe. In total contrast, the villagey streets around rue de la Butte-aux-Cailles make for a charming walk. You can take in its quaint houses, street art, hip bars and eateries, and even an Arts and Crafts–era swimming pool, **Piscine de la Butte-aux-Cailles** (5 pl. Paul Verlaine).

ST-GERMAIN-DES-PRÉS & LUXEMBOURG

Best for: Fine dining, historic cafes, shopping, parks (the Jardin du Luxembourg)
What you won't find here: Penniless intellectuals and artists, low prices
Parameters of the neighborhood: 6th arrondissement

The church of **St-Germain-des-Prés** (p. 189), the heart of this neighborhood, got its name (St. Germain of the Fields) because when it was built in the 11th century, it was in the middle of the countryside. What a difference a

Café Les Deux Magots.

millennium makes. The church became the nucleus of a huge and powerful abbey, which would later constitute an autonomous mini-city complete with a hospital and a prison. The Revolution cut the church down to its current size, and an elegant collection of apartment houses, squares, and parks grew up around it, making it one of Paris' most appealing areas to live in (as real-estate prices will attest). If the neighborhood has always had aristocratic airs (it was a favorite haunt of the nobility during the 17th and 18th c.), during the last part of the 19th century up to the mid–20th century it was also a magnet for penniless artists and intellectuals, who hung out in legendary cafes like the **Café de Flore** (p. 132) and **Les Deux Magots** (p. 134).

Today few struggling creative types can afford either the rents or the price of a cup of coffee around here, and young artists and thinkers have moved north and east to cheaper parts of town. Though the ambience is decidedly bourgeois these days, the neighborhood is still dynamic, and the cafes and shops along the boulevard St-Germain are crowded with a mix of politicians, gallery owners, French celebrities, and editors. This is also a fun neighborhood for shopping—from 500€ pumps on chic rue des St-Pères to 30€ sundresses on the more plebian rue des Rennes. And when you've tired yourself out, you can stroll over to the magnificent **Jardin du Luxembourg** (p. 186) for a timeout by the fountains.

EIFFEL TOWER & LES INVALIDES
Best for: *Iconic monuments, majestic avenues, grand vistas, museums*
What you won't find here: *Affordable restaurants or shopping, nightlife*
Parameters of the neighborhood: *7th arrondissement*

The **Eiffel Tower** (p. 190) reigns over this swanky arrondissement, where the streets that aren't lined with ministries and embassies are filled with elegant apartment buildings and prohibitively expensive stores and restaurants. A large portion of the neighborhood is taken up by the **Champs de Mars,** a park that stretches between the tower and the **Ecole Militaire,** and by the enormous esplanade in front of the **Invalides** (p. 192), which sweeps down to the Seine with much pomp and circumstance. Some of the city's best museums are around here, including the **Musée d'Orsay** (p. 193), the **Musée Rodin** (p. 195), and the **Musée du Quai Branly** (p. 195), whose wacky architecture has added some spice to this very staid area.

While this neighborhood certainly has a lot to see, it is a little short on human warmth—this is not the place to come to see regular Parisians in their natural habitat. One exception is the area around the pedestrian **rue Cler,** a market street that is home to many delightful small restaurants and food stores. Word is out about this cozy corner, however, so expect to see plenty of tourists when you go into that cute *boulangerie* for a couple of croissants.

MONTPARNASSE

Best for: Shopping, historic cafes, nightlife
What you won't find here: Extraordinary architecture, museums, monuments
Parameters of the neighborhood: 14th & 15th arrondissements

In the early 1970s, government officials decided the time had come to make Paris a modern city. They blithely put aside concerns for historic patrimony and architectural harmony, and the old Montparnasse train station and its immediate neighborhood were torn down; a 56-story glass tower and shopping complex was erected in its place. A new train station was constructed behind the tower, as well as a barrage of modern apartment buildings and offices. Fortunately, even ugly contemporary architecture didn't manage to kill the neighborhood—at the foot of the **Tour Montparnasse,** home to a 360-degree rooftop viewing platform (p. 196), life goes on as it always has. A few steps away from the station, stores and cafes still line the tiny old streets; you'll also find many *crêperies* (crepe restaurants), an outgrowth of the large Breton (that is, from Brittany) community that still inhabits this area. Farther down boulevard Montparnasse are legendary brasseries such as **La Coupole** (p. 134) and **Le Select,** where Picasso, Max Jacob, and Henry Miller used to hang out in the 1920s. For a bit of calm, take a walk around the **Cimetiére du Montparnasse** (p. 197), where writers and artists such as Charles Baudelaire and Constantin Brancusi are buried. In the evenings, crowds pour into the many restaurants and movie theaters around the station.

To the south, the arrondissement takes a more residential turn, with the exception of rue Daguerre, a lively market street a block south of the cemetery. The 14th is also home to the new (2019) **Musée de la Libération** (p. 197) war museum, and **Les Catacombes** (p. 197), former limestone mines lined with the bones of millions of Parisians whose remains were moved here in the 18th century when the city's overcrowded graveyards became unhygienic. It makes for a spooky (and intriguing) visit.

PARIS IN CONTEXT

Before there was Paris, there was the Seine. Much wider than it is today, the river looped and curved through the region, and at one point, split into two branches. One branch dried up, leaving a wide band of marshlands to the north, while the other, sprinkled with islands, remained. This swampy bog offered little indication that it had potential for urban grandeur. Yet one day it would become the lifeline of one of the world's greatest cities.

THE MAKING OF PARIS

Origins

Prehistoric Paris did have two things going for it: a river that led to the Atlantic and strategically placed islands, which offered both protection and shelter. The largest island, the core of what would one day become the **Île de la Cité,** attracted a tribe of Celtic people called the Parisii, who fished and traded along its banks somewhere around the 3rd century B.C. Though they weren't the first Parisians (traces of human habitations have been found dating back to Neolithic times), they were the first to firmly implant themselves in the area, and they made ample use of the river not only as a source of food, but as a trade link. Their island had the good fortune of being on the "Pewter Route," a trade route that stretched from the British Isles to the Mediterranean. As a consequence, the Parisii's wealth was such that by the 1st century B.C., they were minting their own gold coins.

Roman Rule (1st c. B.C.–2nd c. A.D.)

No recorded history of Paris exists before the Romans showed up in 52 B.C., but when Caesar and his boys marched in, the Parisii numbered several thousand, and the island bustled with activity. Soon thereafter, however, the Parisii's main activity would be trying to get rid of the Romans. Though they fought valiantly, the Parisii were massacred, and a new Roman town was built on the island and the Left Bank, on the slopes of the **Montagne St-Genevieve** (where the Panthéon now stands; p. 185). The new town, for reasons that remain unclear, was baptized Lutécia and ran along a ramrod-straight north to south axis; the line of this road survives in today's

rue St-Jacques. (The Parisii would eventually get their due, however, as the city would be renamed Civitas Parisiorum in the 4th c., which eventually was whittled down to Paris.) Though there were only around 8,000 inhabitants, by the 2nd century the town boasted three **Gallo-Roman baths** (you can see the ruins of the largest of these at the corner of bds. St-Michel and St-Germain in the Musée de Cluny; p. 181) and a vast amphitheater (the **Arènes de Lutèce,** just off rue Monge in the Latin Quarter).

Barbarian Invasions (3rd–5th c.)

By the 3rd century, the city was subject to waves of barbarian invasions. Most of the population took refuge on the Île de la Cité, which was then encircled by ramparts. Somewhere around this time, St-Denis was decapitated when he was martyred up on a nearby hill, which in time would be dubbed **Montmartre** (p. 28). Legend has it that the saint picked up his severed head and walked with it for several kilometers, preaching all the while; the **Basilica of St-Denis** (just north of Paris) was built on the place where he finally dropped. The event, which supposedly happened around 250, coincides with Christianity's first appearance on the Parisian scene. Another particularly pious Christian, a young nun named Geneviève, was credited with turning Attila the Hun away from Paris in 451. Alerted that the barbarians were approaching, the citizenry was in a state of panic; Geneviève reassured them, telling them that God was with them. In the end, the Huns didn't march on Paris, but on Orléans; the grateful population, convinced it was Geneviève's doing, made her into the city's patron saint. A church was raised in her honor on the hill that's now known as the **Montagne-Ste-Geneviève;** it was pulled down and replaced by a magnificent new one, commissioned by Louis XV in the 18th century, which was subsequently turned into a national mausoleum after the Revolution and renamed the **Panthéon** (p. 185).

Merovingian & Carolingian Dynasties (6th–10th c.)

At the end of the 5th century, the Franks (a Germanic people) invaded and established the Merovingian dynasty of kings; the first, Clovis, made Paris the capital of his new kingdom in 508. The Merovingians were ardent Catholics; under their rule the city sprouted dozens of churches, convents, and monasteries. Childebert I, the son of Clovis, inaugurated a small basilica that would soon be dubbed **St-Germain-des-Prés** after the saint was buried there in 576. Over time, this church would grow into a powerful abbey and intellectual center that would dominate much of the Left Bank up until the Revolution. Even after the abbey was dismantled, and many of its buildings burned, the church lived on, as did the name of the neighborhood. Though the city enjoyed a certain amount of prosperity during this time, it was short-lived; the Merovingians, known as the "do-nothing" kings, were eventually toppled, and by the 8th century, a new dynasty, the Carolingians, had replaced them.

The most famous member of this clan was Charlemagne, who went on to conquer Italy and was crowned emperor by the Pope in 800. Arts and letters

Interior of St-Etienne-du-Mont.

thrived during this period, and the city began to build up on the Right Bank, around the church of **St-Gervais–St-Protais,** and the Port du Grève, where the **Hôtel de Ville** (p. 157) now stands. Starting in the mid–9th century, the city was periodically ravaged by Normans and Vikings, who would sack Paris on their way to plundering Burgundy. The Normans were particularly persistent; after a barricade was erected on the Seine to keep their boats from passing in 885, they laid siege to the city for an entire year. It was only after King Charles the Simple signed a treaty in 911 giving the Normans Normandy that life returned to normal, but by then Paris was in ruins. The age of the Carolingians was drawing quickly to a close.

The Founding of the Capetian Dynasty (11th c.)

In 987, Hugues Capet, the Count of Paris, was crowned king of France; his direct descendants ruled the country for 3½ centuries, and two branches of the Capetian dynasty, the Valois and Bourbons, would continue to rule (with a brief pause during the Revolution) until 1848. With the Capetians came stability, and Paris rebuilt and grew, particularly on the Île de la Cité and the Right Bank. The Left Bank, flattened by the Normans, was left as it was; little by little it was covered with fields and vineyards. The 12th century was a period of economic growth; it saw the birth of **Les Halles** (p. 142), the sprawling central market around which a new commercial quarter developed. In 1163, ground was broken on the **Cathédrale de Notre-Dame de Paris** (p. 137). Finished 200 years later, Notre-Dame remains one of the world's most

Sainte-Chapelle.

exquisite examples of medieval architecture (even after the fire of April 2019, which caused extensive damage to its roof and engulfed its emblematic spire).

The mushy, marshy land on the Right Bank, known as the **Marais** ("swamp"), was partially drained and carpeted with farms. Philippe Auguste, before taking off on a crusade, had a sturdy rampart built around the newly extended city limits; fragments of this wall can still be seen today (see "Walking Tours," p. 275). Philippe's grandson, Louis IX (Saint Louis), added another architectural jewel to the cityscape: the **Sainte-Chapelle** (p. 150), a small church whose upper-story walls are almost entirely made of stained glass. Louis had it built to house a treasure he bought from the debt-ridden Byzantine emperor: Christ's crown of thorns and some fragments of the holy cross (the relics were in Notre-Dame until the 2019 fire; they're now—at time of writing—in the Louvre).

Medieval Glory & Gore (12th–15th c.)

By the 12th century, Paris boasted a population of around 200,000, much larger than other European capitals, as well as a burgeoning reputation as an economic as well as intellectual center. Quality fabrics, leather goods, and metalwork were produced in Paris, as well as art objects. The University of Paris was slowly coming into being, and colleges were popping up all over the Left Bank; in 1257, Robert de Sorbon established the small theological college that became the **Sorbonne** university. The city seemed unstoppable.

But the 14th century would, in fact, put an end to this fruitful period. When the last Capetian king, Charles IV, died in 1328, the succession to the throne was disputed, in part because the closest descendant was Edward III, king of England, who also presided over a chunk of southwestern France. This and many other gripes exploded into the Hundred Years' War, which devastated France for over a century. Expansion in Paris came to an abrupt halt, the endless wars and riots wore down the populace, and in 1348 the Black Plague killed tens of thousands. In the early 1400s, Paris was hit by famine and a string of extremely cold winters. Between one disaster and another during this period, the city lost about half of its population. In 1420, the English occupied Paris; despite the efforts of Joan of Arc and Charles VII, who laid siege to the city in 1429, troops loyal to the Duke of Bedford (the English Regent) didn't leave until 1437. This same duke was responsible for having Joan burned at the stake in Rouen in 1431.

Renaissance Renewal (16th c.)

Slowly, the city came to life again. The population increased, as did commercial and intellectual activity. The invention of the printing press spread new ideas across Europe. After centuries of rejecting the texts and ideas of classical antiquity, scholars embraced the concept of Humanism, which would find a home in Paris. Great thinkers such as Erasmus and John Calvin were drawn to the city's universities. More colleges emerged from the academic landscape: In 1530, François I established a school that would become the prestigious **College de France,** and in 1570 Charles IX founded the **Académie Française.** If the Renaissance made its mark on the intellectual life of the city, it had little impact on its architectural legacy. The Renaissance kings liked Paris but lived and did their building elsewhere. François I, the most construction-happy among them, brought some of the greatest masters of the Italian Renaissance, like Leonardo da Vinci and Benvenuto Cellini, to France, but their genius was mostly displayed in François' châteaux on the Loire and at **Fontainebleau** (p. 262), not in the capital. The king's primary contribution to the cityscape was the remodeling of the **Louvre** (p. 144) and construction of the **Hôtel de Ville** (p. 157), designed by the Italian architect Boccador. The latter building was burned down in 1871 during the fall of the Paris Commune; the existing edifice is a fairly faithful copy erected in 1873. Two glorious churches, **St-Etienne-du-Mont** (p. 185) and **St-Eustache** (p. 151), also were built during this period; their decoration attests to the jubilant spirit of the times.

War once again interfered with the city's development when the bloody struggle between the country's Protestants and Catholics morphed into the Wars of Religion in 1557. Even the marriage of the future king, Henri of Navarre, a Protestant, to Marguerite de Valois, a Catholic, did not diffuse the conflict: A week after their wedding, August 24, 1572, the bells of **St-Germain l'Auxerrois** (p. 151) signaled the beginning of the St-Bartholomew's Day massacre, which resulted in the deaths of between 2,000 and 4,000

Parisian Protestants. When in 1589 Henri was declared King of France (as Henri IV), Parisians would not let the Protestant monarch enter the city. After 4 months of siege, the starving citizens relented and, in the end, to show his goodwill, the king converted, famously declaring that "Paris is worth a mass."

Henri IV lived on to be an enormously popular king, whose structural improvements left a lasting mark on the city. He was the force behind the **Pont Neuf** (p. 158), which straddles the Right and Left banks, as well as the Île de la Cité. To create the bridge, two small islets off the

Place Dauphine.

western tip of the Île de la Cité were filled in and made part of the larger island; the tranquil **Place Dauphine** was also created during this time. Henri also conceived the strikingly harmonious Place Royale (now called **Place des Vosges,** p. 162). The king would not live to see it finished; in 1610, when the royal carriage got stuck in a traffic jam on rue de la Ferronerie, he was stabbed by Ravaillac, a deranged Catholic who was convinced that Henri was waging war against the Pope.

The Age of Louis XIV (17th c.)

The 17th century saw a building frenzy among the aristocracy. Marie de Médicis built the Italian-style **Palais du Luxembourg** in 1615, around the same time that the **Marais** (p. 26) was inundated with splendid palaces and *hôtels particuliers,* or mansions. The new **Île St-Louis,** made from the joining of two previously uninhabited islets to the east of the Île de la Cité, was filled with stately mansions that only the rich could afford. After Marguerite de Valois moved in to the neighborhood, the **St-Germain** quarter also became a place to see and be seen. Finally, in 1632 the powerful Cardinal Richelieu built a huge palace, now called the **Palais Royal** (p. 147), near the Louvre, which encouraged yet another new neighborhood to develop.

In 1643, a 5-year-old boy named Louis XIV acceded to the French throne, where he would stay for the next 72 years. One of the most influential figures in French history, Louis XIV spent his early years in Paris, under the protection of his mother, Anne of Austria. It was not a happy time: The city was writhing under a nasty rebellion called La Fronde, instigated by cranky nobles trying to wrest control back from the powerful prime minister, Cardinal Mazarin. The young monarch and his mother were chased from one royal residence to the next. When Louis grew up and things calmed down, he settled in at the **Louvre,** commanding his team of architects, led by Le Vau, to complete the **Cour Carrée** and other unfinished parts of the palace. The spectacular colonnade on the eastern facade dates from this period. Louis eventually decided to build his own castle, one that was far enough from the noise and filth of the capital and big enough to house his entire court—the better to keep a close eye on political intrigues. The result was the **Château of Versailles** (p. 252), a testament to the genius of Le Vau and that of master landscape architect André Le Nôtre.

Even if Louis XIV didn't live in the city, he certainly added to its architectural heritage. He was responsible for the construction of **Les Invalides** (p. 192), a massive military hospital, and two squares, **Place des Victoires** and Place Louis-le-Grand, today known as **Place Vendôme** (p. 149). Two gigantic entryways, celebrating Louis' military victories, were built at the city gates: the **Porte St-Denis** and the **Porte St-Martin.** Both of these triumphal archways still hover over parts of the 10th arrondissement by Métro Strasbourg–St-Denis, looking somewhat out of place in this working-class district.

From Enlightenment to Revolution (18th c.)

Paris continued to grow and the population density increased. At the turn of the 18th century, some 500,000 Parisians were crammed into a vast network of narrow, mostly unpaved streets. Sewers were nonexistent, and clean drinking water was a luxury. While life in the rarified atmosphere of the aristocratic salons of the **Marais** was brimming with art, literature, and deep thought, down on the ground it was filled with misery. Poverty and want were the constant companions of the vast majority of Parisians. On an intellectual level, the city was soaring—under the reign of Louis XV, Paris became a standard-bearer for the Enlightenment, a school of thought that championed reason and logic and helped construct the intellectual framework of both the American and French Revolutions. Salons—regular meetings of artists and thinkers in aristocratic homes—flourished, as did cafes. Drawn in by the wildly popular new drink called coffee, these cafes were the ideal meeting place for philosophers, writers, and artists, as well as a new breed of politicians with some revolutionary ideas. Political debates were particularly passionate in the cafes in the galleries of the **Palais Royal** (p. 147), which had been filled with shops and opened to the public by Duke Louis Philippe d'Orléans.

Meanwhile, back in Versailles, the court of Louis XVI seemed to be utterly oblivious to the mounting discontent in the capital. As the price of bread skyrocketed and more and more Parisians found themselves on the street (there were more than 100,000 homeless people in the city in 1789, out of an overall population of between 600,000 and 700,000), the disconnect between the aristocracy and the common man threatened to rupture into a bloody conflict. Amazingly, Louis XVI and his wife, Marie Antoinette, continued to live their lives as if the civil unrest in the capital didn't concern them. A financial crisis in the royal treasury prompted a meeting of the Estates-General in Versailles in May 1789, a representative body that had not been convened since 1616. The assembly began demanding a more democratic system of taxation, and better representation of the Third Estate (the people). When the king tried to close down the proceedings, the group, which had renamed itself the National Assembly, dug in its heels and wrote a constitution. The royals kept dithering and trying to break up the assembly, until finally, the Revolution erupted on July 14, 1789, when an angry mob stormed the Bastille prison. There were only seven prisoners in the fortress, but no matter—the genie was out of the bottle, and the pent-up anger of the populace was unleashed.

The royal family was imprisoned and beheaded. After the initial euphoria faded and the high ideals were set down on paper, the Revolution's leaders began to squabble, and factional skirmishes became increasingly deadly. The events of the Revolution are too many to relate here, but within a few years, not only were aristocrats being sent off to the guillotine, but just about anyone who disagreed with the ruling powers, including many of the leaders who wrote the rules. Finally, Robespierre, who directed the bloodiest phase of the Revolution, known as "the Terror," had his turn at the guillotine, and a new government was set up. Called the Directory, this unsuccessful attempt at representational government met its end when a general named Napoleon Bonaparte staged a coup in 1799.

The Empire (early 19th c.)

Under Napoleon, who was crowned emperor in 1804, Paris slowly put itself back together. The economy restarted, and the Emperor turned his attentions to upgrading the city's infrastructure, building bridges (**Pont St-Louis, Pont des Arts, Pont d'Iéna,** and **Pont d'Austerlitz**), improving access to water (the **Canal de l'Ourcq**), and creating new cemeteries like **Père-Lachaise** (p. 175) because the old ones were so crowded that they had become public health hazards. Napoleon was also responsible for the **rue de Rivoli,** a wide east-west boulevard, the first of several that would be laid down later on in the 19th century. The collection of the **Louvre** was greatly enhanced by all the booty the Emperor acquired during his many military campaigns. Napoleon's love of war would eventually be his undoing; after his defeat by the English at Waterloo, he was exiled to the isle of Ste-Helena, where he died in 1821. Paris holds huge monuments to his memory, in particular the **Arc de Triomphe** (p. 162), which honors the Imperial Army. His tomb lies in Les Invalides military complex and museum (p. 192).

The Restoration & Urban Renewal (mid-19th c.)

Incredibly, after all the blood that was spilled in the name of the Republic, Louis XVI's brother (Louis XVIII) became King of France in 1814. What's more, another brother, Charles X, became king after Louis XVIII's death. What both brothers had in common is that they tried to bring back the old days of absolute monarchy. The citizenry, though, had become accustomed to the reforms of the Revolution and the relatively benign rule of Napoleon. This, coupled with the continuing poverty of many Parisians, resulted in two serious uprisings: "Les Trois Glorieuses," the 3 "glorious" days in July 1830, and the Revolution of 1848. In fact, it is these two uprisings, and not the Revolution itself, that are honored on the column in the **Place de la Bastille** (p. 175), the site of the infamous prison. After Charles, a republic was declared, and Napoleon's nephew, Louis-Napoleon, ran for and won the presidency. He liked being president so much that he didn't want to give up power at the end of his term, so he staged a coup and declared the birth of the Second Empire, calling himself Napoleon III.

Under Charles X, the unhygienic state of the city center started to cause serious alarm, particularly after a cholera epidemic in 1832 devastated the population. Many residents fled to the outer limits of the city, away from the overcrowded quarters where many impoverished people lived, and where the filthy streets were often completely clogged with traffic. City administrators began to draft plans for new avenues, in particular the prefect, Rambuteau, who went ahead and started laying down wide boulevards, like the one named after him.

But it was Napoleon III who really changed the face of Paris when he gave urban planner Baron Haussmann free rein to "modernize" the city. Not only did Haussmann lay down wide boulevards that eased congestion and opened up vistas, he cleverly arranged them so that if ever there was yet another popular uprising, the boulevards would facilitate military maneuvers and make it tough for citizens to set up barricades. Over half of the city was ripped up and rebuilt; Haussmann instituted strict regulations for the height of the new buildings and the style of their facades. The result: the elegant buildings and boulevards you see today. On the plus side, the city finally got a decent sewage system and water access, and the squalid slums were knocked down. Several parks sprouted up, such as **Buttes Chaumont** (p. 179) and the

Place de la Bastille.

Bois de Boulogne (p. 205), as well as grand plazas like the **Place de la République** (p. 173) and **Place du Trocadéro.** On the other hand, the character of the city was completely changed, and much of its social fabric was pulled down with the houses. Working-class Paris has been slowly disappearing ever since.

From the Commune to the Belle Epoque (late 19th c.)

The boulevards were put to the test during the Paris Commune of 1871, a brief but bloody episode that was yet another attempt of the French people to construct a democratic republic—though this time it was in the wake of the Franco-Prussian War. The boulevards did their job: The rebellion was crushed, and at least 20,000 Communards were executed. When the smoke cleared, a new government was formed, and to everyone's surprise, it was a republic. The National Assembly had intended to form a constitutional monarchy, but the heir to the throne had no interest in the word "constitutional." As a stopgap measure, a temporary republic was set up—little did anyone know that it would last for 60 years.

There must have been an audible sigh of relief from Parisians, who would finally enjoy a little peace and harmony—or at least enough of a break from war and woe to have a good time. And so they did. During the "Belle Epoque,"

Strolling through Montmartre.

the years at the end of the 19th century and the beginning of the 20th, the arts bloomed in Paris. Groundbreaking art expositions introducing new movements like Impressionism (around 1874) and Fauvism (around 1905) changed people's ways of seeing painting. Up in **Montmartre,** an entire colony of artists and writers (Picasso, Braque, Apollonaire, and others) were filling cafes and cabarets in their off hours. The Lumière brothers and Léon Gaumont showed their newly hatched films in the city's first movie theaters. The city hosted a number of World's Fairs including that of 1889, which created the **Eiffel Tower** (p. 190), and 1900, which left behind the **Pont Alexandre III bridge** (p. 158), as well as the **Grand and Petit Palais** (p. 169). Another great moment in 1900 was the inauguration of the Paris Métro's first underground line.

The World Wars (early 20th c.)

The fun came to an abrupt halt in 1914 with the outbreak of World War I, which killed 1.4 million Frenchmen and wounded 4.2 million others. Calling all Parisians to arms, General Gallieni and his troops fought off the approaching German army (the Battle of the Marne) and saved Paris from occupation. The city did get bombarded, however; on Good Friday, 1918, the church of **St-Gervais–St-Protais** took a direct hit and more than 100 people died.

The city rebounded after the war, both economically and culturally, especially during the 1920s, *les années folles* ("the crazy years"). Paris became a magnet for artists and writers from all over. Americans, in particular, came in droves—F. Scott Fitzgerald, Henry Miller, Ernest Hemingway, and Gertrude Stein were some of the better-known names. They and other European expats like Marc Chagall, James Joyce, and George Orwell gathered in **Montparnasse** cafes like **Le Dôme, Le Select,** and **La Coupole.**

The 1930s brought economic depression and social unrest—a dreary backdrop for the approaching war. The Germans were re-arming, and Hitler was rising to power; in May 1940 Germany invaded the Netherlands, Luxembourg, and Belgium, and then broke through France's defensive Maginot line. The Germans occupied Paris on June 14, and for 4 years the city would know hunger, curfews, and suspicion. The Vichy government, led by Marchal Pétain, in theory governed unoccupied France, but in fact, it collaborated with the Germans. One of the darkest moments of the occupation was in July 1942, when the French police rounded up 13,152 Parisian Jews, including 4,115 children, and parked them in a velodrome before sending them off to Auschwitz; only 30 survived. General Charles de Gaulle became the leader of the Free French and organizer of the Resistance. After the Allies landed in Normandy in 1944, Paris was liberated, and de Gaulle victoriously strode down the **Champs-Élysées** before a wildly cheering crowd. He would later become president of the country (1958–69).

Postwar Paris (mid-20th to early 21st c.)

Writers and artists filtered back to the cafes once the war was over (some had never left), and the **Café de Flore** (p. 132) and **Les Deux Magots** (p. 134) were headquarters for existential all-stars like Jean-Paul Sartre and Simone de Beauvoir. But the late 1940s was also the beginning of the end of French colonial rule, which was punctuated by violent clashes, including a revolt in Madagascar and a war in Indochina (mainland Southeast Asia) that would eventually entangle the United States. In North Africa, Morocco and Tunisia won their independence relatively peacefully, but France would not let go of Algeria without a long and bloody fight, its repercussions still being felt today. The war in Algeria led to the collapse of the French government; de Gaulle was asked to start a new one in 1958. Thousands of Algerian refugees flooded France, with many settling in the Paris region; Algeria finally gained its independence in 1962.

The writer André Malraux was de Gaulle's minister of cultural affairs from 1958 to 1969 and was responsible for protecting and restoring endangered historic districts like the **Marais.** Elsewhere, modern architects were putting their own questionable stamp on the city, like the doughnut-shaped **Maison de Radio France** in the 16th arrondissement, and the vaguely "Y"-shaped **Maison de UNESCO** in the 15th. The late 1960s also marked Paris in less concrete ways. In May 1968, students, hoping to reform the university system, joined a general workers' strike that was paralyzing the nation. The police invaded **La Sorbonne** to calm the protests, and students and sympathizers took to the streets. The confrontations became violent, with students attacking police with cobblestones—**boulevard St-Michel** was subsequently paved with asphalt. This was a period of profound social change; those who participated still proudly refer to themselves as *soixante-huitards* (68ers).

The 1970s was a period of architectural awkwardness—horrified by the idea of becoming a "museum city," then-president Georges Pompidou decided to modernize. One idea that thankfully never came to fruition was to pave over the Canal St-Martin to make way for a freeway that would cut through the center of the city. The dismal **Tour Montparnasse** dates from this period, as does the destruction of the old Les Halles marketplace, which was replaced with an underground shopping mall (**Forum des Halles,** which has been rebuilt and covered over by a massive glass canopy; see box, p. 142). Pompidou's one "success" is the nearby **Centre Pompidou** (p. 155), whose strange, inside-out design provoked howls of outrage when it was built but now has been accepted as part of the Parisian landscape. When François Mitterrand became president in 1981, he too wanted to leave an architectural legacy, and the list of his *grands projets* ("big projects") is lengthy. Fortunately, most were considerably more palatable than his predecessor's. It is to Mitterrand that we owe the **Musée d'Orsay,** the **pyramid** (and underground shopping complex) at the Louvre, and the ultra-modern **Bibliothèque National François Mitterrand,** as well as the **Institut du Monde Arabe** (p. 181) and the **Opéra Bastille** (p. 232). President Jacques Chirac was the force behind the excellent **Musée du Quai Branly** (p. 195), which opened in 2006.

Musée de l'Institut du Monde Arabe.

PARIS TODAY

Recent decades have brought Paris long periods of relative calm, punctuated by seismic upheavals, like the Métro bombings and paralyzing strikes that both hit the city in 1995. More recently, the 2015 terrorist attacks on the satiric newspaper *Charlie Hebdo* and a kosher supermarket, followed by coordinated assaults on restaurant terraces, the Stade de France stadium, and the Bataclan concert hall, shook the city to its core.

In 2018 and 2019, Paris, like the rest of France, was also affected by the grassroots yellow vests (*gilets jaunes*) movement, an anti-elitist, sometimes violent crusade against a whole hodgepodge of issues (including climate-change problems and President Macron's tax reforms). And *then*, in April 2019, a dramatic fire engulfed its most visited monument, the glorious, medieval Cathédrale de Notre-Dame de Paris.

Not a year after that, it was the Covid-19 pandemic's turn to spread chaos. Paris, like most capital cities around the world, was a hotspot for the virus and was thrust into lockdown, with only vital shops and services staying open for most of 2020. In true French style, wine shops were considered vital! Then finally, after a late-starting but hefty vaccine campaign, the city (along with the rest of the country) reopened in 2021 with only a few restrictions. At time of writing, things were looking decidedly upward, largely thanks to the government's social-aid packages. These kept many shops, restaurants, and cafes afloat during the toughest times and allowed numerous museums to use the closure period to implement much-needed renovations. But random acts of terror, freak fires, and worldwide pandemics aside, Paris is still Paris, and then some.

The city has been looking slicker and cleaner in the last few years. Renovation of historic buildings is ongoing, and a vigorous anti-dog-doo campaign has even made some headway on cleaning up the notoriously messy sidewalks. Paris feels younger these days too, with refreshed public spaces, like the new and improved **Place de la République** (p. 173) and the delightfully pedestrianized **banks of the Seine** (p. 206), which now include floating gardens, picnic areas, and sports classes. The city is even home to both the world's largest startup campus, Station F, and Europe's biggest restaurant, the 1,000-seater La Felicità, both set in a converted 1920s industrial building known as the Halle Freyssinet.

The advent of the **Vélib' bike program** in 2007 (p. 290) has slowly transformed Paris into a bike-friendly place. There are now 1,000km (621 miles) of bike lanes. And during lockdown, some extra 60km (37 miles) of lanes—nicknamed "coronapistes"—were set up to relieve crowded public transport too. They have now become permanent fixtures. Paris has backed a host of other green measures as well, including bus lanes and Vélib'-like scooter programs where you can rent an electric scooter to toodle around the city. Other innovative initiatives include the ever-popular **Paris Plage**—an urban beach on the banks of the Seine—and **Nuit Blanche,** an annual all-night cultural party.

In 2014, the Socialist **Anne Hidalgo** was elected Paris' first female mayor. One of her top priorities is air pollution, which is an increasing problem in the capital, so much so that on particularly smoggy days, driving is restricted and the Métro is free. In 2021, she also instated a new speed limit of 30kmph (18mph) on most of Paris' streets to reduce noise pollution. It was under Hidalgo's watch that the city won the bid for the 2024 Olympics too, so don't be surprised if you see lots of renovation underway.

On the surface, at least, the capital seems to be in the pink of good health. Paris has managed to carefully conserve its architectural heritage and its traditional way of life while making a serious effort to enter the modern world. Paris is, after all, the capital of the second-largest economy in the European Union, and a certain dynamism comes with the territory—even if it is framed in Belle Epoque swirls and Mansard roofs. Yet even if the pulse of life in the capital ticks faster than it once did, it still allows for aimless intellectual discussions in cafes, leisurely Sunday strolls through leafy parks, and relaxed lunches over glasses of wine. And maybe it is exactly that gentle aesthetic that makes the city one of a kind. It is rare in today's turbulent world to find an urban center that so harmoniously mixes tradition and modernity, without enslaving itself to either.

Calendar of Events

Paris is an all-year-round kind of city, with great events in every season. No matter when you visit, you will have something to see beyond the traditional sights, be it a sports match, a cycle of museum concerts, or a movie festival. Here is a non-exhaustive list of the best events to look out for month by month. Dates may differ in 2022 and 2023, so always check the events' websites. The Tourist Office (www.parisinfo.com) is also a good resource; click "Going Out," then "Celebrations and Festivals in Paris."

Major holidays are New Year's Day (Jan 1), Easter Sunday and Monday (late Mar/Apr), May Day (May 1), VE Day (May 8), Ascension Thursday (40 days after Easter), Pentecost/Whit Sunday and Whit Monday (7th Sun and Mon after Easter), Bastille Day (July 14), Assumption Day (Aug 15), All Saints Day (Nov 1), Armistice Day (Nov 11), and Christmas Day (Dec 25).

JANUARY

International Circus Festival of Tomorrow. The annual International Circus Festival of Tomorrow at Paris' Pelouse de Reuilly (Métro: Liberté) offers the chance to catch the world's finest circuses under one roof. Young artists from such diverse schools as the Beijing Circus, the Moscow Circus, and France's own *Ecole Fratellini* compete at the festival in a bid to discover the stars of the future. Four days at the end of January. www.cirquededemain.paris.

FEBRUARY

International Agricultural Show. Every February, the *terroir* (France's countryside) comes to Paris for the International Agricultural Show at the Porte de Versailles. It's a real institution (even the French president makes an official call) with exhibits featuring the top models of the animal world, meaty gastronomic delicacies from 18 French regions, and leisure, hunting, and fishing displays. Late February. www.salon-agriculture.com.

Six Nations Rugby. France faces its European rivals (England, Scotland, Wales, Ireland, and Italy) in the Six Nations rugby union internationals at the humongous Stade de France (p. 230). The championship is the oldest rugby tournament in the world, having existed in one form or another since 1883. Since the advent of the Six Nations, France has been the most successful country, so come along and see whether they can be beaten on home territory. February and March. www.stadefrance.com or www.sixnationsrugby.com.

Chinese New Year. Paris celebrates this lively annual event in the 13th arrondissement and Belleville in the 20th, the city's Chinese Quarters. Most of the action is in the 13th, where concerts and screenings are shown alongside the traditional dragon parade, which swirls through avenues such as d'Ivry and Choisy in a flurry of color and sparkle. One day in February.

MARCH

Paris Carnival. The annual *Carnaval de Paris* goes by many names, including the *Pantruche Carnaval,* the *Saint-Fargeau,* and the *Promenade du Boeuf Gras* (Fat Cow Parade). Led by the Fat Cow herself (yes, an actual cow), it revives an age-old tradition begun in 1274. Cheerful Parisians, trumpeters, and other musicians parade through the capital's streets to the Place de la République in the 11th

---

Event Protocols

For up-to-date information on how to enjoy these events, including any reservation or masking requirements, see each event's website and the following official websites (in English): the French government website (www.gouvernement.fr/en/coronavirus-covid-19) and the Paris Tourist Office (https://en.parisinfo.com/practical-paris/info/guides/info-disruption-paris).

arrondissement. Usually the first Sunday of March. www.carnaval-paris.org.

Banlieues Blues. This annual music festival, held in Paris' northern suburb of Pantin, brings top-notch jazz and blues names to the traditionally culture-hungry suburbs. It's a fine way to discover lesser-known theaters as your feet swing to the sound of top-notch international musicians. Mid-March to mid-April. www.banlieuesbleues.org.

APRIL

Festival Chorus. Paris' Festival Chorus brings rock, pop, and French *chanson* to the Seine Musicale (p. 230) in the Hauts-de-Seine suburb of Boulogne-Billancourt, with over 50 different concerts over 6 days. It's a great way to get to know France's music scene as a whole. Six days in early April. https://chorus.hauts-de-seine.fr.

Paris Marathon. The Paris Marathon offers some 55,000 runners the chance to take in some of the city's most famous landmarks (cheered on by thousands of spectators), including the Champs-Élysées, the Tuileries Garden, and Place de la Bastille. If you'd like to get your older kids involved, the 5km (3-mile) breakfast run is for anyone age 12 and over; *La Course du P'tit Déj* is held the day before the marathon. One Sunday in April. www.schneiderelectricparismarathon.com.

Foire du Trône. Europe's largest temporary funfair, the Foire du Trône at the Pelouse de Reuilly attracts around 5 million visitors every year. Though it has roots stretching back to the 12th century, since the 1950s the event has grown to epic proportions: Every year, visitors down enough beer to fill an Olympic swimming pool. With its flashing lights, pumping music, and greasy aromas, the Foire du Trône is a world away from the cultural clichés of the French capital, and sometimes that is the best thing about it. Early April to the end of May. www.foiredutrone.com.

Les Dimanches au Galop. On Sundays, throughout most of April and May, the city's main horse racing stadiums, the Hippodromes de Longchamp and d'Auteuil, open for a family day out. There are children's activities and games galore,

including pony rides, sack races, and pony-cycling (hybrid rocking horses that move like bikes), along with traditional horse races. Early April to the end of May. www.evenements.france-galop.com/en/dimanchesaugalop.

MAY

Nuit Européenne des Musées. During the Nuit Européenne des Musées (Museum Night), the city's museums stay open until 1am, offering you a chance to see the Louvre, and hundreds more, for free. One Saturday in mid-May. http://nuitdesmusees.culturecommunication.gouv.fr.

St-Germain-des-Prés Jazz Festival. The Rive Gauche, Paris' traditional jazz quarter, swings as local and international musicians perform at this jazz festival. Playing everything from boogie-woogie to blues, free concerts are held in St-Germain square; ticketed concerts take place in local libraries, cafes, concert halls, and bars. Two weeks in May. www.festivaljazzsaintgermainparis.com.

The French Open. For 2 weeks, the world's best tennis players battle it out on Roland Garros' clay courts. The event is one of France's biggest sports competitions; book in advance for a decent seat. The main matches are the most expensive, so if you want to save money, watch the unseeded players on the smaller courts: You could be watching the tennis stars of the future. Mid-May to early June. www.rolandgarros.com.

Villette Sonique. Pack a picnic, and head to Parc de la Villette's sprawling lawns for 4 days of free rock and electro concerts, plus numerous big-name shows held in Villette's major concert venues, like the Philharmonie, Le Trabendo, and the Grande Halle (15€–35€). A party atmosphere reigns as music fans gyrate, drink beer, and generally have fun. Kids can attend workshops too, to learn activities like DJ-ing or making music posters. End of May or early June. https://lavillette.com.

JUNE

Jardin Shakespeare. Every year the Jardin Shakespeare in Paris' Bois de Boulogne hosts an open-air theater festival. Plays by the bard are performed in French and

English, as well as works by other playwrights and the occasional concert or opera. The Jardin Shakespeare is so-called because of its five miniature gardens, each named after a Shakespearean work: "Macbeth," "Hamlet," "The Tempest," "As You Like It," and "A Midsummer Night's Dream." June to September. www.jardinshakespeare.com. ✆ **06-12-39-30-69.**

Paris Jazz Festival. This annual summer event presents a program of free jazz concerts in the beautiful surroundings of the Parc Floral. Gigs take place every Saturday and Sunday throughout June and July. The concerts begin at 3 or 4pm and are free to all those who have paid the standard park entry fee. Arrive early to ensure that you get one of the seats available or pack a picnic and bask by the park's miniature lake. June to September. https://festivalsduparcfloral.paris.

Fête de la Musique. In Paris for the Fête de la Musique? Everywhere you go you'll hear music, from opera and jazz to techno and rock. The Fête unites big names at major venues with accordionists on street corners and choirs in church halls. All concerts are free; the website publishes a list of participating venues. June 21. https://fetedelamusique.culture.gouv.fr.

Solidays. Solidarité SIDA is France's main charity promoting the cause of those with HIV. Its annual festival, Solidays, held at Paris' Hippodrome de Longchamp, has fast become one of the city's hippest cultural events, attracting more than 100,000 visitors for a weekend of music and arts. Circus performers, fairground stalls, mime artists, and bungee jumpers create a festive atmosphere, but the real stars of the show are the big names from the international pop and rock scene. Late June. www.solidays.org.

Gay Pride (Marche des Fiertés). The flamboyant Paris Gay Pride parade traditionally goes from République to Beaubourg via the Marais, but final confirmation of the route is not usually given until the last minute. Paris has a large gay and lesbian population, with consequently one of the most liberal attitudes in France. Over the last few years the march has grown into a huge carnival, and the big day itself is the culmination of a series of events, including debates and masked balls. Late June. https://www.gaypride.fr.

Fête des Tuileries. Every summer, the Jardin des Tuileries west of the Louvre turns its northern edge into a good old-fashioned funfair, with a big Ferris wheel, bumper cars, and a rather cheesy ghost train. For smaller kids, a 1900s-era carousel of wooden horses steals the show. The best bit? No tacky pop blasting through speakers. In fact, the fair is entirely music-free, so the relaxing atmosphere of the gardens stays intact. Late June to late August.

JULY

Bastille Day. France's national holiday commemorates the 1789 storming of the Bastille at the start of the French Revolution. Crowds line the Champs-Élysées for a military parade led by the president, during which jets fly in formation as top military brass bands march from the Arc de Triomphe to the Place de la Concorde. Later, Parisians party until dawn as fireworks explode over the Trocadéro. Some of the best spots to watch the action at midnight are Paris' bridges. Try Pont d'Alma and Pont Bir-Hakeim. It'll be crowded, but not as much as elsewhere. July 14.

Paris Plage. Every summer, long, pedestrianized stretches of the Seine (from Sully Morland to Pont Neuf, on the Right Bank, and now also at Port de Solférino on the Left Bank) are turned into Paris Plage, a beach complete with golden sand and tanning beds. There are free sports, such as volleyball, and entertainment from comedy to hip-hop. A second stretch of beach, along the Canal de l'Ourcq, also draws crowds with yet more concerts, outdoor games, canoeing, and sand. July to August. https://quefaire.paris.fr/parisplages.

Open-Air Cinema at La Villette. Each summer, film fans converge on Paris' Parc de la Villette for its 4-week *Cinéma en plein air* (outdoor movie projections). Pack a picnic and watch movies with the locals. Some movies are dubbed or subtitled and are some "VO" (original language). Mid-July to mid-August. https://lavillette.com.

Lollapalooza. The great U.S. music festival has taken root in Paris too, at the Longchamp Racetrack in the Bois de Boulogne. Lineups are excellent—previous headliners have included Depeche Mode, Pearl Jam, and Twenty One Pilots—and the atmosphere is laid-back and good humored. Music aside, the focus is on the nosh, with contemporary street food designed by some of the city's best chefs, many of them taking their signature dishes and adapting them for the festival's takeout system. Mid- to late July. www.lollaparis.com.

Classique au Vert. World-class classical musicians gather to serenade around 1,500 tourists and Parisians in the leafy Parc Floral (Métro: Château de Vincennes). Pack a picnic for a spot on the lawn while the sound fills the air; if you want a spot under the bandstand, get there around an hour before the concert. Weekends in late July, August, and early September. https://classiqueauvert. paris.fr.

AUGUST

Rock en Seine. This music festival, held in the Saint Cloud park just outside Paris (Métro: Boulogne Pont Saint-Cloud), offers a consistently excellent lineup of internationally renowned pop and rock stars, and its chilled-out atmosphere makes it a definite highlight of the city's musical calendar. Kids are welcome too, with a special "mini-rock" stage set aside for 6- to 10-year-olds, and a host of activities, from dressing up sessions and cooking classes to song-writing workshops. If you buy a festival pass, you can camp at the festival campsite (just bring your own tent). Late August. www. rockenseine.com/en.

SEPTEMBER

Techno Parade. The annual Techno Parade has been turning up the volume and quickening the pace on Paris' streets since 1998. Around 20 floats carrying 150 musicians, DJs, and performers turn out to dance their way along the 4.8km (3-mile) route. This huge event attracts 400,000 hardcore partygoers. Top DJs entertain the crowds with their mixing skills and decibel-defying sound systems. You can free your inner party animal afterward too, in numerous bars and clubs across the capital. Mid-September. www.technoparade.fr.

Journées du Patrimoine (Heritage Days). France's Heritage Days give visitors the chance to peek behind the doors of around 17,000 buildings that are usually closed to the public. All over the country visitors can glimpse inside politicians' homes, private crypts and cellars, and the backstage of theaters; many museums open their doors for free as well. Paris has so many wonderful buildings to discover that this event often draws tremendous crowds, so expect to line up and be patient—the wait will be worth it. Late September. www.journeesdupatrimoine. culture.fr.

Paris-Versailles Walk. Walkers and runners have been taking part in the annual Paris-Versailles Walk, *Grande Classique*, since 1977. It starts on the quay in front of the Eiffel Tower and ends 16km (10 miles) away at the Château de Versailles. Changing rooms and refreshments are available all along the route. Anyone over the age of 16 is invited to enter, but French regulations dictate that you need to send in a medical certificate to prove you're up to the challenge. You'll also need to enroll online beforehand. Late September. www. parisversailles.com.

Paris Autumn Festival. Encompassing opera, film, dance, and performing arts, Paris' Autumn Festival (*Festival d'Automne*) incorporates more high-powered contemporary arts events than some other cities see in a whole year. Dip into this festival at any point and you'll discover the best productions Paris has to offer. Languages range from Japanese and Russian to French, German, and English (subtitled where necessary in French), so choose your productions wisely. September to February. www.festival-automne.com.

We Love Green. In the Bois de Vincennes, this is one of the best open-air music festivals of the year: Not only are the stages jam-packed with both international and French stars, performing anything from pop and rock to electro and rap, but there are also workshops and concerts just for kids (led by qualified babysitters, so parents can go off and watch a show). The festival is also eco-responsible, being partly powered by solar panels and offering programming and workshops that promote the environment. Early September. www.welovegreen.fr.

OCTOBER

Nuit Blanche. See Paris as you've never seen it before, when museums, monuments, cinemas, parks, and swimming pools stay open from dusk to dawn (for 1 night only) as thousands of revelers celebrate Nuit Blanche. The Métro stays open later, and night buses serve all the main arteries until dawn. Early October. https://quefaire.paris. fr/nuitblanche.

Qatar Prix de l'Arc de Triomphe. Paris' Hippodrome de Longchamp stages the Qatar Prix de l'Arc de Triomphe, the jewel in the crown of French horse racing, attended by around 48,000 onlookers. Part of the prestigious World Series Racing Championship, the Arc is popular with Brits, who cross the channel to watch the action. In addition to the race, expect a wonderful display of horses, hats, and enough champagne to sink a ship. Early October. www.parislongchamp.com/fr/ qatar-prix-de-larc-triomphe.

Montmartre Grape Harvest Fest. The 5-day Montmartre Grape Harvest Festival (Fête des Vendages de Montmartre) celebrates the new Cuvée Montmartre vintage wine (produced on Montmartre's very slopes). Each year, thousands of revelers come to see short film screenings, listen to concerts, and drink *vin*. Stalls selling regional produce set up shop on the Butte (Montmartre's hill), and a colorful parade in honor of Bacchus fills the cobbled streets. Early to mid-October. www. fetedesvendangesdemontmartre.com.

Salon du Chocolat. The Salon du Chocolat, at Paris' Porte de Versailles, is heaven for thousands of chocolate lovers who come to devour the international ambrosia and learn how it's made. You can also discover the latest in industry trends from a series of chocolate tastings, demonstrations, and symposiums, and watch chocolatiers create their delicacies. This is a popular event, so buy your ticket online before you go. Late October. www.salon-du-chocolat.com

NOVEMBER

Pitchfork Music Festival Paris. Paris' fabulous, 3-day indie music festival takes place in the Grande Halle in Parc de la Villette, attracting thousands of music fans with the promise of edgy bands and after-show DJ parties (until 6am) in the Trabendo concert hall just opposite. Also, look out for "off" Pitchfork concerts in other theaters across the city, usually around Bastille. Early November. https://pitchforkmusicfestival.fr.

DECEMBER

Festival du Merveilleux. The Musée des Arts Forains (p. 173) is a magical ode to the Belle Epoque in Bercy's former wine warehouses. It is home to a vast collection of 19th- and early 20th-century fairground attractions, from carousels to pipe organs. For 10 days after Christmas, the museum hosts a magical festival that adds magicians, street performers, and musicians to its offerings. Late December to early January. http:// arts-forains.com/en/visitors/le-festival-du-merveilleux.

New Year's Eve. The Champs-Élysées is the place to be (if you can stand the crowds) as the City of Lights lives up to its name with a great sound-and-light show at the Arc de Triomphe, starting about 11pm. Arrive by 9pm to grab a good spot. Alternatively, head to Montmartre, where the streets are full of partygoers, and watch midnight strike from the foot of the Sacré-Coeur with Paris at your feet. You might even be lucky enough to spot a few fireworks on the horizon.

WHERE TO STAY

P aris has more than 1,500 hotels, from palaces fit for a pasha to tiny, family-run operations whose best features are their warm welcome and personal touch. In theory, you should be able to find something in line with your budget, timeframe, and personal tastes. But if you can't find the hotel of your dreams in the list that follows, don't despair—at the end of this chapter I list alternative lodging options, like bed-and-breakfasts and short-term apartment rentals.

WHAT TO EXPECT

Parisian lodgings can be many things: charming, opulent, cozy, homey, and even outrageous. But keep in mind the following: **Parisian hotel rooms tend to be small.** Why do I stress this? Because inevitably, tourists who come from countries where hotel rooms are often staggeringly large (does anyone actually need two king-size beds in a double room?) are shocked when they check in to tiny family hotels in ancient buildings. And it's not just budget lodgings—even nifty boutique hotels can have snug rooms.

Don't be too hard on the management, however; most historic Parisian buildings are protected by city regulations that make it difficult, if not impossible, to make structural changes. If you absolutely need room to stretch out, ask for a triple or even a quadruple room (if they're available). Otherwise, consider an international chain hotel, where space and extra amenities are usually not a problem, or an apartment rental.

Amenities

Unless you are staying in a hotel in our "expensive" category, you should be prepared for **minimal amenities.** Washcloths are scarce, toiletries can be few, and a few of the smaller hotels still don't have elevators (and when they do, they're often closet size). Assume that most guest rooms are large enough to sleep in comfortably, but you'll have to do your yoga workout somewhere else. All of the rooms in the hotels listed below have in-room bathrooms with toilets, unless otherwise mentioned.

Now that we've prepared you for the worst, here's what Parisian hotels *do* have (besides charm and personality, *bien sûr*). Almost all have in-room TVs with cable channels and hair dryers in the bathrooms. Irons and hair dryers (if they are not in the room) can

Hotels, B&Bs, and rental apartments must follow strict hygiene protocols to open to the public in Paris. You should find up-to-date information about this on each establishment's website. You can also email hotels with specific questions. For more general information (in English), check the French government website (www.gouvernement.fr/en/coronavirus-covid-19) and the Paris Tourist Office (https://en.parisinfo.com/practical-paris/info/guides/info-disruption-paris).

usually be found at the reception desk. Almost all have hotel-wide Wi-Fi. In more expensive hotels, equipment for making hot drinks is usually standard.

Most hotel rooms have air-conditioning, which—as climate change sets in, making weather less predictable and more extreme—can be a godsend, especially between July and September. Double-check if you're coming in summer; there's nothing worse than a room on a non-air-conditioned top floor facing a noisy street, making it impossible to open the windows at night.

While a continental **breakfast** (juice, coffee, or tea, and a croissant and/or baguette) is still the traditional way to start the day, many hotels now also offer a generous buffet that may include various breads, sweet buns, fruit, yogurt, ham, cereal, juice, and sometimes eggs and bacon. A buffet breakfast might seem pricey at somewhere between 15€ to 25€, but keep in mind that a bare-bones continental version will usually cost at least 9€. If you are a light eater, you'll likely spend less and have more fun at the corner cafe. Romantics will appreciate the fact that at most hotels, you can have your breakfast delivered to your room for no extra charge.

PRACTICAL MATTERS

When & How to Reserve

The Covid-19 pandemic means that the traditional high and low seasons, as well as trade show and festival periods, continue to be up in the air. My advice is to simply book whenever it suits your plans, then make sure you understand the cancellation policy—most hotels will offer free cancellation up to the day before your stay, but often the very lowest rates are non-refundable. One thing that hasn't changed, however, is the need to compare prices. While online travel-booking sites like Expedia, Booking.com, Hotelscombined.com, and Priceline are convenient for searching room rates, often the best place to look is the hotel's official website,

Going Solo

Though the listings below show room rates for two people, single rooms are often available for solo travelers at reduced rates. The best tactic is to ask the hotel directly, since they don't always advertise their smallest rooms, even on their own websites.

particularly in the case of smaller, affordable hotels. Why? Those booking sites charge hotel fees as much as 20%, a percentage that many hotels feel obliged to pass on to the customer.

Perpetually fluctuating prices make it difficult to fix rates in guidebooks; the prices quoted here attempt to offer a realistic range, with the top price reflecting the rack rate (the maximum "official" rate) and the lower figure corresponding to the average discount Internet rate. *Note:* Unless indicated, rates do not include breakfast.

THE RIGHT BANK

Louvre & Île de la Cité (1st Arrondissement)

It was here that Paris began, and it is here that you will still find a great number of the city's most famous sights—and the highest concentration of tourists. While the central location is tempting, be forewarned that this is not where you will find cute neighborhood stores or a slice of typical Parisian life. What's more, the area is pretty dead at night. Admittedly, if you are in town for only 1 or 2 days, a central locale is key, since time will be of the essence. If you have a little more time, you'll find much more comfortable lodgings, at lower prices, just a 10-minute walk away.

EXPENSIVE

Cheval Blanc Paris ★★   Set within the iconic La Samaritaine department store (p. 214) along the Seine, this ultra-refined spot is one of the only hotels in Paris to overlook the Seine—and not just any stretch of the river: the historic part, where the water flows gracefully around the islands, past Notre-Dame and the city's glorious tree-lined quays. If that's not romantic enough for you, romance oozes inside the hotel's Dior spa (home to a 30m/98-ft. pool and a hammam) and in the chic rooftop brasserie, which morphs into an all-day cocktail bar with 360° skyline views—perfect for a panoramic tête-à-tête. Rooms are an elegant mix of Art Deco and contemporary details, and many offer views over the Seine, the rooftops, and/or monuments like the Pompidou Center, the Eiffel Tower, and Montmartre. It's a mega-splurge to stay here, but even if you can't afford a night, stop by for the rooftop or a refined afternoon tea.

8 quai du Louvre, 1st arrond. www.chevalblanc.com. ℂ **01-40-28-00-00.** 72 units. 1,250€–1,450€ double; 1,850€ and up suite. Métro: Louvre-Rivoli or Châtelet. **Amenities:** Restaurant; bar; gym; spa; children's playroom; concierge; room service; free Wi-Fi.

Parisian Hotels & Accessibility

Hotels in centuries-old buildings may be full of charm, but they also often feature narrow staircases and/or tiny elevators. If accessibility is a concern, be sure to check when you reserve. Parisian hotels are evolving: All hotels in the moderate and expensive categories are supposed to have at least one wheelchair-accessible room.

price CATEGORIES

Expensive	300€ and up		**Inexpensive**	Under 150€
Moderate	151€–299€			

Hôtel Brighton ★★★   If you spring for a room with a view at this gracious hotel, you will not be disappointed. A splendid vista from the Louvre to the Tuileries Garden and the Eiffel Tower spreads before you as you loll in your bed. While not every room has the jackpot view, most in the "deluxe" and "executive" categories do, and all have a subdued, sophisticated decor with elegant fabrics draping the windows and tasteful decorative touches. Top-notch bedding, plush bathrobes, and high thread counts are all part of the package. In short, this classy establishment belongs under the arcades of the rue de Rivoli. Rooms are spacious and airy, with roomy bathrooms and a mix of reproduction and real antique pieces. Understandably, rooms with views book up early.

218 rue de Rivoli, 1st arrond. www.paris-hotel-brighton.com. ℂ **01-47-03-61-61.** 61 units. 250€–515€ double; 350€–680€ suite (sleeps 2–4). Métro: Tuileries. **Amenities:** Restaurant; bar; concierge; laundry service; room service; tearoom; free Wi-Fi.

MODERATE

Hôtel Thérèse ★★★   Just a few steps from the Palais Royal and a few more from the Louvre, these beautiful lodgings combine old-fashioned charm with modern chic. Comfy sofas invite you to relax in the lobby, whose decor includes lots of mirrors, bookcases, and unique lighting fixtures. The stylish yet comfortable decor extends to the rooms, which feature pleasing, soft colors, subtle geometric patterns, upholstered headboards, and, on the third floor, very high ceilings. Despite its central location, the tiny street is very quiet, and light floods the building from both sides. Rooms are Parisian size, which means the least expensive are small; the rates go up with the dimensions. A wheelchair-accessible room is on the ground floor.

5–7 rue Thérèse, 1st arrond. www.hoteltherese.com. ℂ **01-42-96-10-01.** 40 units. 157€–370€ double; 380€–417€ family room (up to 4). Métro: Palais Royal–Musée du Louvre or Pyramides. **Amenities:** Bar; bicycles; concierge; laundry service; loaner laptops; room service; free Wi-Fi.

INEXPENSIVE

Hôtel du Cygne ★   Chock-full of exposed beams and stone walls (not to mention narrow stairways—there is no elevator), this 17th-century building has been carefully restored, and the simple lodgings receive ongoing tender loving care from Isabelle Gouge, the friendly owner. Most rooms are predictably small, but are cheerfully decorated with fresh white walls, floral bedspreads, and the owner's personal touches. The reward for the climb to the top floor is a roomy suite that can sleep three. Because the hotel is near Les Halles and the Montorgueil neighborhood (very hip at night), staying on a

Right Bank West Hotels

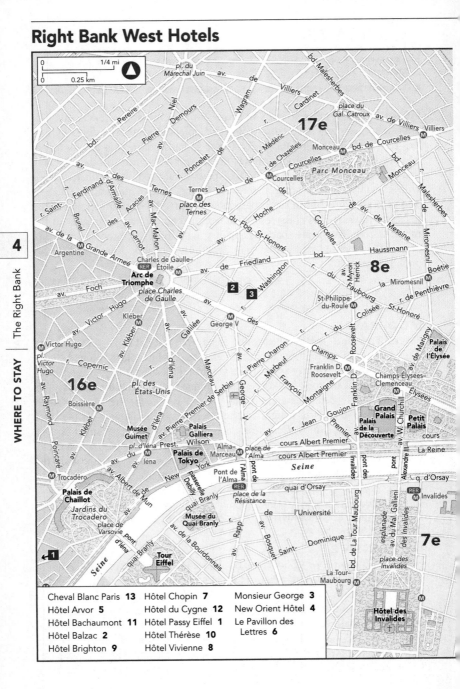

Cheval Blanc Paris **13**	Hôtel Chopin **7**	Monsieur George **3**
Hôtel Arvor **5**	Hôtel du Cygne **12**	New Orient Hôtel **4**
Hôtel Bachaumont **11**	Hôtel Passy Eiffel **1**	Le Pavillon des
Hôtel Balzac **2**	Hôtel Thérèse **10**	Lettres **6**
Hôtel Brighton **9**	Hôtel Vivienne **8**	

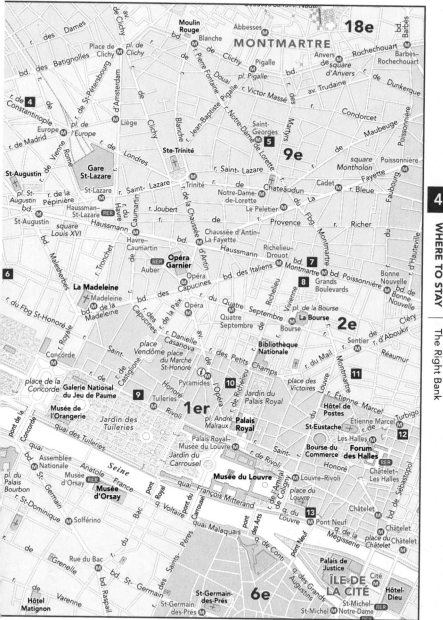

Right Bank East Hotels

Bed & Coworking **11**
Le Citizen **2**
Cosmos Hôtel **3**
Eden Lodge Paris **10**
Generator Paris **1**
Hôtel Caron de
  Beaumarchais **6**
Hôtel de la
  Porte Dorée **12**
Hôtel Jeanne d'Arc
  Le Marais **7**
Hôtel Jules et Jim **5**
Maison Breguet **9**
Pavillon de la Reine **8**
Sinner **4**

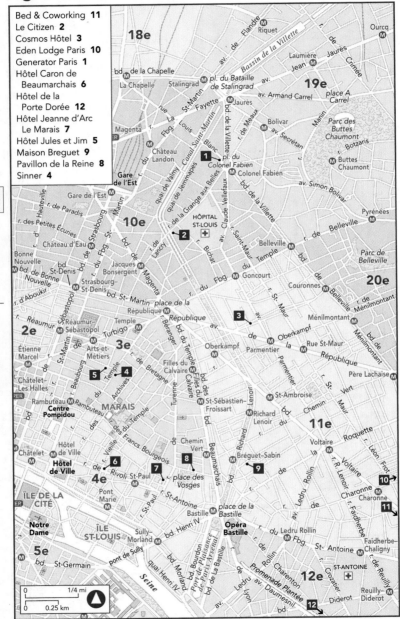

French hotels are graded by a government-regulated system that hands out 0 to 5 stars (plus "Palace" status for upper-end five-starred properties; see p. 63), which the hotels then must post at the entrance to their establishment. Unfortunately, palaces aside, the criteria used often have more to do with quantity than quality. Rooms are rated for size, number of beds, and the presence or absence of items like hair dryers and minibars—overall atmosphere and charm are not necessarily a factor. It's possible to end up in a darling two-star hotel that's much nicer than a three-star down the street with big rooms and a minibar but all the ambience of a rehab center. What's more, the addition of a fifth star prompted everyone to try to jump up a notch, so the most basic hotel might now have three stars. One thing is sure: The more stars it has, the more a hotel is allowed to charge. *Our advice:* Use the French star system as a rough estimate of quality, then do some homework on your own.

By the way, the stars beside the listings below are our own and have no relation to the French star system. You'll find our criteria at the front of the book.

Sunday is much cheaper than other nights. If you're noise sensitive, ask for a room that overlooks the back of the hotel, not the street.

3–5 rue du Cygne, 1st arrond. www.hotelducygne.fr. ℂ **01-42-60-14-16.** 18 units. 80€–135€ double; 155€–185€ suite up to 3 people. Métro: Etienne Marcel. RER: Les Halles. **Amenities:** Free Wi-Fi.

The Marais (3rd & 4th Arrondissements)

Centuries ago, this neighborhood was a swamp (*marais*), but now it's merely swamped with stylish boutiques, restaurants, and people who seem to have just stepped out of a hair salon. Stunning 16th- and 17th-century mansions, which had fallen into disrepair, have been scrubbed down and fixed up over the past few decades, and they shine like pearls along the narrow streets of this fashionable area where clothing stores, cool bars, and restaurants have invaded Paris' historic Jewish quarter. The many excellent museums here include the **Picasso Paris** (p. 161) and the **Musée Carnavalet** (p. 157). In short, this is a great area to stay in, but it's also a victim of its own success. You might not hear a lot of French in some of those cute cafes on rue Vielle du Temple. The northern Marais (in the 3rd arrond.) is generally quieter and less assailed by tourists.

EXPENSIVE

Pavillon de la Reine ★★★ Just off the Place des Vosges, this "Queen's Pavilion" harkens back to when the magnificent square was the home of royalty. You certainly feel like a noble as you pass through an arcade into a small formal garden and enter this elegant mansion, which is set back from the hustle and bustle of the Marais. Despite its 56 rooms, the hotel feels small

Courtyard entrance of Pavillon de la Reine.

and intimate, like a lord's private hunting lodge in the country. The decor is a suave and subtle combination of modern and antique history: Dark period furniture blends with rich colors on the walls and beds, and choice objects and historic details abound. Several of the deluxe rooms are duplexes with a cozy sleeping loft. Guests have access to a full spa, offering sauna and fitness room, as well as massages and treatments. There's also a chic French restaurant, **Anne,** with a 105€ tasting menu that's worth staying in for (Wed–Sat lunch and dinner; Sun lunch only).

28 pl. des Vosges, 3rd arrond. www.pavillon-de-la-reine.com. ℗ **01-40-29-19-19.** 56 units. 340€–550€ double; 600€ and up suite. Métro: Bastille. **Amenities:** Bar; concierge; fitness room; laundry service; room service; sauna; spa; free Wi-Fi.

Sinner ★★★ Looking for a quirky splurge? Celebrated Parisian designer Tristan Auer has turned a standard Parisian building on rue du Temple into a joyously rebellious hotel with daring decor inspired by medieval religious iconography and the Templar knights who once lived in the area. Its dark hallways are lit by lanterns, stained-glass windows add pops of unexpected color, and each room is a different constellation of artwork and wood furnishings. There's even a concept store set in a dark crypt and a spa modeled on Roman baths. A hip cocktail lounge overlooks the restaurant, which has church-style paneling, cathedral ceilings, and a street food–inspired menu.

116 rue du Temple, 3rd arrond. https://sinnerparis.com. ℗ **01-42-72-20-00.** 43 units. 430€–650€ double; 2,000€ suite up to 4 people. Métro: Rambuteau. **Amenities:** Restaurant; bar; spa; room service; laundry service; fitness equipment on request; free Wi-Fi.

MODERATE

Hôtel Caron de Beaumarchais ★★★ In the 18th century, Pierre Augustin Caron de Beaumarchais—author of "The Barber of Seville" and "The Marriage of Figaro"—lived near here, and this small hotel celebrates both the playwright and the magnificent century he lived in. The walls are covered in high-quality reproductions of period fabrics; rooms are furnished with authentic antique writing tables and chandeliers; and period paintings and first-edition pages of "The Barber of Seville" hang on the walls. The rooms are smallish, but the high ceilings (with exposed beams) and tall windows let in lots of light, making them feel spacious. Unlike other parts of the Marais, food stores, buses, and Métro stops are close by, and it's a short walk to the Seine. *Note:* Some beds are not standard sizes.

Guest room and balcony at the Hôtel Caron de Beaumarchais.

12 rue Vieille-du-Temple, 4th arrond. www.carondebeaumarchais.com. ℂ **01-42-72-34-12.** 19 units. 145€–290€ double. Métro: St-Paul or Hôtel de Ville. **Amenities:** Free Wi-Fi.

Hôtel Jules et Jim ★★ The entrance to this gem of a hotel is so discreet you could walk right past it. Find your way inside and you're in for a treat: A cobbled courtyard with an outdoor fireplace merges into a low-key cocktail bar with vintage-inspired furniture, while the guest rooms—all ultra-comfortable—flaunt hip decor such as white walls with clever backlighting and beautiful wall art. Some have bathrooms with floor-to-ceiling windows; others, on the upper floors, provide panoramic rooftop views. For those needing extra room, there's the duplex suite, resplendent in dark woods and retro-chic furniture (but its staircase is not child-proof, so this isn't appropriate for families with toddlers).

11 rue des Gravilliers, 3rd arrond. www.hoteljulesetjim.com. ℂ **01-44-54-13-13.** 23 units. 259€–390€ double; 440€ duplex up to 4 people. Métro: Arts et Métiers. **Amenities:** Cocktail bar; free Wi-Fi.

Hôtel Saint-Louis en l'Isle ★★   Set on the tiny main drag of the tranquil Île Saint-Louis, this friendly place has a prime location on one of the city's most desirable pieces of real estate. The impeccable rooms are done up in a low-key modern style with historic touches: stone floors, dark wood furniture, and framed etchings of 17th- and 18th-century nobles. The streetside rooms are quiet but a little dark; if you want a lot of light, ask for a corner room or splurge on one of the rooms on the top floor. The elevators stop at landings between floors, so you'll have to be able to manage stairs here. A wheelchair-accessible room is on the ground floor.

75 rue St-Louis-en-l'Île, 4th arrond. www.saintlouisenlisle.com. ℂ **01-46-34-04-80.** 20 units. 132€–260€ double; 245€–320€ triple. Métro: Pont Marie. **Amenities:** Free Wi-Fi.

INEXPENSIVE

Hôtel Jeanne d'Arc Le Marais ★★★   Considering its prime location in the southern Marais, right next to the leafy Place du Marché Ste-Catherine, this cozy hotel is an incredible deal. Its simple, tasteful rooms have textured wallpaper and contemporary lighting fixtures. Everything is impeccable, from the quality bedding to the spotless bathrooms. Families will be interested in the spacious and reasonably priced quads. Rooms book up months in advance, especially for fashion weeks (Feb, Mar, July, and Sept). *Note:* Another hotel with the same name is in the 13th arrondissement—make sure you have the right hotel when you reserve, or you will be in for an unpleasant surprise.

3 rue de Jarente, 4th arrond. www.hoteljeannedarc.com. ℂ **01-48-87-62-11.** 34 units. 129€–300€ double; 180€–370€ quad. Métro: St-Paul. **Amenities:** Computer in lobby; free Wi-Fi.

Champs-Élysées, Trocadéro & Western Paris (8th, 16th & 17th Arrondissements)

Even grander than the 7th arrondissement on the Left Bank, the area around the Champs-Élysées is positively mythic. To the south of the boulevard, along avenues Montaigne and George V, are the most exclusive designer shops in the city; to the north, elegant buildings, shops, and restaurants stretch up to Parc Monceau, which has excellent museum neighbors, including **Musée Nissim de Camondo** (p. 168). Affordable lodgings are scarce around here, especially near the Champs and the Arc de Triomphe, where the high prices often have more to do with the location than accommodation quality. Ironically, the location is not particularly central; it's an hour's hike from here to Notre-Dame, but you will be well served by public transport.

EXPENSIVE

Hôtel Balzac ★★★   Chandeliers and yards of rich fabric await you in the lobby of these luxurious lodgings, which were built for the director of the Paris Opéra in 1853. Just a few steps away from the Champs-Élysées, this classy town house features spacious rooms with huge beds, high thread counts, and drapes of chiffon and velour around the bed and windows. The ambience is classic and very French, with antiques, high ceilings, and subtle

The ultimate in upscale Parisian hospitality is the Palace Hotel, a rating given only to establishments able to symbolize "excellence and perfection, luxury and timelessness." It's here you'll find the Michelin-starred restaurants, spas, pools, and big bedrooms, as well as well-to-do Parisians looking for time out in sumptuous surroundings. Palaces also usually occupy historically important buildings, like the **Peninsula** (https://peninsula.com), where George Gershwin wrote "An American in Paris" in 1928.

Our favorites are: **Le Bristol** (www. lebristolparis.com), for its enduring elegance, the best hot chocolate in town, and three-Michelin-starred dining; **Le Crillon** (www.rosewoodhotels.com), for the James Bond–esque spa and pool, decorated with 17,600 gold scales, and the winter garden, which serves one of the best afternoon teas in town; **Le Lutetia** (www.hotellutetia.com), for its brasserie set under a sumptuous glass ceiling, and one afternoon tea; and **La Réserve** (www.lareserve-paris.com), for its wonderful boutique feel, great restaurant, and luxury spa. Rooms in these establishments usually start at around 1,000€, but you can get a "more affordable" feel for the luxury by popping in for a cocktail at the bar (about 25€, but always served with nibbles) or an afternoon tea (expect to pay around 50€ per person).

colors. Visiting dignitaries can opt for a Presidential Suite with views of the Eiffel Tower; lesser mortals will be happy with the junior and corner suites, which feature separate sitting areas. You can enjoy a drink on a plush sofa in the covered interior courtyard. **Pierre Gagnaire,** a gourmet pleasure palace of a restaurant with three Michelin stars, is in the same building.

6 rue Balzac, 8th arrond. www.hotelbalzac.com. ℭ **01-44-35-18-00.** 69 units. 243€–660€ double; 495€ and up suite and junior suite. Parking 30€. Métro: George V. **Amenities:** Restaurant; bar; babysitting; business center; dry cleaning; room service; concierge; free Wi-Fi.

Monsieur George ★★★ Steps from the Champs-Élysées, this hotel (named after George Washington) is as refined as its surroundings and has a lovely young staff to attend to your (almost) every need. Chic rooms in blacks, grays, and blues have a distinct Art Deco feel that continues in the bathrooms, where the marble sinks and gold taps wouldn't look amiss on a luxury 1920s ocean liner. Several rooms have small balconies, and a few even overlook the Sacré-Coeur or the Eiffel Tower; the all-white suites are fresh and airy. The garden suite is a duplex with its own garden courtyard. Guests have access to the hotel's spa and fitness space, set under vaulted ceilings. There's also a hip bar and a gourmet restaurant, **Galanga.**

17 rue Washington, 8th arrond. www.monsieurgeorge.com. ℭ **01-87-89-48-48.** 46 units. 290€–480€ double; 600€ and up suite. Métro: Georges V. **Amenities:** Restaurant; bar; fitness center; spa; concierge; loaner smart devices; room service; laundry service; free Wi-Fi.

MODERATE

Hôtel Passy Eiffel ★★ These colorful lodgings are on a cute shopping street in Passy, previously its own village before it got gobbled up by the city. Rooms are individually decorated in lots of warm neutral colors, blues, and mauves, with most featuring patterned wallpaper. Everything is in tip-top condition, and double-paned windows keep out most street noise. If you are a light sleeper, ask for a courtyard room. For extra romance, request a room with an Eiffel Tower view. For a pre-dinner drink, make a beeline for the small garden courtyard, hidden away from the street.

10 rue de Passy, 16th arrond. www.passyeiffel.com. ⓒ **01-45-25-55-66.** 49 units. 158€–320€ double. Métro: Passy or La Muette. **Amenities:** Bar; concierge; free Wi-Fi.

Le Pavillon des Lettres ★★★ Tastefully chic, this hotel is in the navel of the French political universe, being just across the street from the powerful Ministry of the Interior. The theme here, however, is literature. Each of the 26 exquisite rooms is designated by a different letter and linked to a famous author. If you are in room Z, for example, you might find a copy of Zola's "Nana" on the bedside table and some of the author's text on the wall. The room design is serenely hip, with handsome shades of gray, olive green, beige, and mauve. While the rooms are a little small, the ceilings are mostly high and bathrooms are spacious. Tapas are served at cocktail hour.

12 rue des Saussaies, 8th arrond. www.pavillondeslettres.com. ⓒ **01-49-24-26-26.** 26 units. 225€–430€ double; 330€–590€ junior suite. Métro: Madeleine. **Amenities:** Bar; bicycles; concierge; library; laundry service; room service; loaner iPads; free Wi-Fi.

INEXPENSIVE

New Orient Hôtel ★★★ This lovely hotel offers comfortable rooms with high ceilings, 19th-century moldings, and colorful fabrics. While it may not be on top of the Champs-Élysées, it's not far, and it's close to stately Parc Monceau and a quick trot to the Saint Lazare train station. The friendly owners, who are inveterate flea-market browsers, have refinished and restored the antique furniture themselves. Rooms (many of which have small balconies) are small but in tip-top shape, and the bathrooms sparkle. Though the hotel has an elevator, you'll have to negotiate stairs to get to it. The best rates are on the hotel website.

16 rue de Constantinople, 8th arrond. www.hotelneworient.com. ⓒ **01-45-22-21-64.** 30 units. 90€–230€ double; 130€–250€ triple. Métro: Villiers, Europe, or St-Lazare. **Amenities:** Computer in lobby; concierge; free Wi-Fi.

Opéra & Grands Boulevards (2nd & 9th Arrondissements)

Grands Boulevards (those wide throughways that Baron Haussmann plowed through Paris in the 19th c.) and just below Montmartre is a lovely mix of hip bars and restaurants and old-time Paris, with a good sprinkling of small museums for a dose of culture. While you won't find too many big monuments around here, the area's upsides include lower room rates and a more neighborhood-y feel, at least away from the boulevards.

MODERATE

Hôtel Arvor ★★ These spiffy lodgings are in the charming "New Athens" neighborhood, where 19th-century Romantics like George Sand and Frédéric Chopin lived and worked. Maybe that's why Mme. Flamarion, of the famous French publishing house, decided to open this arty yet relaxed hotel, where fresh white walls show off modern photography and art prints. Rooms are a little small, but simple and chic. Those on the upper floors have nice rooftop views, and some of the suites offer a glimpse of the far-off Eiffel Tower. The airy lobby, with large windows and shelves full of books, is an invitation to kick back and catch up on your reading. Along with alcoholic drinks, the hotel bar offers Kusmi teas and freshly squeezed juices.

8 rue Laferrière, 9th arrond. www.hotelarvor.com. ✆ **01-48-78-60-92.** 30 units. 140€–260€ double; 160€–320€ suite. Métro: St-Georges. **Amenities:** Bar; room service; free Wi-Fi.

Hôtel Bachaumont ★★ Art Deco design gets a colorful, modern twist in this trendy little spot in the Montorgeuil district that draws Parisians as much as travelers, thanks to an excellent brasserie and a cocktail bar run by the team behind the fabulous Experimental Cocktail Club (p. 243). Sit below the beautiful glass ceiling and tuck into delights like juicy steak in wine-rich Bordelaise sauce, and langoustines with sage potatoes. Then sleep it off in sleek, blue-toned rooms set with dark-wood retro furnishings. Standard rooms are larger than most (if you're a light sleeper, ask for a courtyard room overlooking the brasserie's atrium), while suites are downright big for Paris, with a loftlike vibe. One even has a balcony for extra romance and rooftop views.

18 rue Bachaumont, 2nd arrond. www.hotelbachaumont.com. ✆ **01-81-66-47-00.** 49 units. 202€–300€ double; 405€–550€ suite. Métro: Sentier or Etienne-Marcel. **Amenities:** Restaurant; bar; room service; free Wi-Fi.

INEXPENSIVE

Hôtel Chopin ★★ Nestled at the back of the delightful Passage Jouffroy, this budget hotel has remarkably quiet rooms considering its location in the middle of the rush and bustle of the Grands Boulevards. The staircase is a little creaky (you will have to climb a flight to get to the elevator), but the refreshed rooms are clean and colorful, and the bathrooms are spotless. Rooms on the upper floors get more light; many have nice views of Parisian rooftops. Across the street from the Passage Jouffroy is Passage des Panoramas, a maze of hip bistros and shops.

10 bd. Montmartre or 46 passage Jouffroy, 9th arrond. www.hotel-chopin.com. ✆ **01-47-70-58-10.** 36 units. 102€–150€ double; from 155€ triple. Métro: Grands Boulevards or Richelieu-Drouot. **Amenities:** Free Wi-Fi.

Hôtel Vivienne ★★★ Right around the corner from restaurant-filled Passage des Panoramas, this family-run hotel offers comfortable, spotless lodgings at great prices. Most of the rooms have a modern decor and accents in muted purple, chocolate, or gray; some have a more classic look with floral prints or stripes. A few rooms have balconies with space for a small table;

some have connecting doors, and a handful of large suites are great for families. If you don't mind sharing a toilet down the hall, several doubles go for 81€. The service is friendly, as is the hotel's cat, Romero. Light sleepers will want a courtyard-facing room—the street can be noisy.

40 rue Vivienne, 2nd arrond. www.hotel-vivienne.com. ⓒ **01-42-33-13-26.** 44 units. 90€–160€ double; 165€–220€ suite for 2–4. Métro: Grands Boulevards or Richelieu–Drouot. **Amenities:** Concierge; free Wi-Fi.

Montmartre (18th Arrondissement)

If you're looking for a romantic setting, you can't do much better than Montmartre. Once you get away from the tourist hordes that invade Sacré-Coeur and Place du Tertre, you'll find lovely little lanes and small houses that harken back to the days when Picasso and the boys were at the Bateau Lavoir. Unfortunately, the pickings are a bit slim if you want to actually sleep here. If you are determined to stay up on the Butte, book early, as the few quality lodgings are generally in high demand.

EXPENSIVE

Hôtel Particulier Montmartre ★★ If your vision of Montmartre involves secret little cobbled lanes and old town houses with tree-filled gardens, this chic, arty hotel is for you. To get to it, you must buzz in from the street, then take a narrow, private path—Passage de la Sorcière (aka the "witch's alley")—to an elegant former mansion. Each of the five suites was designed by a different artist: One evokes a fancy bordello, with jewel-studded velvet walls; another has psychedelic floral wallpaper and stunning views over the garden; all are sumptuous. For extra pizzazz, the loftlike top-floor suite is awash in natural light and flaunts an open bathroom with a clawfoot bathtub. Into food? You may want to consider dining in: The hotel's on-site restaurant, **Le Grand Salon,** offers exquisite French dishes with a modern twist and has an old world–style courtyard—a glorious treat on a sunny day.

23 av. Junot (Pavillon D), 18th arrond. https://hotelparticulier. com. ⓒ **01-53-41-81-40.** 5 units. 390€–590€ suite. Métro: Lamarck Caulincourt. **Amenities:** Restaurant; bar; garden; laundry service; room service; free Wi-Fi.

Art-themed room at Hôtel Particulier.

Montmartre Hotels

L'Ermitage Sacré-Coeur **5**
Hôtel des Arts Montmartre **3**
Hôtel Particulier **4**
Le Relais Montmartre **1**
Terrass" Hotel **2**

MODERATE

Terrass" Hotel ★   Most upper-floor rooms in this trendy hotel (once frequented by Dalí and Renoir) afford amazing cityscapes, from the steel-gray rooftops in the east to the filigreed silhouette of the Eiffel Tower in the west. Can't get enough of the views? Head to the rooftop bar-restaurant to continue your gazing over cocktails and delicious Mediterranean dishes. Or, after a busy day sightseeing, wind down in the hotel's Nuxe spa, with its massage rooms, hammam, sauna, and a rain shower. Another perk is the fitness center, where guests can sign up for weekend lessons of yoga or Pilates. If you're looking for gifts, hit the lobby shop, where you won't find products more local than the hotel's own honey (from its rooftop hives) and hip T-shirts by Montmartre Parisian designer Fils de Butte.

12 rue Joseph de Maistre, 18th arrond. https://terrass-hotel.com. ℂ **01-46-06-72-85.** 100 units. 170€–285€ double; 890€ suite. Métro: Place de Clichy or Blanche. **Amenities:** Restaurant; bar; spa; fitness center; room service; free Wi-Fi.

Suite at Terrass" Hotel.

INEXPENSIVE

Hôtel des Arts Montmartre ★★ On a narrow street just off lively rue des Abbesses, this unassuming hotel once hosted artists and sculptors and even a few dancers from the Moulin Rouge. It's currently run by the third generation of the Lameyre family. Today's guests are generally tourists, who enjoy the great rates, comfortable lodgings, and welcoming atmosphere. Rooms are small yet spotless, with firm mattresses and cheerful colors on the walls. A few have distant views of the Eiffel Tower over Parisian rooftops; the "Romantic" room comes with a bottle of champagne and has a small balcony. Montmartre's two remaining windmills, Moulin de la Galette and Moulin du Radet, are just up the street. Not all rooms are air-conditioned; check upon reservation.

5 rue Tholozé, 18th arrond. www.arts-hotel-paris.com. ℂ **01-46-06-30-52.** 50 units. 79€–150€ double; 140€–220€ triple. Parking 20€. Métro: Blanche or Abbesses. **Amenities:** Concierge; room service; free Wi-Fi.

Le Relais Montmartre ★★ These comfortable lodgings include small but impeccable rooms decked out in light, warm colors and a stylish, classic decor of tasteful floral prints. The hotel is on a peaceful little side street, right around the corner from a delicious stretch of food shops on rue Lepic. Families can book into the adjoining rooms. In good weather, breakfast is served on a lovely little patio; speaking of breakfast, this is one of the few hotels around to serve a really decent one, thanks to products brought in from the aforementioned gourmet shops. If you're in a hurry, the *lève tôt* (early bird) option in reception is a very good value at just 6€.

6 rue Constance, 18th arrond. www.hotel-relais-montmartre.com. © **01-70-64-25-25.** 26 units. 85€–230€ double. Métro: Blanche. **Amenities:** Concierge; laundry service; loaner iPad; free Wi-Fi.

L'Ermitage Sacré-Coeur ★★★   Built in 1890 by a rich gentleman for his mistress, this elegant town house has been lovingly converted into intimate guest lodgings. Tucked behind Sacré-Coeur, the small mansion still feels like a private home. In fact, it virtually is: The Canipel family has run these unconventional lodgings since the 1980s. Each room is decorated with different period prints and draperies, as well as handsome antique bedsteads and armoires. The hallways and entry are done up in deep blues and gold leaf; wall murals and paintings are the works of a local artist. The hotel has no elevator and no TVs in the rooms. The Canipels also rent nearby studios and apartments that sleep one to four. All reservations are made by e-mail.

24 rue Lamarck, 18th arrond. www.ermitagesacrecoeur.fr. © **06-12-49-05-15.** 5 units. 110€ double; 130€ triple; 140€ quad. Parking 25€. Métro: Lamarck-Caulaincourt. **Amenities:** Free Wi-Fi.

République, Bastille & Eastern Paris (11th & 12th Arrondissements)

Just north of the Marais, this shabby-chic, up-and-coming area offers low rates and proximity to the nightlife around rue Oberkampf. Nearby, the Faubourg St-Antoine area is an El Dorado for exciting new restaurants and has nice lodging options; though it doesn't look central on the map, it has excellent public transport. This historic workers' neighborhood was where revolutionary fervor came to a head on July 14, 1789, when irate citizens stormed down the boulevard and took over the Bastille. Things have calmed down considerably since then, and outside of the festive bar and club scene around the Bastille and rue de Charonne, it's a pretty laid-back area.

MODERATE

Bed & Coworking ★★   Want to see Paris' forward-thinking side? This high-concept hotel occupies a former distillery on a mini-campus that includes a fitness center, a fabulous Mediterranean restaurant, **Laïa** (see p. 110), and—as the hotel's name suggests—a coworking space (run by Deskopolitain). In fact, at time of writing, this was the city's only hotel to include unlimited time at a coworking desk for the price of the room—a godsend if you're mixing business and pleasure. Rooms are comfy and colorful, with a kitchenette and garden views, plus you're a short stroll from the foodiest street in the 11th, **rue Paul Bert.** The hotel is tucked away from the street; you enter through large doors and walk to the back of a courtyard.

226 bd. Voltaire, 11th arrond. © **01-88-45-30-12.** 15 units. 155€–300€ double. Métro: Rue des Boulets. **Amenities:** Coworking access; free Wi-Fi.

Eden Lodge Paris ★★★   Hidden from the street in the back of a beautiful garden, this modern wooden structure combines environmental awareness with extremely comfortable lodgings. There are only five rooms and breakfast is free, so some might call this a bed-and-breakfast instead of a hotel. Quality insulation, LED lighting, solar panels, and zero-carbon output give these lodgings their ecological cred, as well as self-cleaning tiles that absorb air pollution. There's no skimping on comfort, though: Rooms are chic, warm, and minimalist, with vintage-esque furniture and high-tech Japanese toilets. A microwave and refrigerator are available for guests in the breakfast room, which is open all day. Bicycles are on hand, as well as a 500 sq. m (5,381 sq. ft.) garden for communing with nature.

175 rue de Charonne, 11th arrond. www.edenlodgeparis.net. ℂ **01-43-56-73-24.** 5 units. 225€ double; 350€ suite. Rates include breakfast. Métro: Alexandre Dumas. **Amenities:** Bicycles; garden; free Wi-Fi.

Maison Breguet ★★★   The 11th arrondissement is getting more chic by the day, as this hip, relatively new (2018) five-star proves. The hotel comes complete with a slick glass-roofed cocktail bar and a neo-bistro (a bistro serving modern versions of traditional French dishes) offering beautifully executed dishes like langoustines poached with mandarin oranges and roasted apples with pecans. You can dine in the peaceful courtyard on sunny days, and the rooms are as cool as can be, with a classy retro-Scandinavian vibe and an earthy color palette. The other draw here (aside from the price, which is lower than most other five-starred properties) is the wellness area, with a lovely indoor pool, sauna, hammam, and gym.

8 rue Breguet, 11th arrond. www.maisonbreguet.com. ℂ **01-58-30-32-31.** 53 units. 187€–297€ double; 250€–550€ suite. Métro: Breguet Sabin or Chemin Vert. **Amenities:** Restaurant; bar; indoor pool; sauna; fitness rooms; hammam; free Wi-Fi.

INEXPENSIVE

Cosmos Hôtel ★★   Just around the corner from the animated Oberkampf neighborhood, this budget option is a terrific deal. The modern rooms are spotless, and everything from the bed linens to the floor covering looks spanking new. And such a deal: only 82€ to 92€ for a double. Furthermore, the staff is friendly and helpful. The only downside is possible weekend-night noise as people spill out of nearby bars and restaurants. Ask for a room at the back if you're noise sensitive.

35 rue Jean-Pierre Timbaud, 11th arrond. www.cosmos-hotel-paris.com. ℂ **01-43-57-25-88.** 36 units. 82€–92€ double; 102€ triple. Métro: Parmentier. **Amenities:** Free Wi-Fi.

Hôtel de la Porte Dorée ★★   True, it's a little out of the way, but these lovely lodgings are well worth the Métro fare. Soothing neutral tones, antique headboards, high ceilings, wood floors, and original curlicue moldings are all part of the package at this hotel, which is owned by a friendly Franco-American couple. The hotel goes the extra mile for both the environment

Guest room at Hôtel de la Porte Dorée.

(ecologically correct policies) and babies (toys, playpens, and even potty seats available). And you'll pay less for all this than you will for something utterly basic in the center of town. What's more, it is right next to the verdant **Bois de Vincennes,** where you can rent bikes, picnic, or visit the Paris zoo (p. 174). The nearby Métro will get you to the city center in about 15 minutes.

273 av. Daumensil, 12th arrond. www.hoteldelaportedoree.com. ✆ **01-43-07-56-97.** 43 units. 99€–185€ double; 120€–195€ triple. Métro: Porte Dorée. **Amenities:** Babysitting; bicycles; free Wi-Fi.

Belleville, Canal St-Martin & La Villette (10th, 19th & 20th Arrondissements)

When historic arty neighborhoods like St-Germain and Montmartre became far too expensive for up-and-coming artists, many of them moved to these more proletarian neighborhoods, giving the area a funky, bohemian feel. Though it's gentrifying, gritty Belleville is still known for artists' studios, while dozens of hip cafes and restaurants now line the Canal St-Martin and the Bassin de la Villette. The young and adventurous will appreciate this part of town, but you will need to use the Métro to get to the city's more central areas—though the Marais is just a 10-minute walk from the start of Canal St-Martin.

MODERATE

Le Citizen ★★ Maybe it's the smiling young staff in jeans or the ecological ethos, but there's something alternative about this adorable boutique hotel on the Canal St-Martin. While the rooms are on the small side, they are light and airy, with lots of blond wood, clean lines, and views out onto the tree-lined canal. Each floor has only two rooms, ranging from the snug "City" to the spacious "Suite Zen," which can accommodate a couple with two children. On some floors, two rooms can be connected to form a large "apartment." At check-in, you'll be handed a loaner iPad loaded with information on Paris, as well as restaurant recommendations. The buffet breakfast and movies on demand are included in your room rate. The cool restaurant serves lunch and nighttime tapas until 11pm.

96 quai de Jemmapes, 10th arrond. www.lecitizenhotel.com. ✆ **01-83-62-55-50.** 12 units. 129€–290€ double; 250€–300€ suite; 400€–520€ apartment. Rates include breakfast. Métro: Jacques Bonsergent. **Amenities:** Restaurant; loaner iPad; free Wi-Fi.

INEXPENSIVE

Generator Paris ★★ A 20-minute walk from Gare du Nord (the Eurostar terminal) and 5 minutes from the picturesque quays and bars of Canal St-Martin, this trendy establishment (opposite Oscar Niemeyer's iconic French Communist Party HQ) blurs the lines between hotel and hostel by offering both private rooms and dormitories (for 8 or 10 people). It also offers perks that many of the city's standard hotels can't provide: namely, a rooftop bar with views onto Sacré-Coeur and a Métro-themed basement "club" with a fab cocktail happy hour. Breakfast is served in a light-filled cafe overlooking a small urban garden. The bright dorms are filled with young, mostly English-speaking travelers, but the more expensive private rooms attract a more demanding set of mature clients with extras like terraces. Female-only dorms are available.

9–11 pl. du Colonel Fabien, 10th arrond. https://generatorhostels. com. ✆ **01-70-98-84-00.** 199 units. 19€–50€ per person in dormitories; 78€–150€ double. Métro: Colonel Fabien. **Amenities:** Cafe; bar; in-room lockers; laundromat; towel rental; free Wi-Fi.

Métro-themed breakfast area at the Generator hostel.

THE LEFT BANK

Latin Quarter (5th & 13th Arrondissements)

Central and reasonably priced, the Latin Quarter is a longtime favorite for travelers in search of affordable accommodations. As a consequence, a few corners of this famously academic neighborhood are overrun with tourists and trinket shops. The streets immediately surrounding Place St-Michel (especially around rue de la Huchette) are where you'll find the worst tourist traps, in terms of both hotels and restaurants. Better prices and quality are to be had in the quieter and more authentic areas around the universities (College de France, La Sorbonne, Faculté de Sciences), a little farther from Notre-Dame but still within easy walking distance.

EXPENSIVE

Hôtel Monte Cristo ★★★ This hotel woos with wonderful decor themed around Alexandre Dumas' adventure novel "The Count of Monte Cristo." Stunning hand-painted fabrics combine with antiques, paintings, and beautiful mirrors to create a plush and rather exotic setting. Bathrooms are a contemporary take on Napoleon III–style, with terrazzo tiles mixed with vintage-style porcelain. With a nod to Dumas' Caribbean roots, you can sample rum neat (there are some one-off vintages worth sipping) or in a lip-smacking cocktail at the rum bar. Don't forget your swimsuit: The Asian-themed indoor pool and sauna, rarities in this part of the city, are fab places to wind down after a day of sightseeing.

20–22 rue Pascal, 5th arrond. www.hotelmontecristoparis.com. ℂ **01-47-07-41-92.** 50 units. 170€–500€ double; 350€ and up suite. Métro: Censier-Daubenton or Les Gobelins. **Amenities:** Bar; indoor pool; sauna; free Wi-Fi.

MODERATE

Hôtel Design Sorbonne ★★ In the thick of the student quarter facing La Sorbonne, this cozy boutique hotel combines comfort with unusual but classy decor. Period furniture is covered in lively green, blue, and dark brown stripes; colorful wall fabrics put a modern spin on Victorian patterns, and excerpts from French literary classics are woven into the carpets. Each room has a desk with an iMac for guests' use. As pretty as they are, the rooms are small, and some have tiny bathrooms. If you need space, opt for a deluxe with a bathtub or the large room on the top floor with a view of the Sorbonne and the Panthéon.

6 rue Victor Cousin, 5th arrond. www.hotelsorbonne.com. ℂ **01-43-54-58-08.** 38 units. 115€–380€ double; 180€–400€ top-floor double. Métro: Cluny–La Sorbonne. RER: Luxembourg. **Amenities:** Free Wi-Fi.

Hôtel Les Jardins du Luxembourg ★★ Just around the corner from its glorious namesake and down the street from the university, these intimate lodgings are tucked away on a quiet cul-de-sac, making it a favorite with the professorial crowd. The building's claim to fame is that Sigmund Freud stayed here on his first visit to Paris. Today it exudes elegance, from the nature-themed wallpaper behind the beds to the dark paint and glossy tiles in the bathrooms. While the standard rooms are pretty, the superior rooms, which cost only a few euros more, have nicer views and small balconies.

5 impasse Royer-Collard, 5th arrond. www.hoteljardinsluxembourg.com. ℭ **01-40-46-08-88.** 26 units. 140€–205€ double. Métro: Cluny–La Sorbonne. RER: Luxembourg. **Amenities:** Sauna; free Wi-Fi.

Hôtel Saint-Jacques ★★   The spacious rooms in this delightful hotel retain lots of architectural details from its Belle Epoque past. Most of the ceilings are adorned with masses of curlicues, and some have restored 18th-century murals. Modern reproductions of famous French paintings hang on the walls, and Second Empire–themed murals decorate the lobby and breakfast room. The romantic decor has a light, feminine feel, in shades of light blue, cream, and gray—considerably more inviting than when the hotel served as a set for the Audrey Hepburn/Cary Grant classic, "Charade." One wheelchair-accessible room is on the ground floor.

35 rue des Ecoles, 5th arrond. www.paris-hotel-stjacques.com. ℭ **01-44-07-45-45.** 36 units. 125€–270€ double; 155€–300€ triple. Métro: Maubert-Mutualité. **Amenities:** Bar; babysitting; free Wi-Fi.

OFF Paris Seine ★★★   Feel like taking a cruise but don't want to leave the city? Try Paris' first floating hotel, docked on the banks of the Seine at the foot of the Gare d'Austerlitz. Once inside, you'll feel like you're on a trendy ocean liner, especially as the music blasts when you are having a drink on one of the two decks over the water. On warm days, you can even paddle in a narrow outdoor pool that separates the bar areas. The chic, cabinlike rooms are small but well thought out; it's worth paying for a Seine-side room so you can gaze at the lights that reflect on the river at night. There's no room service per se, but if you pay at the bar in advance, you can have goodies delivered to your room. If you're a light sleeper, bring ear plugs as you can sometimes hear the Métro passing on the bridge over the water.

20–22 Port d'Austerlitz, 13th arrond. www.offparisseine.com. ℭ **01-44-06-62-65.** 58 units. 215€–285€ double; 270€–440€ suite. Métro: Gare d'Austerlitz or Gare de Lyon. **Amenities:** Bar; free Wi-Fi; outdoor pool.

INEXPENSIVE

Familia Hôtel ★★   Perfectly located, close to rue Mouffetard but far from the maddening crowds, this is a budget hotel that doesn't feel like one. The rooms are snug and a little outdated, but every detail has been scrupulously considered, from the carved cherrywood headboards to the period fabrics on the windows to the top-quality mattresses on the beds. Some rooms have exposed beams, others have wall murals, and those on the second, fifth, and sixth floors have small balconies with lovely views of the Latin Quarter. If there's no room, try the slightly higher-end version of the Familia next door, **Hôtel Minerve** (www.parishotelminerve.com; ℭ **01-43-26-26-04**), with similar detailing and larger rooms (150€–280€ double; 212€ triple).

11 rue des Ecoles, 5th arrond. www.familiahotel.com. ℭ **01-43-54-55-27.** 30 units. 75€–95 double; 110€–190€ triple. Métro: Jussieu or Cardinal Lemoine. **Amenities:** Free Wi-Fi.

4

WHERE TO STAY | The Left Bank

Left Bank Hotels (Eiffel Tower Area)

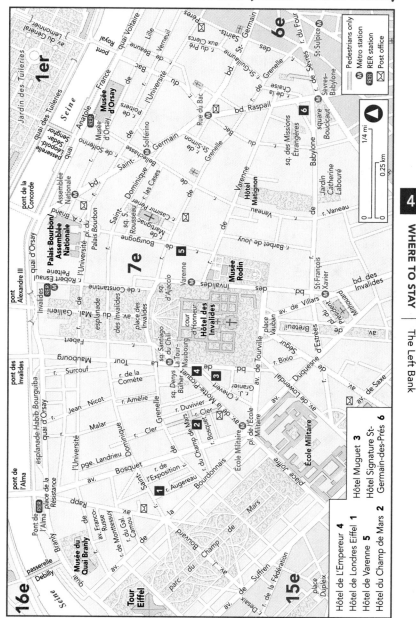

Hôtel de L'Empereur **4**
Hôtel de Londres Eiffel **1**
Hôtel de Varenne **5**
Hôtel du Champ de Mars **2**

Hôtel Muguet **3**
Hôtel Signature St-Germain-des-Prés **6**

Pedestrians only
Métro station
RER station
Post office

Left Bank Hotels (Latin Quarter, St-Germain, Montparnasse)

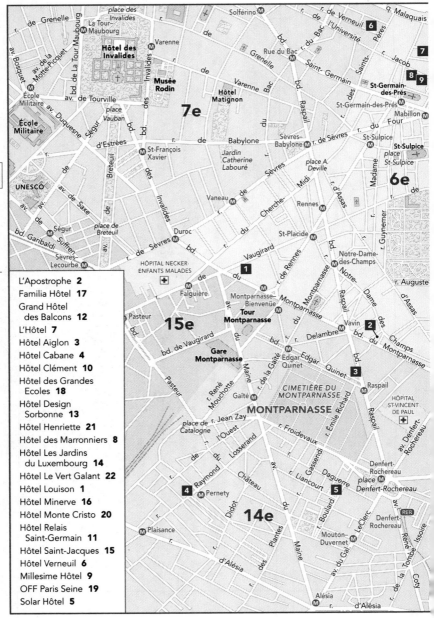

L'Apostrophe **2**
Familia Hôtel **17**
Grand Hôtel
   des Balcons **12**
L'Hôtel **7**
Hôtel Aiglon **3**
Hôtel Cabane **4**
Hôtel Clément **10**
Hôtel des Grandes
   Ecoles **18**
Hôtel Design
   Sorbonne **13**
Hôtel Henriette **21**
Hôtel des Marronniers **8**
Hôtel Les Jardins
   du Luxembourg **14**
Hôtel Le Vert Galant **22**
Hôtel Louison **1**
Hôtel Minerve **16**
Hôtel Monte Cristo **20**
Hôtel Relais
   Saint-Germain **11**
Hôtel Saint-Jacques **15**
Hôtel Verneuil **6**
Millesime Hôtel **9**
OFF Paris Seine **19**
Solar Hôtel **5**

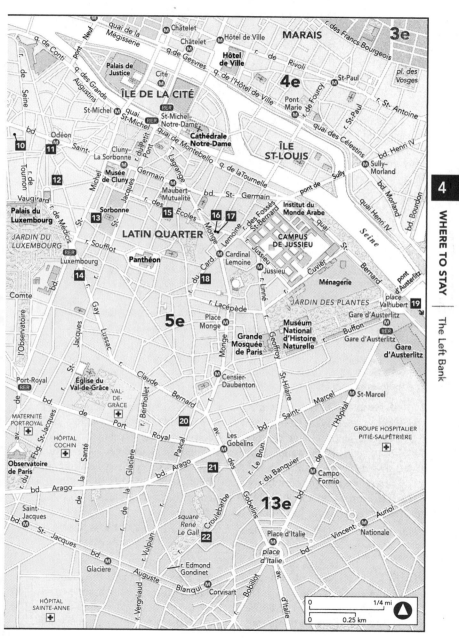

Hôtel des Grandes Ecoles ★★★   Tucked into a private garden on the slope of the Montagne Ste-Geneviève, this lovely hotel gives you the impression you have just walked out of Paris and into the countryside. A path leads to a flower-bedecked interior courtyard, where birds chirp in the trees; the reception area adjoins an inviting breakfast room with potted plants and an upright piano. The spotless rooms are filled with country-style furniture and papered in old-fashioned prints; quilted bedspreads and framed etchings complete the look. Views from most windows are of either the garden or surrounding trees. The calm is such that the hotel has nixed TVs. What's more, this unique ambience comes at a reasonable price. Rooms in the "Garden Building" are more modern, with newer bathrooms; families will appreciate the six suites that each sleep four.

The garden at Hôtel des Grandes Ecoles.

75 rue de Cardinal-Lemoine, 5th arrond. https://en.hoteldesgrandesecoles.com. ℰ **01-43-26-79-23.** 51 units. 140€–170€ double; 185€ family room. Parking 30€. Métro: Cardinal Lemoine or Place Monge. **Amenities:** Free Wi-Fi.

Hôtel Henriette ★★★   On a narrow, cobbled street that harks back to the Paris of yesteryear, this quaint hotel is made for those looking for a Parisian experience without the tourists. Room decor has a vintage slant, from bold, 1940s-style floral wallpaper to walls paneled with discreet 1970s natural wood. Downstairs, a lovely walled courtyard has wrought-iron furniture and plants creeping up old, crumbly walls. Breakfast is served buffet-style in a light-filled dining area, and includes gluten-free and handy express options (coffee and pastries for just 6€). It's a real find.

9 rue des Gobelins, 13th arrond. https://hotelhenriette.com. ℰ **01-47-07-26-90.** 32 units. 99€–159€ double; 195€–250€ suite. Métro: Les Gobelins. **Amenities:** Room service; free Wi-Fi.

Hôtel Le Vert Galant ★★★   In a quiet green corner near the Manufacture Nationale des Gobelins (p. 181), this lovely haven is only minutes away from rue Mouffetard and three Métro lines. Since it wraps around a small garden, all the rooms in this family-run operation look out on greenery, and the hotel has an unfussy, country feel. The recently renovated guest rooms have oak floors and Italian tiled showers. The Basque restaurant next door, **Auberge Etchegorry,** is run by the same management; eat here and you get a free glass of wine and coffee.

41 rue Croulebarbe, 13th arrond. www.vertgalant.com. © **01-44-08-83-50.** 17 units. 92€–150€ double. Parking 15€. Métro: Corvisart, Gobelins, or Place d'Italie. **Amenities:** Restaurant; free Wi-Fi.

St-Germain-des-Prés & Luxembourg (6th Arrondissement)

Sleek boutiques and restaurants abound in this legendary (and expensive) neighborhood; historic cafes and monuments lend plenty of atmosphere. Unlike some other Parisian neighborhoods, this one is lively even late at night; it is also centrally located and within walking distance of many top sights. The highest concentration of noise and tourist traps is around boulevard St-Germain and Carrefour de l'Odéon; once you turn down a side street, things quiet down.

EXPENSIVE

Hôtel Relais Saint-Germain ★★★ Fashioned out of three adjoining 17th-century town houses, this intimate hotel mixes old-world charm and jazzy modern ideas. Exposed beams abound in the spacious rooms, even the smallest of which is equipped with a comfortable sitting area. And yet there is nothing fussy or boring about the decor, which artfully blends period

Blondin twin room at Hôtel Relais Saint-Germain.

furniture with modern prints, like a Louis XV armchair covered in zigzagged leather. The effect is both stylish and deeply comforting. You'll want to fling yourself onto the king-size bed, cover yourself with a fake-fur throw, and just stare out the window at the lovely Carrefour de l'Odéon. There are some extra stairs between floors, so if you have mobility issues, make that clear when you reserve. Guests have priority at the hotel's restaurant, **Le Comptoir** (p. 124), where you might otherwise wait a month for a reservation. Rooms book up far in advance here.

9 carrefour de l'Odéon, 6th arrond. www.hotel-paris-relais-saint-germain.com. © **01-44-27-07-97.** 22 units. 250€–330€ double; 415€ and up suite. Rates include breakfast. Métro: Odéon. **Amenities:** Restaurant; babysitting; concierge; laundry service; room service; free Wi-Fi.

L'Hôtel ★★★ The hotel where Oscar Wilde famously lived above his means, and died in 1900 (on the ground floor) is now a gorgeous boutique hotel dressed up like a Belle Epoque boudoir. Each guest room is different, and all are set around a remarkable, six-story spiral staircase. Some rooms have fireplaces; some have fabric-covered walls; all come with lush period antiques, including one with a pair of gigantic, 19th-century Chinese vases. The Oscar Wilde room features a peacock-themed mural. The bijou cocktail bar (named after—you guessed it—Wilde) has live jazz on the first Thursday of the month, while downstairs in the cellar, you'll find a hammam pool, a steam room, and a massage room.

13 rue des Beaux Arts, 6th arrond. www.l-hotel.com. © **01-44-41-99-00.** 20 units. 290€–480€ double; 650€–780€ suite. Métro: St-Germain-des-Prés. **Amenities:** Restaurant; bar; concierge; laundry service; room service; free Wi-Fi.

MODERATE

Hôtel des Marronniers ★★ If you are looking for old-fashioned Parisian charm, head for these cozy lodgings just a few minutes away from the church of St-Germain-des-Prés. Nestled in the back of a courtyard behind the galleries and antique stores of chic rue Jacob, rooms here feature rich fabrics, (mostly) high ceilings, warm colors, and reproduction antiques, as well as a dash of quirky *je ne sais quoi.* Rooms are so quiet it's hard to believe you are in the city center; those facing the garden get more light. While the bedrooms have all been renovated, bathrooms could use an overhaul. Guests are invited to have breakfast or just relax in the lush garden behind the hotel, which doubles as a tearoom during the day; if it's raining, you can do the same on the covered veranda. The triples and quads are particularly well laid out for families.

21 rue Jacob, 6th arrond. www.hoteldesmarronniers.com. © **01-43-25-30-60.** 36 units. 179€–194€ double; 220€–285€ triple; 230€–350€ quad. Métro: St-Germain-des-Prés. **Amenities:** Garden; laundry service; library; tearoom; free Wi-Fi.

Hôtel Louison ★★ Hovering on the invisible border between the Montparnasse and St-Germain neighborhoods, this adorable hotel is a quick walk to the Luxembourg Gardens and the delights of the Bon Marché department store. While maintaining the original detailing and mood of this

19th-century building, the period decor is spiced up with contemporary colors and textures, like a gold and purple version of traditional *toile de jouy* wallpaper, or old-fashioned stripes cheered up with lush velvet pillows and contemporary headboards. Off the lobby, a cozy reading room is available for quiet pursuits and discussion; the breakfast room is open all day with a microwave for guests. Connecting rooms are available, as well as a furnished apartment for rent by the week or the month.

105 rue de Vaugirard, 6th arrond. www.louison-hotel.com. ℂ **01-53-63-25-50.** 42 units. 90€–199€ double; 175€–199€ triple. Parking 38€. Métro: Duroc or St-Placide. **Amenities:** Concierge; loaner iPad; laundry service; free Wi-Fi.

Hôtel Verneuil ★★★ Both historic and chic, this intimate hotel has conserved the exposed beams and architectural details of the 17th-century building it inhabits. In a nod to the neighborhood's literary roots, manuscripts and scrolls are tucked into niches in the walls. Neutral colors and cozy period touches give it the feel of a private home—perhaps that of an eminent editor. While the hallways are painted in somber shades of brown and beige, the rooms are bright and friendly, if small. If you need to stretch out, go for the deluxe room, which has space for a desk and chairs; there are a few connecting rooms for families. *Fun facts:* Author James Baldwin used to live in the building, and music icon Serge Gainsbourg lived across the street (as the fan graffiti shows).

8 rue de Verneuil, 7th arrond. www.hotel-verneuil-saint-germain.com. ℂ **01-42-60-82-14.** 26 units. 219 €–298€ double; 250€–480€ triple. Métro: St-Germain-des-Prés or Rue du Bac. **Amenities:** Bar; babysitting; business corner with printer; massages; laundry service; smartphone with apps and local information; room service; free Wi-Fi.

Millesime Hôtel ★★ These cozy lodgings defy their historic surroundings with a set of modern, chic rooms in soothing shades of beige and gray. A 21st-century take on Parisian elegance that includes unusual wood headboards and soft flannel upholstery, the decor is contemporary without being overbearing. Desks are unusually functional here if you need to work or write, especially in the superior doubles and suites. Post-sightseeing drinks can be sipped in the small bar or, if the weather is nice, in the pretty courtyard patio.

15 rue Jacob, 6th arrond. www.millesimehotel.com. ℂ **01-44-07-97-97.** 20 units. 190€–280€ double; 310€–450€ suite. Métro: St-Germain-des-Prés. **Amenities:** Bar; concierge; iPhone docks; mobile phones for guests; room service; free Wi-Fi.

INEXPENSIVE

Grand Hôtel des Balcons ★ For the neighborhood, the rooms in this simple hotel are remarkably spacious. Most have small balconies, and if you look up the street you'll see the columns of the 18th-century Odéon theater. The roomy triples and quads are a good bet for families, and a wheelchair-accessible room is on the ground floor. The lobby has an Art Nouveau feel, and the well-kept rooms are impeccably clean, if not particularly stylish.

3 rue Casimir Delavigne, 6th arrond. www.balcons.com. ℂ **01-46-34-78-50.** 49 units. 108€–180€ double; 219€ triple; 240€ quad. Métro: Odéon. **Amenities:** Free Wi-Fi.

Hôtel Clément ★★ Facing the chic boutiques of Marché St-Germain, these charming and impeccably maintained rooms offer exceptional value about two blocks from St-Germain-des-Prés and a warren of restaurant-filled streets. Walls are covered in traditional prints, and beds are decked out in white quilted spreads. Doubles tend to be small, but the mini-suites are good for families. The Marché is closed at night, so all is calm in the evenings; rooms on the upper floors enjoy views of Parisian rooftops. You'll need to be able to manage a few stairs to get to the elevator.

6 rue Clément, 6th arrond. www.hotelclementparis.com. © **01-43-26-53-60.** 28 units. 91€–180€ double; 125€–270€ triples and suites. Métro: Mabillon. **Amenities:** Babysitting; laundry service; room service; free Wi-Fi.

Eiffel Tower & Nearby (7th Arrondissement)

For some reason, many visitors to Paris clamor for hotels near the Eiffel Tower, perhaps under the impression that this is a central location. It isn't. Not only that, the 7th arrondissement is one of the grandest in Paris, filled with government ministries and posh residences—not exactly the ideal spot to experience a typical slice of Parisian life. That said, this is undeniably a beautiful, quiet area, and there is something magical about wandering out of your hotel and seeing the Eiffel Tower looming in the background.

EXPENSIVE

Hôtel Signature St-Germain-des-Prés ★★★ Run by the friendly Prigent family (also of the Hôtel de Londres Eiffel; see below), this stylish boutique hotel has a homey, retro charm. Bright colors on the walls blend harmoniously with subdued bedspreads and linens; vintage mid-20th-century reproduction furniture and faux antique phones take the edge off sleek modern lines. The "Prestige" rooms cost more but are especially roomy (30 sq. m/323 sq. ft.), a rarity even in upscale Parisian hotels. In addition to the attentive service, this hotel is blessed with an excellent location for shopping addicts: It's just down the street from Bon Marché.

5 rue Chomel, 7th arrond. www.signature-saintgermain.com. © **01-45-48-35-53.** 26 units. 280€–480€ double; 360€–490€ triple; 440€–650€ 2-room connecting family suite. Métro: Sèvres-Babylone or St-Sulpice. **Amenities:** Concierge; free Wi-Fi.

MODERATE

Hôtel de L'Empereur ★★ All the rooms facing the street in this perfectly manicured hotel (run by the same meticulous management as the Hôtel Muguet; see below) have swell views of the nearby golden dome of Les Invalides, which hovers over the tomb of Napoleon (hence the name of the hotel). The best views are from the fifth and sixth floors. If views aren't your priority, consider the larger rooms facing the courtyard, which get lots of light, have less street noise, and are less expensive. The hotel has connecting rooms for families.

2 rue Chevert, 7th arrond. www.hotelempereur.com. © **01-45-55-88-02.** 31 units. 160€–210€ double; 200€ triple; 330€ quad. Métro: Ecole Militaire. **Amenities:** Concierge; guest computer; free Wi-Fi.

Hôtel de Londres Eiffel ★★★ From the moment you enter, you feel like you are in a private home, and you'll probably be greeted by the friendly owners, the Prigents, as well as their dog, a polite golden retriever named Samba. Knickknacks line the wood bookshelves in the neo-retro lobby, an old-fashioned yet cheerfully modern look that extends to the guest rooms. Walls are covered with tasteful printed fabrics featuring slightly kitsch 19th-century motifs, while the furniture harkens back to the 1940s, with lots of wood in soft shades of beige and brown. Two of the rooms have views of the Eiffel Tower (which is just steps away), but these book up early. For even more quiet and intimacy, request a spot in the Pavillion, a small, elevator-less building in the back with six rooms. Adjoining rooms are available for families.

1 rue Augereau, 7th arrond. www.hotel-paris-londres-eiffel.com. ✆ **01-45-51-63-02.** 30 units. 185€–390€ double; 290€–390€ triple; 350€–680€ quad. Métro: Ecole Militaire. **Amenities:** Free Wi-Fi.

Hôtel de Varenne ★★ This hotel maintains an atmosphere of refined serenity and caters to the ministerial crowd that frequents the area. Set back from the street, rooms are noiseless, and the pretty garden patio is perfect for breakfast alfresco in the warmer months. The decor is stately without being stuffy, with custom-made furniture inspired by the Louis XVI and Empire styles. Considering the quality of the lodgings and the self-importance of the neighborhood, rates are very reasonable. A wheelchair-accessible suite is on the ground floor.

44 rue de Bourgogne, 7th arrond. www.hoteldevarenne.com. ✆ **01-45-51-45-55.** 26 units. 154€–310€ double; 250€–380€ triple; 340€–500€ suite. Free breakfast when booking directly through the hotel's website. Parking 30€. Métro: Varenne or La Tour Maubourg. **Amenities:** Concierge; babysitting; laundry service; free Wi-Fi.

Hôtel Muguet ★★★ Known for its impeccable service and comfort level, this personable hotel is as classically chic as it is cozy. Modern wood headboards have a lily-of-the-valley (*muguet*) motif, and bright bathrooms have vintage-style washstands and Italian showers. Rooms are relatively large for Paris, and the triples are downright spacious. Five doubles have a great view of the Eiffel Tower, two others of Les Invalides; needless to say, they book up months in advance. The others, which are less expensive, look out on either the quiet street or the courtyard. Two wheelchair-accessible rooms on the ground floor face directly into a small but lush garden.

11 rue Chevert, 7th arrond. www.hotelparismuguet.com. ✆ **01-47-05-05-93.** 40 units. 100€–280€ double; 249€–350€ triple; 410€-800€ quad or quint. Métro: Varenne or La Tour Maubourg. **Amenities:** Computer and printer in lobby; concierge; free Wi-Fi.

INEXPENSIVE

Hôtel du Champ de Mars ★★ An adorable and affordable little inn right around the corner from the food shops of rue Cler—what more could you ask for? The impeccably maintained rooms are tastefully decorated with the kind of care people generally reserve for their own homes: thick cotton bedspreads, framed etchings, and printed fabrics in warm colors on the walls and windows. Two rooms have a tiny courtyard, while those on the upper floors get lots of light. *Note:* Food is not allowed in the rooms.

7 rue du Champ de Mars, 7th arrond. www.hotelduchampdemars.com. © **01-45-51-52-30.** 25 units. 110€–170€ double. Métro: Ecole Militaire. **Amenities:** Concierge; loaner laptop; free Wi-Fi.

Montparnasse & Nearby (14th & 15th Arrondissements)

Montparnasse is more centrally located than it might seem—it's right on the border of St-Germain and close to the Luxembourg Gardens. Also, the train station is a major transit hub for a bundle of Métro lines and bus routes. Though the utterly unaesthetic **Tour Montparnasse** now casts a shadow over this former writers' and artists' haunt (Henry Miller, Man Ray, Chagall, Picasso . . .), riding the lift to the top provides the best views in the city (p. 196) and the neighboring streets are still full of personality.

MODERATE

Hôtel Aiglon ★★★   Once upon a time, the likes of Jean-Paul Sartre, Luis Buñuel, and Albert Giacometti frequented this Art Deco hotel at the heart of what was once the city's most vibrant artistic scene. While the hotel has since had a makeover, with resolutely modern interior design, it is still a favorite of artists, filmmakers, and writers. It's close enough to the train station to be convenient but well out of the shadow of the Tour Montparnasse, and south-facing rooms enjoy leafy views of the Montparnasse cemetery. While the rooms share a palette of discreet shades of gray, beige, and blue, each has a different custom-made mosaic in the bathroom, the works of a local artist. The hotel also offers 12 spacious family rooms that accommodate three to four people, as well as an apartment that sleeps five.

232 bd. Raspail, 14th arrond. www.paris-hotel-aiglon.com. © **01-43-20-82-42.** 46 units. 84€–240€ double; 130€–390€ triple; 260€–470€ quad; 200€–600€ apartment for 5. Parking: 34€/day. Métro: Raspail. **Amenities:** Concierge; laundry service; room service; portable Wi-Fi hotspot rental; free Wi-Fi.

L'Apostrophe ★★   The intimate "poem" hotel honors the neighborhood's literary history (Henry Miller wrote across the way at La Coupole, and Hemingway set up shop at Closerie des Lilas down the street). Each of the 16 rooms has a theme: "Calligraphie" has Chinese characters splashed on royal blue walls; "Musique" features stenciled sheet music, instruments, and giant piano keys; and "Paris–Paradis" pays homage to the city's skyline. The larger rooms include a Jacuzzi right in the room—very romantic, but not for anyone who doesn't want to get naked in front of his or her roommate (the toilet is private). The other rooms come with jet massage in the (private) shower.

3 rue de Chevreuse, 6th arrond. www.apostrophe-hotel.com. © **01-56-54-31-31.** 16 units. 93€–250€ double with jet-massage shower; 180€–270€ double with Jacuzzi. Métro: Vavin. **Amenities:** Bar; free Wi-Fi.

INEXPENSIVE

Hôtel Cabane ★★★ This friendly hotel is one of the Left Bank's best deals, especially for families: It offers kids a small gift upon arrival; there's reduced-rate breakfast for children 4 to 12 (free for ages 3 and under); and baby cribs, bottle warmers, and highchairs are always available. Room decor is understatedly elegant, with feature walls painted in relaxing turquoise, and there are either garden views or vistas over the typically Parisian street below. If you're in Paris for romance, book La Cabane, a hidden wooden cabin with cool, rustic-chic decor, a two-person light-therapy shower, and its own garden terrace. The hotel bar, open until 2am, is the place to be for "Le happyhour" (7-9:30pm) for a pre-dinner drink.

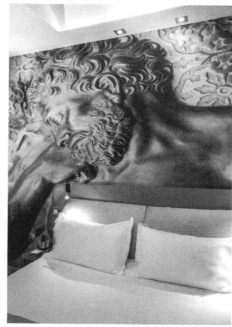

Every room at L'Apostrophe has a different design.

76 rue Raymond Losserand, 14th arrond. www.hotelcabane.com. ✆ **01-40-52-12-40.** 43 units. 81€–140€ double; from 199€ for La Cabane. Métro: Pernety. **Amenities:** Bar: free Wi-Fi.

Solar Hôtel ★ Declaring itself "the first ecological, economical, and activist hotel," these basic lodgings feature energy-efficient lighting, water-saving measures, and composting and recycling. Breakfast, included in the low rate, is organic; bicycles are available for guests; and there is a nice garden for sipping your fair-trade tea. The bright rooms have a hostel-like feel (although they are private), but the mattresses are firm and everything is clean and tidy. Just around the corner from rue Daguerre, a cute pedestrian market street, the hotel has two buildings. One has free Wi-Fi and small refrigerators in the rooms but no elevator; the other has an elevator but Wi-Fi only in the common areas.

22 rue Boulard, 14th arrond. www.solarhotel.fr. ✆ **01-43-21-08-20.** 34 units. 89€ double. Rates include breakfast. Métro: Denfert-Rochereau. **Amenities:** Bicycles; free Wi-Fi.

ALTERNATIVE LODGINGS

Hotels are all very well and good, but for some, nothing beats staying in a private home or apartment, particularly if you are a family on a budget. Fortunately, travelers with an independent streak have several options, including short-term rentals, B&Bs, and "aparthotels."

Short-Term Rentals

Recent years have seen a boom in short-term rentals, and the Internet is now swimming in websites and agencies proffering hundreds of apartments smack in the center of the City of Light. Though the rates for two people can be close to what you'd pay at a hotel, the advantages include cooking some of your meals at home, saving yourself money. Other benefits are privacy, independence, and a chance to see what it's like to live like a Parisian, even if it's just for a week.

If your group includes more than two people, and especially if you are traveling *en famille,* the benefits can be huge. Family suites and/or adjoining rooms are rare in Parisian hotels, so you'll often end up paying for two doubles—somewhere around 250€ to 500€ per night—whereas you could rent a one-bedroom apartment with a foldout couch and/or extra bed for anywhere from 85€ to 285€ per night.

So how should you book? While agencies like the ones listed below come with more services and guarantees, rates also tend to be more expensive than Internet rental platforms like **Airbnb.com, Flipkey.com,** and **Vrbo.com,** as many of the rentals listed on these sites are done by the owners directly, so there's no middleman to pay. Agencies justify their costs by having cleaning staff, all-inclusive rates, and an office you can call when something goes wrong. They also can vet all of their apartments to make sure they are legal and compliant with hygiene measures, and they can check that there is no funny business on the owners' side. That said, there is no denying that thousands of people happily use Airbnb and similar sites and find great accommodations for reasonable rates. Plus, most platforms have introduced obligatory Covid-19 safety practices for both hosts and guests.

The problem is that hugely popular sites like Airbnb cannot check up on every owner, so you cannot be entirely sure that your rental is legal or indeed as good or clean as it looks in the photos.

Bottom line: If you want to minimize risk and are willing to pay more for it, go with a well-established agency such as **Parisian Home** (www.parisianhome.com; ℂ **01-45-08-03-37**), **Paris Attitude** (www.parisattitude.com; ℂ **01-42-96-31-46**), or **Paris Appartements Services** (www.paris-appartements-services.com; ℂ **01-40-28-01-28**). **Apartments Actually** (http://apartmentsactually.com; reservations@apartmentsactually.com) also has some stunning properties in the Marais. In most cases, you will deal directly with the agency (not the owners), and the minimum stay is usually 4 days to 1 week.

IN impressionist FOOTSTEPS: A WORTHY NIGHT JUST OUTSIDE THE CENTER

Fancy a night in a hidden gem, away from the tourists, in verdant surroundings that inspired Impressionist painter Jean-Baptiste Camille Corot? Jump on a train from Gare Saint-Lazare to the suburb of Ville d'Avray (just a 15-min. ride to Sevres Ville d'Avray station), where hotel **Les Etangs de Corot**, 55 rue de Versailles, Ville d'Avray, overlooks one of the lakes the great artist painted. Bedrooms are classically chic, with a French country style and plenty of bold patterns. You can stroll Corot's lake at sunset, watching the sky turn from pastel blue to pink as herons fish for supper. Your dinner awaits in the Michelin-starred restaurant, dressed up like a contemporary hunting lodge; then it's cocktail time in the 19th-century *guinguette* (outdoor bar) on the water's edge. www.etangs-corot.com. ✆ **01-41-15-37-00.** 170€–260€ double; 225€ family room; 300€–390€ suite.

Bed & Breakfasts

Though bed-and-breakfasts (*chambres d'hôtes*) are common in the French countryside, in the big city, where privacy and anonymity are treasured, they are still relatively rare. Three B&Bs I wholeheartedly recommend are:

- **52 Clichy** (www.52clichy.com) in the new foodie quarter, the 9th arrondissement. Run by a British expat, Rosemary, there's a lovely room (125€–145€) and a whole apartment to rent (160€–200€). On sunny days breakfast is served on a balcony overlooking rooftops.

- **La Villa Paris** (www.la-villa-paris.com) in a 1920s villa in the residential 13th arrondissement. This place feels like a secret boutique hotel with five warmly decorated rooms and luxurious bathrooms, not to mention a leafy breakfast terrace (100€–200€).

- **Bonne Nuit Paris** (www.bonne-nuit-paris.com) in a 17th-century house in the hip end of the Marais (3rd arrond.). It's right by the Marché des Enfants Rouges food market, and the four rooms and an apartment all have a chic, old-world vibe (170€–275€).

Aparthotels

These utilitarian lodgings are a cross between a hotel and an apartment. Short on charm, *aparthotels* are decidedly practical: Units come with kitchenettes as well as hotel services like fresh towels, dry cleaning, and a concierge. Rates are generally higher than short-term rentals, but you do have the comfort of knowing you are dealing with a large company (if that makes you comfortable) with standardized apartments, organized websites, and customer service.

The best-known *aparthotel* company is **Citadines** (www.citadines.com; ✆ **01-41-05-79-05;** 125€–350€), with its clean, comfortable units in excellent locations. Another good one to try is **Adagio** (www.adagio-city.com; ✆ **08-25-01-20-11,** 0.15€/min), which has several locations in central Paris and offers bright, modern, fully equipped spaces (100€–350€ a night).

WHERE TO DINE

Everywhere you look in Paris, someone is doing his or her best to ruin your waistline. *Boulangeries* (bakeries) with buttery croissants and decadent pastries lurk on every street corner, open-air markets tempt the senses, and terrific restaurants with intriguing menus sprout up on every block.

In France, food is not a pastime; it's an art. Eating and drinking is a topic of serious discussion, the subject of radio shows, newspaper columns, and even feature films. It's not surprising that Paris, navel of the French universe, should boast some of the best food on the planet. Fortunately, you don't have to have a king-size budget to dine like royalty. But you do have to choose wisely. Once upon a time, you could wander into just about any restaurant in Paris and sit down to a good meal; today, this is no longer the case. Try not to notice all the fast food and don't even think about eating in one of the ubiquitous Chinese restaurants that serve a bland version of this marvelous Asian cuisine reheated in microwaves.

Fortunately, the guardians of good food are fighting back. Sick of the pressure and fuss of the temples of *haute cuisine,* a clutch of famous chefs (like Christian Constant and Yves de Camdeborde) kickstarted the "bistronomy" movement, opening dressed-down bistros that serve dressed-up versions of traditional workers' cuisine at relatively reasonable prices. In general, these restaurants are affordable and hip, and serve excellent food. One outgrowth of this movement is the obsession with "noble" ingredients, such as high-quality, regional produce or products, often from a specific small-scale farm or artisan, sometimes organic.

You'll also find a puzzling interest in American food. Gourmet hamburgers are ubiquitous on bistro menus, and you'll find bagels and smoked salmon at "le brunch," a newfangled meal (for the French) that is currently all the rage.

The coffeeshop movement has finally hit Paris too, and not just Starbucks (though you will, alas, find plenty of those). I'm talking American-style coffeeshops offering free Wi-Fi, and menus full of lattes and "le carrot cake." It's an inevitable part of globalization, and a welcome trend for both the city's freelance workers and visitors looking for familiar food and an Internet connection. Plus, the city still has plenty of Belle Epoque beauties to feast your eyes on and fill your stomachs in.

5

This chapter offers a sampling of Paris' gourmet delights; we've listed the best cafes, tearooms, and other places to find sinful sweets at the end. Since Covid-19, most of these restaurants also offer click 'n' collect or takeout options, so if you ever feel like eating in, check out individual websites for details.

PRACTICAL MATTERS

Eating Hours & Annual Closings

In Paris, unless you see a sign that says SERVICE CONTINU, meals are usually restricted to set hours. This is one of the reasons it's a good idea to reserve, if you can (the other is that dining rooms tend to be small). Don't expect to wander in someplace for a bowl of soup at 4pm. Lunch is generally served between noon and 2pm (sometimes 2:30pm), and dinner is from 7 to 10:30pm (sometimes 11pm). Many restaurants close on Sundays and/or Mondays, though some have started serving Sunday brunch, generally from 11am to 3pm. Cafes and restaurants with a bar tend to stay open between mealtimes, serving drinks and coffee; if you are starving, you can usually order a light sandwich or a *croque-monsieur* (a French take on a grilled ham and cheese sandwich). Some brasseries serve late into the night. For late-night dining options, see p. 103.

Many restaurants close in August (normally the first 2 weeks), and some shut down between Christmas and New Year's; see listings for details.

Tip: If you didn't reserve and you want to avoid waiting in line, try to arrive at the very beginning of the service, noon or around 7:30pm. Most French people eat later than that, so you'll have a better chance if you avoid the rush.

Reservations

Most restaurants in Paris are small, so if you have your heart set on eating at one in particular, reserving ahead, even if it is the same day, is essential. If you are looking to dine at one of Paris's hip neo-bistros or famous gourmet temples, you may have to reserve weeks in advance. Ask your hotel receptionist to help if you can't manage the telephone or try reserving online through www.thefork.com (which also offers discounts). Otherwise, you can often reserve on the restaurant's site via email.

Dejeuner sur L'Herbe (Picnics)

Although restaurants are all very well and good, there's a lot to be said for a quick and easy outdoor meal in one of Paris' many lovely parks and squares. Picking up picnic ingredients is a pretty easy affair, though you should familiarize yourself with a bit of terminology. For good takeout food, look for the nearest *charcutier* (these specialize in smoked meat, pâtés, and other pork products) or *traiteur* (a store that sells prepared takeout dishes and salads). At almost any *boulangerie* (bakery), you can find what may well be **the best lunch bargain in the city:** their lunch *formule* (set menu). For around 8€ or 9€, you can get a long sandwich (usually half a baguette), amply filled with chicken, ham, or tuna and *crudités* (tomato, lettuce, and other salad-like items), a drink, and a pastry. Often you can substitute a slice of quiche for the sandwich. *Formules* and sandwiches are usually only available from 11am to 2pm. **Eric Kayser** (www.maison-kayser.com) and **Paul** (www.paul.fr) are reliable bakery chains serving salads, sandwiches, and even hot dishes. But your best bet is to use your *nez* (nose) and find a place on your own. The telltale signs of a good bakery are an attractive window display and a queue at mealtimes.

Choosing a Restaurant

Below is a selective list of restaurants, wine bars, and tearooms that serve the type of excellent food you came specifically to Paris to try. But since the city has thousands of restaurants, you're bound to wander into something wonderful and unexpected on your own. Finding a good restaurant is extremely subjective, considering any number of variables and a good dose of what the French call *le feeling.*

That said, I recommend you take some precautions if you go beyond the suggestions in this guide. Unfortunately, Paris has many restaurants geared solely to tourists that shovel out food that is unmemorable at best, and

Eatery Protocols

Dining and drinking establishments must follow strict hygiene protocols, which means you may be asked to wear a mask when you are not in your seat at the restaurant. You may also need to show an E.U. Digital Covid vaccination certificate (see p. 285) or proof of a negative PCR test in order to get in.

Many restaurants include this type of information on their websites; for more general information (in English), check the French government website (www.gouvernement.fr/en/coronavirus-covid-19) and the Paris Tourist Office (https://en.parisinfo.com/practical-paris/info/guides/info-disruption-paris).

indigestible at worst. Shun places that advertise English menus and look instead for places that are full of happy customers speaking French. And don't avoid places with lines out front (that's a *good* sign). And if there are delicious smells issuing from the kitchen, it's likely the food will be good (restaurants lacking in appetizing aromas may be relying on prepackaged foods and microwaves).

THE RIGHT BANK

Louvre & Île de la Cité (1st Arrondissement)

Dining near the Louvre can be expensive and frustrating. Since almost every tourist visiting the city comes to this part of town, it's rife with overpriced, mediocre tourist restaurants (you can identify them by their menus printed in at least five languages). However, on some of the smaller streets away from the museum, you'll find more authentic eateries.

EXPENSIVE

Verjus ★ MODERN FRENCH Okay, the chef's American, but that doesn't stop this nosh nirvana from being utterly Parisian, from the setting (an all-white dining room, nestled at the top of a hidden staircase, with Art Deco-style furniture and views onto Théâtre du Palais Royal) to the food (contemporary takes on French classics). The dishes are served in tasting menus that list the ingredients in each dish—chicken, asparagus, and wild garlic or artichoke with caviar. But don't be fooled: On the plate, this simplicity translates to perfectly executed delicacies that may well be the highlight of your trip. Paris has few "gastronomique" restaurants where you can eat like a king for under 100€, and this, along with Septime (p. 109) and Pierre Sang in Oberkampf (p. 111) is one of the best. Needless to say, the wine

price CATEGORIES

Expensive	Main dishes 35€ and up	**Inexpensive**	Main dishes under 20€
Moderate	Main dishes 20€–34€		

Right Bank West Restaurants

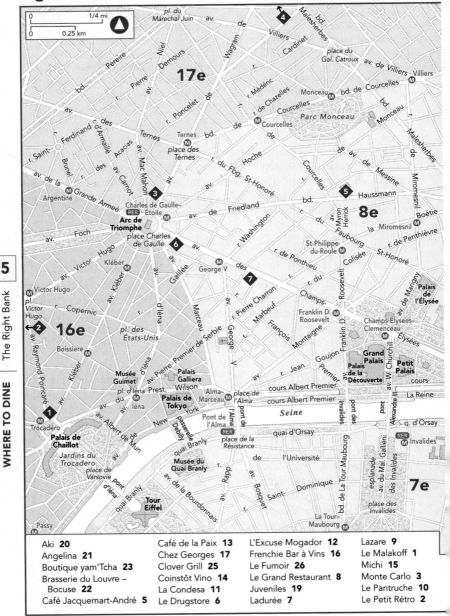

Aki **20**	Café de la Paix **13**	L'Excuse Mogador **12**	Lazare **9**
Angelina **21**	Chez Georges **17**	Frenchie Bar à Vins **16**	Le Malakoff **1**
Boutique yam'Tcha **23**	Clover Grill **25**	Le Fumoir **26**	Michi **15**
Brasserie du Louvre – Bocuse **22**	Coinstôt Vino **14**	Le Grand Restaurant **8**	Monte Carlo **3**
Café Jacquemart-André **5**	La Condesa **11**	Juveniles **19**	Le Pantruche **10**
	Le Drugstore **6**	Ladurée **7**	Le Petit Rétro **2**

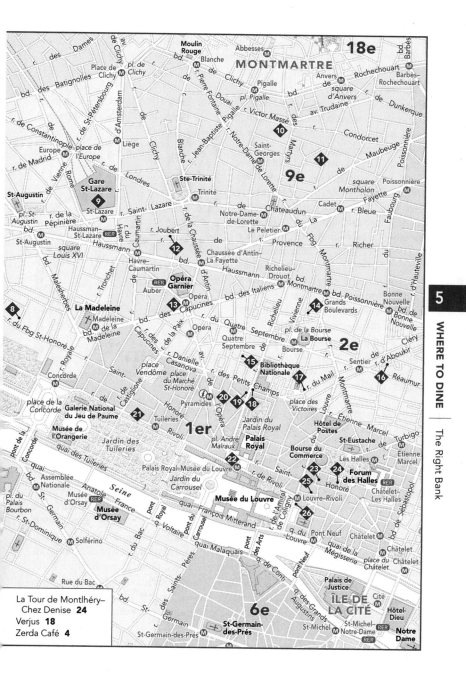

La Tour de Montlhéry–
Chez Denise **24**
Verjus **18**
Zerda Café **4**

list is a treat, filled with biodynamic and organic wines. The 55€ wine pairing option is worth the splurge. Reservations required.

52 rue Richelieu, 2nd arrond. www.verjusparis.com. ℭ **01-42-97-54-40.** Tasting menu 78€. Mon–Fri 7–11pm. Closed 2 weeks in Aug. Métro: Palais Royal–Musée du Louvre or Pyramides.

MODERATE

Brasserie du Louvre–Bocuse ★★ MODERN BRASSERIE Lyonnais

cooking legend Paul Bocuse (nicknamed the "Pope of Gastronomy") passed away in 2018, but his legacy lives on in this vintage-chic brasserie on the ground floor of the Hôtel du Louvre. Tuck into wonderfully executed versions of his signature regional dishes, like hot pistachio-studded sausage (rolled in a soft brioche), sole meunière, and pike quenelle with Nantua (lobster) sauce, while admiring the views of the Comédie Française and Louvre through the bay windows or arcaded terrace. All of the desserts are excellent, but I have a particular fondness for the crème brûlée (vanilla custard topped with caramelized sugar)—it's possibly the best in the city. *Note:* There are copious breakfast buffet options, too.

Dining at Brasserie du Louvre–Bocuse.

1 pl. du Palais Royal, 1st arrond. www.hyatt.com (then search for Hôtel du Louvre). ℭ **01-44-58-37-21.** Main courses 19€–36€; fixed-price breakfast 20€–30€. Wed–Sun noon–3pm and 6–11pm. Closed first 3 weeks of Aug. Métro: Palais-Royal–Musée du Louvre.

Clover Grill ★★★ FRENCH/STEAKHOUSE Grill restaurants are all the

rage, but few can compete with this refined BBQ joint near Les Halles, which turns the concept of American-style grilling into something resolutely French: beech-smoked beef rib for two with mashed potato, fresh fish from *petit pêcheurs* (artisanal fishermen) with sauce *choron* (béarnaise sauce with tomatoes), and blue lobster with seasonal vegetables *en papillote*—all hands-down delicious. Even the fruit gets grilled, from brochettes of pineapple to apples in caramel sauce with Breton butter biscuits. Other desserts to look out for include the sticky pavlova, and fluffy *churros* (fried dough fingers) with chocolate. Chef Jean-François Piège is known for his playful approach to cooking, and the *churros* embody this, as he turns something simple into a gourmet dish.

6 rue Bailleul, 1st arrond. www.clover-grill.com. ℭ **01-40-41-59-59.** Main courses 20€–70€; fixed-price menu 69€. Daily noon–2:15pm and 7–10:30pm. Métro: Louvre–Rivoli.

Right Bank East Restaurants

Les Arlots **1**
L'As du Fallafel **16**
Astier **10**
Au Bascou **9**
Aux Bons Crus **19**
Benoit **15**
Biglove Caffè **14**
Bob's Juice Bar **6**
Bouillon Julien **7**

Buffet **21**
Café des Musées **17**
Chez Michel **2**
Clamato **22**
L'Ebauchoir **25**
ELMER l'Epicerie **8**
Fulgurances **24**
Ground Control **26**
Hôtel du Nord **4**

Laia **24**
Marché des Enfants Rouge **13**
MijoT **11**
Noglu **20**
Pierre Sang in Oberkampf **12**
Le Potager du Marais **18**

Le Pure Café **23**
Rosa Bonheur **3**
Septime **22**
Le Verre Volé **5**

Juveniles ★★ WINE BAR   This lively wine bar has been around since 1987, but since the owner's daughter and son-in-law took over in 2014, people come just as much for the food as they do for the wine. You might start with chanterelle mushrooms with chives and poached egg, followed by panfried pork with sage-infused polenta, and finish up with a chocolate mousse, for example. Wash that down with a berry-rich Languedoc red or a light and fruity Beaujolais, and you've got yourself one memorable and gourmet meal. Prices are extremely reasonable, considering the close proximity to the chic Palais Royal. You can also buy wines to go, making this a great stop if you're picnicking. Reservations required for dining. Drinking at the bar is first-come, first-served.

47 rue de Richelieu, 1st arrond. www.juvenileswinebar.com. ℂ **01-42-97-46-49.** Main courses 17€–22€. Tues–Sat noon–2:30pm and 7:30–10:30pm. Closed 2 weeks in Aug. Métro: Pyramides.

La Tour de Montlhéry–Chez Denise ★★ TRADITIONAL FRENCH/ BISTRO   One of the last remnants of the bustling atmosphere that used to surround the old Les Halles central market, Chez Denise stays open through the night until 5am and serves sturdy platters of *côte de boeuf* (a giant rib steak), grilled marrow bones, and brochettes of grilled meat so long they look like swords. The long-aproned waiters are used to encountering English speakers, but that hasn't changed the vibe, which is local and lively. If you are not a carnivore, the menu has a few fish dishes, and you can always enjoy homemade fries, which are delicious.

5 rue des Prouvaires, 1st arrond. ℂ **01-42-36-21-82.** Main courses 23€–30€. Mon–Fri noon–3pm and 7:30pm–5am. Closed July 15–Aug 15. Métro: Les Halles.

Le Fumoir ★★ FRENCH-SCANDINAVIAN   With its high ceilings, subdued lighting, and large windows, this understated, hip spot is a good place to regroup. During the day (except at lunchtime), dawdling is encouraged: Magazines and newspapers are available at the front entry, and a small lending library/ book exchange is in the back room. At night, well-dressed 30-somethings

---

Rude Waiters: Myth or Reality?

When people ask me about the legendary rudeness of Parisian waitstaff, I have to fight the urge to do the French shrug. It really depends. It is undeniable that Parisian customer service can be frosty, but here's how I see it: With Parisians, you are guilty until proven innocent. If you can weather the initial chilly blast and show them you are not easily flustered, they'll usually warm up—and they will be charming your socks off. Also, don't mistake cultural differences for rudeness. The ultimate faux pas in Paris is rushing you off your table, so if the waiters take forever to bring you your check, they're not being rude, they're saying "feel free to stay a little longer."

crowd around the magnificent wood bar—which in a former life stood in a Philadelphia speakeasy—as they wait for their table. You'll eat well here too: The offerings might include Nordic poached cod with smoked potato purée or a very French and very tender lamb *navarin* (stew) with fresh peas. On Sundays, the 29€-brunch comes complete with pancakes and eggs Benedict, and on Sunday nights, the Swedish chef (Henrik Andersson) returns to his roots with an all-Swedish menu.

Let's Do Lunch

Many restaurants in Paris serve a set-price menu at lunch that is considerably cheaper than the same food served at dinnertime. It is not unusual to find a two- or three-course lunch prix-fixe, also called a *formule*, or a menu for 17€ to 28€. The only downside is that your choice of dishes will usually be limited on the *formule*. **Note:** Set-price lunches are usually only served Monday through Friday.

6 rue de l'Amiral Coligny, 1st arrond. www.lefumoir.com. ✆ **01-42-92-00-24.** Main courses 13€–28€; fixed-price lunch 26€–30€ or dinner 36€–40€. Mon–Sat 9am–1am; Sun 9am–11pm. Métro: Louvre–Rivoli.

INEXPENSIVE

Aki ★★ JAPANESE   The specialty here is *okonomiyaki*, a sort of grilled omelet topped with meat or seafood and a yummy sauce. Watch the cooks create yours on a griddle in the open kitchen before diving into your meal. You can also order excellent udon or soba noodles. Get here early or be prepared to stand in line.

11 bis rue Ste-Anne, 1st arrond. www.akirestaurant.fr. ✆ **01-42-97-54-27.** Main courses 12€–15€; fixed-price menu 13.50€–17€. Mon–Sat 11:30am–10:45pm. Métro: Pyramides.

Boutique yam'Tcha ★★★ FRENCH-ASIAN STREET FOOD   Book a table at renowned chef Adeleine Grattard's Michelin-starred restaurant yam'Tcha and you'll certainly have a fabulous meal (121 rue St-Honore, 1st arrond.; ✆ **01-40-26-08-07;** tasting menus 70€–150€; reservations 2 months in advance): Grattard works miracles with simple ingredients such as lobster, sea bass, truffles, and pork. But her second place near the Louvre—a dual take-out *bao* bar (steamed Taiwanese brioches) and tearoom—lets you taste her cooking for a fraction of the price. The bar section is a window open to the street, where foodies queue for *bao* buns filled with delectables such as smoked tofu or crab with vegetables, plus unexpected mixes like Stilton and cherries. The tearoom, run by Grattard's Hong Kong–born husband Chi Wah Chan (a veritable tea guru who pairs teas with dishes in the same way sommeliers pair wines), serves excellent main courses such as Peking soup and fish tartare, both for around 14€.

4 rue Sauval, 1st arrond. www.yamtcha.com. ✆ **01-40-26-06-06.** Bao buns 6€–9€; main courses 10€–16€. Wed–Fri noon–6pm; Sat noon–8pm. Métro: Louvre–Rivoli.

You are wandering around the streets near the Opéra, when you take a sharp turn onto the rue Ste-Anne. Suddenly, everything is in Japanese, with noodle shops everywhere! Plunge into a bowl at one of these restaurants:

o **Udon Jubey,** 39 rue Ste-Anne, 1st arrond. (℃ **01-40-15-92-54;** Métro: Pyramides), makes some of the best udon in town; slurp at the counter or grab one of the limited number of tables.

o **Higuma,** 32 bis rue Ste-Anne, 1st arrond. (www.higuma.fr; ℃ **01-47-** **03-38-59;** Métro: Pyramides), features an open kitchen, ramen soups, and a long line out the front door.

o **Aki Café,** 75 rue Ste-Anne, 1st arrond. (www.facebook.com/ akicafeparis; ℃ **01-40-41-95-27),** is a canteen with takeout service run by the same management as the restaurant (described above). It's the place to go for sweet Katsu curry and terrific Franco-Japanese pastries, such as adzuki bean tarts and matcha tea éclairs.

Le Marais (3rd & 4th Arrondissements)

Between its working-class roots and its more recent gentrification, the Marais has a wide range of choices, from humble falafel joints to trendy brasseries. Unlike the shops here, which have become so hip it hurts, a good selection of midrange restaurants still attracts both the sleek set and just regular folks.

EXPENSIVE

Benoit ★ TRADITIONAL FRENCH This historic restaurant had hosted a century's worth of Parisian notables when renowned chef Alain Ducasse took the helm in 2005. Mirrors, zinc, and tiles still line the venerable dining room, while the menu features beautifully executed bistro classics. *Escargots* (snails) in garlic butter and brill braised with Jura wine share the stage with homemade cassoulet and beef filet bordelaise. Save room for the *profiteroles,* puff pastry filled with ice cream and drizzled with chocolate sauce.

20 rue St-Martin, 4th arrond. www.benoit-paris.com. ℃ **01-42-72-25-76.** Main courses 34€–50€; fixed-price lunch 39€. Mon–Thurs noon–2pm and 7:30–10pm; Fri–Sun noon–2pm and 7–10pm. Closed between Christmas and New Year's and in Aug. Métro: Hôtel-de-Ville.

MODERATE

Au Bascou ★★ BASQUE Basque cuisine, like the province, is not entirely French. Using lots of tomatoes, onions, and sweet Espelette pepper, Basque dishes have a decidedly different tang to them. But while the name of this restaurant refers to Basque country, the menu covers the entire southwest. Traditional Basque dishes like *pipérade* (a tasty omelet loaded with peppers and onions) and *axoa* (a stew of veal shoulder, peppers, and onions) mingle with southwestern classics like duck foie gras and roast *palombe* (wood pigeon). Everything is handled with great care by the chef Renaud Marcille, who used to be the right-hand man of Alain Sederens.

38 rue Réaumur, 3rd arrond. www.au-bascou.fr. *(C)* **01-42-72-69-25.** Main courses 18€–30€; fixed-price lunch 19€ and 25€; fixed-price dinner from 40€. Mon–Fri noon– 2pm and 8–10:30pm. Closed between Christmas and New Year's and in Aug. Métro: Arts-et-Métiers.

Café des Musées ★ TRADITIONAL FRENCH/BISTRO Weary culture vultures who've just finished the Picasso museum will appreciate this bustling corner cafe with its appealing sidewalk tables. I recommend it not just for the atmosphere, however, but because the young chef does terrific things with bistro classics like steak frites with béarnaise sauce, or *andouillette* (tripe sausage), as well as lighter fare like seasonal vegetable casserole with basil oil, or a *grand aioli,* poached cod with aioli mayonnaise and vegetables. If you're here early enough (8–11:30am), it's a top spot for breakfast too: think hot drink, pastry, and fruit juice for 8€. Or come for afternoon tea, when cakes and hot drinks are served for 12.50€.

49 rue de Turenne, 3rd arrond. www.lecafedesmusees.fr. *(C)* **01-42-72-96-17.** Main courses 12€–26€; fixed-price lunch 19.50€ and 21€. Daily noon–3pm and 7–11pm. Closed last 2 weeks of Aug. Métro: St-Paul or Chemin Vert.

Le Potager du Marais ★ VEGAN The shoebox-size dining room fills up quickly, as Paris doesn't have many vegan eateries, so make sure you reserve in advance. But even omnivores enjoy the delicious veggie offerings here, which might include seitan *bourguignon,* mushroom pâté, and pumpkin Parmentier. Many items are gluten-free. Finish off with a simple but scrumptious apple compote or crème brûlée.

26 rue Saint-Paul, 4th arrond. www.lepotagerdumarais.fr. *(C)* **01-57-40-98-57.** Main courses 16€–19€. Wed–Sun noon–3pm and 7–10.30pm. Métro: St-Paul.

INEXPENSIVE

BigLove Caffé ★ ITALIAN Jars of preserved fruit line the walls, and hams hang from the ceiling—yes, you're still in Paris, but this place sure feels like Napoli. It tastes like it, too. For brunch, patrons tuck into pancakes with *bufflonne* ricotta and passion fruit, or eggs Benedict with 24-month-matured Parma ham. For lunch and dinner, pizza reigns supreme (the gluten-free versions are just as good), as does pasta. Whatever you choose, everything is made with only the choicest and freshest of ingredients, many of them direct from *petits producteurs* (small producers) in Italy. Set in a frighteningly hip part of the northern Marais, it is a popular place, so reserve ahead—especially on Saturday and Sunday when this neighborhood is a brunch hot spot.

30 rue Debelleyme, 3rd arrond. www.bigmammagroup.com. *(C)* **01-42-71-43-62.** Main courses 13€–18€. Mon–Fri noon–2:30pm and 6–10:45pm; Sat–Sun noon–3:30pm and 6:30–10:45pm (until 11pm Sun). Métro: Filles de Calvaire.

ELMER l'Epicerie ★★ DELI If you're into pâté, this narrow deli is the place for *pâté en croute* (pastry-encased pâté) and lip-smacking foie gras and

Eating Vegetarian in Paris

Though the French still love their meat, times are a-changing, and an increasingly large number of Parisian restaurants now cater to vegetarians, offering at least a couple of appropriate dishes on the menu. Even basic cafes will usually serve *salades composées*, meal-size salads that often come in meat-free versions. If you eat fish, most restaurants offer at least one or two pescatarian selections too. And, of course, Paris does have vegetarian restaurants. We've listed a few (**Bob's Juice Bar,** p. 114; **Le Potager du Marais,** p. 99; **Noglu,** p. 112; and **Jardin des Pâtes,** p. 122). For more options, visit the **Happy Cow** (www.happycow.net), a veggie and vegan online network with extensive listings for Paris.

chicken liver terrine, served with homemade gherkins and pickled onions. There's a grocery section where you can buy fruit, veggies, and all sorts of meats, cheeses, and olive oils direct from small regional producers. And at lunch time, they serve doorstop-size takeout sandwiches, filled with cheeses, meats, and more of that aforementioned foie gras pâté (from 10.50€). Or for an all-out neo-bistro experience, reserve a table at ELMER, the chic, Nordic-inspired sister restaurant across the street, where Modern French delights like lobster ravioli and barbecued suckling lamb are reeled out of the kitchen with real panache (fixed-price lunch 29€; fixed-price dinner 60€).

19 rue Notre-Dame de Nazareth, 3rd arrond. www.elmer-restaurant.fr. ℂ **01-40-09-80-47.** Main courses 6€–14€. Tues–Fri noon–3pm. Métro: République or Arts et Métiers.

L'As du Fallafel ★★ FALAFEL/ISRAELI   This Marais institution offers, without a doubt, the best falafel in Paris. And they're kosher too. True, falafel joints are scarce in this city, but that doesn't take away from the excellence of these overstuffed beauties, brimming with cucumbers, pickled turnips, shredded cabbage, tahini, fried eggplant, and those crispy balls of fried chickpeas and spices. Other arrangements of similar ingredients *sans* pita can be found in the *assiettes* (platters). Wash it down with an Israeli beer. Service is fast and furious, but basically friendly—just be prepared to deal with hordes of tourists and locals at lunch.

34 rue des Rosiers, 4th arrond. http://l-as-du-fallafel.zenchef.com. ℂ **01-48-87-63-60.** Main courses 8€–20€. Sun–Thurs noon–11pm; Fri noon–4pm. Métro: St-Paul.

Marché des Enfants Rouge ★★ STREET FOOD   On rue de Bretagne, this quaint, 400-year-old food market (the oldest in Paris) is a bustling, fragrant labyrinth of ready-to-eat food stalls hawking everything from Caribbean curries to couscous, sushi, and pasta. A hugely popular spot (if the queues are anything to go by) is Alain Miam Miam's organic crepe stand, which serves made-to-order paninis and pancakes dripping in tasty cheese and ham. This is also where you'll find some of the best burgers in town: Burger Fermier makes the bread on-site, slathers the burgers in French cheese such as cider-infused

Tomme, and only uses hand-picked beef from a farm in northern France. Come late afternoon and you can join the post-shopping crowd over a glass of wine.

39 rue de Bretagne, 3rd arrond. No phone. Main courses 7.50€–16€. Tues–Sat 8am–8:30pm; Sun 8:30am–5pm. Métro: Saint Sébastien-Froissart.

Champs-Élysées & Western Paris (8th, 16th & 17th Arrondissements)

Mobbed with tourists, oozing with opulence, the Champs-Élysées is a difficult place to find a good meal unless you are willing to spend a lot of money. Mediocre chain restaurants abound on the grand avenue itself; kebab joints mingle with frighteningly expensive gourmet palaces on the surrounding side streets. Many two- and three-Michelin star restaurants are here too; before you splurge on a dinner table, remember that lunch in one of these same eateries often costs half the price.

EXPENSIVE

Le Grand Restaurant ★★★ MODERN FRENCH   Chef Jean-François Piège is—in my humble opinion—the most exciting chef in France right now. His ultramodern take on traditional "bourgeois" cuisine is playful, delicious, and wholly unlike anything you'll taste anywhere else. Book ahead for a table in his swank, gray dining room (decked in concrete walls and geometric ceiling panels that wouldn't look amiss in Kubrick's "2001: A Space Odyssey"), then sit back for a roller-coaster ride of haute cuisine: shellfish-stuffed potato with caviar, Parmesan-infused spaghetti with truffles and fall-off-your-fork pork, and a delightful bergamot-flavored custard cream to finish. Don't be fooled by the simplicity of the descriptions; Piège's cooking is as complex as it is satisfying. His place is near the Élysée palace,

Le Grand Restaurant.

so you might spot politicians out for a business meal—though Piège's devoted fans are never far away.

7 rue d'Aguesseau, 8th arrond. www.jeanfrancoispiege.com. ℂ **01-53-05-00-00.** Main courses 72€–155€; fixed-price lunch 121€; fixed-price dinner 231€ and 281€. Wed–Sat 12:30–1:30pm and 7:30–9:30pm. Closed 3 weeks in Aug and last week in Dec. Métro: Concorde or Madeleine.

MODERATE

Lazare ★★★ MODERN BISTRO   Before the Gare St-Lazare train station had its 2012 makeover, about the only thing you could get to eat was a limp sandwich. Today, you can eat like a king as you wait for your train to come in, and we're not talking Burger King. Eric Frechon, a three-Michelin-starred chef, is the great mind behind this gourmet enterprise, which serves as cafe, bar, and restaurant. The lofty ceilings, wood furnishings, and white walls give the place a relaxed air, as does the menu, which features French comfort food like *boeuf bourguignon*, cod *brandade* (a sort of fish shepherd's pie), and Toulouse sausage with mashed potatoes. A gaggle of young, intense cooks bustles about, preparing each dish with the best ingredients and designing each plate with care. Breakfast is served from 7:30 to 11am, and teatime is 3 to 6pm.

Inside the Gare St-Lazare shopping gallery, 8th arrond. https://lazare-paris.fr. ℂ **01-44-90-80-80.** Main courses 19€–49€; Sun fixed-price lunch 39€. Mon–Sat 7:30am–midnight; Sun 11:45am–midnight. Métro: Gare St-Lazare.

Le Drugstore (Publicis) ★★ MODERN BRASSERIE   You won't find toothpaste at the Publicis "drugstore," whose name comes from a former 1950s incarnation that consisted of a warren of shops, restaurants, and services "à l'americaine." This ultramodern, oh-so-chic complex has replaced the funky original, keeping the multifunctional concept intact with shops, restaurants, and a cinema. The Brasserie is the most accessible eating option: a light-filled expanse with an incredible street-side view of the Champs-Élysées and the Arc de Triomphe. The food is high-end casual, featuring items like gourmet hamburgers, grilled fish, steak tartare, and filet of sole, all delivered by a young and beautiful waitstaff. Meals are served nonstop until 1am, making this a good bet for a late-night meal. Up early? The long daily breakfast menu is available from 8 to 11:30am.

133 av. des Champs-Élysées, 8th arrond. www.publicisdrugstore.com. ℂ **01-44-43-77-64.** Main courses 19€–46€. Mon–Fri 8am–2am; Sat–Sun 10am–2am. Métro: Charles de Gaulle–Étoile.

Le Malakoff ★ BRASSERIE   While the brasseries on the Place du Trocadéro are generally overpriced and sniffy, this one is accessible, both in terms of price and service. The menu is standard Parisian brasserie fare—steak tartare, grilled chicken, *choucroute garni,* steak frites—executed with skill and supplemented with a wide variety of tasty *salades composées* (meal-size salads). Best of all, you get a front row view of the grandiose Place and the Palais de Chaillot (and, if you lean over, the Eiffel Tower). The same management runs **Le Wilson** (www.le-wilson.fr), a smaller operation at 2 place du Trocadéro at the corner of avenue du Président Wilson, which offers a similar menu.

6 pl. du Trocadéro, 16th arrond. www.le-malakoff.com. (✆) **01-45-53-75-27.** Main courses 14€–25€; fixed-price lunch 19€. Daily 7am–1am. Métro: Trocadéro.

Le Petit Rétro ★★ TRADITIONAL FRENCH This gorgeous little restaurant, dolled up in original Art Nouveau tiles, a zinc bar, and vintage wooden tables, captures the essence of Belle Epoque Paris, and not only in terms of decor. The menu harks back to days gone by with traditional dishes like cod in langoustine cream sauce and veal blanquette. Make sure you mop up all that sauce with some wildly delicious bread and butter. The butter is by Bordier, the last butter maker in France to churn its butter with a wooden paddle. Dessert? You'll be hard-pushed to find a finer *pain perdu* (bread pudding), made with brioche and vanilla cream.

5 rue Mesnil, 16th arrond. https://petitretro.fr. (✆) **01-44-05-06-05.** Main courses 19€–32€; fixed-price lunch 26€ and 31€; 5-course tasting menu 95€. Mon–Sat noon–2pm and 7:30–10pm. Closed 2 weeks in Aug. Métro: Victor Hugo.

INEXPENSIVE

Monte Carlo ★★ SELF-SERVICE/FRENCH Hitting a self-serve canteen might not be your idea of Parisian dining, but if you're on a budget, don't dismiss this handy spot by the Arc de Triomphe. Monte Carlo has been a favorite with local police officers, office workers, and tourist bus drivers alike since the 1970s—largely because it serves food all day, but also because it's one of the cheapest spots around the Champs-Élysées. A mere 12.40€ gets you a two-course menu of dishes like chicken in mustard sauce or Alsatian sauerkraut, plus either a salad starter or a dessert (think panna cotta with fruit coulis). This won't be the culinary highlight of your stay, but the food is well prepared and tasty, and I honestly cannot name anywhere else in the area with such a good quality/price ratio.

9 av. de Wagram, 17th arrond. www.monte-carlo.fr. (✆) **01-43-80-02-20.** Fixed-price menus 12.40€–17.50€. Daily 11am–11pm. Closed 2 weeks in mid-Aug. Métro: Charles de Gaulle–Étoile.

After-Hours Dining

Not many restaurants stay open until the wee hours of the night, but a few stalwarts are around Les Halles. **Le Tambour,** 41 rue de Montmartre, 2nd arrond. ((✆) **01-42-33-06-90;** Métro: Les Halles), serves reliable dishes like steak frites (main courses 16€–20€) 24/7 in a dining room filled with kitschy Paris memorabilia. Nearby, **Au Pied de Cochon,** 6 rue Coquillière, 1st arrond. (www.pieddecochon.com; (✆) **01-40-13-77-00;** Métro: Les Halles), is a 24/7 brasserie specializing in pork and more pork (main courses 22€–50€). Au Pied de Cochon also has some good seafood dishes, and a restorative onion soup is ideal after a night on the town. For a late-night beef fix, head to **La Tour de Montlhéry–Chez Denise** (p. 96; usually open until 5am), where the steak is as juicy as it is huge.

Zerda Café ★★ NORTH AFRICAN   Intricately carved Moorish designs cover the walls of this friendly restaurant, which serves some of the best couscous in Paris. Zerda offers a choice of lamb, chicken, and *merguez* (spicy lamb sausage) versions; my favorite is the meltingly tender "lamb cooked in sauce," but all are good. If you prefer one of the scrumptious *tagines* (stews seasoned with such ingredients as dried fruits, olives, or preserved lemons), be patient: They take 20 minutes to prepare.

125 rue de Toqueville, 17th arrond. www.zerdacafe.fr. ℂ **09-81-42-69-00.** Main courses 15.50€–22€. Mon–Sat 6–10pm. Closed 2 weeks in Aug. Métro: Pont Cardinet or Wagram.

Opéra & Grands Boulevards (2nd & 9th Arrondissements)

Buzzing with cafes and theaters in the 19th century, the long-overlooked Grands Boulevards are finally coming back to life, especially where these wide avenues intersect with the Opéra and the hip and happening part of the 9th arrondissement that borders Montmartre, nicknamed SoPi (as in South of Pigalle). Less trendy, but also less expensive, the little streets around the Bourse (the French stock exchange) have a wide range of restaurant options, especially at lunchtime. The covered passages that crisscross parts of the 2nd arrondissement (p. 211), especially Passage des Panoramas, also harbor some excellent dining options.

EXPENSIVE

Chez Georges ★★ TRADITIONAL FRENCH   A step back in time, this is how Parisian restaurants were before cuisine became nouvelle. The room is crowded and lively, the cooking old-fashioned and delicious. Many of the customers are regulars who work in nearby offices. The handwritten menu features beautifully executed classics like filet of sole, *pot-au-feu* (beef simmered with vegetables), and sweetbreads with morels. Save room for the profiteroles at dessert.

1 rue du Mail, 2nd arrond. www.facebook.com/chezgeorges1965. ℂ **01-42-60-07-11.** Main courses 21€–45€. Mon–Fri noon–2:30pm and 7–11pm. Closed Aug and the last week of Dec. Métro: Bourse.

La Condesa ★★★ MODERN BISTRO   On an up-and-coming street in SoPi, this joint is emblematic of Paris' cosmopolitan dining scene: At the helm is a Mexican chef who trained at Lyon's legendary Institut Paul Bocuse, worked in three-star restaurants in Paris, whizzed off to learn more in Japan, then came back to launch his own restaurant. And what a restaurant it is: Green tones and natural wood provide a slick backdrop for beautifully executed dishes like celery granita, kombu-marinated veal, and yellow pollock with spiced pineapple. Take it all in with wines from France and Italy, Mexican mezcal, and even Japanese whisky.

17 rue Rodier, 9th arrond. https://lacondesa-paris.com. ℂ **01-53-20-94-90.** Fixed-price lunch 45€ or dinner 75€–95€. Tues–Sun noon–2pm and 7–10pm. Closed 2 weeks in Aug. Métro: Anvers or Notre-Dame de Lorette.

A WORD ABOUT kids IN RESTAURANTS

Many foreigners wonder how French people manage to make their kids behave so well in restaurants. While the ritual of long Sunday family lunches probably trains them to sit still at an early age, there's also the fact that childhood rowdiness is not well tolerated in eating establishments. If the kids can't sit still, the parents simply don't eat out with them. It's rare to find crayons, puzzles, and other kid-friendly items in Parisian restaurants, though they usually have high-chairs (*chaise-haute*, shehz-oht), if not booster seats (*réhausseur*, ray-hoh-sur). That said, by and large French people are kid-friendly, so small, family-owned restaurants will usually be pretty understanding, as long as you don't let your kids run wild. Ask if there's a children's menu (*menu enfant*). While french fries are not particularly nutritious, restaurants usually keep small ones busy with plenty of these treats. You might want to bring along your own kiddie-size

forks and spoons, however, as they are never provided. Below is a short list of some restaurants that are particularly amenable to the kid contingent:

o **Le Relais de l'Entrecôte** (p. 124) Serving unlimited helpings of steak and fries, this lively place is a no-brainer for the kid set.

o **Rosa Bonheur** (p. 115) Located inside the Parc des Buttes-Chaumont, this cool cafe has a beautiful outdoor terrace where parents can nibble on tapas while watching their kids roll down the hill.

o **Wepler** (p. 107) On Place de Clichy, by Montmartre, this traditional brasserie offers a 9€ kids menu that goes beyond fries and burgers, featuring ham and cheese pasta, fish of the day, and green beans as an alternative to *frites*.

MODERATE

Coinstôt Vino ★★ WINE BAR   What's in a name? In this case, an amalgam of French and Italian words for "corner bistro" and "wine," which pretty much sums things up. This tiny place, which sits on the corner of two covered alleyways in the lovely Passage des Panoramas, has a generous and excellent selection of wines. While much of the menu is top-quality nibbles to enjoy while you savor your wine, like oysters and plates of smoked ham, pâté, and cheese, you can also choose from a few *plats du jour* (daily specials) like grilled sea bass and steak with mushrooms. In season, the oysters come from Utah Beach, of Normandy landings fame. A pizza chef was imported from Italy, and you can sample his excellent wares with your glass of *vino*.

26 bis passage des Panoramas, 2nd arrond. https://coinstotvino.business.site/. ℂ **01-44-82-08-54.** Main courses 15€–30€; fixed-price lunch 16€–20€. Mon–Fri noon–2pm and 6–11pm; Sat 6–11pm. Closed first 3 weeks of Aug and last week of Dec. Métro: Grands-Boulevards or Bourse.

Frenchie Bar à Vins ★★ WINE BAR   If you're looking for a quiet night of nibbles and wine, don't go to this wine bar in the up-and-coming Sentier district north of Les Halles. The sister establishment of chef Gregory March-and's ultra-sucessful Frenchie restaurant (where you still have to reserve well in advance) is a raucous, crowded spot, where you'll be lucky to get a table unless you arrive at 6:30pm when it opens. But that's part of the fun. The wonderful reds, whites, and rosés are the perfect social lubricant for getting to know the tipsy locals spilling out onto the sidewalk. And the plates that fly out of the kitchen like wildfire—mussels with chorizo, black truffle pasta, and *croque madame* (bread with ham, cheese, truffles, and white béchamel sauce)—are pure delights (many cost around 13€). If you miss the 6:30pm start, come for a post-dinner drink after 10pm, when you can usually waltz straight in.

6 rue du Nil, 2nd arrond. www.frenchie-bav.com. ℂ **01-40-39-96-19.** Mains 11€–34€. Daily 6:30–11pm. Closed 2 weeks in Aug. Métro: Sentier.

Le Pantruche ★★ TRADITIONAL FRENCH/BISTRO The name is old-fashioned slang for Paris, but this little bistro has a decidedly modern feel to it. Maybe it's the mirrored column near the bar. In yet another case of runaway chefs from Michelin-starred restaurants, here you'll find flavorful updated bistro fare like braised sweetbreads with carrots in a licorice glaze, or suckling pig with pears, celery root, and chestnuts. It's hard to resist indulging in dessert when the Grand Marnier soufflé is on the menu. The fixed-price menus at lunch and dinner are a terrific value, and the tiny dining room fills quickly; definitely reserve ahead.

3 rue Victor Massé, 9th arrond. ℂ **01-48-78-55-60.** Main courses 19€–26€; fixed-price lunch 22€ or dinner 40€. Mon–Fri 12:30–2:30pm and 7:30–9:30pm. Closed first 3 weeks of Aug. Métro: Pigalle.

INEXPENSIVE

L'Excuse Mogador ★ CREPES In the hustle-bustle of clothing stores and lunch spots that line the streets in this crowded quarter, this tiny crêperie is a must if you're hankering after classic Breton flavors. The crepes are generously filled with fresh ingredients like goat cheese, spinach, eggplant, and of course, ham and cheese; the zinc bar and vinyl banquettes make the ambience that much more Parisian. It's open only at lunchtime, when it fills up quickly with shoppers and office workers.

21 rue Joubert, 9th arrond. ℂ **01-42-81-98-19.** Main courses 9€–13€. Mon–Sat 11:30am–4pm. Métro: Havre-Caumartin. RER: Auber.

Michi ★ JAPANESE So discreet is Michi's facade (on rue Ste-Anne, the hub of Paris's "Little Tokyo") that you'd be forgiven for walking past without so much as batting an eyelid. But miss it and you'll miss one of the best sushi joints in town, a tiny spot where fish is as fresh as it gets, and the chef works tirelessly to prepare every dish in front of a seven-seater counter, the best seat in the house if you can get it (there's also a basement). In addition to the sushi and sashimi, look out for delicacies like sea urchin. There's also a good choice of sake and Japanese beer.

58 bis rue Ste-Anne, 2nd arrond. ℂ **01-40-20-49-93.** Main courses 13€–19€; fixed-price menu 13€–17€. Tues–Sat noon–2:30pm and 7–10:30pm. Métro: Quatre-Septembre or Bourse.

Montmartre (18th Arrondissement)

When you get away from the tourist traps of Place du Tertre, you start to understand why people love this neighborhood, and why it's become a favorite with the arty-hipster set. To the north and west of the basilica is where you will find the villagey atmosphere you've heard so much about; to the east and south, Montmartre gives way to Barbès, a lively immigrant neighborhood where you are just as likely to see women donning headscarves and African prints as smart Parisian apparel. Either way, you're bound to come across good food.

MODERATE

Le Coq Rico ★★★ ROTISSERIE   At the top of the Butte de Montmartre, this popular rotisserie is where renowned chef Antoine Westerman proves that poultry can go way beyond the nugget. When raised in the right conditions (in the open air, with space and nutritious food), poultry can be just as delicious as the finest cut of beef. On the menu are such delicacies as guinea fowl in a hazelnut crumb, succulent whole duck from the Dombes region (to share), and tantalizingly juicy Challans chicken—the lot accompanied by crispy, hand-cut fries or macaroni and cheese. The desserts are worth leaving space for, too: lemon crumble, caramelized brioche with poached pears and beer ice cream, and one of the best chocolate *mille-feuille* (layers of pastry and chocolate) in town.

98 rue Lepic, 18th arrond. https://lecoqrico.com. ✆ **01-42-59-82-89.** Main courses 15€–45€; fixed-price lunch 27€; whole birds to share 87€–115€. Daily noon–11:30pm. Métro: Abbesses or Lamarck-Caulincourt.

Wepler ★★ FRENCH BRASSERIE   Picasso and Modigliani used to hang out at this venerable brasserie on Place de Clichy, as did writer Henry Miller, who made it his headquarters. "I knew it like a book," he wrote. "The faces of the waiters, the managers, the cashiers, the whores, the clientele, even the attendants in the lavatory, are engraved in my memory as if they were illustrations in a book which I read every day." Today the atmosphere is quite sedate, but it's still a wonderful place to sit and watch the world go by, and the prices are accessible enough that it is still frequented by artists and writers. The restaurant even offers an annual literary prize. The classic brasserie menu (steak tartare, shellfish platters, poached haddock in *beurre blanc*) has a light, gourmet touch. For a smaller meal, ask for the less expensive cafe menu, which features delicate omelets, a *plat du jour,* and meal-size salads served on the covered terrace.

14 pl. de Clichy, 18th arrond. www.wepler.com. ✆ **01-45-22-53-24.** Main courses 18€–30€; fixed-price lunch or dinner 26.50€–38€. Daily 8am–12:30am. Métro: Place de Clichy.

INEXPENSIVE

Bouillon Pigalle ★★ TRADITIONAL FRENCH   The word *bouillon* refers to the workers' restaurants, found all over Paris back in the 19th century. The idea was to offer good food at modest prices, a concept that still

Montmartre Restaurants

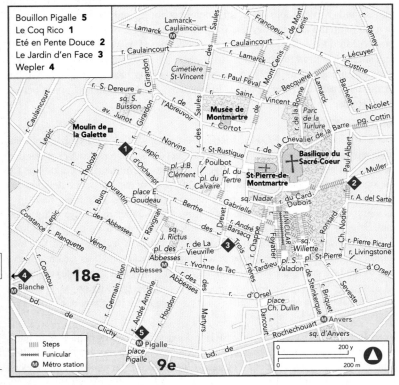

Bouillon Pigalle **5**
Le Coq Rico **1**
Eté en Pente Douce **2**
Le Jardin d'en Face **3**
Wepler **4**

18e

9e

||||| Steps
••••••• Funicular
Ⓜ Métro station

speaks to working Parisians more than 100 years later, if the line out the door of this 300-seat joint is any indication. You come here to tuck into classics like leeks in vinaigrette, *boeuf bourguignon*, and chocolate eclairs at prices so low (think 3€ for a starter, 8.50€ for a main, and less than 3.50€ for dessert) that you wonder how the place makes a profit. The menu covers a wide variety of traditional dishes like steak with fries or rum baba. Service is fast and furious, but it's all part of the atmosphere, which is something that belongs to another time and place. You cannot make a reservation, so be prepared to wait.

22 bd. de Clichy, 18th arrond. www.bouillonpigalle.com. 🕽 **01-42-59-69-31.** Main courses 8.50€–13.50€. Daily noon–midnight. Métro: Pigalle.

Le Jardin d'en Face ★★ BISTRO   This dinner-only place is in tourist central, just off Place des Abbesses, yet it's jam-packed with locals, which is always a good sign—and the reason you'll probably have to reserve ahead. The draw? Excellently executed bistro classics are served at low prices—like a delicious starter of runny egg *cocotte* with foie gras for 7.50€, a main of cheesy, potato-ey *tartiflette* served with magret of duck, or filet mignon of pork in port sauce for 14€, and simple but soul-satisfying desserts like red-fruit crumble and crème brûlée for 6€. The menu has other delectable meat and fish dishes, as well as soups and terrines, and service is with a smile. What more can you ask for?

29 rue des Trois Frères, 18th arrond. https://eater.space/le-jardin-d-en-face. ℰ **01–53–28–00–75.** Main courses 13€–14€. Daily 7:30pm–midnight. Métro: Abbesses.

République, Bastille & Eastern Paris (11th & 12th Arrondissements)

With a mix of working-class families, hipsters, and *bobos* (bourgeois bohemians), the area between République and Nation is diverse, young, and fun. It's also one of the most exciting places for food right now, with a plethora of young chefs opening restaurants that Parisians cross the city for.

EXPENSIVE

Septime ★★★ MODERN FRENCH   With its seafood tapas bar next door (**Clamato**) and its tiny wine bar across the street (**Septime la Cave**), Septime has done more to gentrify this stretch of the 11th arrondissement than years of town planning ever could. With reservations made well in advance, people cross the entire city for a table in Bertrand Grébaut's retro-chic neo-bistro. But that's not why you should come. The progressive, seasonal dishes—anything from line-caught squid with mustard and leek sauce to pigeon with beetroot and Morello cherries—are consistently delicious, and the menus change daily according to what's freshest in the produce market. If you can't score a dinner reservation, try lunchtime. And if all else fails, nip next door to Clamato, where fabulous small plates of crab fritters, clams, or trout roe are washed down with lip-smacking wine that starts for as little as 5.50€ a glass. You won't be disappointed.

80 rue de Charonne, 11th arrond. www.septime-charonne.fr. ℰ **01-43-67-38-29.** Fixed-price lunch 60€ (wine pairing 45€) or dinner 95€ (wine pairing 60€). Mon–Fri 12:15–2pm and 7:30–10pm. Closed 3 weeks in Aug. Métro: Charonne or Ledru-Rollin.

MODERATE

Astier ★★ TRADITIONAL FRENCH/BISTRO   This vintage restaurant has kept up its polished wood and checked napkins as well as its classic menu. Marinated herring, garlicky snails, braised pork in mustard sauce, rib steak with anchovy toasts, pike *quenelles* (a sort of elegant dumpling), and *tarte tatin* (caramelized apple tart) are menu regulars, plus the legendary cheese tray. It's your quintessential Paris bistro, without the surly waiters. The wine list is delectable, too.

44 rue Jean-Pierre Timbaud, 11th arrond. www.restaurant-astier.com. ℰ **01-43-57-16-35.** Main courses 22€–24€; fixed-price lunch 25€ and 46€; fixed-price dinner 36€–56€. Mon–Fri 12:15–2:15pm and 7–10:30pm; Sat 12:15–2:15pm and 7–11pm; Sun 12:30–2:15pm and 7–10:30pm. Métro: Parmentier or Oberkampf.

Buffet ★★ TRADITIONAL BISTRO   After more than a decade of neo-bistro cooking (modern takes on traditional French dishes), Parisians have finally started to long for the classics that the city's next-generation chefs have been subverting (albeit so deliciously) for so long. When nothing but smoked *Morteau* sausage and lentils or veal blanquette will do, those in the know head to Buffet. This small, no-frills dining room is run by a young, talented team of chefs and waitstaff, yet it exudes pre-war nostalgia, from the gingham paper tablecloths and the globe lights, to the piped mayonnaise on the popular hard-boiled egg starter. Save room for dessert: The gooey chocolate fondant and rum baba are superlative.

8 rue de la Main d'Or, 11th arrond. www.restaurantbuffet.fr. ℂ **01-83-89-63-82.** Main courses 20€–24€. Tues–Sat 7–11pm. Closed part of Aug. Métro: Ledru Rollin.

Fulgurances ★★ BISTRO   Fulgurances looks like any other hip neighborhood bistro: natural wood tables, open kitchen, and a quaint spiral staircase tucked away at the back. However, something exciting is afoot. This place is an "incubator," a testing ground for sous chefs looking to become head chefs and open their own restaurants. For a limited number of weeks, they get free run of the kitchen, concocting their own menus, honing their styles, and seeing diners' reactions just meters from the kitchen counter. Menus are limited to what the chef decides to cook that day, usually a choice of two starters, mains, and desserts at lunch, and an evening tasting menu. As this is a cooking "playground," your taste might not always fit with the chef's vision, but this is undoubtedly one of the most interesting dining experiences in the city.

10 rue Alexandre Dumas, 11th arrond. https://fulgurances.com. ℂ **01-43-48-14-59.** Fixed-price lunch 19€, 25€, and 42€ or dinner 58€. Tues–Fri 12:30–2pm and 7:30–10pm. Closed part of Aug. Métro: Rue des Boulets.

Laïa ★★★ MEDITERRANEAN   An ex-team from the George V palace hotel set up this wonderful Mediterranean restaurant, tucked away in a hidden garden along the tourist-free boulevard Voltaire, on the site of a former distillery. It's like a slice of urban paradise—just you, the flowers, and not a peep from the traffic—not to mention that you get some of the most competitive menus on the block: 16€ for a two-course lunch and 35€ for the fixed-priced dinner. And boy, are the dishes delicious: marinated grilled chicken, beef with mint and blackberries, and barbecued octopus. In fact, much of the food is barbecued on a robata (a Japanese-Spanish grill), with herbs and vegetables from the restaurant's rooftop garden. Classic cocktails are given a Mediterranean spin (from 8€). And the service? Well, it's what you'd expect from an ex-palace team: relaxed yet ultra-attentive, and always with a smile. The place is open for coffee from 10am. There are some vegetarian options too.

226 bd. Voltaire, 11th arrond. https://laia-restaurant.com. ℂ **09-75-65-27-21.** Main courses 15€–23€; fixed-price lunch 16€; fixed-price dinner 35€. Mon–Sat 10am–midnight. Closed 2 weeks in Aug. Métro: Rue des Boulets or Voltaire.

Pierre Sang in Oberkampf ★★★ BISTRO   Pierre Sang was a finalist in France's TV cooking competition "Top Chef," yet there's nothing pretentious or showy about this restaurant. The open kitchen does provide entertainment, as Sang's chefs chop, sizzle, and steam all sorts of spice-infused delights that send fragrant scents wafting over the long, shared tables. Expect an inventive selection of Franco-Korean tapas made with whatever market-fresh ingredients have come in that week (though they'll cater for allergies obviously; tell them as soon as you arrive). This might include a tender chicken and tarragon terrine, a crispy herring tempura, or spicy shrimp with *gochujang* (Asian chili sauce). Reserve in advance; it's as popular as can be. If you can't get in, Sang owns two other restaurants on rue Gambey (the street the restaurant looks out onto): **On Gambey** is a more upmarket version of "in Oberkampf" (menus cost 49€ to 88€), while **Pierre Sang Express** is a takeout bibimbap counter (from 12€).

55 rue Oberkampf, 11th arrond. www.pierresang.com. ✆ **09-67-31-96-80.** Fixed-price lunch 20€–25€; tapas 6€–13€. Daily noon–3pm and 7–11pm. Closed part of Aug. Métro: Parmentier or Oberkampf.

INEXPENSIVE

Aux Bons Crus ★★★ BISTRO   Back in the 1960s France was peppered with *Routiers*, roadside restaurants that catered to truck drivers and holidaymakers on their way from the cities to the coast or countryside. As the ancestor of the service station, Routiers were known for serving cheap, homemade food, hearty enough to get you through the long journey ahead. While most have disappeared, Aux Bons Crus at Voltaire is alive and kicking, sporting the Routiers famous red, white, and blue logo, and serving low-price classics like steak in pepper sauce on checkered tablecloths. Today you're more likely to run into people pushing strollers and zipping around on electric scooters than you are truck drivers, but that doesn't detract from the authentic, old-time Paris feel you get as you tuck into beetroot salad, roast chicken, and chocolate profiteroles for around 29€.

54 rue Godefroy Cavaignac, 11th arrond. www.auxbonscrus.fr. ✆ **01-45-67-21-13.** Main courses 15€–21€. Daily noon–2pm and 7–10pm. Closed part of Aug. Métro: Voltaire.

Ground Control ★★ STREET FOOD   There's an underground feel to this sprawling venue near Gare de Lyon, a vast multidisciplinary arts center with its own radio station, exhibition spaces, and a food hall set in disused SNCF hangars. The food court is the place to get delicious Chinese, Mexican, and Central African Republic dishes, plus coffee and cake for dessert. Outside, converted buses hawk everything from British fish and chips, to ham and cheese crepes, to fresh oysters, with seating at vintage benches and tables. Just make sure you get your drink before you order food. None of the stalls sell beverages, and it's annoying to have to leave your hot food tray for some water or beer.

81 rue du Charolais, 12th arrond. www.groundcontrolparis.com. No phone. Main courses 8€–16€. Wed–Fri noon–midnight (last entry through the gate 10:30pm); Sat 11am–midnight; Sun 11am–10:30pm (late entry 9:15pm). Métro/RER: Gare de Lyon.

Funky and fun, Ground Control provides an alternative take on dining in Paris.

WHERE TO DINE | The Right Bank

L'Ebauchoir ★★★ MODERN FRENCH   Located in an unlikely corner of the 12th arrondissement, this atmospheric neighborhood hangout offers a fab selection of modern bistro cooking at decidedly reasonable prices. The high ceilings, sunny yellow walls, and wooden fixtures create a warm and friendly environment for vaguely Mediterranean-inspired dishes like roast lamb with sweet spices and Thai basil, or *magret* (breast) of duck with vanilla and pineapple. You can usually find a nice vegetarian option here, like a vegetable "cake" with sautéed shiitake mushrooms, asparagus, and hummus. With a two-course lunch deal at 15€, this place gets jammed at noon, so try to reserve.

43 rue des Citeaux, 12th arrond. www.lebauchoir.com. ✆ **01-43-42-49-31.** Main courses dinner 19€–24€; fixed-price lunch 15€–26€. Mon 8–11pm; Tues–Thurs noon–2:30pm and 8–11pm; Fri–Sat noon–2:30pm and 7:30–11pm. Closed 1 week mid-Aug. Métro: Faidherbe Chaligny or Reuilly Diderot.

Noglu ★★ GLUTEN-FREE   This small restaurant is where gluten-intolerant people bring their friends because the home-cooked gluten-free food is so tasty you don't have to have a food allergy to appreciate it. Dishes might include cod with lentils, vegetable lasagna, and warm chocolate cake. Though not vegetarian per se, Noglu always has meat- and fish-free dishes on the menu. If you're in a hurry, everything can be made to take out. Like what you eat? Sign up for a pastry-making lesson (70€). There's now another address on the Left Bank (69 rue de Grenelle, 7th arrond.).

15 rue Basfroi, 11th arrond. www.noglu.fr. ✆ **01-42-36-52-50.** Main courses 12€–17€; fixed-price breakfast 10.50€. Mon–Fri 9am–4pm; Sat 10am–5pm; Sun 10am–4pm. Closed 2 weeks in Aug. Métro: Voltaire, Charonne, or Ledru Rollin.

Belleville, Canal St-Martin & Northeast Paris (10th, 19th & 20th Arrondissements)

Between the two parks of Belleville and Buttes Chaumont and along the Canal St-Martin lie some of the city's most quirky and delightful restaurants. In one of the last strongholds of Paris' bohemian set, you can find both gourmet bistros and funky cheap eats, as well as a good number of wine bars that serve nibbles along with the fruit of the vine. One Thursday evening every month boulevard de Belleville morphs into a street food market where around 20 stands sell everything from Vietnamese *bò bún* (a beef and noodle salad) to Mexican street tacos (www.lefoodmarket.fr).

MODERATE

Chez Michel ★★★ BRETON/SEAFOOD Diners come from all over Paris, as well as from across the channel (via the nearby Eurostar train hub at Gare du Nord), to sample Thierry Breton's superb cooking at affordable prices that have barely budged in a decade. A native of Brittany, Breton improvises on recipes from back home, including lots of seafood dishes like *kaotriade,* a Breton ("Breton" means from Brittany, by the way) fish stew, and fresh crab salad. For dessert, try the copious rice pudding or the awe-inspiring Paris-Brest (a choux pastry filled with praline cream).

10 rue de Belzunce, 10th arrond. www.restaurantchezmichel.fr. ℂ **01-44-53-06-20.** Fixed-price lunch 32€–38€ or dinner 38€. Mon–Fri 11:45am–2pm and 6:45–11pm. Closed Aug. Métro: Gare du Nord.

Les Arlots ★★★ WINE BAR/BISTRO You'll need to reserve several days in advance to get a table in this tiny, noisy bistro by Gare du Nord, quite simply because it serves some of the best comfort cuisine in town—everything from langoustines in mayonnaise to foie gras–stuffed cabbage to perfectly cooked (that is, pink) veal with braised carrots. Locals wax lyrical about the homemade sausage and mash, and desserts are just as tempting: The cinnamon and orange is both creamy and tangy, the *fraisier* (strawberries, shortbread, and sour cream) has just the right crunch-to-cream ratio. Only the freshest products are used, so the menu changes regularly, but these are staples to look out for when the season's right. Wash them down with a crisp sauvignon blanc or a berry-red syrah and you'll be smiling before you can say "bon appetit!"

136 rue du Faubourg Poissonnière, 10th arrond. ℂ **01-42-82-92-01.** Main courses 19€–24€; fixed-price lunch 19€. Tues–Sat noon–2:30pm and 7:30–10:30pm. Closed last 3 weeks in Aug and first week of May. Métro/RER: Gare du Nord or Métro Anvers, Poissonnière, or Barbès-Rochechouart.

MijoT ★★ MODERN FRENCH/BISTRO On busy nights, chef Isabelle Bouillon calls in a kitchen aide, but the rest of the time MijoT is a one-woman show, with Isabelle doing everything, from the cooking to the waiting, and even the washing up. But sample this tiny bistro's delectable fare—carrot and orange soup, duck ravioli, and chocolate tart with thyme cream and champagne sorbet, perhaps—and you'll soon see that the restaurant's much more than just an ode to multitasking. Not only are the dishes delicious, but all ingredients also come directly from local producers (except the duck, which is sourced in the Nouvelle Aquitaine region); proceeds go to a charity dedicated to feeding the poor.

6 rue Victor Letalle, 20th arrond. http://mijot.fr. © **01-47-97-25-77.** Main courses 19€–32€. Tues–Sat 7–10:30pm. Closed part of August. Métro: Ménilmontant.

INEXPENSIVE

Bob's Juice Bar ★ VEGETARIAN   Hipsters are tripping all over themselves to try "smoossies" (that is, smoothies) and juices these days, and some of the best can be found at this terrific vegetarian restaurant, which has become *the* place to sample muffins, bagels, soups, and other delicious vegetarian goodies. The brainchild of Marc Grossman (alias "Bob"), an erstwhile New Yorker, this may not be the most authentically French experience, but it certainly is a tasty one. You can sit down or take out here, or try the **Bob's Bake Shop** in La Chapelle (Halle Pajol, 12 Espl. Nathalie Sarraute, 18th arrond.) or in the famous Shakespeare and Company bookshop cafe, 37 rue de la Bûcherie, 5th arrond. (p. 221).

15 rue Lucien Sampaix, 10th arrond. www.bobsjuicebar.com. © **09-50-06-36-18.** Smoothies and juices 5€–7.50€; main courses 6€–8€. Mon–Fri 8am–3pm; Sat 9:30am–4:30pm. Métro: Jacques Bonsergent.

Bouillon Julien ★★★ BISTRO/TRADITIONAL FRENCH   Resplendent in original 1906 moldings, mosaics, and a stained-glass ceiling, Bouillon Julien (in the up-and-coming 10th arrond.) is a place where postcard-perfect decor matches scrumptious dishes that remind you of the good old days, even if you're not that old. You might find comfortable classics like rabbit terrine with *ravigote* sauce (mayonnaise with mustard, pickles, and herbs) and shallots, or something a little more challenging, like *andouillette* (pungent tripe sausage). This is definitely a surf-and-turf lover's hangout, while the wine list features many affordable bottles from small wine producers. Look for the mahogany bar: It's an Art Nouveau original by Louis Majorelle (a furniture designer and one of the pioneers of the style) and a pure work of art.

16 rue du Faubourg Saint-Denis, 10th arrond. www.bouillon-julien.com. © **01-47-70-12-06.** Main courses 9.90€–14€. Daily 11:45am–midnight. Closed 2 weeks in Aug. Métro: Strasbourg Saint-Denis or Bonne Nouvelle.

Hôtel du Nord ★★ FRENCH   Overlooking Canal St-Martin, just across from where Amélie threw pebbles in Jean-Pierre Jeunet's acclaimed 2001 movie, this vintage bistro is a hip place for a meal. For casual dining, book the front section, reminiscent of a 1930s cafe with tiled floors and an Art Deco zinc bar; for something more sophisticated, the back section's red banquettes, white tablecloths, and mirrors create a boudoir-chic ambience. Wherever you sit, the food is good: classic dishes like beef carpaccio with fries, sausage-rich cassoulet, or vegetarian options such as ricotta and spinach ravioli. The

24.50€ brunch is popular on Sundays, when the streets outside become pedestrian-only.

102 quai de Jemmapes, 10th arrond. www.hoteldunord.org. ℗ **01-40-40-78-78.** Main courses 14€–23€; fixed-price lunch 15.50€–19.50€. Daily 10:30am–1am. Métro: Jacques Bonsergent.

Le Verre Volé ★ WINE BAR/MODERN FRENCH The sun is shining, the leafy trees are posing prettily along the Canal St-Martin, and you are walking one of the pretty footbridges that curve over the water. All that's missing is a table and a glass of wine.

Hôtel du Nord.

Luckily, this wine bar/restaurant is on hand with a vast selection of bacchic and gustatory delights. You could just share a plate of sliced smoked meats and sausage, the usual accompaniment to a glass of red, or you can explore the menu, which might include a slice of milk-fed veal or mullet ceviche. Then select a bottle of wine from the shelves that line the walls and enjoy it (for a nominal corkage fee) in this informal, if crowded, setting.

67 rue de Lancry, 10th arrond. www.leverrevole.fr. ℗ **01-48-03-17-34.** Fixed-price lunch 19€–21€; main courses 16€–24€. Mon–Fri 4–8pm; Sat 11am–7pm; Sun 11am–3pm. Métro: Jacques Bonsergent.

Rosa Bonheur ★ TAPAS This unconventional space is named after an unconventional 19th-century painter/sculptor. Yes, it's a tapas bar, but it's also a sort of off-the-wall community center, hosting various expositions and events, not to mention its own chorus and soccer team. Located in an old *buvette* (refreshment pavilion) inside the Parc des Buttes Chaumont that dates from the Universal Exposition of 1900, the restaurant boasts a sprawling terrace and one of the best panoramic views in town. Late afternoon, a huge crowd gathers to drink and nibble tapas both indoors and out. The ambience is relaxed and friendly; coming here is a good excuse to stroll through the lush Buttes Chaumont park. That park, plus an indoor play area and kids menu, makes Rosa Bonheur a great family option. A second location is on a docked barge on the Seine, **Rosa Bonheur Sur Seine** (right near the Pont des Invalides on the Left Bank; open year-round Wed–Fri 5pm–1:30am; Sat–Sun noon–1:30am). From April to October it has outdoor seating and a pizza stand on the quay.

2 allée de la Cascade, 19th arrond. www.rosabonheur.fr. ℗ **01-42-00-00-45.** Tapas 4€–10€. Wed–Sun 5–11:30pm. Closed first 2 weeks in Jan. Métro: Botzaris.

Rosa Bonheur, inside the Parc des Buttes Chaumont.

THE LEFT BANK

Latin Quarter (5th & 13th Arrondissements)

For more than 700 years, this lively neighborhood has been overrun with students, a population that is forever on the lookout for a good, cheap meal. As a result, the area is full of inexpensive snack shacks of varying quality, from souvlaki huts to Vietnamese noodle shops to Breton crêperies. Steer clear of the unbearably touristy area around rue de la Huchette, where you are bound to pay too much for a mediocre product, and be wary of rue Moufftard, which was once a good bet for good food but has since become a victim of its own success. If you want to eat well, you'll need to venture a little farther afield, where innovative restaurateurs have been cultivating a knowledgeable clientele of professors, professionals, and savvy tourists.

EXPENSIVE

La Tour d'Argent ★★★ CLASSIC FRENCH   Everyone from Queen Elizabeth II to Orson Welles has dined in this venerable restaurant, famed for its history (a restaurant has stood here since 1582), its impeccable service, and its sweeping view of the Seine and Notre-Dame (still under scaffolding). And since the appointment of chef Philippe Labbé in 2016, the food's back on track again (after a dip in quality), wooing well-dressed crowds with the promise of inventive French cuisine and the establishment's coveted signature dish of pressed duck (each duck has been numbered since 1890). Five or six different waiters will visit your table at one time or another, accomplishing various tasks (opening wine bottles, pulling out your chair, and even leading you to the bathroom) with utmost professionalism and not a hint of snobbery. They then discreetly disappear into the rich decor as you gaze through the huge windows. The fixed-price lunch is a good way to enjoy this singular experience without busting your budget. Be sure to reserve at least a week in advance; jackets are required for men at dinner.

15–17 quai de la Tournelle, 5th arrond. www.latourdargent.com. ℂ **01-43-54-23-31.** Main courses 80€–140€; fixed-price lunch 105€ or dinner 295€ and 350€. Tues–Sat noon–1:30pm and 7–9pm. Closed Aug. Métro: St-Michel or Maubert-Mutualité.

La Truffière ★★ CLASSIC FRENCH   An atmospheric 17th-century dining room near the Seine with exposed stone walls and wooden beams is the setting for the sort of French cuisine you crave when you think of Paris—langoustines, suckling lamb, ultra-ripe cheeses, and the "black diamonds" (truffles) that the restaurant takes its name from, prepared with panache by talented chef Antoine Coutier. If you're into wine, you'll be hard-pressed to find a better restaurant: The menu has some 3,200 bottles. Thank goodness for the sommelier, who takes into account both your budget and the dishes you've ordered. Tasting menus cost up to 155€ in the evening, so the 39€ lunch menu is one of the best deals in town.

4 rue Blainville, 5th arrond. www.la-truffiere.fr. ℂ **01-46-33-29-82.** Main dishes 62€– 95€; fixed-price lunch 39€ or dinner 68€–155€. Tues–Sat noon–1:30pm and 7–10pm. Closed Aug. Métro: Place Monge or Cardinal Lemoine.

MODERATE

Au Petit Marguery ★★ TRADITIONAL FRENCH/BISTRO   This place has everything you always wanted in a French bistro: antique tile floors, banquettes, vested waiters, and a dark rose color scheme. The menu also reflects the traditions of yesteryear, with an emphasis on game dishes in autumn and fresh produce in summer. Appetizers include several different terrines, including homemade foie gras; main dishes feature meaty items like 7-hour lamb and lighter fare like sea bream with fennel and star anise. Top it all off with a Grand Marnier soufflé (a specialty of the house). The restaurant has a smaller and more relaxed version of itself next door, the **Comptoir Marguery,** where prices are lower and the menu is a little more basic; another outpost of the main restaurant, **Au Petit Marguery Rive Droite,** is at 64 avenue des Ternes on the Right Bank.

9 bd. du Port-Royal, 13th arrond. www.petitmarguery.com. ℂ **01-43-31-58-59.** Fixed-price lunch 26€–32€ or dinner 43.50€. Daily 11:30am–3pm and 6–11pm (bar service nonstop 11:30am–11pm). Métro: Gobelins.

Bistroy Les Papilles ★★ BISTRO/WINE BAR   Lined with shelves upon shelves of delectable bottles, this bustling wine shop/bistro/gourmet grocery matches simple but excellent fare with terrific samples of the fruit of the vine. At dinnertime, the fixed-price menu offers great value—four courses for 36€—but no choices. If you don't want the menu, try the *marmite du marché,* the stew of the day served in a cast-iron pot (around 20€). At lunch you can choose between a fixed-price menu or lighter fare: a variety of salads, open-faced sandwiches, and charcuterie plates. Wine is available by the glass, but patrons are encouraged to choose a bottle from the nearby shelves and pay

Au Petit Marguery.

just a small corkage fee—a great way to try a good bottle without the usual restaurant markup on the wine.

30 rue Gay-Lussac, 5th arrond. www.lespapillesparis.fr. ℂ **01-43-25-20-79.** Main courses 20€; fixed-price lunch 29€ or dinner 36€. Tues–Sat 9:30am–midnight. Closed Aug and between Christmas and New Year's. RER: Luxembourg.

Le Petit Pontoise ★ BISTRO Looking for somewhere authentic and friendly in the tourist heart of the Latin Quarter? Le Petit Pontoise is just a 5-minute walk from Notre-Dame and even closer to the Seine, but it's coveted by locals who come for foie gras with figs, Provençal scallops, and honey-fried pigs' cheeks. The setting's lovely too—all red leather banquettes and country-style wooden tables. Sample the luscious food with (many) glasses of great French wines, from golden-hued Sancerre white to light, fruity, organic Bourguil red. The place is packed in the evening, so get there early or reserve a table online beforehand.

9 rue Pontoise, 5th arrond. www.lepetitpontoise.fr. ℂ **01-43-29-25-20.** Main dishes 25€–36€; fixed-price lunch 23€–34€. Daily noon–2:30pm and 6:30-10:30pm. Closed last week of Dec, first week of Jan, and 2 weeks in Aug. Métro: Maubert-Mutualité.

L'Ourcine ★★ MODERN FRENCH A great choice for wine lovers, L'Ourcine has a long list of bottles from small, little-known French vineyards. A personal favorite is the 2012 Fitou by Château de Nouvelles in the Aude region, a full-bodied red with notes of violet and rosemary (35€). And ready to soak it all up are reasonably priced, delicious dishes that might include Brittany lobster (fresh off the boat and whizzed into Paris), foie gras–stuffed chicken, and (in autumn) venison, the latter served in a rich berry and red wine sauce. Dessert could follow with creamy, vanilla-infused *riz au lait* (rice

Left Bank Restaurants (Eiffel Tower Area)

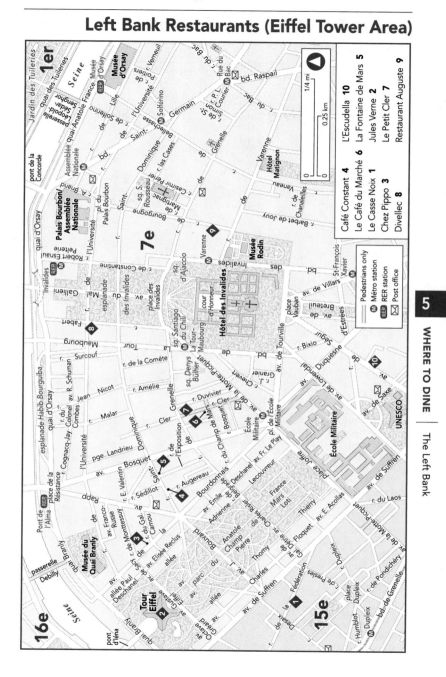

Café Constant **4**
Le Café du Marché **6**
Le Casse Noix **1**
Chez Pippo **3**
Divellec **8**
L'Escudella **10**
La Fontaine de Mars **5**
Jules Verne **2**
Le Petit Cler **7**
Restaurant Auguste **9**

Pedestrians only
Ⓜ Métro station
RER RER station
⊠ Post office

Left Bank Restaurants (Latin Quarter, St-Germain, Montparnasse)

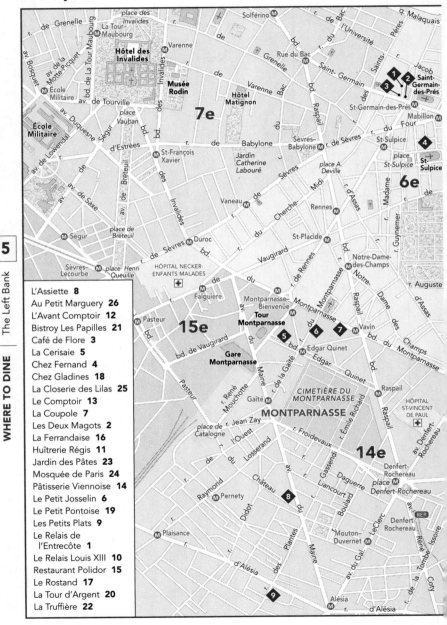

L'Assiette **8**
Au Petit Marguery **26**
L'Avant Comptoir **12**
Bistroy Les Papilles **21**
Café de Flore **3**
La Cerisaie **5**
Chez Fernand **4**
Chez Gladines **18**
La Closerie des Lilas **25**
Le Comptoir **13**
La Coupole **7**
Les Deux Magots **2**
La Ferrandaise **16**
Huîtrerie Régis **11**
Jardin des Pâtes **23**
Mosquée de Paris **24**
Pâtisserie Viennoise **14**
Le Petit Josselin **6**
Le Petit Pontoise **19**
Les Petits Plats **9**
Le Relais de
  l'Entrecôte **1**
Le Relais Louis XIII **10**
Restaurant Polidor **15**
Le Rostand **17**
La Tour d'Argent **20**
La Truffière **22**

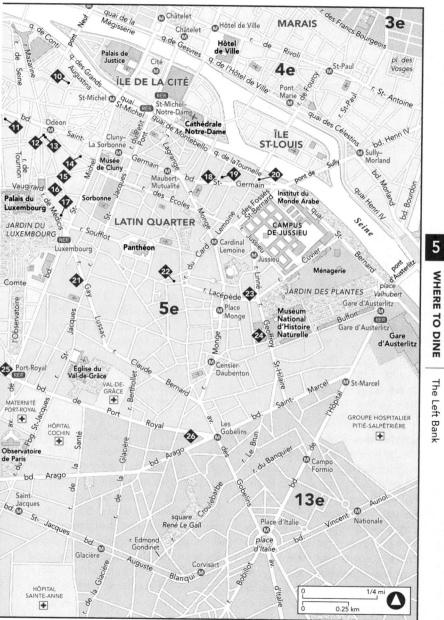

pudding) or apples flamed in Calvados and served with caramel ice cream. The 29€ menu is a particularly great deal.

92 rue Broca, 13th arrond. www.restaurant-lourcine.fr. © **01-47-07-13-65.** Fixed-price menu 29€–39€. Tues–Sat noon–2:30pm and 7–11pm. Closed 2 weeks in Aug. Métro: Les Gobelins or Glacière.

INEXPENSIVE

Chez Gladines Saint-Germain ★ SOUTHWESTERN Hungry? Come here for enormous and tasty portions of rib-sticking southwestern French specialties. That means crispy duck confit with sautéed potatoes; Basque-style chicken (with tomatoes and bell peppers); *pipérade* (a casserole of eggs with smoked ham, sliced and sautéed potatoes, bell peppers, and a bright tomato sauce); and the like. Even the salads are gargantuan, filled with goodies like bacon, goat cheese, smoked ham, and foie gras. The success of the original Gladines in the 13th arrondissement (30 rue des Cinq Diamants) has spawned two other locations: 11 bis rue des Halles, 1st arrond.; and 74 bd. des Batignolles, 17th arrond.

44 bd. St-Germain, 5th arrond. www.gladines.com. © **01-46-33-93-88.** Main courses 10€–15€. Mon–Thurs noon–11pm; Fri–Sat noon–11:45pm; Sun noon–11:30pm. Métro: Maubert-Mutualité.

Jardin des Pâtes ★ PASTA/VEGETARIAN This quaint restaurant by the Jardin des Plantes specializes in pasta. But this is no ordinary pasta—not only are the rice, wheat, rye, and barley noodles made fresh every day, but the organic flour that goes into them is ground daily on the premises. The focus on wholesome ingredients is menu-wide—even the ice cream is 100% natural. While you won't find the usual Italian sauces, you will find original creations like rye pasta with ham, cream, sweet onions, white wine, and Comté cheese or barley pasta with fresh salmon, leeks, seaweed, and crème fraîche. Vegetarians have ample choices here, and the relaxed atmosphere makes it a good place to bring (well-behaved) kids. Pastas are made to order, so don't be in a hurry. Reservations are advised, especially on weekends.

4 rue Lacépède, 5th arrond. © **01-43-31-50-71.** Main courses 12€–15€. Daily noon–2:30pm and 7–11pm. Métro: Place Monge.

St-Germain-des-Prés (6th Arrondissement)

St-Germain is a mix of expensive eateries that only the lucky few can afford and smaller bistros that bring back the days when intellectuals and artists frequented the Café de Flore. Overpriced tourist restaurants cluster around boulevard St-Germain near the Carrefour de l'Odéon; as you head south and north of this major boulevard, your choices will expand. Though the Marché St-Germain has been transformed into a type of mall, the restaurants hugging its perimeter offer a wide range of possibilities.

EXPENSIVE

La Ferrandaise ★★ TRADITIONAL FRENCH/BISTRO   Named after a particularly tasty breed of cow, this carnivore's paradise serves beef that comes direct from Puy du Dôme, the center of France's green heartland. The young chef is also a great believer in local products (all vegetables are local and/or organic) and authentic bistro cuisine. Menu highlights could include shoulder of lamb with spinach, or a juicy steak with sautéed carrots, but if meat is not your game, then equally delectable fish and poultry dishes are also on offer. To finish, try a fresh Auvergne cheese like Saint Nectaire or Fourme d'Ambert. Bring your appetite, as you must order one of the three-course fixed-price menus; there's no a la carte.

8 rue de Vaugirard, 6th arrond. www.laferrandaise.com. ✆ **01-43-26-36-36.** Fixed-price lunch 16€–37€ or dinner 37€ and 65€. Mon–Fri noon–2:30pm and 7–10:30pm; Sat 7–11pm. Closed evenings in Aug. Métro: Odéon.

Le Relais Louis XIII ★★★ TRADITIONAL FRENCH   In an ancient building on the site where Louis XIII was crowned back in 1610, this acclaimed restaurant pays homage not only to the monarch, but to traditional French cuisine at its most illustrious. No tonka beans or reduced licorice sauce here— Chef Manuel Martinez trains his formidable talents on classic sauces and time-honored dishes like sea bass *quenelles* and roast duck, though he's not opposed to topping off the meal with a little lemon-basil sherbet at dessert. Signature dishes include lobster and foie gras ravioli and braised sweetbreads with wild mushrooms. The dining room, crisscrossed with exposed beams and ancient stonework, makes you wonder if the Three Musketeers might not tumble through the doorway bearing your *mille-feuille* with bourbon vanilla cream.

8 rue des Grands-Augustins, 6th arrond. www.relaislouis13.fr. ✆ **01-43-26-75-96.** Main courses 58€–59€; fixed-price lunch 65€–145€ or dinner 95€–145€. Tues–Sat 12:15–2:30pm and 7:15–10:30pm. Closed 1st week Jan, 1st week May, and all of Aug. Métro: Odéon or St-Michel.

MODERATE

Chez Fernand ★★ TRADITIONAL FRENCH/BISTRO   This neighborhood institution packs a flavorful punch. Red-checkered tablecloths provide a homey background for excellent bistro dishes like thick steak with a pepper sauce and creamy mashed potatoes, veal liver with caramelized onions, or the *boeuf bourguignon,* the specialty of the house. You could start with a nice, light sea bass tartare or a rich, grilled marrowbone. Whatever your choice, it will be executed with loving care and quality ingredients, which is why this restaurant has a devoted clientele.

13 rue Guisarde, 6th arrond. www.chezfernand-guisarde.com. ℂ **01-43-54-61-47.** Main courses 22€–34€. Daily noon–2:30pm and 7–11pm. Métro: Mabillon.

Huîtrerie Régis ★ OYSTERS/SEAFOOD   Like oysters on the half shell? Good, because that's pretty much all they have here: delicious bivalves that come straight from the Marennes-Oléron region on France's Atlantic coast. The brief and to-the-point menu gives you a choice of various sizes and grades of oysters, as well as sea urchins, clams, and shrimp. You'll have to order at least a dozen oysters to sit down in the tiny restaurant; considering the price, you may as well order a *formule,* or fixed-price menu, which includes various combinations of oysters, wine, and coffee. These oysters are fresh, oceany mouthfuls of flavor that deserve a good glass of Sancerre.

3 rue de Montfaucon, 6th arrond. http://huitrerie-regis.com. ℂ **01-44-41-10-07.** Oysters per dozen 30€–39€; fixed-price lunch or dinner 34.50€–49€. Mon–Fri noon–2:30pm and 6:30–10:30pm; Sat–Sun noon–10:45pm. Closed mid-July to mid-Sept. Métro: Mabillon or St-Germain.

Le Comptoir ★★★ TRADITIONAL FRENCH/BISTRO   The brainchild of super-chef Yves de Camdeborde, this small and scrumptious bistro set below the Relais Saint-Germain hotel (p. 79) is still bringing in the crowds more than a decade after its opening in 2005. Camdeborde is often credited with starting the bistronomy movement in the 1990s, when he walked out on the Crillon and opened his own bistro. He wanted to offer the French equivalent of "down home" cooking, using the best ingredients and charging affordable prices. During the day, Le Comptoir is a bistro, serving relatively traditional fare, like a slice of lamb with thyme sauce or *panier de cochonaille,* a basket of the Camdeborde family's own brand of sliced smoked ham, dried sausage, and other pork-based delectables. On weeknights, it's a temple to haute cuisine, with a tasting menu that includes as many as five different dishes. Reserve weeks in advance for this fixed-price meal, which changes nightly. If you can't get a seat, try **L'Avant Comptoir,** the restaurant's adjacent wine bar/counter serving small plates of charcuterie and seafood (see below).

9 carrefour de l'Odéon, 6th arrond. www.hotel-paris-relais-saint-germain.com. ℂ **01-44-27-07-50.** Main courses 17€–32€; fixed-price dinner Mon–Fri 65€. Daily noon–11pm. Métro: Odéon.

Le Relais de l'Entrecôte ★ TRADITIONAL FRENCH/STEAK   You won't have to trouble yourself with deciding what to eat here: The only thing on the menu is steak. Just tell the waiter how you want it cooked (*bien cuit* for medium-well, à point for medium-rare, or *saignant* for rare), and sit back and wait. First comes a fresh green salad, and then the main event: a giant silver platter of steak, doused in an addictive "secret sauce," and served with crispy golden fries. Expect to see your server return with a second helping once you've finished. Desserts, if you can find the strength, are classic and delicious, including profiteroles and crème brûlée. Get here early; you can't reserve, and a line snakes out the door. If the line looks too long, you can try one of the two other locations: 101 bd. Montparnasse in the 6th, or 15 rue Marbeuf in the 8th.

20 rue St. Benoît, 6th arrond. www.relaisentrecote.fr. ✆ **01-45-49-16-00.** Daily noon–2:30pm and 7–11:30pm. Fixed-price lunch and dinner 27€. Métro: St-Germain-des-Prés.

INEXPENSIVE

L'Avant Comptoir ★ WINE BAR/TAPAS/CREPES   This shoebox-size wine-bar-cum-crepe stand is an outcropping of the venerable Le Comptoir next door. Hungry diners descend on the bar-and-tapas component while waiting for a table at the restaurant; those in search of quick and portable bites can order takeout crepes and salads (by ordering from the takeout menu, you give up your right to stand and eat at the counter). The decidedly hip atmosphere trumps the low-key "this is just a typical southwestern bar" decor. Goodies include fried croquettes stuffed with Iberian ham, *brandade* (mashed potatoes with cod), oxtail canapés with horseradish cream, and chicken hearts grilled with garlic and parsley. If there's no room, or you're in the mood for seafood, try its sister joint next-door, **L'Avant Comptoir de la Mer.**

3 carrefour de l'Odéon, 6th arrond. www.hotel-paris-relais-saint-germain.com. No phone. Tapas 7€–10€. Daily noon–midnight. Métro: Odéon.

Pâtisserie Viennoise ★★ BAKERY   Squeezed between two medical schools, this old-fashioned pastry shop gets its share of students and professors in need of a nosh. And this is a nosher's heaven: It has a huge selection of pastries, including Viennese classics like Linzer torte and strudel, and the hot chocolate is one of the best in the city (4.50€–5.50€). It's thick and dark and bitter—sugar cubes are provided so you can adjust the sweetness—and if you ask for it à la *viennoise,* it will come with a dollop of real whipped cream. The tiny dining area looks like it hasn't changed in at least 50 years: a collection of wooden booths and small tables that might have been shipped in from Vienna. You can also lunch here on inexpensive quiches, salads, and pasta dishes, including some nice vegetarian choices.

8 rue de l'Ecole de Médecine, 6th arrond. ✆ **01-43-26-60-48.** Main courses 7€–10€; pastries 3.50€–6€. Mon–Fri 8:30am–7:30pm. Closed mid-July through 3rd week of Aug. Métro: Odéon or Cluny La Sorbonne.

Restaurant Polidor ★ TRADITIONAL FRENCH/BISTRO   An unofficial historic monument, Polidor is not so much a restaurant as a snapshot of a bygone era. The decor has not changed substantially for at least 100 years, when Verlaine and Rimbaud, the bad boys of French poetry, would come here for a cheap meal. The bistro would continue to be a literary lunchroom for decades: In the 1950s, it was dubbed "the College of Pataphysics" by a rowdy group of young upstarts that included Max Ernst, Boris Vian, and Eugene Ionesco; André Gide and Ernest Hemingway were reputed regulars. The menu features hefty bistro standbys like *boeuf bourguignon* and *blanquette de veau* (veal stew with white sauce), but if you look carefully you'll also find lighter fare like salmon with basil and chicken breast with morel sauce. These days, the arty set has moved elsewhere; you'll probably be sharing the long wood tables with other tourists, along with a dose of locals and fans of Woody Allen's "Midnight in Paris," as certain shots were filmed here. Though the food is not particularly memorable, the ambience is unique.

41 rue Monsieur-le-Prince, 6th arrond. www.polidor.com. ℭ **01-43-26-95-34.** Main courses 12€–20€; fixed-price menu 22€–35€. Daily noon–3pm and 7pm–midnight. Métro: Odéon.

Eiffel Tower & Nearby (7th Arrondissement)

Crowded with ministries and important people, this neighborhood is so grand, you half expect to hear trumpets blowing each time you turn a corner. Eating here on a budget takes some skill, or at least a bit of insider knowledge. Though this is a rather staid neighborhood, a few streets are fairly lively, namely rue Cler, a pretty market street, and rue St-Dominique, home to some of the best restaurants on this side of the Seine. You're likely to get fleeced if you insist on eating right next to the Eiffel Tower—that is, if you can find a restaurant, as the pickings are pretty slim in the Iron Lady's immediate vicinity. If it's a nice day, buy a sandwich at a bakery and have a picnic on the Champs de Mars, where you can't beat the price or the view.

EXPENSIVE

Divellec ★★ MODERN FRENCH/SEAFOOD Close your eyes and you're at the seaside, Deauville or Trouville perhaps (famed posh spots along the Normandy coast), for you can smell the salt as you step into this ultrachic, seafood-only restaurant near Les Invalides, where truffles and oysters top pillowy Saint Jacques scallops bathed in delicate watercress sauce. Fish, as is customary in France, comes with sauces—monkfish gets *ravigote* cream (herby, mustardy emulsion), sole gets walnut butter—but they never overpower the "pure" taste of the flesh. The *navarin d'homard,* lobster in a creamy sauce, is possibly the best in town. The sharing plates include sardine rillettes for 18€, sushi for 28€, and sashimi for 28€–35€. On a sunny day, reserve a terrace spot with a view of the tree-filled Esplanade des Invalides.

18 rue Fabert, 7th arrond. www.divellec-paris.fr. ℭ **01-45-51-91-96.** Main courses 38€–75€. Daily noon–1:45pm and 7–9:45pm. Closed 3 weeks in Aug. Métro/RER: Les Invalides.

Jules Verne ★★★ MODERN FRENCH Sometimes Paris is about embracing the clichés, and dining on the second floor of the Eiffel Tower is definitely a cliché worth embracing. Not only are the views magnificent, with the city's iconic rooftops undulating in graceful higgledy-piggledydom between Trocadéro, Les Invalides, and La Défense's skyscrapers, but now that award-winning chef Frédéric Anton has taken over the kitchen, the food is worth writing home about, too. Try wonders like langoustine ravioli in tarragon sauce, vanilla-salted pigeon, and a bitter chocolate soufflé—all beautifully presented to evoke (in the words of the chef) "the cogs, the nuts, and bolts" of the Eiffel Tower. The 135€ weekday three-course lunch menu is a steal. For an extra dose of romance, splurge at night when the city sparkles at your feet. Reservations are required at least 2 months in advance.

2nd floor of the Eiffel Tower, av. Gustave Eiffel, 7th arrond. www.restaurants-toureiffel. com. No phone. Main courses 74€–165€; fixed-price lunch 135€ (Mon–Fri only); tasting menu (lunch and dinner) 190€ and 230€. Daily noon–1:30pm and 7–9pm. Métro: Bir-Hakeim or Trocadéro. RER: Champs de Mars Tour Eiffel. Closed 14 July dinner.

Restaurant Auguste ★★ MODERN FRENCH/SEAFOOD   It's not every famous chef who can call himself "Mr. Goodfish." Gael Orieux's love of the sea and everything in it has led him to become spokesperson for an association dedicated to protecting the oceans. Naturally, that means that what you see on your plate is not only delicious, but also ecologically correct. Let's hope he makes an impact on his clientele, many of whom are politicians taking a break from the nearby Assemblée Nationale. Aside from protecting fish, Orieux cooks it, serving some of the best seafood in town, and plates it with real flair. A dish of scallops with foie gras and enoki mushrooms might look like a Jackson Pollock abstract; a lacquered monkfish with lobster oil and nutmeg will be equally artistic. Meat eaters are taken care of with dishes like blackened lamb with Cajun spices, white cherry juice, and yellow zucchini.

54 rue de Bourgogne, 7th arrond. www.restaurantauguste.fr. ℂ **01-45-51-61-09**. Main courses 40€–58€; fixed-price lunch 39€ or dinner 90€, with wine 154€. Mon–Fri noon–2:30pm and 7:30–10:30pm. Closed 3 weeks in Aug. Métro: Varenne.

MODERATE

La Fontaine de Mars ★★ BISTRO/SOUTHWESTERN FRENCH   Red and white checks are everywhere at this old-school bistro: on the tablecloths, the wicker chairs, and even the curtains. A venerable institution that first opened in 1908, it continues to draw crowds with its classy, low-key decor and traditional menu. The kitchen turns out reliable and succulent southwestern dishes like cassoulet, foie gras, and duck breast with black cherry sauce. Starters include *escargots* (snails) and *oeufs au Madiran* (eggs baked with red wine and bacon). The dessert list is full of such classics as île *flottante* ("floating island," a puffy meringue floating on vanilla cream), crème brûlée, and dark chocolate mousse.

129 rue St-Dominique, 7th arrond. www.fontainedemars.com. ℂ **01-47-05-46-44**. Main courses 18€–50€. Daily noon–3pm and 7:30–11pm. Métro: École Militaire.

Le Casse Noix ★★ TRADITIONAL FRENCH/BISTRO   Chef Pierre-Olivier Lenormand brings his high-caliber food to a casual, affordable setting. The decor is nostalgic (note the nutcracker collection and vintage advertisements), and the traditional French cooking is sincere and generous. Perhaps a roast pork shoulder Ibaïona with olive purée will fit the bill? Or try a classic *petit salé* (lentils with smoky ham) followed by a crowd-pleasing dessert like île *flottante*. About a 10-minute walk from the Eiffel Tower, this is a good bet for those looking for a bit of authenticity in an otherwise very touristy neighborhood. At dinnertime, the fixed-price menu is *obligatoire;* there is no a la carte ordering. Lunch is more flexible.

56 rue de la Fédération, 15th arrond. www.le-cassenoix.fr. ⓒ **01-45-66-09-01.** Main courses lunch 19€–23€; fixed-price lunch and dinner 37€. Mon–Fri noon–2:30pm and 7–10:30pm. Closed Aug and between Christmas and New Year's. Métro: Dupleix.

L'Escudella ★★ MODERN FRENCH This smart neo-bistro is located on a quiet residential street between UNESCO and Les Invalides. Its name means "plate" in Occitan—a nod to both chef Paul-Arthur Berlan's origins and the southwest-inspired dishes you're about to tuck into: delights like tomato and mustard gazpacho, sea bass with chorizo and artichoke risotto, and lip-smacking Paris-Carcassonne (choux pastry filled with hazelnut cream, a southwest version of the Paris-Brest). If you fancy sharing starters, L'Escudella serves excellent tapas: homemade paté, *jambon de bayonne* (cured ham), or spicy Wagyu beef chorizo. The lunchtime dish of the day is an absolute steal at 16€. In fact, this place is so lovely, it's a mystery it hasn't attracted more attention—especially since the chef was a semifinalist on France's version of "Top Chef," the American TV cooking show.

41 av. de Ségur, 7th arrond. www.escudella.fr. ⓒ **09-82-28-70-70.** Main courses 22€–36€; fixed-price lunch and dinner 46€–55€. Tues–Fri noon–2pm and 7–8:30pm. Métro: École Militaire or Saint François Xavier.

INEXPENSIVE

Café Constant ★★ TRADITIONAL FRENCH/BISTRO At this relaxed bistro you are quite likely to find the chef and owner Christian Constant himself at the bar during his off hours. The restaurant serves a modern version of French comfort food like tangy poached cod with aioli, melt-in-your-mouth beef daube (stew) with carrots, or steak with shallots and creamy potato purée. While the low prices and great food are no longer a traveler's secret (you might be sharing the dining room with Asian and American tourists), that's no reason not to make the most of it: This is still one of the best deals in town. At lunch on weekdays you can even get a two-course meal (chef's choice) for 27€—a terrific deal for this level of quality. Reservations are not accepted.

139 rue St-Dominique, 7th arrond. www.maisonconstant.com. ⓒ **01-47-53-73-34.** Main courses 16€–29€; fixed-price lunch 27€–30€. Daily 8am–11pm. Métro: École Militaire.

Chez Pippo ★★★ ITALIAN/PIZZERIA This down-to-earth, child-friendly Italian eatery is a handy address to have up your sleeve when visiting the Eiffel Tower or Musée du Quai Branly. Despite being in the heart of tourist central, it's well off the radar, drawing in-the-know locals, many from the American Library in Paris just around the corner, and just a handful of visitors. Pop by for a quick pizza (13€–25€)—the Miranda (Parma ham and olives) or a Diavola (spicy sausage) are very good. If you're in the mood for something fancy, I recommend splurging on the creamy lobster risotto (32€).

31 av. de la Bourdonnais, 7th arrond. www.chezpippo.com. ⓒ **01-73-70-54-50.** Main courses 7€–32€. Daily 9am–1am. Métro: École Militaire. RER: Gare du Pont de l'Alma.

5

The Left Bank

WHERE TO DINE

Though Paris is peppered with market streets and old-word *passages* (18th-century precursors to today's shopping malls, see p. 211), Beaupassage in the chic 7th arrondissement is the city's first ever arcade entirely dedicated to the glories of food. Opened in 2018 on the site of a former convent and a car show-room, it marries ultramodern design and contemporary art installations with res-taurants and food shops run by the city's top chefs. Though the 7th is as chic as can be, and the chefs have 17 Michelin stars among them, you'll actu-ally find food for all budgets—breadma-kis (maki-style club sandwiches, rolled and cut into big slices) from 6.50€ in Thierry Marx's **Boulangerie;** a 29€ lunch menu at the **Allénothèque** (the bistro award-winning chef Yannick Alleno runs with his wife); and a 19€ fixed-price sea-food menu at **Mersea** (famed for its fish and chips). Capping things off are a butcher, a cheese shop, an organic supermarket, and a gym. Beaupassage is at 53–57 rue du Grenelle, 7th arrond. (https://www.facebook.com/beaupas-sageparis; daily 7am–midnight.)

Le Café du Marché ★ TRADITIONAL FRENCH/BISTRO   Located on rue Cler, a pedestrian market street, this bustling cafe has one of the nicest sidewalk terraces in the area. You can do some serious people-watching here without inhaling excess car exhaust. The menu is nothing to shout about, but features pleasant bistro dishes like crispy duck confit, snails, and onion soup, as well as more modern turns like salmon brochettes with dill cream, and crowd pleasers like burgers. Meals are served "nonstop" all day.

38 rue Cler, 7th arrond. https://menuonline.fr/cafedumarche75007. ✆ **01-47-05-51-27.** Main courses 13.50€–18€. Daily 7am–1am. Métro: École Militaire.

Le Petit Cler ★ TRADITIONAL FRENCH/BISTRO   This cute little cafe tumbles out onto the rue Cler pedestrian market street and serves high quality but simple food at very reasonable prices. While you won't find many red and white checks, you will find classic cafe fare (steaks with sautéed potatoes, omelets, open-faced grilled sandwiches, and the like) as well as a daily special, which might be roast chicken (Sun) or fresh fish (Fri). You can also get a complete breakfast (including eggs) for 14€, and (later in the day) cheese and cold meat platters (from 8.50€) to soak up all the wine on the menu.

29 rue Cler, 7th arrond. ✆ **01-45-50-17-50.** Main courses 11€–18€. Daily 8am–11:30pm. Closed 2 weeks in Aug. Métro: École Militaire.

Montparnasse & Nearby (14th & 15th Arrondissements)

The famous cafes and brasseries (Le Dôme; Le Select; La Coupole, p. 134; and Closerie des Lilas, where struggling writers and artists like Picasso, Hemingway, and Chagall once hung out) make for atmospheric spots for a drink or meal. This is also the most Breton (that is, from Brittany) section of

Paris. The trains from Brittany arrive and depart from Montparnasse, and the story goes that between the World Wars, fresh-off-the-train Bretons, not knowing where else to go, settled in the immediate vicinity—hence the high density of crêperies along rues du Montparnasse and d'Odessa (the crepe having its origins in Brittany). In recent years, the neighborhood has woken up, gastronomically speaking, and a bundle of new gourmet bistros are tantalizing local taste buds. Check out rue Daguerre, a quaint street market by Denfert Rochereau Métro that's peppered with restaurants.

EXPENSIVE

Closerie des Lilas ★★ TRADITIONAL FRENCH/BRASSERIE This restaurant, brasserie, and piano bar was a favorite of Picasso and Gertrude Stein, not to mention Ernest Hemingway, who downed whiskey here so often that both the bar and a signature dish (panfried steak in creamy whiskey sauce) bear his name. With such history, you'd expect this to be on every tourist's radar, but the Closerie has managed to remain resolutely Parisian, drawing in locals with the promise of indulgent dishes like fresh seafood platters, panfried sweetbreads, and even caviar with steamed potatoes and cream. Literary fans will be pleased to learn that every year, the Closerie awards female writers with prestigious literary prizes, the Prix de la Closerie, Prix Lilas, and Lilas du Livre.

161 bd. du Montparnasse, 6th arrond. www.closeriedeslilas.fr. ⓒ **01-40-51-34-50.** Mains 28€–52€; seafood platters 50€–115€. Daily noon–2pm and 7–11pm; piano bar 11am–1:30am. Closed Aug. Métro: Raspail or Vavin. RER: Port-Royal.

MODERATE

La Cerisaie ★★ SOUTHWESTERN FRENCH/BISTRO A shoebox-size dining room near the Tour Montparnasse, La Cerisaie serves a classy version of the soul-warming cuisine of southwestern France. In autumn and winter, Chef Cyril Lalanne does amazing things with wild game, and his menu features every animal in the forest from hare to partridge to boar. Other regional dishes include breast of goose with roasted pears and sautéed foie gras. It's best to reserve ahead.

70 bd. Edgar-Quinet, 14th arrond. www.restaurantlacerisaie.com. ⓒ **01-43-20-98-98.** Main courses 18€–21€; fixed-price menu 60€. Mon–Fri noon–2:30pm and 7–10:30pm. Closed mid-July to mid-Aug. Métro: Montparnasse-Bienvenüe or Edgar Quinet.

L'Assiette ★★ TRADITIONAL FRENCH There's a whiff of the Belle Epoque in this old-fashioned dining room with its mirrors and ceiling ornaments. The menu appeals to culinary nostalgia as well, with dishes like homemade cassoulet and pike quenelles (long and delicate fish dumplings) with Nantua sauce, as well as *escargots* and homemade foie gras for starters. For dessert, indulge in crème caramel made with salted butter or profiteroles with chocolate sauce.

181 rue du Château, 14th arrond. www.restaurant-lassiette.com. ⓒ **01-43-22-64-86.** Main courses 26€–39€; fixed-price lunch 23€. Wed–Sun noon–2:30pm and 7–10:30pm. Closed Aug. Métro: Gaîté.

The Left Bank

WHERE TO DINE

Les Petits Plats ★★ MODERN FRENCH/BISTRO   Not especially hungry but you still want to eat well? This friendly bistro offers all of its main courses in full or half-sizes (at full- and half-prices). The blackboard lists the day's offerings, which might include a juicy slab of Aubrac beef, lightly sizzled cod with compote of roasted fresh vegetables, or sautéed squid and scallops with black rice. Finish it off with a meltingly rich chocolate *mi-cuit* (a not-quite-cooked cake). The ambience is relaxed and the young staff is downright charming. At dinner a tasting menu of five different dishes costs 47€.

39 rue des Plantes, 14th arrond. ⓒ **01-45-42-50-52.** Main courses 22€–26€; half-dishes 11€–15€; fixed-price lunch 19€ or dinner 38€–47€. Mon–Sat noon–2pm and 7:30–10pm. Closed 3 weeks in Aug. Métro: Alésia.

You'll find many crêperies along rues Montparnasse and d'Odessa.

INEXPENSIVE

Le Petit Josselin ★★ CRÊPERIE   Of the dozens of crêperies concentrated near the Montparnasse train station, this tiny dining room is one of the best. The *galettes* and crepes are perfectly cooked with lacy, crispy edges, and include fillings like bacon and egg, smoked salmon, and the can-do-no-wrong classic, ham and cheese. Try to save room for a sweet crepe after—the salted caramel butter crepe is a wonder. Tradition demands that this meal be accompanied by a bowl of "brut" cider (low alcohol content, for adults only). If there's no room, try La Crêperie Josselin (the restaurant's big sister) farther up the road.

59 rue du Montparnasse, 14th arrond. ⓒ **01-43-22-91-81.** Main courses 6€–15€; fixed-price menu 15€. Mon–Sat noon–3pm and 7–11pm. Métro: Edgar Quinet.

THE TOP TEAROOMS

It may surprise you to know that despite their famous cafe culture, many French people are closet tea fanatics. Thus, it is only fitting that some of the world's loveliest tearooms are in Paris.

Angelina ★★ TEAROOM   This Belle Epoque beauty under the arcades on the rue de Rivoli was once frequented by Proust and Coco Chanel, among other notables. Famous for its hot chocolate and its chestnut-y Mont Blanc pastry, this is also a great (if not touristy) spot for a chic breakfast or lunch. Be prepared to wait in line to get in.

226 rue de Rivoli, 1st arrond. www.angelina-paris.fr. ⓒ **01-42-60-82-00.** Main courses 16€–30€; fixed-price breakfast 20€–30€; brunch 40€. Daily 9am–7pm. Métro: Tuileries.

Café Jacquemart-André ★★ TEAROOM   Peek up at the Tiepolo ceiling as you sip your tea in what was once the dining room of Edouard André and Nélie Jacquemart. This beautiful tearoom serves excellent teas and delicious pastries from Stroher and La Petite Marquise. Lunch (or brunch Sun) from 11am to 2:30pm, tea and pastries 3 to 5:30pm. No reservations.

Musée Jacquemart-André, 158 bd. Haussmann, 8th arrond. www.musee-jacquemart-andre.com. ✆ **01-45-62-11-59.** Main courses 14€–19€; fixed-price lunch 18€–29€; brunch 30€. Mon 11:45am–6:30pm; Tues–Fri 11:45am–5:30pm; Sat 11am–5:30pm; Sun 11am–2:30pm. Métro: Miromesnil or Saint-Augustin.

Ladurée ★ TEAROOM   This luxury pastry shop has boutiques everywhere these days, but there's nothing quite like a cup of tea and macarons (Ladurée's famous light-as-air filled cookies) in one of its elegant Parisian tearooms. The rue Royale location, with its original 1862 *boiseries* (decorative wood paneling), and the grandiose Champs-Élysées site with its upstairs salon are the most impressive.

75 av. des Champs-Élysées, 8th arrond. www.laduree.fr. ✆ **01-40-75-08-75.** Main courses 20€–40€. Daily noon–8pm. Métro: George V.

Mosquée de Paris ★ TEAROOM   For an altogether different cup of tea, have a seat at the lovely tearoom attached to the grand Paris Mosque. Sip a glass of sweet mint tea and nibble on a *corne de gazelle* (a crescent-shaped, powdered-sugar-covered delight) on the patio or in the beautifully tiled tearoom and dream that you're in the Casbah. Couscous is served too (18€). Note that the entrance is not the same as the one for the mosque; it's on the corner of rue Daubenton and rue Geoffroy St-Hilaire.

39 rue Geoffroy St-Hilaire, 5th arrond. www.la-mosquee.com. ✆ **01-43-31-38-20.** Mint tea 2.80€; three pastries 7€; main courses 18€. Daily 9am–midnight. Métro: Censier-Daubenton.

THE TOP CAFES

It would be a crime to come to Paris and not stop for a coffee (or other drink) in a cafe. Despite the onslaught of American-style coffee shops, classic cafe life is still an integral part of the Parisian scene, and it simply won't do to visit the capital without at least participating once. ***Important note:*** Cafes are not bars in the North American sense—though they generally serve alcohol, they are not places where people come to get smashed. They are places where people come to just "be," to sip a drink, to take a break, to read a book, or to simply watch the world go by. Most cafes open very early in the morning and close between midnight and 2am.

Paris must have thousands of cafes. Though you could probably have a basic cafe experience in just about any corner operation, here are a few sure-fire options to choose from.

Historic Cafes

Café de Flore ★★★ CAFE   A monument to the St-Germain quarter's intellectual past, Café de Flore is a must-sip on the cafe tour circuit.

This is a particularly tough call, since new pastry shops open frequently, but here are a few classics where not even the snootiest gourmands will turn up their noses.

- **Arnaud Larher,** 93 rue de Seine, 6th arrond. (https://arnaudlarher.com; © 01-43-29-38-15; Métro: Odéon or Mabillon), is a gâteaux and chocolate wiz, with everything made by hand. Try the chocolate éclair; it's a dream.
- **La Pâtisserie de Cyril Lignac,** 24 rue Paul Bert, 11th arrond. (www.gourmand-croquant.com; © 01-55-87-21-40; Métro: Faidherbe-Chaligny or Rue des Boulets), is where cakes look like pieces of contemporary art. Try the Equinoxe, a gray, circular creation filled with vanilla cream and caramel.
- **Pierre Hermé,** 72 rue Bonaparte, 6th arrond. (www.pierreherme.com; © 01-43-54-47-77; Métro: St-Sulpice), may look like a chic jewelry store, but the goods are edible here. Exquisite and fashionable pastries include the Ispahan series, based on lychee, rose, and raspberry flavors.
- **Sébastien Gaudard,** 1 rue des Pyramides, 1st arrond. (www.sebastiengaudard.com; © 01-71-81-24-70; Métro: Pyramides), makes exquisite French cakes, from classic *millefeuilles* (puff pastry layered with vanilla cream) to playful sharing cakes, like the cherry and chocolate *shirt*, with a marzipan collar and nuts crumbled on top like patterned fabric.
- **Stohrer,** 51 rue Montorgueil, 2nd arrond. (www.stohrer.fr; © 01-42-33-38-20; Métro: Sentier or Les Halles), was opened by Louis XV's pastry chef in 1730. This is the place to sample the ultimate *baba au rhum,* the famous rum-soaked sponge cake; Stohrer invented it in the 18th century.

5

WHERE TO DINE | The Top Cafes

Seemingly every great French intellectual and artist has had his or her moment here: Poets Apollinaire and André Breton wrote here; artists Zadkine, Picasso, and Giacometti came to take refuge from Montparnasse; literary and theatrical stars came to preen; and of course, philosophers gathered to figure out the meaning (or nonmeaning) of life. During World War II, Simone de Beauvoir and Jean-Paul Sartre more or less moved in, and Sartre is said to have written his trilogy "Les Chemins de la Liberté" ("The Roads to Freedom") here. The atmosphere now is less thoughtful and more showbiz, but it still may be worth an overpriced cup of coffee just to come in and soak it up. 172 bd. St-Germain, 6th arrond. www.cafedeflore.fr. © **01-45-48-55-26.** Daily 7:30am–1:30am. Métro: St-Germain-des-Prés.

Café de la Paix ★ CAFE   A Parisian institution ever since it was inaugurated by Empress Eugenie in 1862, this is the home of one of the most expensive cups of coffee in the city (6€). Everyone from Emile Zola to Yves Montand has done time at this Second Empire marvel, whose gold leaf and curlicues have been meticulously renovated. Its outdoor terrace offers a magnificent view of the Palais Garnier—the perfect place for a drink before a night at the Opéra. It won't be cheap, but it will be memorable. Corner of pl. de l'Opéra and bd. des Capucines, 9th arrond. www.cafedelapaix.fr. © **01-40-07-36-36.** Daily 9am–midnight. Métro: Opéra.

La Coupole ★★ CAFE   The artistic legacy of this brasserie is almost as vast as its square footage: Marc Chagall, Josephine Baker, Henry Miller, Salvador Dalí, and Ernest Hemingway are just some of the stars that lit up this converted charcoal depot. One of the largest restaurants in France, this Art Deco mastodon first opened in 1927 and has been hopping ever since. Thirty-three immense painted pillars hold up the ceiling; huge murals and paintings cover the walls. Though the food is decent (the lamb curry is the signature dish), it's best to just come here for a drink or a snack, grab a table by the windows, and watch the world go by. It's also a fun place to have breakfast.

102 bd. du Montparnasse, 14th arrond. www.lacoupole-paris.com. ℂ **01-43-20-14-20.** Tues–Sat 8:30am–midnight; Sun–Mon 8:30am–11pm. Métro: Vavin.

Les Deux Magots ★★ CAFE   After the war, de Beauvoir and Sartre moved from Café de Flore to this nearby artists' haunt, where they continued to write and think and entertain their friends for a good chunk of the rest of their lives. The literary pedigree here is at least as impressive as that of its neighbor: Poets Verlaine and Rimbaud camped out here, as did François Mauriac, André Gide, Paul Eluard, Albert Camus, and Ernest Hemingway. The outdoor terrace is particularly pleasant early in the morning before the crowds wake up.

6 pl. St-Germain-des-Prés, 6th arrond. www.lesdeuxmagots.fr. ℂ **01-45-48-55-25.** Daily 7:30am–1am. Métro: St-Germain-des-Prés.

Cafes for People-Watching

Eté en Pente Douce ★ CAFE   On a delightful corner facing the tranquil eastern side of Sacré-Coeur, this colorful cafe features a lovely sidewalk terrace where you can relax away from the tourist hordes. Don't bother with

The historic cafes of Paris are hard to resist—particularly Café de Flore, one of Picasso's old haunts.

coffee TALK

Ordering a cup of coffee in Paris is not quite as simple as it sounds. Most any cafe has delightful caffeinated (and decaffeinated) java possibilities. Cappuccinos, by the way, are rare in Parisian cafes, and when you do get one, chances are it won't resemble anything you'd get in Italy. **Important tip:** Drinks at the bar (coffee or otherwise) can cost half what you will pay at a table—as little as 1€ for an espresso.

The following miniglossary will help you navigate once your waiter makes it over to your table.

Café (ka-*fay*): Coffee. This is pure, black espresso, albeit lighter than the Italian version, served in a small demitasse cup. The equivalent of a "long shot," in Starbucks-speak.

Allongé (all-on-*jay*): Coffee. This is black espresso with a shot of hot water, served in a slightly bigger cup.

Décaf (*day*-ka): Decaf, or decaffeinated coffee. An unleaded version of the above.

Café serré (ka-*fay* sehr-*ay*): Though smaller in volume, packs a bigger punch. Resembles an Italian espresso.

Noisette (*nwa*-zet): Café with a dash of steamed milk (my favorite). You could also order an **Allongé Noisette** for a splash of milk in a longer coffee.

Café crème (crem): Café with an equal amount of steamed milk, served in a larger cup.

Café au lait (ka-*fay* oh lay): Virtually identical to the above, sometimes with a bit more milk. The biggest difference is the time of day; in the morning, they call it a *café au lait*, in the afternoon a *crème*.

---

the food here, which is fair to middling; just order a *café* or a nice, cool beer, look out on the greenery, and watch people huffing and puffing up the stairs to the basilica. You'll have to huff and puff a little yourself to get here.

23 rue Muller, 18th arrond. www.parisresto.com. ℂ **01-42-64-02-67.** Daily noon–midnight. Métro: Anvers.

Le Pure Café ★★ CAFE   In the heart of the residential 11th arrondissement, this is a neighborhood cafe in the truest sense: With a small V-shaped terrace that looks out over a trio of relatively quiet roads (for Paris), it's the place to watch an odd assortment of local hipsters, pensioners, freelancers, and arty types slurp espressos and spritzes (a cocktail made with Aperol and prosecco). Indoors, it's Art Deco revisited with a huge zinc-topped, circular bar, turquoise metro tiles, and 1930s light fittings.

14 rue Jean Macé, 11th arrond. www.lepurecafe.fr. ℂ **01-43-71-47-22.** Mon–Fri 7am–1am; Sat 8am–1am; Sun 9am–midnight. Métro: Faidherbe-Chaligny, Rue des Boulets, or Charonne.

Le Rostand ★★ CAFE   This quintessentially Parisian cafe has a swell terrace directly opposite the entrance to the Jardin du Luxembourg, and despite its touristy location, it draws oodles of chic locals. It's the ideal spot for a before- or after-promenade drink, a book-reading session, or just taking a load off after a visit to the park or the Panthéon.

6 pl. Edmond Rostand, 6th arrond. https://lerostand.fr. ℂ **01-43-54-61-58.** Daily 8am–midnight. RER: Luxembourg.

EXPLORING PARIS

With more than 130 world-class museums to visit, scores of attractions to discover, extraordinary architecture to gape at, and wonderful neighborhoods to wander, Paris is an endless series of delights. The hardest part is figuring out where to begin. Fortunately, you can have a terrific time even if you don't see everything. Some of your best moments may be simply roaming around the city without a plan. Lolling on a park bench, dreaming over a drink at a sidewalk cafe, or noodling around an unknown neighborhood can be the stuff of your best travel memories.

The following pages will highlight the best that Paris can offer area by area, from iconic sights known the world over to quirky museums and hidden gardens, from 1,000-year-old castles to galleries celebrating the most challenging contemporary art, and from the must-sees to the only-if-you've-seen-everything-else. Just remember that it is always advisable to reserve advance tickets for the bigger attractions. You will not get into the Louvre without a pre-paid, time-stamped ticket, for instance. Also bear in mind that at time of writing, late-night openings had been canceled at many museums, but they could well be reinstated. Here, then, are the best of Paris' attractions.

THE RIGHT BANK
Louvre & Île de la Cité (1st Arrondissement)

It all started here: Back in the city's misty and uncertain beginnings, the Parisii tribe set up camp on the right bank of the Seine, and then started hunting on the **Île de la Cité.** Many centuries later, the **Louvre** popped up, first as a fortress, and now one of the world's mightiest museums. The city's epicenter, this area packs in a high density of must-see monuments and museums, but don't miss the opportunity for aimless strolling in the magnificent **Tuileries Gardens** or over the **Pont Neuf.** This section includes the entire Île de la Cité, though technically half of it lies in the 4th arrondissement.

Sightseeing Protocols

Since early 2020, museums and attractions have limited the number of visitors per day. At many attractions, you may be required to book your tickets in advance with a time slot, especially for popular museums like the Louvre. You may also be required to wear a mask or show proof of Covid vaccination or a negative PCR test in order to enter. Information and protocols change like the wind, so check each attraction's website before you travel. You'll also find up-to-date information in English on the French government website (www.gouvernement.fr/en/coronavirus-covid-19) and the Paris Tourist Office (https://en.parisinfo.com/practical-paris/info/guides/info-disruption-paris).

Bourse de Commerce—Pinault Collection ★★ MUSEUM/ART GALLERY   At the western tip of the Les Halles gardens, the city's stunning former Chamber of Commerce building (on the site of an 18th-century corn exchange) is the city's newest contemporary art space. This museum/art gallery houses the Pinault Collection, the personal 3,000-piece contemporary art holding of billionaire François Pinault (the honorary chairman of Kering, the luxury group that owns YSL, Gucci, and Alexander McQueen). The third-floor restaurant offers sweeping views over Paris' rooftops and St-Eustache church.

2 rue Viarmes, 1st arrond. www.pinaultcollection.com. ✆ **01-83-75-10-00.** Admission 14€ adults (audioguide included), 10€ ages 18–25, free for children 17 and under. Wed–Sun 11am–7pm (until 9pm Fri). Métro: Louvre-Rivoli or Les Halles. RER: Châtelet-des-Halles.

Cathédrale de Notre-Dame ★★★ CATHEDRAL   One of France's most brilliant expressions of medieval architecture, this remarkably harmonious ensemble of carved portals, huge towers, and flying buttresses has survived close to a millennium's worth of French history and served as a setting for some of the country's most solemn moments. Even the vast fire that consumed its spire and gutted the entire roof in 2019 didn't bring it down (thanks to 400 firefighters). Access to the cathedral and its surrounding gardens is prohibited at least until 2026, though the forecourt, the Parvis Notre Dame—Place Jean-Paul II, is open. If you'd like to see the exterior in all its former glory, take the virtual reality flight at **FlyView** (p. 152), which jetpacks you over the Seine to Notre-Dame (and other monuments) using 360-degree film footage shot by drone several years before the tragedy.

Napoleon crowned himself and Empress Joséphine here, Napoleon III was married here, and some of France's greatest generals (Foch, Joffre, Leclerc) had their funerals here. In August 1944, the liberation of Paris from the Nazis was commemorated in the cathedral, as was the death of General de Gaulle in 1970.

The story of Notre-Dame begins in 1163, when Bishop Maurice de Sully initiated construction, which lasted over 200 years. (The identity of the architect who envisioned this masterpiece remains a mystery.) The building

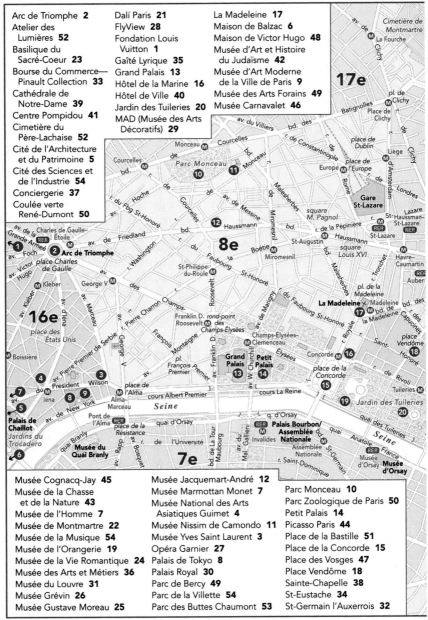

Arc de Triomphe **2**
Atelier des Lumières **52**
Basilique du Sacré-Coeur **23**
Bourse du Commerce—Pinault Collection **33**
Cathédrale de Notre-Dame **39**
Centre Pompidou **41**
Cimetière du Père-Lachaise **52**
Cité de l'Architecture et du Patrimoine **5**
Cité des Sciences et de l'Industrie **54**
Conciergerie **37**
Coulée verte René-Dumont **50**

Dalí Paris **21**
FlyView **28**
Fondation Louis Vuitton **1**
Gaîté Lyrique **35**
Grand Palais **13**
Hôtel de la Marine **16**
Hôtel de Ville **40**
Jardin des Tuileries **20**
MAD (Musée des Arts Décoratifs) **29**

La Madeleine **17**
Maison de Balzac **6**
Maison de Victor Hugo **48**
Musée d'Art et Histoire du Judaïsme **42**
Musée d'Art Moderne de la Ville de Paris **9**
Musée des Arts Forains **49**
Musée Carnavalet **46**

Musée Cognacq-Jay **45**
Musée de la Chasse et de la Nature **43**
Musée de l'Homme **7**
Musée de Montmartre **22**
Musée de la Musique **54**
Musée de l'Orangerie **19**
Musée de la Vie Romantique **24**
Musée des Arts et Métiers **36**
Musée du Louvre **31**
Musée Grévin **26**
Musée Gustave Moreau **25**

Musée Jacquemart-André **12**
Musée Marmottan Monet **7**
Musée National des Arts Asiatiques Guimet **4**
Musée Nissim de Camondo **11**
Musée Yves Saint Laurent **3**
Opéra Garnier **27**
Palais de Tokyo **8**
Palais Royal **30**
Parc de Bercy **49**
Parc de la Villette **54**
Parc des Buttes Chaumont **53**

Parc Monceau **10**
Parc Zoologique de Paris **50**
Petit Palais **14**
Picasso Paris **44**
Place de la Bastille **51**
Place de la Concorde **15**
Place des Vosges **47**
Place Vendôme **18**
Sainte-Chapelle **38**
St-Eustache **34**
St-Germain l'Auxerrois **32**

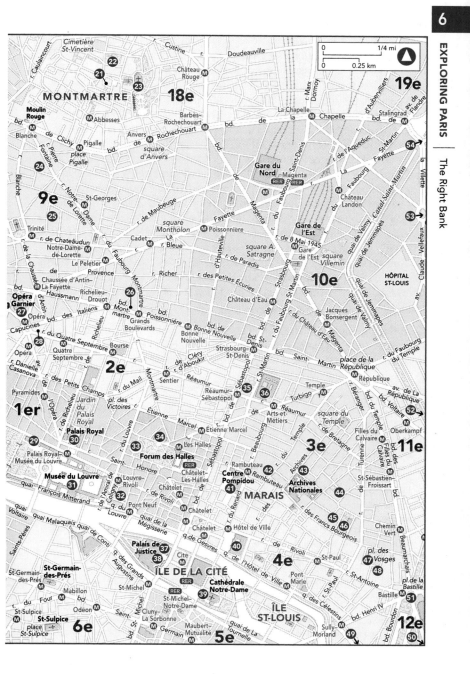

was relatively untouched up until the end of the 17th century, when monarchs started meddling with its windows and architecture. By the time the Revolutionaries decided to convert it into a "Temple of Reason," the cathedral was already in sorry condition—and the pillaging that ensued didn't help. The interior was ravaged, statues were smashed, and the cathedral became a shadow of its former glory.

We can thank the famous "Hunchback" himself for saving Notre-Dame. Victor Hugo's novel "The Hunchback of Notre-Dame" drew attention to the state of disrepair, and other artists and writers began to call for the restoration of the edifice. In 1844, Louis-Phillipe hired Jean-Baptiste Lassus and architect/archaeologist/writer/painter Eugène Viollet-le-Duc to restore the cathedral, which they finished in 1864. Though many criticized Viollet-le-Duc for what they considered to be overly romantic and inauthentic excesses, he actually took extreme care to remain faithful to the historic Gothic architecture.

Over 1 billion euros were donated to the cathedral in the first week following the fire, so money for repairs shouldn't—for once—be lacking. For now, however, rest assured that though some treasures were lost, the organ, Quasimodo's bell (the Bourdon), and relics such as the **Crown of Thorns** (brought back from Constantinople by Saint Louis in the 13th century) are safe. Many treasures have been housed for protection and/or restoration in the Louvre. Place du Parvis Notre-Dame. www.notredamedeparis.fr.

Conciergerie ★ HISTORIC SITE Despite looking like a turreted, fairytale castle, the Conciergerie is in fact a relic of the darker side of the Revolution, where some of its most famous participants spent their final days before

---

Should You Pass on the Pass?

Paris is a walkable city with numerous free museums and serendipitous experiences, so paying for its sightseeing pass, the **Paris Passlib'**, might not make sense. It comes down to the math. Introduced in 2021, the fully digitized pass is valid for a year and comes in four versions: **Mini** (32€ for 3 activities from 14 offered), **City** (69€ for 5 attractions from 33 offered), **Explore** (119€ for 6 attractions from 38), and **Prestige** (189€ for 6 attractions from 57). An activity is classed as anything from entry to a museum to an experience like a boat trip or a cabaret show, depending on the pass you choose. The passes claim that buying one can save you roughly 15%. However, if you look at the details,

this is mostly true only if you select the most expensive activities on the list. Take the Mini pass: If you use it to book a river cruise with Bateaux Parisiens, a ticket to the Monnaie de Paris, and the Musée Rodin, the pass will save you 7€. If, however, you use it on the Musée du Quai Branly, the Conciergerie, and the Château de Vincennes, you will lose 4€. In short, don't dismiss the pass, but do your homework: Deciding which activities you'd like to experience and totting up the sums before you buy is a time-consuming activity, but worth it to save some cash. And don't forget that Paris has multiple museums that offer free entry (see below). For more information, visit www.parisinfo.com.

Most museums offer free entry to students and young adults ages 25 and under from the European Union with valid ID. If this is you, ask when you buy your ticket. Children, typically ages 17 and under, but sometimes only up to age 7, often get in for free too. See the listings below for details. With only a few exceptions, all city museums are free (permanent collections only), all the time. That includes the following cultural cornucopias:

o Musée d'Art Moderne de la Ville de Paris (p. 165)
o Maison de Balzac (p. 165)
o Musée Bourdelle (p. 198)
o Musée Cognacq-Jay (p. 158)
o Petit Palais (p. 169)
o Maison de Victor Hugo (p. 157)
o Musée Zadkine (p. 188), except during temporary exhibits
o Musée de la Vie Romantique (p. 152)

You can also get into all national museums free of charge on the first Sunday of every month (seasonal restrictions may apply). Expect even bigger crowds than your usual Sunday. National museums include:

o Musée du Louvre (p. 144), October to March
o Musée National des Arts Asiatiques Guimet (p. 167)
o Musée National Eugène Delacroix (p. 188)
o Musée National du Moyen Age/ Thermes de Cluny (p. 181)
o Musée de l'Orangerie (p. 144)
o Musée d'Orsay (p. 193)
o Musée Rodin (p. 195)
o Picasso Paris (p. 161)

making their way to the guillotine. Danton, Desmoulins, Saint-Just, and Charlotte Corday passed through these doors, but perhaps its most famous guest was Marie Antoinette, who spent her time here in a dismal cell, reading and praying while she awaited her fate. After doing away with the monarchy, the Revolution began to eat itself alive; during the particularly bloody period known as the Terror, murderous infighting between the various revolutionary factions engendered panic and paranoia that led to tens of thousands of people throughout the country being arrested and executed. Eventually Robespierre, the main force behind the Terror and an ardent advocate for Marie Antoinette's execution, found himself in the cell next door to the one she stayed in.

Though it's been a prison since the 15th century, the building itself is actually what remains of a 14th-century royal palace built by Philippe le Bel. Even before the Revolution, the Conciergerie was notorious: Henry IV's murderer, Ravaillac, was imprisoned here before an angry crowd tore him apart alive. The enormous **Salle des Gens d'Armes,** with its 8.4m-high (28-ft.) vaulted ceiling, is an impressive reminder of the building's palatial past. As for the prison itself, though the cells have been outfitted with displays and re-creations of daily life (including wax figures), it's a far cry from the dank hell it once was. Fresh paint and lighting make it a little difficult to imagine what it was like in the bad old days, but a few areas stand out, like the **Cours des Femmes** (the women's courtyard), which virtually hasn't changed since the days when female prisoners

Famously called "the belly of Paris," **Les Halles** was the city's primary wholesale food market for 8 centuries. The smock-clad vendors, beef carcasses, and baskets of vegetables all belong to the past, as the market was relocated to the suburb of Rungis in the early 1970s. In a fit of modernity, all the pretty 19th-century pavilions were torn down, and in their place a weird, partly underground shopping mall was constructed: the **Forum des Halles,** 1–7 rue Pierre-Lescot, 1st arrond. In 2010, the city embarked on a massive renovation program to overhaul the shopping center and the surrounding gardens by building "the canopy," an immense, undulating sheet of glass and metal that floats over the Forum. Despite its multimillion price tag, most Parisians complain that it's unattractive, but it does house brand-new shops and restaurants, and it opens onto a wonderful, immense garden that sweeps across lawns and kids' play areas over to 16th-century **Eglise St-Eustache** (p. 151)—a masterpiece of Gothic architecture. The underground has started getting its makeover too, so some areas may be under construction. For info, visit www.forumdeshalles.com.

did their washing in the fountain. **Marie Antoinette's cell** was converted into a memorial chapel during the Bourbon Restoration; a re-creation of her cell, containing some original objects, is on display. Other worthwhile historical exhibits include a list of the names of all those guillotined during the Revolution, 2,780 in Paris alone. If you can, hire a Histopad (5€), a smart tablet with augmented reality functions that lets you see parts of the building as it would have looked in the 14th century and during the Revolution. The Conciergerie can be visited in conjunction with the **Sainte-Chapelle,** which lies along the same road (p. 150; joint tickets with time slots 17€ adults, free for children 17 and under, also free ages 18–25 from E.U. countries).

2 bd. du Palais, 1st arrond. www.paris-conciergerie.fr. © **01-53-40-60-80.** Admission 9.50€ adults, free for children 17 and under. Daily 9:30am–6pm. Métro: Cité, Châtelet, or St-Michel. RER: St-Michel.

Jardin des Tuileries ★★★ PARK   This exquisite park spreads from the Louvre to the Place de la Concorde. One of the oldest gardens in the city—and the first to be opened to the public—it's also one of the largest. In the Middle Ages, a factory here made clay tiles (*tuiles*), a word that was incorporated into the name of the palace that Catherine de Médicis built at the far end of the Louvre in 1564. Such a grand palace needed equally splendid Italian gardens; later in the mid-1600s, Louis XIV had master landscape artist André Le Nôtre—the man behind the gardens of Versailles—give them a more French look. Le Nôtre's elegant geometry of flowerbeds, parterres, and groves of trees made the Tuileries Gardens the ultimate stroll for well-to-do Parisians.

Though the Tuileries Palace burned down during the Paris Commune in 1871, the landscaping lived on. During World War II, furious fighting went on here, and many statues were damaged. Little by little in the postwar years, the garden was put back together. Seventeenth- and 18th-century representations of various gods and goddesses were repaired, and the city added new works by modern masters such as Max Ernst, Alberto Giacometti, Jean Dubuffet, and Henry Moore. Rodin's *The Kiss* and *Eve* are here, as well as a series of 18 of Maillol's curvaceous women, peeking out of the green **labyrinth** of hedges in the Carousel Gardens near the museum.

Pulling up a metal chair and sunning yourself on the edge of the large **fountain** in the center of the gardens (the **Grande Carrée**) is a delightful respite after a day in the Louvre.

Near pl. de la Concorde, 1st arrond. Free admission. Daily 7:30am–dusk. Métro: Tuileries or Concorde.

MAD (Musée des Arts Décoratifs) ★★ MUSEUM   Possessing some 150,000 items in its rich collection, this fascinating museum offers a glimpse of history through the prism of decorative objects, with a spectrum that ranges from medieval traveling trunks to Philippe Starck stools. The collection is organized by period and style, so on your journey you will pass by paintings from the First Italian Renaissance, through a room filled with exquisite 15th-century intarsia ("paintings" made out of intricately inlaid wood), before gaping at huge, intricately carved 17th-century German armoires. Other highlights include a tiny room covered in gilded woodwork from an 18th-century mansion in Avignon; a stunning Art Nouveau/Art Deco section, showcasing elaborately carved pianos, beds, and dining room furniture; and fashion designer Jeanne Lanvin's decadent, purple Art Deco boudoir.

Two other worthy collections are the Publicité/Graphisme collection on the history of advertising and the Mode/Textile fashion displays. While the

Jardin des Tuileries, outside the Louvre.

former will be of interest primarily to those who are in the biz, the latter hosts a terrific range from famous couture houses like Jean-Paul Gaultier and Dior. Another intriguing addition is a collection of wallpaper through the ages—the earliest of which dates from 1864 and depicts a bucolic hunting scene. *Note:* Tickets can be combined with the Musée Nissim de Camondo (p. 168; 20€).

Palais du Louvre, 107 rue de Rivoli, 1st arrond. https://madparis.fr. ✆ **01-44-55-57-50.** Admission 14€ adults (audioguide included), free for ages 25 and under. Tues–Sun 11am–6pm (until 9pm Thurs for some temporary exhibitions only). Métro: Palais-Royal–Musée du Louvre or Tuileries.

Musée de l'Orangerie ★★ MUSEUM   Since 1927, this former royal greenhouse has been the home of Monet's stunning *Nymphéas*, or water lilies, which he conceived as a "haven of peaceful meditation." Two large oval rooms are dedicated to these masterpieces, in which Monet tried to replicate the feeling and atmosphere of his garden at Giverny. He worked on these enormous canvases for 12 years, with the idea of creating an environment that would soothe the "overworked nerves" of modern men and women—in what might be called one of the world's first art installations.

The other highlight here is the Walter–Guillaume collection, an impressive assortment of late-19th- and early-20th-century paintings that once belonged to art collectors Jean Walter and Paul Guillaume. It's on the lower level, where the first, light-filled gallery displays mostly portraits and still lifes, such as Renoir's glowing, idyllic *Femme Nu dans un Paysage* and Cézanne's rather dour-looking *Madame Cézanne*. This collection has a stormy history—after Guillaume's death, his rather flamboyant wife rearranged the collection to her own taste, selling off some of the more "difficult" paintings. The result is a lovely collection that lacks a certain bite; truly impressive works by these masters can be seen elsewhere.

Jardin des Tuileries, 1st arrond. www.musee-orangerie.fr. ✆ **01-44-77-80-07.** Admission 12.50€ adults, 10€ ages 18–25, free for children 17 and under. Wed–Mon 9am–6pm. Métro: Concorde.

Musée du Louvre ★★★ MUSEUM   The best way to thoroughly visit the Louvre would be to move in for a month. Not only is it one of the largest museums in the world, with more than 35,000 works of art displayed over 60,000 sq. m (645,835 sq. ft.), but it's also packed with enough artistic masterpieces to make the Mona Lisa weep. Rembrandt, Reubens, Botticelli, Ingres, and Michelangelo are all represented here; subjects range from the grandiose (Antoine-Jean Gros's gigantic *Napoleon Bonaparte Visiting the Plague-Stricken in Jaffa*) to the mundane (Vermeer's tiny, exquisite *Lacemaker*). You can gape at a diamond the size of a golf ball in the gilded Galerie d'Apollon or marvel over exquisite bronze figurines in the vast Egyptian section. There's something for everyone here.

Today, the building is divided into three wings: Sully, Denon, and Richelieu, each one with its own clearly marked entrance, found under I. M. Pei's glass pyramid. Get your hands on a free museum map, choose your personal

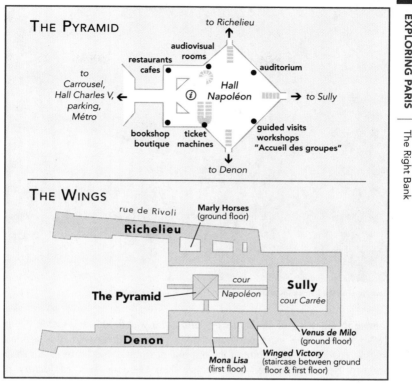

THE PYRAMID

to Richelieu

audiovisual rooms

restaurants cafes

to Carrousel, Hall Charles V, parking, Métro

auditorium

Hall Napoléon

→ to Sully

bookshop boutique

ticket machines

guided visits workshops "Accueil des groupes"

to Denon

THE WINGS

rue de Rivoli

Marly Horses (ground floor)

Richelieu

cour Napoléon

The Pyramid

Sully cour Carrée

Denon

Venus de Milo (ground floor)

Mona Lisa (first floor)

Winged Victory (staircase between ground floor & first floor)

"must-sees," and plan ahead. There's no way to see it all; you'll be an instant candidate for early exhaustion if you try. Mercifully, the museum is well organized and has been very reasonably arranged into color-coded sections. There's also a handy app (the Louvre Museum Visitor Guide) you can download ahead of your visit to help you plan what to see. If you're really in a rush, or you just want to get an overall sense of the place, you can take the introductory "Welcome to the Louvre" guided tour in English (17€; 1½ hr; check the website for times or call ✆ **01-40-20-52-63**). You won't see as much as you would on your own, but at least you'll know what you are seeing. Most important of all, reserve admission at least 14 days in advance.

The museum's three biggest stars are all in the Denon wing. *La Joconde*, otherwise known as the ***Mona Lisa*** (see the "Men Have Named You . . ." box, below), has an entire wall to herself, making it easier to contemplate her enigmatic smile, despite her surprisingly small size. While everyone's gawping at her, look behind you at the gigantic and sublimely beautiful 16th-century painting *Wedding Feast at Cana* by Paolo Veronese. Another inscrutable

Courtyard of the Louvre Museum.

female in this wing is the *Venus de Milo,* who was found on a Greek isle in 1820. Possibly the most photographed woman in the world, this armless marble goddess gives no hint of the original position of her limbs or her exact identity. Recently restored and lovelier than ever, the *Winged Victory of Samothrace* is the easiest to locate. Standing atop a majestic flight of stairs, her powerful body pushing forward as if about to take flight, this headless yet magnificent Greek sculpture once guarded the Sanctuary of the Great Gods on the island of Samothrace.

Because a complete listing of the Louvre's highlights would fill a book, below is a decidedly biased selection of our favorite areas:

13TH- TO 18TH-CENTURY ITALIAN PAINTINGS A few standouts in the immense Italian collection include Botticelli's delicate fresco *Venus and the Three Graces Presenting Gifts to a Young Woman,* Veronese's aforementioned and enormous *Wedding Feast at Cana,* and of course, the *Mona Lisa.* The Divine Miss M is in a room packed with wonders, including several Titians and Tintorettos. Once you've digested this rich meal, stroll down the endless Grande Galerie, past more da Vincis (*Saint John the Baptist, The Virgin of the Rock*), as well as works by Raphael, Caravaggio, and Artemisia Gentileschi.

GREEK & ROMAN SCULPTURE While the *Winged Victory of Samothrace* and the *Venus de Milo* are not to be missed, the Salle des Caryatides (the room itself is a work of art) boasts marble masterworks such as *Artemis* hunting with her stag and the *Sleeping Hermaphrodite*, an alluring female figure from behind—and something entirely different from the front.

THE GALERIE D'APOLLON The gold-encrusted room is an excellent example of the excesses of 17th-century French royalty. Commissioned by Louis XIV, aka "the Sun King," every inch of this gallery is covered with gilt stucco sculptures and flamboyant murals invoking the journey of the Roman sun god Apollo (ceiling paintings are by Charles Le Brun). The main draw here is the collection of crown jewels. Among necklaces bedecked with quarter-sized sapphires and tiaras dripping with diamonds and rubies are the **jewel-studded crown** of Louis XV and the **Regent,** a 140-carat diamond that decorated his hat.

THE EGYPTIANS This is the largest collection outside of Cairo, thanks in large part to Jean-François Champollion, the 19th-century French scientist and scholar, who first decoded Egyptian hieroglyphs. Sculptures, figurines, papyrus documents, steles, musical instruments, and of course, mummies fill numerous rooms in the Sully wing, including the colossal *statue of Ramses II* and the strangely moving *Seated Scribe.* He gazes intently out of intricately crafted inlaid eyes: A combination of copper, magnesite, and polished rock crystal creates a startlingly lifelike stare.

LARGE-FORMAT FRENCH PAINTINGS Enormous floor-to-ceiling paintings of monumental moments in history cover the walls in these three rooms. The overcrowded and legendary *Coronation of Napoléon* by Jacques-Louis David depicts the newly minted Emperor crowning Joséphine, while the disconcerted pope and a host of notables look on. On the facing wall, *Madame Récamier* (also by David), one of Napoleon's loudest critics, reclines fetchingly on a divan. Farther on are several tumultuous canvases by Eugène Delacroix, including *Liberty Guiding the People,* which might just be the ultimate expression of French patriotism. In the painting, which evokes the events of the revolution of 1830, Liberty—breast exposed, a rifle in one hand, the French flag in the other—leads the crowd over a sea of dead bodies. High ideals and gore—it sort of sums up the French revolutionary spirit.

Note: When visiting the museum, **watch your wallets and purses**—there has been an unfortunate increase in pickpockets; thieves even use children to prey on unsuspecting art lovers. On a more positive note, the Louvre has made great strides in improving **accessibility for travelers with disabilities,** including special programs, ramps, free wheelchairs, and folding chairs. For more info, click "visit" and then "accessibility" at the top of the museum's website.

1st arrond. Main entrance in the glass pyramid, cour Napoléon. www.louvre.fr. © **01-40-20-50-50.** Admission 17€ adults, free for children 17 and under. Wed–Mon 9am–6pm. Métro: Palais-Royal–Musée du Louvre.

Palais Royal ★★ HISTORIC SITE/GARDEN The gardens and long arcades of the Palais Royal are not only a delight to stroll through but were also witnesses to one of the most important moments in French history.

MEN HAVE named YOU . . .

Everything about the *Mona Lisa* is mysterious—the identity of the sitter, how long it took to paint, and how it got into the French royal collection, among other things. Most scholars agree that it is a portrait of Lisa Gheradini, the wife of one Francesco del Giocondo, but Ms. Lisa could also be Isabella of Aragon (as suggested by the patterning of her dress) or simply an embodiment of beauty and happiness (hence the smile), as suggested by the Italian word *gioconda*.

In 2006, researchers found evidence of a fine, translucent veil around the subject's shoulders, a garment women in Renaissance Italy wore when they were expecting, provoking an onslaught of speculation that her secret smile had to do with her being pregnant.

What's certain is that the painting created a sensation. The overall harmony of the composition, the use of a distant landscape in the background, the lifelike quality of the subject, had a huge impact on early-16th-century Florentine art. As Giorgio Vasari, a Renaissance painter and biographer, lamented, "It may be said that it was painted in such a manner as to make every valiant craftsman, be he who he may, tremble and lose heart."

The painting's history is action packed. One morning in 1911, an artist named Louis Béroud entered the museum to sketch a copy of the famous portrait and found a bare spot with four hooks in the wall. After a concerted effort, he convinced the lackadaisical guard to find out what happened. In fact, the *Mona Lisa* had been stolen. The thief had entered the museum posing as a visitor, hid in the building overnight, and in the morning disguised himself as a workman and made off with the painting while the guard went out to smoke a cigarette. Needless to say, panic ensued. There was a nationwide investigation, and the

But first the backstory: Built by Cardinal Richelieu, the lavish palace was left to the king upon his prime minister's death in 1642. It was subsequently occupied by a number of royal family members (including Louis XIV as a child) until it came into the hands of a certain Duke Louis Philippe d'Orleans at the end of the 18th century. An inveterate spendthrift, the young lord soon found himself up to his ears in debt. To earn enough money to pay off his creditors, he came up with the shockingly modern idea of opening the palace gardens to development, building apartments on the grounds. The bottom floor of these lodgings, which make up three sides of the enclosure you see today, were let out as shops, cafes, and boutiques. Though the neighbors screamed, their cries were drowned out by the success of the new project, which made the area into a commercial hub. What's more, since the police had no power over these royal grounds, all sorts of usually illegal activities were given free reign here. Gambling houses and bordellos sprang up between the shops and cafes, and the gardens became the central meeting place for Revolutionaries. Things came to a head on July 12, 1789, when Camille Desmoulins stood up on a table in front of the Café de Foy and called the people to arms—2 days later, the mob would storm the Bastille, igniting the French Revolution.

borders were sealed. What the police didn't realize is that the painting was at first hidden only a mile from the Louvre. Conspiracy theories spread through the newspapers—some thought it was merely a publicity stunt. There was a lot of criticism about the Louvre's lax security, in particular from the poet Apollinaire. He soon found himself arrested as a suspect, and his friend Pablo Picasso was also brought in for questioning after they were caught in possession of some other art objects of dubious origins. After they both broke down in tears before the bench, the judge let them go with a slap on the wrist.

After 2 years of false leads and bungled investigations, the *Mona Lisa* was finally found when the thief, Vincenzo Perugia, tried to sell it to an art dealer in Florence. What was the motive for the crime? It seems that Perugia, an Italian patriot who had once worked at the museum, simply felt that the *Mona Lisa* belonged in her country of birth, Italy. During his trial, Perugia claimed to have been bewitched by the painting—and indeed, who hasn't been?

The life of a superstar certainly isn't easy. With millions of admirers around the world, at least a couple are bound to have a few screws loose. Once she was back at the museum (under increased security), things calmed down until 1956, when a deranged visitor threw acid on the painting, severely damaging its lower half (restoration took several years). A few months later, someone threw a rock at her. The painting is now covered with bulletproof glass, and a full-time guard stands at the ready. So be patient with the lines and velvet ropes—if *Mona Lisa* gets the kind of security usually reserved for rock stars or heads of state, she has certainly earned it.

The glory days of the Palais Royal would end abruptly in 1815, when a new Louis-Philippe showed up, decided this was not the way to treat the home of his ancestors, and kicked everyone out. Once the royals finally left in the 19th century, the palace was taken over by various government ministries, and the apartments in the galleries were let out to artists and writers, among them Collette and Jean Cocteau.

Today the shops in the arcades are very subdued, mostly a smattering of high-end designer clothes and a couple of pricey restaurants. The *cour d'honneur* on the south end is filled with black-and-white-striped columns by Daniel Buren; though most Parisians have now gotten used to this unusual installation, when it was unveiled in 1987 it caused almost as much of a stir as Camille Desmoulins.

Rue St-Honoré, 1st arrond. Free admission to gardens and arcades, buildings closed to public. Daily 7:30am–dusk. Métro: Palais-Royal–Musée du Louvre.

Place Vendôme ★★ SQUARE   In 1686, Louis XIV decided the time had come to design a magnificent square, at the center of which would stand a statue of His Royal Highness. Though the statue is long gone, this is still one of the classiest squares in the city. The work of Jules Hardouin-Mansart, today this über-elegant octagonal ensemble of 17th-century buildings is the home of the original Ritz Hôtel, as well as the world's most glitzy jewelry makers, including Cartier, Van Cleef and Arpels, and Boucheron. The famous statue reigned over the square up until the Revolution, when it was melted down for scrap. When Napoleon took over, he decided it was the perfect place for a huge Roman-style column honoring his glorious army (yes, once again), this time documenting its victory at Austerlitz. A long spiral of bas-reliefs recounting the campaign of 1805 marches up the Colonne de la Grande Armée, which was crowned by a statue of the Emperor himself. The original statue did not survive the regime; a few decades later, Napoleon III replaced it with the existing copy.

Enter by rue de Castiglione, 1st arrond. Métro: Tuileries or Concorde.

Sainte-Chapelle ★★★ CHURCH   A wall of color greets visitors who enter this magnificent chapel. Stained-glass windows make up a large part of the walls of the upper level of the church, giving worshippers the impression of standing inside a jewel-encrusted crystal goblet. What isn't glass is elaborately carved and painted in gold leaf and rich colors: vaulting arches, delicate window casings, and an intricate wainscoting of arches and medallions. The 15 stained-glass windows recount the story of the Bible, from Genesis to the Apocalypse, as well as the story of Saint Louis, who was responsible for the chapel's construction. Back in the early 13th century, Louis IX (who was later canonized) spent 2 years bargaining with Emperor Badouin II of Constantinople for some of the holiest relics in Christendom: the Crown of Thorns and a piece of the Holy Cross. The relics were finally purchased for a princely sum, and Louis decided that they should be housed in an appropriately splendid chapel in the royal palace (the relics are currently at the Louvre Museum; p. 144). The record is not clear, but the architect may have been the illustrious Pierre de Montreuil, who worked on the cathedrals of St-Denis and Notre-Dame. Whoever it was, he was a speed demon; the chapel was built in record time for the Middle Ages, from 1241 to 1248. He was also quite brilliant; he managed to support the structure with arches and buttresses in such a way that the walls of the upper chapel are almost entirely glass.

The lower chapel, which was meant for the servants, has a low, vaulted ceiling painted in blue and red and gold and covered with fleur-de-lis motifs. Up a small staircase is the upper chapel, clearly meant for the royals. This masterpiece suffered both fire and floods in the 17th century and was pillaged by zealous Revolutionaries in the 18th. By the mid–19th century, the chapel was being used to store archives—2m (6½ ft.) of the bottom of each window was removed to install shelves. Fortunately, renewed interest in medieval art staved off plans for Sainte-Chapelle's demolition, and eventually led to a conscientious restoration by a team that was advised by master restorer Viollet-le-Duc. The quality of the work on the windows is such that it is almost impossible to detect the difference between the original and the reconstructed stained glass (which makes up about one-third of what you see).

Sainte-Chapelle stages evening **concerts** March to November (13€–70€). And they're very popular, so I recommend reserving in advance online at www.classictic.com.

If you plan to visit the Conciergerie (p. 140), you can save money by buying a joint ticket with time slots: 17€ adults, free for children ages 17 and under.

Palais de Justice, 4 bd. du Palais, 1st arrond. www.sainte-chapelle.fr. © **01-53-40-60-80.** 11.50€ adults, free for children ages 17 and under. Daily Oct–Mar 9am–5pm; Apr–Sept 9am–7pm. Métro: Cité, St-Michel, or Châtelet–Les Halles. RER: St-Michel.

St-Eustache ★ CHURCH A Gothic church with a Renaissance decor, St-Eustache is one of the largest in the city, at more than 105m long (344 ft.) and 43m wide (141 ft.). It was built from 1532 to 1640 along the plan of Notre-Dame (the intertwined arches of the ceiling give a similar sense of exalted elevation) and has found new fame since the latter closed after the 2019 fire. These dimensions result in excellent acoustics for the church's huge 8,000-pipe organ. The church's musical reputation stretches back centuries; Berlioz and Liszt both conducted their works here, among others. Before the Revolution, St-Eustache was a parish where both the nobility and working class came to worship—Cardinal Richelieu and Madame de Pompadour were baptized here, as was the playwright Molière. After the Revolution, it was turned into a temple to agriculture, and, like many Parisian churches, its interior suffered mightily. It has subsequently been restored to its former glory and is truly breathtaking, not least on the outside, where (if you stand in the new Les Halles gardens) you can see an unusual figure for a church, a giant stag's head. The story goes that a Roman general called Placidus was hunting deer when a stag appeared with a crucifix hanging between its antlers. The vision caused Placidus to convert to Christianity and change his name to Eustathios, or "Eustache," after whom the church is now named. You can hear the organ and the choir in action Sunday at 5pm before (and during) the 6pm mass; other concerts are listed on the church's website.

2 impasse St-Eustache, 1st arrond. www.st-eustache.org. © **01-42-36-31-05.** Free admission. Mon–Fri 9:30am–7pm; Sat 10am–7:15pm; Sun 9am–7:15pm. Sun organ recitals 5pm. Métro: Les Halles.

St-Germain l'Auxerrois ★ CHURCH This is a church with a checkered past. St-Germain was designated the royal church when the Valois moved in across the street at the Louvre in the 14th century, and kings, queens, and their entourages often attended mass here. Many of the artists who worked on the Louvre are buried here, including architects Le Vau and Soufflot. But its most infamous moment came at dawn on August 24, 1572, when the church's bells sounded the signal that began the Saint Bartholomew's Day massacre. Despite her erstwhile tolerance, Catherine de Médicis and her son Charles IX gave their blessing to a plot to slaughter the Huguenot (Protestant) leaders. The crowd murdered every Protestant in sight—between 2,000 and 4,000 were killed over the following 5 days.

The church has been rebuilt several times over the centuries, resulting in a mix of architectural styles. The 12th-century Romanesque tower hovers over a 15th-century Flamboyant Gothic porch embellished with human and animal figures. The vaulted interior is relatively simple and shelters some interesting works of art, among which are a monumental **sculpted wooden pew,** designed for the royal family in 1684 by Le Brun, and a 16th-century carved wood **retable** depicting scenes from the life of Christ.

2 pl. du Louvre, 1st arrond. www.saintgermainauxerrois.cef.fr. ⓒ **01-42-60-13-96.** Free admission. Daily 9am–7pm. Métro: Louvre-Rivoli.

Opéra & Grands Boulevards (2nd & 9th Arrondissements)

The grandiose **Opéra Garnier** reigns over this bustling neighborhood, which teems with office workers, tourists, and shoppers scuttling in and around the *grands magasins* ("big stores") on boulevard Haussmann. The 2nd arrondissement has more outstanding retail experiences than cultural ones, but the hip 9th has a few small museums worthy of your time.

FlyView ★★★ VIRTUAL REALITY EXPERIENCE Just steps from the Garnier opera house, this virtual reality city tour presents itself as a futuristic mini-airport, with flight times displayed on screens and flight attendants in quaint turquoise uniforms. Once in the flight room, you strap yourself into a jetpack, put on the headset, and then hold on (white-knuckled) for 13 minutes of virtual sightseeing. There are several "flights" to choose from, but for sweeping city vistas, I recommend "The Incredible Flyover," where you take off from a Paris rooftop before whooshing through the air to Concorde's needle, then float under the Arc de Triomphe, dash between the Eiffel Tower's filigree girders, and zip over the Seine to Notre-Dame. FlyView uses impressively detailed 360-degree images taken by drone. By filming Notre-Dame before its roof burned down (and after, for the "Rebuilding Notre-Dame" ride), FlyView has become the only way you can see the edifice close up—reason alone to book a ticket. Minimum height is 1.2m (4 ft.).

30 rue du Quatre Septembre, 2nd arrond. www.flyview360.com. ⓒ **01-83-62-12-36.** Admission 19.50€, family pack (2 adults and 2 children) 66€. Wed 2:30–7pm; Sat–Sun and daily during French school holidays 10:30am–7pm. Métro: Opéra, Chaussée d'Antin-Lafayette or Quatre Septembre. RER: Auber.

Musée de la Vie Romantique ★ MUSEUM This quaint villa, with painted shutters and a fragrant rose garden, is where Romantic painter Ary Scheffer (1795–1858) once entertained such illustrious guests as Baronne Aurore Dupin (George Sand), Eugène Delacroix, Chopin, and Charles Dickens. Today, the tiny museum gives an inkling as to what life might have been like in the company of these iconic artists, with atmospheric period rooms, one of which is dedicated to George Sand and displays moving mementos from her life—jewelry, trinkets, paintings, and even a plaster cast of her right arm. In summer, the rose garden doubles as one of Paris' most charming tearooms—a slice of countryside in the heart of what was once known as La Nouvelle Athènes (New Athens) after the classical-style mansions that mushroomed in the early 19th century to house Paris' prestigious artist community.

16 rue Chaptal, 9th arrond. www.vie-romantique.paris.fr. 🕐 **01-55-31-95-67.** Free admission to permanent collection except during certain temporary exhibits. Tues–Sun 10am–6pm. Métro: Saint-Georges, Pigalle, or Blanche.

Musée Grévin ★ MUSEUM

This vast, kitsch cavern of wax figures—movie stars, historical figures, sports heroes, rock 'n' rollers, notables from the political scene—is a fun place to take the kids. If you're not up on French history or pop culture, you might not recognize some of the faces, but don't worry, Marilyn Monroe, Brad Pitt, and Pope Francis are here, too. Stars appear in their natural habitats: chic brasseries, cocktail parties, and fashion shows. Historical tableaus feature such scenes as Joan of Arc being burned at the stake and Louis XIV holding court at Versailles. Also here: a light show in the renovated Palais des Mirages, a leftover from the Universal Exposition of 1900. *Tip:* If you're traveling with 2 adults and 2 children (ages 5 to 15), save money by buying the family ticket online from 17€ per person.

10 bd. Montmartre, 9th arrond. www.grevin-paris.com. 🕐 **01-47-70-85-05.** Admission varies with the season, starting at 25€ adults, 18.50€ ages 6–17, free for children 5 and under. Daily 10am–6:30pm (hours vary with seasons; check website for exact times). Métro: Grands Boulevards.

Musée Gustave Moreau ★★★ MUSEUM

Symbolist painter Gustave Moreau was a contemporary of the Impressionists, but he worked against the grain, rejecting realism and naturalism to draw inspiration from the Bible, Greek mythology, Leonardo da Vinci, and Indian miniatures. This quaint museum, set in the elegant town house where he once lived and worked, has atmospheric period rooms that reveal Moreau's obsession for Second Empire and Restoration-era knickknacks and furniture, and galleries filled with his fabulous mythical beasts and fantasy worlds. It's a little-known gem.

14 rue de la Rochfoucauld, 9th arrond. www.musee-moreau.fr. 🕐 **01-48-74-38-50.** Admission 7€ adults, 5€ students 18–25, free for children 17 and under. Wed–Mon 10am–6pm. Métro: Trinité.

Opéra Garnier ★★ OPERA HOUSE

Flamboyant, extravagant, and baroque, this splendid example of Second Empire architectural excess, built by architect Charles Garnier between 1862 and 1875, sits on the underground lake that inspired Gaston Leroux's 1911 novel, "The Phantom of the Opera." Corinthian columns, loggias, busts, and friezes cover the facade of the building, which is topped by a flattened gold dome. Seventy-three sculptors worked on the decoration, which includes portraits of composers, Greek gods, and symbolic representations of Music, Poetry, Drama, and Dance.

The interior is no less dramatic. The vast lobby, built in a spectrum of different colored marble, holds a spectacular double staircase that sweeps up to the different levels of the auditorium, as well as an array of glamorous

Opéra Garnier National de Paris.

antechambers, galleries, and ballrooms that make you wonder how the opera scenery could possibly compete. Mosaics, mirrors, gilt, and marble line these grand spaces, whose painted ceilings dance with fauns, gods, and nymphs. The largest room, the grand foyer, is drenched in gold leaf and hung with gigantic chandeliers, looking something like a real palace, which was, in fact, the effect Garnier was going for. The main event, of course, is the auditorium, which might seem a bit small, considering the size of the building. In fact, it holds not even 2,000 seats. The horseshoe shape of the seating area ensures that viewers see both the stage and each other—19th-century operagoers were equally concerned with what was on the stage and who was in the house. The beautiful ceiling was painted by Marc Chagall in 1964 with colorful images from various operas and ballets.

All of this (with the exception of the Chagall ceiling) sprang from the mind of a young, unknown architect named Charles Garnier, who won a competition launched when Napoleon III decided the time had come to build himself an opera house. Though the first stone was laid in 1862, work was held up by war, civil unrest, and a change in regime; the **Palais Garnier** was not inaugurated until 1875. Some contemporary critics found it a bit much (one called it "an overloaded sideboard"), but today it is generally acknowledged as a masterpiece of the architecture of the epoch.

You can visit the building on your own (for a fee), but with so much history and so many good stories, you might want to take advantage of the **guided** visits in English (17€ adults, 12.50€ ages 10–25, 9.50€ children 9 and under; check website for times). Or simply **buy tickets to a show.**

Corner of rue Scribe and rue Auber, 9th arrond. www.operadeparis.fr. ✆ **08-25-05-44-05** (.35€/min.). Admission 14€ adults, 10€ students and ages 12–25, free for children 11 and under. Daily Oct to mid-July 10am–5pm; mid-July to Sept 10am–6pm. Métro: Opéra.

Le Marais (3rd & 4th Arrondissements)

Home to royalty and aristocracy between the 14th and 17th centuries, the Marais still boasts remarkable architecture, some of it dating back to the Middle Ages. One of the few neighborhoods that was not knocked down during Baron Haussmann's urban overhaul, its narrow streets are lined with magnificent *hôtels particuliers* (mansions) as well as humbler homes from centuries past. The **Pompidou Center** and **Picasso Paris** are probably the biggest attractions, but the Marais also harbors a wealth of terrific smaller museums, as well as the delightful **Place des Vosges.** Remnants of the city's **historic Jewish quarter** can be found on rue des Rosiers, which has seen an influx of clothing shops in recent years. Nowadays, the real Jewish neighborhood is in the 19th arrondissement.

Centre Pompidou ★★ MUSEUM The bizarre architecture of this odd building provokes such strong emotions that it's easy to forget that there is something inside. Believe it or not, President Pompidou searched far and wide to find an architect. In 1971, an international design competition was held with entrants from 49 countries, and the winners were the Italo-British design team of Renzo Piano and Richard Rogers. Their concept was to put the support structure and transport systems on the outside of the building, thereby liberating space on the inside for a museum and cultural center. The result was a gridlike exoskeleton with a tubular escalator inching up one side, and huge multicolored pipes and shafts covering the other. To some, it's a milestone in contemporary architecture; to others, it's simply a horror. Either way, it's one of the most visited structures in France.

The Pompidou is much more than an art museum. Its over 100,000 sq. m (1,076,390 sq. ft.) of floor space includes a vast **reference library,** a **cinema archive, bookshops,** and a **music research institute,** as well as a **photography** and **children's** gallery, a **performance hall,** and areas for educational activities.

The actual museum, the **Musée National d'Art Moderne,** is on the fourth and fifth floors. Getting there is half the fun as you glide up the exterior escalators. Since the collection is in constant rotation and **temporary exhibitions** are a huge draw, it's impossible to say what you are likely to see on your visit. The emphasis is generally on works from the second half of the 20th century, with a good dose of surrealism, Dada, and other modern movements from the first half. This is not "pretty" art, but art that is designed to make you think. It might make you think about heading straight for the exit, but if nothing else, there are works here that will surprise you and get your juices flowing. Pieces range from relatively tame abstract works by **Picasso** and **Kandinsky** to **Andy Warhol**'s multiheaded portrait of Elizabeth Taylor (*Ten Lizes*) to a felt-wrapped piano by **Joseph Beuys.** Video installations are often highlighted, as well works by new artists.

Just outside is the **Atelier Brancusi,** where the sculptor's workshop has been reconstituted in its entirety; in his will, Brancusi left the workshop's contents to the museum on the condition that every sculpture and object be displayed exactly as it was found in his studio on the day of his death.

Don't miss the view from the top floor—a wonderful opportunity to gaze at the city's higgledy-piggledy roof-

Facade of the Centre Pompidou.

tops. Even if you don't visit the museum, you can buy a ticket to the top for 5€. Or you can admire it from within **Georges** (https://restaurantgeorgesparis. com), the museum's oh-so-chic rooftop cafe/restaurant, which flaunts decor just as avant-garde as the artworks inside the museum. The staff is a little snooty, however. *Note:* The Centre Pompidou is set to close for renovations in 2023 and reopen in 2027.

pl. Georges-Pompidou, 4th arrond. www.centrepompidou.fr. ℂ **01-44-78-12-33.** Admission 14€ adults, 11€ students ages 18–25, free for children 17 and under; admission may vary depending on exhibits. Wed–Mon 11am–10pm (Thurs until 11pm during temporary exhibitions). Métro: Hôtel de Ville. RER: Châtelet–Les Halles.

Gaîté Lyrique ★ CULTURAL INSTITUTION One of the newer additions to the city's cultural scene, this gallery space/concert hall/educational center is devoted to exploring mixed-media and digital art forms. Set in an abandoned 19th-century theater (hence the name), the building has been restored and transformed to host rotating exhibits that range from music and multimedia performances to design, fashion, and architecture to new media. There's even an interactive room dedicated to video games.

3 bis rue Papin, 3rd arrond. www.gaite-lyrique.net. ℂ **01-53-01-52-00.** Admission varies depending on the event or exhibition. Tues–Fri 2–8pm; Sat–Sun noon–7pm. Métro: Réaumur-Sébastopol or Arts et Metiers.

Hôtel de Ville ★ HISTORIC SITE   No, it's not a hotel. This enormous neo-Renaissance wedding cake is Paris' city hall, and the only way to see the inside is to make friends with the mayor, though it does host regular art exhibits on subjects linked to Paris' history, usually for free (access is through the back entrance on rue Lobau). Even if you can't get inside, you can feast on the lavish exterior, which includes 136 statues representing VIPs of Parisian history. Since the 14th century, this spot has been an administrative seat for the municipality; the building you see before you dates from 1873, but it is an accurate copy of an earlier Renaissance version that was burned down in 1870 during the Paris Commune. The vast square in front of the building, formerly called the Place du Grève, was once used for municipal festivals and executions. It was also the stage for several important moments in the city's history, particularly during the Revolution: Louis XVI was forced to kiss the new French flag here, and Robespierre was shot in the jaw and arrested here during an attempted coup. Today the square hosts more peaceful activities: There's a merry-go-round, and in winter an ice-skating rink is sometimes set up.

29 rue de Rivoli, 4th arrond. www.paris.fr. ✆ **01-42-76-63-01.** Free admission to exhibits. Métro: Hôtel-de-Ville.

Maison de Victor Hugo ★ MUSEUM   The life of Victor Hugo was as turbulent as some of his novels. Regularly visited by both tragedy and triumph, the author of "The Hunchback of Notre-Dame" lived in several apartments in Paris, including this one on the second floor of a corner house on the sumptuous Place des Vosges. From 1832 to 1848, he lived here with his wife and four children, during which time he wrote "Ruy Blas" and part of "Les Misérables"; met his lifelong mistress and muse, Juliette Drouet; was elected to the Académie Française; lost his 19-year-old daughter in a boating accident on the Seine; and entered the political arena. When Napoleon III seized power in 1851, this passionate advocate of free speech, universal suffrage, and social justice was made distinctly unwelcome, particularly after he declared the new king a traitor of France. Fearing for his life, Hugo left the country and lived in exile until 1870, when he triumphantly returned to France and was elected to the senate. By the time he died in 1885, he was a national hero; his funeral cortege through the streets of Paris is the stuff of legend, and his body was one of the first to be buried in the Panthéon (p. 185). The museum's collection charts this dramatic existence through the author's drawings, original manuscripts, notes, furniture, and personal objects, all displayed in small rooms that re-create the ambience and the spirit of the original lodgings. The museum's latest addition is a charming cafe.

6 pl. des Vosges, 4th arrond. www.maisonsvictorhugo.paris.fr. ✆ **01-42-72-10-16.** Free admission to permanent collection except during certain temporary exhibits. Tues–Sun 10am–6pm. Métro: St-Paul, Bastille, or Chemin Vert.

Musée Carnavalet ★★★ MUSEUM   Paris has served as a backdrop to centuries' worth of dramatic events, from Roman takeovers to barbarian invasions, from coronations to decapitations to the birth of the modern French

6 | THE bridges OF PARIS

Despite its name (*neuf* means "new"), the **Pont Neuf** (Quai du Louvre to Quai de Conti) is the oldest bridge in Paris. The bridge was an instant hit at its inauguration by Henri IV in 1607 (its ample sidewalks, combined with the fact that it was the first bridge sans houses, made it a delight for pedestrians), and it still is. For a quiet picnic spot, take the stairs by the statue of Henri IV (in the center of the span) down to the **Square du Vert Galant.**

The **Pont des Arts** (Quai François Mitterrand to Quai de Conti) was originally constructed at the beginning of the 19th century. Delicately arching over the river, the iron pedestrian bridge is still the most romantic bridge in the city—with its splendid view of the Île de la Cité and its itinerant artists sketching along the railing—in spite of the fact that over-enthusiastic lovers attached so many locks to the railing that the barrier actually fell over and has now been replaced with plastic screens. It's best to avoid any symbolic gestures (like writing your names on a lock, attaching it to the railing, and throwing away the key) and opt for romantic selfies instead.

A modern way to get from the Left to the Right bank is via the **Passerelle Simone de Beauvoir** (Quai de Bercy to Quai François Mauriac). A graceful pedestrian passage, the bridge consists of two arching bands of oak and steel, which intertwine and cross the river without the support of a central pillar. The central lens-shaped structure was constructed by the Eiffel factory (founded by Gustave).

With its enormous pillars topped by gilded statuary, it's hard to miss the **Pont Alexandre III** (Cours de la Reine to Quai d'Orsay). Linking the vast esplanade of the Invalides with the glass-domed Grand Palais, this elegant bridge fits right in with its grand surroundings. The span was named after Czar Alexander III of Russia and inaugurated at the opening of the Paris Exposition of 1900.

Incredibly, the small and lovely **Pont Marie** (Quai des Célestins to Quai d'Anjou–Ile St-Louis), composed of three gentle arches, was once loaded down by some 50 houses. The structure could not hold its charge, and during a flood in 1658, the Seine washed away two of its arches and 20 houses fell into the water. The tragedy, which claimed 60 lives, got city officials to thinking, and finally, in 1769, homesteading on bridges was outlawed.

republic. These stories and others are told at this fascinating museum through objects, paintings, and interiors. The collection is displayed in two extraordinary 17th-century mansions—works of art in their own right. Starting with a prehistoric canoe from 4600 B.C. and continuing into the 21st century, the history of Paris is illustrated with items as diverse as Gallo-Roman figurines, Napoleon's toiletry kit, and an 18th-century portrait of Benjamin Franklin painted when he was the U.S. ambassador to France.

16 rue des Francs-Bourgeois, 3rd arrond. www.carnavalet.paris.fr. ℂ **01-44-59-58-58.** Free admission to permanent collection except during certain temporary exhibits. Tues–Sun 10am–6pm. Métro: St-Paul or Chemin Vert.

Musée Cognacq-Jay ★ MUSEUM This bite-size museum offers a bite-size taste of the finer side of 18th-century France. Its founder, Ernest Cognacq, led a rags-to-riches life: At 12 years old, he was selling odds and ends as an itinerant merchant, and by the end of his life he was the owner of a fabulously successful department store (today's La Samaritaine building) with a prodigious private art collection. His rich assortment of 18th-century art and furniture make up the contents of this small museum, which is housed in a lovely *hôtel particulier* (mansion). The collection leans heavily toward the romantic side of the century, with many lesser works by famous artists such as Chardin and Fragonard, but what's most impressive here is the furniture, such as the bed à la polonaise draped in blue damask and framed in gilt, or the exquisite Louis XVI–era writing table with geometric wood inlay.

8 rue Elzévir, 3rd arrond. www.cognacq-jay.paris.fr. ☏ **01-40-27-07-21.** Free admission to permanent collection except during certain temporary exhibits. Tues–Sun 10am–6pm. Métro: St-Paul or Chemin Vert.

Musée d'Art et d'Histoire du Judaïsme ★★ MUSEUM   Housed in the magnificent Hôtel de Saint Aignan, one of the many palatial 17th-century mansions that dot the Marais, this museum chronicles the art and history of the Jewish people in France and in Europe. It features a superb collection of objects of both artistic and cultural significance (a splendid Italian Renaissance Torah ark, a German gold and silver Hanukkah menorah, a 17th-century Dutch illustrated Torah scroll, documents from the Dreyfus trial), which is interspersed with texts, drawings, and photos telling the story of the Jews and explaining the basics of both Ashkenazi and Sephardic traditions. You'll do a

Couple overlooking the Seine.

lot of reading here; documentation is translated in English, but if you're feeling lazy you can get the informative audioguide. The final rooms include a collection of works by Jewish artists, including Modigliani, Soutine, Lipchitz, and Chagall. Be prepared for airportlike security at the entrance.

71 rue du Temple, 3rd arrond. www.mahj.org. ℭ **01-53-01-86-60.** Admission 10€ adults, 7€ ages 18–25, free for children 17 and under. Mon–Fri 11am–6pm; Sat–Sun 10am–6pm. Métro: Rambuteau or Hôtel de Ville.

Musée de la Chasse et de la Nature ★ MUSEUM   If you can get over the fact that it's a museum dedicated to hunting, this small museum makes for a pleasant outing. You'll find the expected taxidermied animals, but they are discreetly presented among an elegant collection of paintings, tapestries, sculptures, and even contemporary art. Each room has a theme: For example, the blond wood–paneled Salle Cerf et Loup takes on the imagery of the stag and the wolf, illustrated in paintings by artists as disparate as Renaissance-era Lucas Cranach and 20th-century fauvist André Derain. The emphasis is not so much on the kill as the symbolism behind the images: In the Middle Ages, the stag, which represented Christ, and the wolf, which represented the Devil, could coexist, a theme that is echoed in the 16th- and 17th-century tapestries that cover the walls. Once you've sauntered through rooms dedicated to dogs, birds, horses, and even unicorns, you will walk smack into the trophy room, where discretion is abandoned and hunting is blatantly celebrated in all its gory glory. Still, there is something intriguing about this place. It reminds you that the relationship between humans and animals dates to well before there were naturalists and environmentalists, and if that relationship was filled with animosity and fear, it was also tinged with a sort of mystical respect.

62 rue des Archives, 3rd arrond. www.chassenature.org. ℭ **01-53-01-92-40.** Admission 12.50€ adults, 10.50€ E.U. citizens ages 18–26, free for children 17 and under. Tues, Thurs–Sun 11am–6pm; Wed 11am–9:30pm. Métro: Rambuteau.

Musée des Arts et Métiers ★★★ MUSEUM   If you've read Umberto Eco's novel "Foucault's Pendulum," you'll probably want to come here just to see Foucault's original pendulum swing in the church of St-Martin-des-Champs, but there are plenty of other reasons to spend a couple of hours at this temple of technology. The Musée harbors sterling examples of just about every discovery that made the mechanical world possible. True techies will linger over the many displays of gearboxes, steam engines, and other historic gizmos; the less technically inclined will probably prefer the first versions of telephones, movie cameras, and toasters. A lot of "firsts" are here, like the first omnibus (a "high-speed" steam vehicle built in 1873), and the Blériot XI (the first plane to cross the English Channel), as well as the earliest examples of phonographs, lightbulbs, and tape decks. Those "new" antiques—the typewriters, record players, and VCRs on display in those old wooden cases— drive home the fact that the technological revolution is ongoing, and today's wonders will be tomorrow's curiosities.

60 rue Réaumur, 3rd arrond. www.arts-et-metiers.net. 📞 **01-53-01-82-00.** Admission 8€ adults, 5.50€ students, free for children 17 and under. Tues–Thurs and Sat–Sun 10am–6pm; Fri 10am–9pm. Métro: Arts et Métiers.

Picasso Paris ★★★ MUSEUM   This shrine to all things Picasso is in the stunning Hôtel Salé, a 17th-century mansion built by salt-tax farmer Pierre Aubert, whose position gave the mansion its name—*salé* means "salty." This unique institution valiantly strives to make sense of the incredibly diverse output of this prolific genius: Some 400 carefully selected paintings, sculptures, collages, and drawings are presented in a more or less chronological and thematic order, no small task when dealing with an artist who experimented with every style, from neoclassicism to surrealism to his own flamboyantly abstract inventions. Impressionist portraits (*Portrait of Gustave Coquiot*, 1901), Cubist explorations (*Man with Guitar*, 1911), mannerist allegories (*The Race*, 1922), and deconstructionist forms (*Reclining Nude*, 1932) make up only part of his oeuvre, which has been estimated to include some 50,000 works. Not only that, Picasso often worked in wildly different styles during the same period, sometimes treating the same subjects. For example, the rounded yet realistic lovers dancing in *La Danse des Villageois,* painted in 1922, hang next to two forms in a blaze of color representing *The Kiss,* painted in 1925. There's also a sampling of the somewhat disturbing portraits of the many women in his life, including portraits of Dora Maar and Marie-Thérèse, both painted in 1937. On the top floor is Picasso's private collection, which includes works by artists he admired like Courbet and Cézanne, as well as paintings by his friends, who included masters like Braque and Matisse.

All in all, what you see on the walls is less than 10% of the 5,000 works in the museum's collection; the presentation rotates every couple of years.

5 rue de Thorigny, 3rd arrond. www.museepicassoparis.fr. 📞 **01-85-56-00-36.** Admission 14€ adults, free for children 17 and under. Tues–Fri 10:30am–6pm; Sat–Sun 9:30am–6pm. Métro: St-Paul or Chemin Vert.

Picasso Paris museum.

Place des Vosges ★★★ SQUARE   Possibly the prettiest square in the city, the Place des Vosges combines elegance, greenery, and quiet. Nowhere in Paris will you find such a unity of Renaissance-style architecture; the entire square is bordered by 17th-century brick town houses, each conforming to rules set down by Henri IV himself. Arched arcades run under the houses. In the center is a garden with a geometric arrangement of lush lawns, fountains, and trees. At the epicenter is a huge equestrian statue of Louis XIII, during whose reign (1610–43) the square enjoyed a golden age of festivals and tournaments. But it was a tournament in a previous century that proved pivotal to the creation of this square. In the 16th century, a royal palace called the Hôtel des Tournelles stood on this site. In 1559, an organized combat was held there, during which the current monarch, feisty Henri II, defeated several opponents. Feeling pleased with himself, he decided to fight Montgomery, the captain of his guard. A badly aimed lance resulted in Henri's untimely death; his wife, Catherine de Médicis, was so distraught that she had the palace demolished. His descendant, Henri IV, took advantage of the free space to construct a royal square. Over the centuries, a number of celebrities lived in the 36 houses, including Mme. de Sévigny and Victor Hugo (now the Maison de Victor Hugo; p. 157). Today the homes are for the rich, as are many of the chic boutiques under the arcades, but the park, the fountains, and the children's playground are for everyone.

4th arrond. Métro: St-Paul.

Champs-Élysées, Trocadéro & Western Paris (8th, 16th & 17th Arrondissements)

Decidedly posh, this is one of the wealthiest parts of the city in both per capita earnings and cultural institutions. While the **Champs-Élysées** is more glitz than glory, the surrounding neighborhoods offer high-end shops and restaurants as well as some terrific museums and concert halls. This is also where you will find grand architectural gestures, like the **Arc de Triomphe** and the **Place de la Concorde,** which bookend the Champs, and the **Grand Palais** and **Petit Palais,** leftovers from the legendary 1900 Universal Exposition.

Arc de Triomphe ★★★ MONUMENT   If there is one monument that symbolizes "La Gloire," or the glory of France, it is this giant triumphal arch. Crowning the Champs-Élysées, this mighty archway both celebrates the military victories of the French army and memorializes the sacrifices of its soldiers. Over time, it has become an icon of the Republic and a setting for some of its most emotional moments: the lying in state of the coffin of Victor Hugo in 1885, the burial in 1921 of the ashes of an unknown soldier who fought in World War I, and General de Gaulle's pregnant pause under the arch before striding down the Champs-Élysées before the cheering crowds after the Liberation in 1944.

It took a certain amount of chutzpah to come up with the idea to build such a shrine, and sure enough, it was Napoleon who instigated it. In 1806, still glowing after his stunning victory at Austerlitz, the Emperor decided to erect a monument to the Imperial Army, along the lines of a Roman triumphal arch. The architect chosen was Jean-François Chalgrin, who drew inspiration from Rome's Arch of

Titus, though he abandoned the columns and made Napoleon's arch a whopping 50m (163 ft.) high and 45m (147 ft.) wide, the largest of its type on the planet. Unfortunately, the defeat at Waterloo put an end to the Empire before the arch was finished, and construction came to an abrupt halt. It wasn't until 1823 that building got going again; it was finally finished in 1836 by Louis-Philippe.

The arch is covered with bas-reliefs and sculptures, the most famous of which is the enormous *Departure of the Volunteers* of 1792, better known as the Marseillaise, by François Rude, showing winged, female Liberty leading the charge of Revolutionary soldiers. Just above is one of the many smaller panels detailing Napoleonic battles—in this case, Aboukir—wherein the Emperor treads victoriously over the Ottomans. At the base of the arch is the Tomb of the Unknown Soldier, over which a flame is relit every evening at 6:30pm. The inscription, added after World War I, reads ICI REPOSE UN SOLDAT FRANÇAIS MORT POUR LA PATRIE, 1914–1918 ("Here lies a French soldier who died for his country").

Don't even think about crossing the traffic circle; instead take the underpass near the Champs-Élysées Métro entrance. You can visit the area under the arch free of charge, but if you want to enjoy the view from the rooftop terrace, you have to pay. You also have to climb 284 stairs to get there (only the very young, the very old, and those with disabilities get to use the elevator). Though you are not as high up as the viewing platforms on the Eiffel Tower, the panorama is quite impressive. Directly below, 12 boulevards radiate from the star-shaped intersection (hence the moniker "Étoile"), and out front is the long sweep of the Champs-Élysées, ending at the obelisk of the Place de la Concorde, behind which lurks the Louvre. You can pick out many of the most famous monuments, including Sacré-Coeur and the Eiffel Tower; to the west are the skyscrapers of La Défense, including the huge, hollowed-out Grande Arche, a modern version of the one you are standing on. The viewing terrace is closed in bad weather and July 14th (Bastille Day).

pl. Charles de Gaulle, 8th arrond. www.paris-arc-de-triomphe.fr. ✆ **01-55-37-73-77.** Admission 13€ adults, free for children 17 and under. Apr–Sept daily 10am–11pm; Oct–Mar daily 10am–10:30pm. Métro: Charles-de-Gaulle–Étoile.

Fondation Louis Vuitton ★ MUSEUM In a building designed by mega-architect Frank Gehry, this stunning contemporary art museum is swathed in a mass of billowing "sails" of glass, giving the impression that it is about to sail off into the lush greenery of the Bois de Boulogne, a large park on the western edge of the city (p. 205). Once you've taken in the arty outside, you have two choices: (1) stand in line to see the sophisticated temporary collections of ultra-contemporary art, or (2) go explore the Bois de Boulogne's alleys, gardens, and lakes. If you are big on heady modern and conceptual art, it's a must; if not, stick to option number 2.

8 av. du Mahatma Gandhi, Bois de Boulogne, 16th arrond. www.fondationlouisvuitton. fr. ✆ **01-40-69-96-00.** 16€ adults, 10€ ages 18–26, 5€ artists and children 3–17, free for children 2 and under. Mon, Wed–Thurs noon–7pm; Fri noon–11pm; Sat–Sun 11am–8pm. Métro: Les Sablons or Porte Maillot. Shuttle bus 1€ one-way from pl. Charles de Gaulle–Etoile, corner of av. Friedland.

Hôtel de la Marine ★ MUSEUM   Standing in the center of Place de la Concorde, with your back to the Seine, you can't miss three wonderful monuments: the Hôtel de Crillon (a palace hotel), the Madeleine church at the end of rue Royale, and the Hôtel de la Marine, the 18th-century neoclassical beauty (the Crillon's twin) that once stored the king's furniture before becoming the naval ministry's HQ. Its history is fascinating: here, in 1792, France's crown jewels—more than 10,000 gemstones of diamonds, topazes, rubies, emeralds, sapphires, and pearls—were stolen under the guards' noses. In 1848, it was here that minister François Arago abolished slavery in the colonies. For years the building was off-limits to the public, but in 2021 it opened as a museum, with period rooms showcasing 18th-century design, hitherto unseen royal furniture, and the Qatarian Al Thani Collection, an assembly of over 6,000 works of art, including the 17th-century Idol's Eye, the world's largest blue diamond. The museum's inner courtyard is open to the public from 9am to midnight and displays contemporary floor lights that at night make you feel as though you're walking on stars.

2 pl. de la Concorde, 8th arrond. www.hotel-de-la-marine.paris. ✆ **01-58-51-52-00.** Admission 13€–17€ adults, free for children 17 and under. Daily 10:30am–7pm (until 10pm on Fri). Métro: Concorde.

La Cité de l'Architecture et du Patrimoine ★ INSTITUTE/ MUSEUM   Created to promote French architecture and showcase evolving trends, this vast institution (located in the Palais de Chaillot) includes a museum, a research facility, and a top-notch school of architecture. On the ground floor, the enormous Galerie des Moulages with its vaulting skylights, exhibits casts of the gems of French architecture from the 12th to the 18th centuries. Commissioned in the late 19th century as a way of documenting France's architectural heritage, the project turned out to be an invaluable tool when it came to restoring the ravages of two world wars. The cast of the beautiful Queen of Sheba, for example—the original of which graced the face of Reims Cathedral—made it possible to create a faithful reproduction after the original was seriously damaged in World War I.

On the second floor, you'll dip into the cool waters of 20th- and 21st-century architecture, represented by intricate architectural models of structures like Piano and Rogers' Centre Pompidou (p. 155) and Rem Koolhaus' Maison Lemoine, a three-layer home built in Floriac, France, for a man who was paralyzed and his family. Don't miss clambering through a reconstruction of an apartment from Le Corbusier's Cité Radieuse, a shockingly (for the late 1940s) modern approach to urban housing.

1 pl. du Trocadéro, 16th arrond. www.citedelarchitecture.fr. ✆ **01-58-51-52-00.** Admission 9€ adults, 6€ ages 18–25, free for children 17 and under. Wed and Fri–Mon 11am–7pm; Thurs 11am–9pm. Métro: Trocadéro.

La Madeleine ★ CHURCH   As you peer up the rue Royale from the Place de la Concorde, you'll see something that very closely resembles a Roman temple. It is in fact a church, one that owes its unusual form to its equally singular history. In 1763, architect Pierre Constant d'Ivry laid the first stone of a church that would include a neoclassical facade with multiple columns. He didn't get very far. First the architect died, and then the Revolution broke out, during which construction ground to a halt. No one knew what to do with the site until Napoleon finally strode onto the scene and declared that it would become the Temple de la Gloire, to honor the glorious victories of his army. He wanted something "solid" because he was sure that the monument would last "thousands of years." Unfortunately for him, military defeats and mounting debt would again delay construction. Once Napoleon was out of the picture for good, inertia took over the project again, and it wasn't until 1842, under the Restoration, that La Madeleine was finally consecrated.

The inside of the church is pretty dark, thanks to a lack of windows, but there are actually some interesting works of art here, if you can make them out in the gloom. On the left as you enter is François Rude's *Baptism of Christ*; farther on is James Pradier's sculpture *La Marriage de la Vierge*.

pl. de la Madeleine, 8th arrond. www.eglise-lamadeleine.com. ✆ **01-44-51-69-00.** Free admission. Daily 9:30am–7pm. Métro: Madeleine.

Maison de Balzac ★ MUSEUM Fleeing his creditors in 1840, writer Honoré de Balzac rented this small house in what was then the village of Passy, where he lived for 7 years under an assumed name. He also worked like a demon: He was capable of writing for up to 20 hours a day for weeks at a time. The five rooms of Balzac's dwellings are hung with paintings and portraits of his family and friends, including several of Madame Hanska, whom he finally married after 18 years of passionate correspondence. There are also a few manuscripts and personal objects, including his turquoise-encrusted cane, which was the talk of Paris, and his monogrammed coffee pot, which kept him going through the marathon work sessions. In his office is the little table where he wrote *The Human Comedy,* "a witness," he wrote to Madame Hanska, "to my worries, my miseries, my distress, my joys, everything . . . my arm almost wore out its surface from taking the same path over and over again."

47 rue Raynouard, 16th arrond. www.maisondebalzac.paris.fr. ✆ **01-55-74-41-80.** Free admission to permanent collection. Tues–Sun 10am–6pm. Métro: Passy or La Muette.

Musée d'Art Moderne de la Ville de Paris ★ MUSEUM Housed in a wing of the massive Palais de Tokyo, this municipal modern-art museum covers ground similar to that of the Pompidou Center but on a smaller scale. Picasso, Rouault, Picabia—the big names are all here, but the works are often lesser-known, making the museum a fab spot for discovering significant paintings you may never have seen before. Highlights include a room dedicated to surrealism (the personal collection of André Breton) and a series of paintings by Delaunay and Léger. The contemporary section, from 1960 on, covers seriously abstract movements like Fluxus and Figuration. In recent years, the collection has acquired several new works from the 1980s on, but for the latest cutting-edge ideas, you are probably better off at the Palais de Tokyo museum (p. 169) in the wing next door. One huge room is covered with brilliant wall murals by Raoul Dufy (*La Fée Electricité*), as well as another vast room with two enormous versions of *La Danse* by Matisse.

11 av. du Président-Wilson, 16th arrond. www.mam.paris.fr. © **01-53-67-40-00.** Free admission to permanent collections. Tues–Sun 10am–6pm (Thurs until 10pm during temporary exhibitions). Métro: Iéna or Alma-Marceau.

Musée de l'Homme ★★ MUSEUM   The African and Pacific art housed in this museum once inspired Picasso. Today, it is a state-of-the-art anthropology museum showcasing the richness of human culture and the evolution of mankind. In true existential Sartre fashion, this is where you come to reflect on the hard questions: What does it mean to be human? Where do we come from? And where are we headed—especially in the light of climate change? The answer is there's no one answer, but it's great thinking about it as you work your way around the exhibits—everything from a Cro-Magnon skull to André Pierre Pinson's anatomical waxworks (fabulous, intricate examples of anatomy from the French Enlightenment) and a gallery of 19th-century busts designed to illustrate the diversity of human beings. The building itself is a showpiece. Set in the Passy wing of the Palais de Chaillot—built for the 1937 World's Fair on the site of the former 1878 Trocadéro Palace—it is an Art Deco treasure filled with natural light, thanks to rows of floor-to-ceiling windows that look out onto the most famous icon of all, the Eiffel Tower. For the best tower views, head to **Café Lucy,** an ultra-modern cafeteria on the second floor and the **Café de l'Homme,** a chic brasserie with a terrace offering undisrupted vistas (www.cafedelhomme.com).

17 pl. du Trocadéro, 16th arrond. www.museedelhomme.fr. © **01-44-05-72-72.** Admission 10€ adults, free for age 25 and under. Wed–Mon 11am–7pm. Métro: Trocadéro.

Musée Jacquemart-André ★★★ MUSEUM   The love child of a couple of passionate art collectors, Nélie Jacquemart and Edouard André, this terrific, bite-size museum takes the form of a 19th-century mansion filled with fine art and decorative treasures, including Botticelli's *Virgin and Child.* And because of its size, you can see a wide range here without wearing yourself to a frazzle.

The house itself is a work of art: At its inauguration in 1875, the marble Winter Garden with its spectacular double staircase was the talk of the town, and the awe-inspiring second floor—with works by masters such as Bellini, Uccello, and Mantegna—is like walking into a felt-lined jewel box. An impressive assortment of Louis XV– and Louis XVI–era decorative objects are also in evidence, as are the paintings of Fragonard, Boucher, and Chardin. To honor the artists that influenced these French painters, the couple also amassed a number of 17th-century Dutch paintings, including a jaunty *Portrait of a Man* by Frans Hals and Rembrandt's shadowy and powerful *Supper at Emmaus,* where the figure of Christ is backlit and it is only the look on his tablemate's face that reveals the identity of the mysterious guest.

Leave time to eat a light lunch or have tea in the Jacquemart-André's lovely dining room, where you can gaze up at a magnificent fresco by Tiepolo on the ceiling (see "The Top Tearooms," p. 131).

158 bd. Haussmann, 8th arrond. www.musee-jacquemart-andre.com. (*) **01-45-62-11-59.** Admission 15€ adults, 9.50€ students and children 7–25, free for children 6 and under. Daily 10am–6pm (Mon until 8:30pm during temporary exhibitions). Métro: Miromesnil or St-Philippe-du-Roule.

Musée Marmottan Monet ★★ MUSEUM Boasting the world's largest collection of Monets, this museum offers an in-depth look at this prolific genius and some of his talented contemporaries. Among the dozens of canvases by Monet is the one that provided the name of an entire artistic movement. Pressed to give a name to this misty play of light on the water for the catalog for the 1874 exposition that included Cézanne, Pissarro, Renoir, and Degas, Monet apparently said, "Put 'impression.'" The painting, *Impression, Sunrise,* certainly made one, as did the show—thereafter the group was referred to as the Impressionists. Monet never stopped being fascinated with the interaction of light and water, be it in a relatively traditional portrait of his wife and daughter against the stormy sea in *On the Beach at Trouville,* or in an almost abstract blend of blues and grays in *Charing Cross Bridge.* Monet was also interested in light's transformation; he often painted the same subject at different times of the day. One of his famous series on the Cathedral of Rouen is here: *Effect of the Sun at the End of the Day.* Fans of the artist's endless water-lily series will not be disappointed; the collection includes dozens of paintings of his beloved garden in Giverny.

Paintings by Renoir, Sisley, Degas, Gauguin, and other contemporaries can also be seen in the light-filled rooms of this 19th-century mansion, which belonged to art collector Paul Marmottan. Upstairs is a room dedicated to the only female member of the group, Berthe Morisot, known for her intimate portraits and scenes of family life.

2 rue Louis-Boilly, 16th arrond. www.marmottan.fr. (*) **01-44-96-50-33.** Admission 12€ adults, 8.50€ students 25 and under and ages 8–18, free for children 7 and under. Tues–Wed and Fri–Sun 10am–6pm; Thurs 10am–9pm. Métro: La Muette. RER: Bouilainvilliers.

Musée National des Arts Asiatiques Guimet ★★ MUSEUM Founded in 1889 by collector and industrialist Emile Guimet, this vast collection of Asian art is one of the largest and most complete in Europe. Here you'll find room after room of exquisite works from Afghanistan, India, Tibet, Nepal, China, Vietnam, Korea, Japan, and other Asian nations. You could spend an entire day here, or you could pick and choose regions of interest (displays are arranged geographically); the audioguide is a good bet for finding standouts and providing cultural context. Highlights include a marvelous Tibetan bronze sculpture (*Hevajra and Nairâtmya*) of a multiheaded god embracing a ferocious goddess with eight faces and 16 arms; a blissfully serene stone figure of a 12th-century Cambodian king (*Jayavarman VII*) who presided over a short-lived Khmer renaissance; and superb Chinese scroll paintings, including a magnificent 17th-century view of the Jingting mountains in autumn. Admission prices vary during temporary exhibitions.

6 pl. d'Iéna, 16th arrond. www.guimet.fr. ℂ **01-56-52-53-00.** Admission to permanent collection 8.50€ adults, 6.50€ ages 18–25, free for children 17 and under. Wed–Mon 10am–6pm. Métro: Iéna.

Musée Nissim de Camondo ★★ MUSEUM

Having made a fortune in his business ventures, in 1914 Count Moïse de Camondo built a mansion in the style of the Petit Trianon at Versailles and furnished it with rare examples of 18th-century furniture, paintings, and art objects (like a series of six Aubusson tapestries illustrating the fables of La Fontaine and a pair of bronze vases covered with petrified wood that once belonged to Marie Antoinette). After the count's death in 1935, the house and everything in it was left to the state as a museum, named after the count's son, who was killed fighting in World War I. The family's troubles did not stop there—in 1945, the count's daughter and her family were deported and died at Auschwitz. This little-visited museum is a delight. The count's will stipulated that the house be left exactly "as is" when it was transformed into a museum; as a result, you can wander through a fully equipped kitchen, a gigantic tiled bathroom, and salons filled with gilded mirrors, inlaid tables, and Beauvais tapestries—all in the same configuration as when Camondo lived there. Be sure to pick up a free English audioguide. Tickets can be combined with the Musée des Arts Décoratifs (p. 143; 20€).

63 rue de Monceau, 8th arrond. https://madparis.fr. ℂ **01-53-89-06-40.** Admission 12€ adults, free for ages 25 and under. Wed–Sun 10am–5:30pm. Métro: Villiers.

Musée Yves Saint Laurent ★★ MUSEUM

This wonderful museum for fashion lovers is set in the sumptuous 19th-century mansion Yves Saint Laurent used as his HQ from 1974 to 2002. The king of couture planned for a museum from the 1980s onward, marking important items with an "M" (for Musée). There are some 5,000 in all, plus over 15,000 accessories—which are now part of the Fondation Pierre Bergé – Yves Saint Laurent (which he started with his partner Pierre Bergé in 2002). Though Saint Laurent died in 2008 and didn't see the opening of the museum (in 2017), he would undoubtedly have been happy with the result: Successions of temporary retrospectives highlight both his career and his creative genius, resulting in rich and fascinating displays of game-changing outfits—like the Mondrian dress and the "smoking" tuxedo—as well as lesser-known pieces designed for the ballet and the theater. The spaces are beautiful, especially Saint Laurent's studio, filled with his books and sketches, unchanged, as if the great designer is about to come home.

5 av. Marceau, 16th arrond. https://museeyslparis.com. ℂ **01-44-31-64-00.** Admission 10€ adults, 7€ ages 10–18, free for children 9 and under. Tues–Thus and Sat–Sun 11am–6pm; Fri 11am–9pm. Métro: Alma Marceau.

Palais de Tokyo ★★ MUSEUM/PERFORMANCE SPACE If you're traveling with cranky teenagers who've had enough of La Vieille France, or if you're also sick of endless rendezvous with history, this is the place to come for a blast of contemporary madness. This vast art space not only offers a rotating bundle of expositions, events, and other happenings but is also one of the only museums in Paris that stays open until 10pm. While some might quibble about whether or not the works on display are really art, there's no denying that this place is a lot of fun. You'll find a completely different crowd here, one that is generally young and intense. There's no permanent collection, just continuous temporary exhibits, installations, and events, such as live performances and film screenings. The center, whose mission includes nurturing, promoting, and providing studio space for emerging artists, is one of the largest sites devoted to contemporary creativity in Europe. Check the website for what's on during your visit. In warm weather, you can eat on the splendid terrace of its chic, neo–Art Deco brasserie, **Monsieur Bleu,** which has Eiffel Tower views, or sip cocktails in its restaurant/bar **Bambini.** Both stay open until 2am.

13 av. du Président-Wilson, 16th arrond. www.palaisdetokyo.com. ⓒ **01-81-97-35-88.** Admission 12€ adults, 9€ ages 18–25, free for children 17 and under. Wed–Mon 10am–10pm. Métro: Iéna.

Parc Monceau ★★ PARK/GARDENS Located in a posh residential neighborhood and ringed by stately mansions, this small park is the brainchild of the duke of Chartres (the future Philippe Egalité), who commissioned a fanciful garden in 1769 filled with *folies,* faux romantic ruins, temples, and antiquities inspired by exotic faraway places. Don't be surprised to stumble upon a minaret, a windmill, or a mini-Egyptian pyramid here; the most famous *folie* is the **Naumachie,** a large oval pond surrounded in part by Corinthian columns. The park has had several makeovers over the centuries, but it is still essentially an English-style garden, complete with wooded glens and hillocks. A sizable **playground** is in the southwest corner, and there's a **merry-go-round** near the north entrance, where columns surround a **round pavilion;** the Duke of Chartres used to keep a small apartment on the second floor from which he could see the entire park.

35 bd. de Courcelles, 8th arrond. www.paris.fr. Free admission. 8am–sundown. Métro: Monceau or Villiers.

Petit Palais ★★ MUSEUM The collection may not be exhaustive, and you may not see any world-famous works, but you will enjoy a wonderful mix of periods and artists at this bijou fine arts museum, set in a sumptuous "little" palace built for the 1900 Paris Exposition (opposite the sumptuous, glass-roofed **Grand Palais** across the street, which is closed for renovations until 2024) . Its chronology stretches from the ancient Greeks to World War I, with paintings by masters like Monet, Ingres, and Rubens, an Art Nouveau dining room by Hector Guimard, and the exquisite multilayered glass vases of Emile Gallé. Those interested in earlier works will find Greek vases, Italian Renaissance majolica, and a small collection of 16th-century astrolabes and gold-and-crystal traveling clocks. Intricately carved ivory panels and delicately carved wood sculptures (including a grinning, long-locked Saint Barbara who looks like she is about to burst out in a fit of the giggles) stand out in the small medieval section, and a series of rooms dedicated to 17th-century Dutch painters like Steen and van Ostade is considered one of the best collections of its kind in France (after the Louvre). Refresh yourself after your visit at the cafe in the gorgeous inner courtyard.

av. Winston Churchill, 8th arrond. www.petitpalais.paris.fr. © **01-53-43-40-00.** Free admission to permanent collection. Tues–Sun 10am–6pm (Fri until 9pm during temporary exhibitions). Métro: Champs-Élysées–Clémenceau.

Place de la Concorde ★★★ SQUARE   Like an exclamation point at the end of the Champs-Élysées, the Place de la Concorde is a magnificent arrangement of fountains and statues, held together in the center by a 3,000-year-old Egyptian obelisk (a gift to France from Egypt in 1829). When it was inaugurated in 1763 during the reign of Louis XV, this vast plaza was on the outer edges of the city; today, though part of an urban landscape, it still gives the impression of open space. If it weren't for the cars hurtling around the obelisk like racers in the Grand Prix, this would be a delightful spot for a breath of fresh air (if you feel compelled to cross to the obelisk and you value your life, find the stoplight and cross there).

It's hard to believe that this magnificent square was once bathed in blood, but during the Revolution, it was a grisly stage for public executions: King Louis XVI and his wife, Marie Antoinette, both bowed down to the guillotine here, as did many prominent figures of the Revolution, including Danton, Camille Desmoulins, and Robespierre. Once the monarchy was back in place, the plaza hosted less lethal public events like festivals and trade expositions. In 1835 the *place* was given its current look: Two immense fountains, copies of those in St. Peter's Square in Rome, play on either side of the obelisk; 18 sumptuous columns decorated with shells, mermaids, sea horses, and other sea creatures each hold two lamps; and eight statues representing the country's largest cities survey the scene from the edges of the action. On the west side are the famous **Marly Horses,** actually copies of the originals, which were suffering from erosion and have since been restored and housed in the Louvre. On the north side of the square are two palatial buildings that date from the square's 18th-century origins: On the east side is the **Hôtel de la Marine** (p. 164, which opened in 2021 as a vast art museum to house the Qatarian Al Thani Collection), and on the west side is the **Hôtel Crillon,** where on February 6, 1778, a treaty was signed by Louis XVI and Benjamin Franklin, among others, wherein France officially recognized the United States as an independent country and became its ally.

8th arrond. Métro: Concorde.

Montmartre (18th Arrondissement)

Few places in this city will fill you with the urge to belt out sappy show tunes like the *butte* (hill) of Montmartre. Admiring the view from the esplanade in front of the oddly Byzantine **Basilique du Sacré-Coeur,** you'll feel like you have finally arrived in Paris, and that you now understand what all the fuss is about. Try to ignore the tour buses and crowds mobbing the church and the hideously touristy **Place du Tertre** behind you; instead, wander off into the warren of streets toward the **Place des Abbesses,** or up **rue Lepic,** where you'll eventually stumble across the **Moulin de la Galette** and **Moulin du Radet,** the two surviving windmills (of 30 that once stood on this hill). We have a walking tour on p. 268 which will lead you to these less-touristed gems and others.

Basilique du Sacré-Coeur ★ CHURCH   Poised at the apex of the hill like a *grande dame* in crinolines, this odd-looking 19th-century basilica has become one of the city's most famous landmarks. After France's defeat in the Franco-Prussian War, prominent Catholics vowed to build a church consecrated to the Sacred Heart of Christ as a way of making up for whatever sins the French may have committed that had made God so angry at them. Since 1885, prayers for humanity have been continually chanted here (the church is a pilgrimage site, so dress and behave accordingly). This multi-domed confection was inspired by the Byzantine churches of Turkey and Italy. Construction began in 1875, and the church was completed in 1914, though it wasn't consecrated until 1919 because of World War I. The white travertine

Stairs in Montmartre.

stone was chosen for its self-cleaning capabilities: In the rain, it secretes a chalky substance that acts as a fresh coat of paint. The interior of the church includes a breathtaking mosaic ceiling, installed in the 1920s. Most visitors climb the 300 stairs to the dome, where the splendid view of the city extends over 48km (30 miles).

Parvis de la Basilique, 18th arrond. www.sacre-coeur-montmartre.com. ℓ **01-53-41-89-00.** Free admission to basilica, joint ticket to dome and crypt 8.50€ adults, 5.50€ ages 4–16, free for children 3 and under. Basilica daily 6am–10:30pm; crypt and dome June–Sept daily 10:30am–8:30pm. Métro: Abbesses; take elevator to surface and follow signs to funicular.

Dalí Paris ★ MUSEUM   This tiny museum dedicated to the works of sur-realist Salvador Dalí won't take more than 45 minutes to visit, but what a 45 minutes you'll spend! The space is littered with erotic engravings, dreamlike objects, and whimsical furniture, not to mention Dalí's theatrical sculptures (the most important assembly in France), including a spindly-legged Space Elephant and several of his iconic soft watches, which seem to drip phantas-magorically to the floor. The man with the iconic moustache lived in Mont-martre with his wife and muse Gala, in an apartment at 7 rue Becquerel. It was from here in 1956, following a commission for Dalí to illustrate Cervantes' novel "Don Quixote," that the Catalan artist staged one of the *butte*'s most memorable artistic moments: the filming of him creating the first engravings. Against a windmill backdrop rose forth a knight on horseback, and Dalí true to form used two rhinoceros' horns and bread dipped in ink to create the illustrations. You can see some engravings from the series alongside others from the Bible and "Alice in Wonderland."

11 rue Poulbot, 18th arrond. www.daliparis.com. ℓ **01-42-64-40-10.** Admission 13€ adults, 9€ ages 8–26, free for children 7 and under. Wed–Fri 1–5pm; Sat–Sun 11am–5pm. Métro: Anvers, Abbesses, or Lamarck-Caulincourt.

Musée de Montmartre ★★ MUSEUM   The main reason to visit this small museum is to get an inkling of what Montmartre really was like back in the days when Picasso, Toulouse-Lautrec, Van Gogh, and others were painting and cavorting up on the *butte*. While there are few examples of the artists' works here, plenty of photos, posters, and even films document the neighborhood's famous history, from the days when its importance was mainly religious to the glory days of the Paris Commune, and finally to the artistic boom in the 19th and 20th centuries. Next to an original poster of dancer Jane Avril by Toulouse-Lautrec, for example, you'll see a photo of the real Jane Avril, as well as other Montmartre cabaret legends like Aristide Bruant and La Goulue. The few paintings and drawings by famed painters like Utrillo and Modigliani are supplemented by works by lesser-known Montmartrois like Steinlen, Léandre, and de Belay. The 17th-century house that shelters the museum was at various times the home of Auguste Renoir and Raoul Dufy, as well as Susan Valadon and her son, Maurice Utrillo, whose studio can now be visited. Surrounded by gardens and greenery, the site offers a lovely view of the last scrap of the Montmartre vineyard. English-language audioguides are a big help here. On a sunny day, stop for coffee in the garden cafe—it's a heavenly setting and great for small kids to run around without your having to worry about traffic.

12 rue Cortot, 18th arrond. www.museedemontmartre.fr. © **01-49-25-89-39.** Admission garden only 5€; museum 13€ adults, 10€ ages 18–25, 7€ ages 10–17, free for children 9 and under. Wed–Fri 11am–6pm; Sat–Sun 10am–7pm. Métro: Lamarck-Caulaincourt.

République, Bastille & Eastern Paris (11th & 12th Arrondissements)

While you can't really point to any major tourist attractions in this area, this part of town is seriously up-and-coming and has great nightlife and clothing stores, not to mention a booming restaurant scene. Some important historical sites are also here: The French Revolution was brewed in the workshops of the **Faubourg St-Antoine** and was ignited at the **Place de la Bastille.** The former stomping grounds of the medieval Knights Templar, the recently remodeled **Place de la République** is a potent symbol of the French Republic.

Atelier des Lumières ★★★ IMMERSIVE MUSEUM   If you've ever watched a light show projected onto the facade of a building, you'll know just how impressive they can be. But few shows can top this museum's offerings: Set in a converted foundry, the entire indoor space—floors, walls, and ceilings—is one monumental, moving canvas. Around 140 projectors and a high-tech sound system transport you smack-dab into famous paintings, as if you've shrunk and become part of the work. The first space covers the history of art, the second, smaller in size but no less impressive, is for today's emerging digital artists. Because of flashing lights and the overwhelming nature of the exhibits, people with epilepsy and kids ages 2 and under should not visit.

38 rue St-Maur, 11th arrond. www.atelier-lumieres.com. © **01-80-98-46-00.** 15€ adults, 12€ students 12–25, 10€ ages 5–25. Daily 10am–8pm.

Coulée Verte René-Dumont ★ WALKING TRAIL   Transformed from an unused train viaduct, this beautiful elevated garden walkway (also known by its former name, the Promenade Plantée) runs from the Place de la Bastille to the Bois de Vincennes. The 4.5km (2.8-mile) pedestrian path traces flower gardens, tree bowers, rose trellises, and fountains, taking you over the 12th arrondissement, past the Gare de Lyon, and through the Reuilly Gardens (home to fizzy drinking-water fountains). At ground level along avenue Daumesnil, the brick archways now shelter the **Viaduc des Arts,** a series of galleries and workshops that show off the work of highly skilled artisans.

Enter by the staircase on av. Daumesnil just past the Opéra Bastille, 12th arrond. www. parisinfo.com.

Musée des Arts Forains ★★ MUSEUM   This offbeat museum in Bercy's former wine warehouses is the largest of its kind in Europe, packed to the rafters with fairground memorabilia from the 19th and 20th centuries. It's a magical place, where Belle Epoque carousels populated by mermaids, horses, and fantastical carriages sit alongside weird and wonderful automated mannequins, Venetian carnival costumes, and even a hot-air balloon with an elephant-shaped basket. Light shows that make you feel you've stepped into a surreal version of the 2017 movie "The Greatest Showman" complete the offerings. English tours are during the summer only; tours are in French the rest of the year, but with English printouts, so you'll still be able to follow. Entrance is by tour only; reserving by phone or online is mandatory.

53 av. des Terroirs de France, 12th arrond. http://arts-forains.com. © **01-43-40-16-22.** Admission 18€ adults, 12€ ages 4–11, free for children 3 and under. Wed, Sat, and Sun times vary (reserve beforehand); daily during school vacations. Métro: Cour Saint-Emilion.

Parc de Bercy ★★ PARK Sandwiched between the AccorHotels Arena and Bercy Village (shops and movie theaters in former wine warehouses), Parc de Bercy is well off most tourists' radar. However, it bursts with photogenic, tree-shaded walkways, pretty lakes where herons strut their stuff, and themed gardens of roses and color-coded flower beds. The area around the Maison du Jardinage, a quaint house assimilated into the greenery, makes you feel as though you're in the countryside. The carousel (2.5€ ticket; cash only) provides a bit of extra excitement for small kids.

128 quai de Bercy, 12th arrond. Free admission. Mon–Fri 8am to sundown; Sat–Sun 9am to sundown. Métro: Bercy or Cour Saint-Emilion.

Parc Zoologique de Paris ★★ ZOO Lush and ecologically correct, this animal reserve invites visitors to five regions of the world, from the plains of Sudan to Europe, via Guyana, Patagonia, and Madagascar. Going for quality instead of quantity, the zoo may not have room for elephants and bears, but it does introduce visitors to animals they might not be familiar with, like the fossa, a catlike carnivore from Madagascar, or the capybara, a giant South American rodent. There is also a good sampling of zoo favorites like lions, baboons, penguins, and a troupe of giraffes—if you are lucky, you can get an up-close look while the latter lunch in the giraffe house. The enclosures are well adapted to their inhabitants, so much so that at times it's hard to see them. But if you are patient, you'll spy wolves peeking out of the foliage, or a bright red tomato frog gripping a vine. Home to more than 1,000 animals in all, the zoo still manages to feel human-sized—you can see the whole thing in a couple of hours. Don't miss the huge aviaries, one of which is home to a large flock of flamingos. In summer, the zoo stays open until 11:30pm on Thursdays, offering a great chance to catch the nocturnal animals at play.

Parc de Vincennes, 12th arrond. www.parczoologiquedeparis.fr. © **01-44-75-20-10.** Admission 20€ adults, 17€ students 12–25, 15€ children 3–11, free for children 2 and under. Mid-Oct to mid-Mar Wed–Mon 10am–5pm; mid-Mar to mid-May and Sept to mid-Oct Mon–Fri 10am–6pm, Sat–Sun and school holidays 9:30am–7:30pm; mid-May to end Aug daily 9:30am–8:30pm and night hours Thurs 7–11:30pm. Métro: Porte Dorée.

Place de la Bastille ★ SQUARE   The most notable thing about this giant plaza—aside from architect Carlos Ott's Opéra Bastille, a modern opera house opened in 1989—is the building that's no longer here: the Bastille prison. Now a revamped traffic circle with bike lanes and steps down to the Canal St-Martin, this was once the site of an ancient stone fortress that became a symbol for all that was wrong with the French monarchy. Over the centuries, kings and queens condemned rebellious citizens to stay inside the cold walls, sometimes with good reason, other times on a mere whim. By the time the Revolution started to boil, though, the prison was barely in use; when the angry mobs stormed the walls on July 14, 1789, only seven prisoners were left to set free. Be that as it may, the destruction of the Bastille came to be seen as the ultimate revolutionary moment; July 14 is still celebrated as the birth of the Republic. Surprisingly, the giant bronze column, the Colonne de Juillet, in the center honors the victims of a different revolution, that of 1830. Even more surprisingly, below the column is a crypt containing a mummy. Why the mummy is there is somewhat of a mystery, one that will hopefully be solved when the crypt opens its doors to the public in 2022.

12th arrond. Métro: Bastille.

Belleville, Canal St-Martin & La Villette (10th, 19th & 20th Arrondissements)

One of the most picturesque attractions in this area is the **Canal St-Martin** itself, which extends up to **La Villette,** a former industrial area that has been transformed into a gigantic park and cultural compound. Other intriguing outdoor attractions include the romantic **Père-Lachaise cemetery,** the resting place of France's most noteworthy notables, and the verdant **Buttes Chaumont park.** The Belleville neighborhood is home to one of the city's bustling Chinatowns, as well as many artists' studios.

Cimetière du Père-Lachaise ★★★ CEMETERY   Cemeteries are not usually on the top of anyone's must-see list, but this is no ordinary cemetery. Romantic and rambling as a 19th-century English garden, this hillside resting place (open in 1804) is wonderfully green, with huge, leafy trees and narrow paths winding around the graves, which include just about every French literary or artistic giant you can imagine, plus several international stars. Proust, Apollinaire, Colette, Delacroix, Seurat, Modigliani, Bizet, and Rossini are all here, as well as Sarah Bernhardt, Isadora Duncan, and Simone Signoret and Yves Montand (buried side by side, of course). Though some graves have simple tombstones, many are miniature architectural marvels, embellished with exquisite marble and stone figures, or even phone-booth-size chapels, complete with stained-glass windows. Some of the standouts include:

o **Héloïse and Abélard:** These two legendary lovers actually existed, and their 12th-century remains were brought here in 1817, when the city built them this monument. It's covered by an openwork Gothic chapel taken from an abbey in southwestern France.

The pretty Canal St-Martin waterway connects the Seine, near Bastille, to the Canal de l'Ourcq, near the Villette in the 19th arrondissement. When Parisians talk about *le canal*, they are usually referring to the popular stretch of the quays Jemmapes and Valmy, which begins just above République and runs up to Jaurès Métro. Inaugurated in 1825 with the aim of bringing fresh drinking water to the city center, the canal narrowly escaped being paved over in the 1970s. Canal St-Martin was listed as a historic monument in 1993, and today its tree-lined banks and arched bridges make it a delightful place to stroll, especially on Sundays when the east side is closed to cars. You can take a boat tour with **Paris Canal** (www.pariscanal.com; ℂ **01-42-40-29-00**) or **Canauxrama** (p. 199) or explore in a self-drive boat with **Marin d'Eau Douce** (p. 199).

o **Molière and La Fontaine:** Although there was no romantic link, the celebrated playwright and noted fable writer were also brought here in 1817 and placed in nearby sarcophagi, both of which stand appropriately high on pillars. If the authenticity of the remains is in doubt, they still make a fitting memorial to these two brilliant talents.

o **Oscar Wilde:** This huge stone monument is topped with a winged figure that resembles an Aztec deity. It's an elegant homage to the brilliant writer, who died a pauper in Paris in 1900. For many years it was covered in lipstick kisses, which eroded the stone, hence today's protective see-through barrier.

Celebrity graves can be hard to find, so a map is essential. You can usually find one at the newsstand at the exit of Père Lachaise Métro, or use the one in this book (see below). The website also has good maps, as well as the Paris municipal site (www.paris.fr; search for "Père Lachaise"). *Note:* Entry is via the gate opposite rue de la Roquette; the other entrances are generally closed.

16 rue de Repos, 20th arrond. www.pere-lachaise.com. Free admission. Mon–Fri 8am–6pm; Sat–Sun 8:30am–6pm (Nov to early Mar until 5pm). Métro: Père-Lachaise or Philippe Auguste.

Cité des Sciences et de l'Industrie ★★ MUSEUM   This gigantic and terrific science and industry museum was built upon the site of the city's former 19th-century slaughterhouse auction room, which had closed in 1974 due to competition from the suburban Rungis food market, leaving the city with derelict land to fill. Today it includes a planetarium, a 3D movie theater, and a multimedia library, not to mention a real submarine and a shopping mall. The heart of the museum is its permanent collection, which flaunts huge floors of interactive exhibits and displays on subjects like sound, mathematics, and human genes. On the ground floor, parents will be delighted to find the **Cité des Enfants** (separate admission, 12€ adults, 9€ under age 25 or over 65, for a 90-min. session; see website for hours; reservations essential, particularly during French school vacations), which has separate programs for 2- to 7-year-olds and 5- to

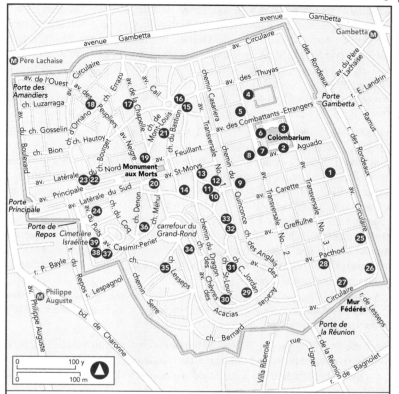

Abélard & Héloïse **37**

Guillaume Apollinaire **5**

Pierre-Auguste Beaumarchais **30**

Hans Bellmer **24**

Sarah Bernhardt **9**

Georges Bizet **17**

Maria Callas **3**

Frédéric Chopin **36**

Colette **23**

Auguste Comte **34**

Jean Baptiste Camille Corot **11**

Honoré Daumier **10**

Jacques-Louis David **19**

Honoré de Balzac **16**

Eugène Delacroix **15**

Gustave Doré **14**

Isadora Duncan **6**

Paul Eluard **26**

Max Ernst **2**

Théodore Géricault **20**

Jean-Auguste-Dominique Ingres **13**

Jean La Fontaine **33**

René Lalique **12**

Lefebvre Masséna **29**

Amedeo Modigliani **28**

Molière **32**

Jim Morrison **35**

Alfred de Musset **21**

Edith Piaf **27**

Camille Pissarro **38**

Marcel Proust **4**

Gioacchio Antonio Rossini **22**

Rothschild family plot **39**

Henri de Saint-Simon **31**

Georges Seurat **18**

Simone Signoret & Yves Montand **8**

Gertrude Stein & Alice B. Toklas **25**

Oscar Wilde **1**

Richard Wright **7**

12-year-olds. Kids get to explore the world around them in a series of hands-on activities and displays. If all this isn't enough, outside you can clamber into the **Argonaut** (access included with your ticket; must be over age 3 to enter), a real submarine that was one of the stars of the French navy in the 1950s, or dip inside the gigantic metal sphere called the **Géode** (12€ adults, 9€ age 25 and under; www.lageode.fr), an IMAX-type movie theater showing large-screen films.

Parc de La Villette, 30 av. Corentine-Cariou, 19th arrond. www.cite-sciences.fr. ✆ **01-40-05-80-00.** Varied ticket packages 12€ adults, 9€ visitors 25 and under, free for children 2 and under. Tues–Sat 9:15am–6pm; Sun 9:15am–7pm. Métro: Porte de La Villette.

Musée de la Musique ★ MUSEUM   Located on the north end of the Parc de la Villette, and part of the striking Philharmonie de Paris concert complex (p. 232), this museum has a permanent collection of over a thousand instruments, sculptures, paintings, and other objects that recount the history of music in Europe from the 16th to 20th centuries. Study a beautiful and rare 17th-century guitar with ivory inlay, a clutch of Stradivarius violins, or a concert piano that Franz Liszt once played on. A separate section on world music includes another 700 objects, mostly from Africa and Asia. As you wander about, you will probably come across live demonstrations by local musicians. The temporary exhibitions are always big hits here and include a program of top-notch concerts.

In the Cité de la Musique, 221 av. Jean-Jaurès, 19th arrond. https://philharmoniedeparis. fr. ✆ **01-44-84-44-84.** Admission 8€ adults, 7€ ages 27–28, free for visitors 26 and under. Mon–Sat 11am–7pm; Sun 11am–6pm. Métro: Porte de Pantin.

Parc de la Villette ★★ PARK   This vast complex, which includes a park, museums, concert halls, and other cultural institutions, was built on the site of the city's slaughterhouses, abandoned since the mid-1970s. Construction

---

Long Live the Lizard King

Though the grave itself is unexceptional, the tomb of 1960s rock star **Jim Morrison** is possibly the most visited, or at least the most hyped, in the cemetery. For years, fans made pilgrimages, leaving behind so much graffiti, litter, and mind-altering substances that families of those buried nearby began to complain, and the tomb was surrounded by a fence. Still, nothing can dispel the enduring attraction of the Morrison legend. In 1971, battling a variety of drug, alcohol, and legal problems, the singer/musician came to Paris, ostensibly with the goal of taking a break from performing and getting his life back on track. Four months later, he was found dead in a Parisian bathtub, at age 27. Since no autopsy was performed, the exact cause of his death was never known (although there was good reason to suspect a drug overdose), which has led to wild speculation on the part of his fans. Rumors still circulate that he was a target of the CIA or murdered by a witch, that he committed suicide, or that he faked his own death and is currently residing in India, Africa, or New Jersey under the name "Mr. Mojo Risin'."

The Géode in the Parc de la Villette is a 3D-IMAX cinema.

began in 1980, when Bernard Tschumi, a French-Swiss architect, was chosen to create an urban cultural park accessible to one and all. The park is certainly a success on the cultural end: It harbors **Cité de la Musique** and **Cité des Sciences et de l'Industrie**—two excellent museums—as well as the **Zénith** and **Cabaret Sauvage** concert halls, not to mention the **Philharmonie de Paris** (p. 232). As far as the green spaces go—well, let me put it this way: If it is possible for a park to have a sense of humor, this one definitely has one. Eleven themed gardens are dotted with 25 red *folies*—oddball contemporary structures that sometimes house a drink stand or an information booth, and sometimes are just there for the heck of it. The gardens range from the sublime to the silly; a few are strictly reserved for children (who can bring along their parents).

From mid-July to mid-August the **Cinéma en Plein Air** takes place Tuesday to Sunday at sundown, presenting classic movies for free.

19th arrond. www.villette.com. ⓒ **01-40-03-75-75.** Daily 6am–1am. Métro: Porte de Pantin or Porte de la Villette.

Parc des Buttes Chaumont ★ PARK   Up until 1860, this area was home to a deep limestone quarry, but thanks to Napoleon III, the gaping hole was turned into an unusual park, full of hills and dales, rocky bluffs, and cliffs. It took 3 years to make this romantic garden; over 1,000 workers and 100 horses dug, heaped, and blasted through the walls of the quarry to create green lawns, a cool grotto, cascades, streams, and even a small lake. By the opening of the 1867 World's Fair, the garden was ready for visitors. The surrounding area was, and still is, working-class; the Emperor built it to give this industrious neighborhood a green haven and a bit of fresh air. **Pony rides** are available for the kids on weekends and Wednesdays (3–6pm; www.animaponey.com); the park also has a **puppet theater,** a **carousel,** and **two playgrounds.** The *guinguette*-style (open-air) bar/cafe—**Rosa Bonheur** (p. 115), named after the 19th-century feminist artist—is a bucolic spot for drinks and snacks, staying open even after the park has closed.

Rue Botzaris, 19th arrond. Daily 7am–dusk. Métro: Botzaris or Buttes Chaumont.

THE LEFT BANK

Latin Quarter (5th & 13th Arrondissements)

For several hundred years, the students who flocked to this quarter spoke Latin in their classes at the **Sorbonne** (founded in the 13th c.). Today students still abound around the Sorbonne, and even though classes are taught in French, the name stuck. Intellectual pursuits aside, this youth-filled neighborhood is a lively one, with lots of cinemas and cafes. History is readily visible here, with remains dating back to the Roman occupation: The **rue St-Jacques** and **boulevard Saint-Michel** mark the former Roman *cardo* (main street), and you can explore the remnants of the **Roman baths** at the **Cluny Museum** (see below).

Jardin des Plantes ★★ GARDEN This delightful botanical garden, tucked between the Muséum National d'Histoire Naturelle (p. 184) and the Seine, is one of our favorite spots for a picnic and a stroll. Created in 1626 as a medicinal plant garden for King Louis XIII, in the 18th century it became an internationally famed scientific institution thanks to naturalist, mathematician, and biologist Georges-Louis Leclerc, Count of Buffon, with the help of fellow naturalist Louis Jean-Marie Daubenton. Today the museums are still part academic institutions, but you don't need to be a student to appreciate these lush grounds.

The garden also harbors a small but well-kempt zoo, the **Ménagerie, le Zoo du Jardin des Plantes** (www.mnhn.fr; ✆ **01-40-79-56-01;** 13€ adults, free for children 3 and under; daily 9am–6pm, until 6.30pm in summer). Created in 1794, this is the second-oldest zoo in the world (after the Tiergarten Schönbrunn in Vienna). Because of its size, the zoo showcases mostly smaller species, in particular birds and reptiles. But the healthy selection of mammals (240 to be exact) includes rare species like red pandas, Przewalski horses, and even Florida pumas. If you're interested in tropical plant life, don't miss the park's **Grandes Serres** (✆ **01-40-79-56-01;** 7€ adults, 5€ children and students ages 4–25, free for children 3 and under; Oct–Mar Wed–Mon 10am–5pm, Apr–Sept Wed–Mon 10am–6pm)—four magnificent 19th-century greenhouses that take you on a botanical journey from the jungle to the desert via a prehistoric plant section and a special area on New Caledonia's unique vegetation (76% of its plants cannot be found anywhere else in the world). It's fascinating if you've got a green thumb, and a good bet on a cold day.

Rue Geoffroy-St-Hilaire, 5th arrond. www.jardindesplantes.net. © **01-40-79-56-01.** Free admission to gardens. Daily 8am–dusk. Métro: Gare d'Austerlitz.

Manufacture Nationale des Gobelins ★ TAPESTRY FACTORY TOUR   Back in the 17th century, Louis XIV purchased this famed tapestry factory with the aim of furnishing his new château (Versailles) with the most splendid tapestries around. France's most skilled workers created sumptuous carpets and wall coverings using designs sketched by the top artists of the era. The workshop's reputation has survived the centuries, and the factory is still active, working with the same materials used in the time of Louis XIV (wool, cotton, silk). Still state-owned, today the factory operates under the auspices of the French Ministry of Culture and produces modern tapestries to hang in some of France's grandest public spaces. This is definitely not a mass-market operation—these tapestries take several years to finish. Highly skilled workers (who study for 4 years at the on-site school) work from paintings by contemporary artists to create enormous works of art. During the tour you'll watch weavers in action at their giant looms. To visit the ateliers, you must take a guided, 90-minute tour (in French; purchase tickets online).

42 av. des Gobelins, 13th arrond. www.mobiliernational.culture.gouv.fr. No phone. Tours 13€ adults, 8.50€ students. Tues–Thurs 3pm (tour). Métro: Gobelins.

Musée de l'Institut du Monde Arabe ★ MUSEUM   While it harbors a substantial collection, one of the biggest draws to this museum/library/research center is the building itself, designed by architect Jean Nouvel in 1987. The south facade is covered by a metallic latticework echoing traditional Arab designs, with 30,000 light-sensitive diaphragms that open and close according to how bright it is outside. The airy museum space presents a collection that emphasizes the diversity of peoples and cultures in the Middle East, reminding us, among other things, that it was the birthplace of all three major Western religions. While the collection is intellectually stimulating, if art is what you are after, the Islamic Art section of the Louvre will be more satisfying. Still, there's a terrific view of the Seine and Notre-Dame from the rooftop restaurant, plus an interesting cycle of concerts (12€–26€; tickets available online).

1 rue des Fossés St-Bernard, 5th arrond. www.imarabe.org. © **01-40-51-38-38.** Admission 8€, 4€ ages 12–26, free for children 11 and under. Tues–Fri 10am–6pm; Sat–Sun 10am–7pm. Métro: Jussieu, Cardinal Lemoine, Sully-Morland.

Musée National du Moyen Age/Thermes de Cluny (Musée de Cluny) ★★ MUSEUM   Ancient Roman baths and a 15th-century mansion set the stage for a terrific collection of medieval art and objects at this museum. Built somewhere between the 1st and 3rd centuries, the baths (visible from bd. St-Michel) are some of the best existing examples of Gallo-Roman architecture. They are attached to what was once the palatial home of a

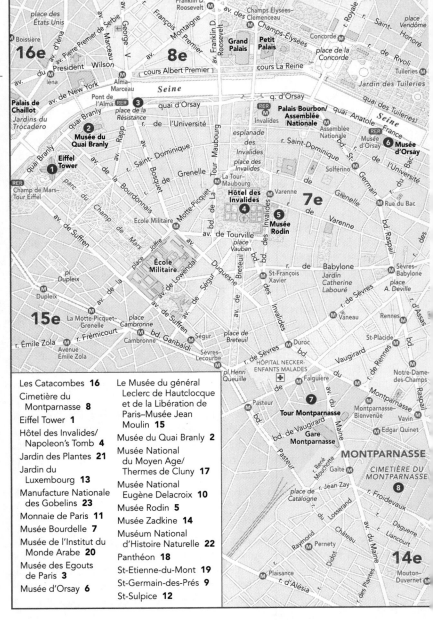

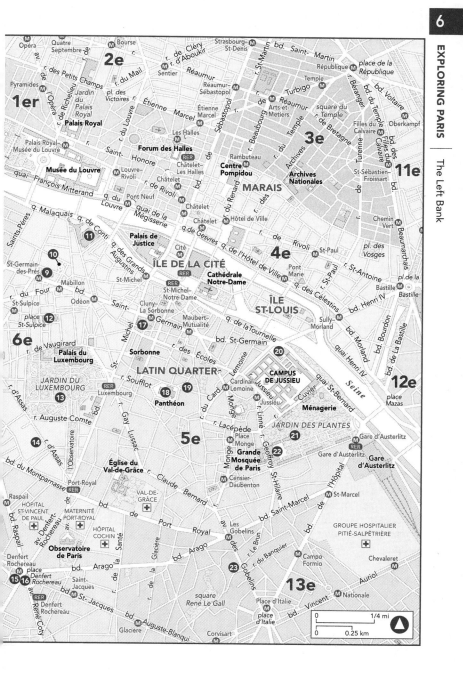

15th-century abbot, whose last owner, Alexandre du Sommerard, amassed a vast array of medieval masterworks. When he died in 1842, his home was turned into a museum and his collection put on display. Sculptures, textiles, furniture, and ceramics are shown, as well as gold, ivory, and enamel work. Of the several magnificent tapestries, the biggest draw is the *Lady and the Unicorn* series, one of only two sets of complete unicorn tapestries in the world (the other is at the Met Cloisters in New York City). In five of these late-15th-century tapestries, the lady, her unicorn, a lion, and various other symbolic representations of the animal and vegetable kingdoms illustrate the five senses. In the sixth she stands before a tent bearing the inscription "To My Only Desire" while placing a necklace in a case held by her servant. The meaning of this last tapestry remains an enigma—the mystery merely adds to its beauty.

6 pl. Paul Painlevé, 5th arrond. www.musee-moyenage.fr. *①* **01-53-73-78-00.** Admission 9€ adults, 5€ ages 18–24, free for children 17 and under. Wed–Mon 9:15am–5:45pm. Métro/RER: Cluny–La Sorbonne or St-Michel.

Muséum National d'Histoire Naturelle ★★ MUSEUM This natural history museum was established in 1793, under the supervision of two celebrated naturalists, Georges-Louis Leclerc, Count of Buffon, and Louis Jean-Marie Daubenton. Originally (and still) an academic research institution, this temple to the natural sciences contains a series of separate museums, each with a different specialty. The biggest draw is the **Grande Galerie de l'Evolution,** where a sort of Noah's ark of animals snakes its way around a huge hall filled with displays that trace the evolution of life and man's relationship with nature. It also has a virtual reality room that lets you get up close and personal to all sorts of animals (5€). One intriguing hall, the **Galerie de Minéralogie et de Géologie,** includes a room full of giant crystals, and another with eye-popping precious stones from the Royal Treasury, as well as various minerals and even meteorites. For dinosaurs, saber-toothed tigers, ancient humans, and thousands of other fossilized skeletons, repair to the **Galeries de**

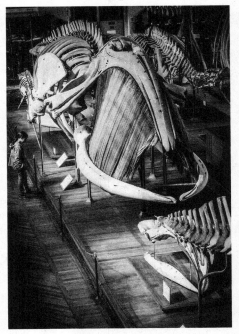

Galerie de l'Evolution in the Natural History Museum, Jardin des Plantes.

Paléontologie et d'Anatomie Comparée. The museum's **Galerie des Enfants** (children's gallery) offers hands-on interactive displays for little tykes. Except for the Grande Galerie, which has a joint ticket deal with the Galerie des Enfants, you'll have to pay for each *galerie* separately, but a ticket to one gives you a reduced rate at the others.

36 rue Geoffrey, 5th arrond. www.mnhn.fr. *©* **01-40-79-54-79.** Admission to each galerie 7€–13€ adults, free for visitors 26 and under. Wed–Mon 10am–6pm. Métro: Jussieu or Gare d'Austerlitz.

Panthéon ★★ CHURCH/MAUSOLEUM   High atop the "montagne" (actually a medium-size hill) of St-Geneviève, the dome of the Panthéon is one of the city's most visible landmarks. This erstwhile royal church has been transformed into a national mausoleum—the final resting place of luminaries such as Voltaire and Rousseau, Marie and Pierre Curie, World War II heroes of the Résistance, and (since 2021) the American-born entertainer and activist Josephine Baker, the first Black woman to be given a place in the monument. Initially dedicated to St-Geneviève, the church was commissioned by a grateful Louis XV, who attributed his recovery from a serious illness to the saint. The work of architect Jacques-Germain Soufflot, who took his inspiration from the Pantheon in Rome, it must have been magnificent—the vast interior was clearly created with a higher power in mind. However, during the Revolution its sacred mission was diverted toward a new god—the Nation—and it was converted into a memorial and burial ground for notable citizens of the Republic. The desired effect was achieved—the enormous empty space, lined with huge paintings of great moments in French history, resembles a cavernous tomb. The star attraction in the nave is **Foucault's Pendulum** (named after the French physicist Léon Foucault, who invented it in 1851), a simple device—a heavy ball suspended on a long wire above markers—that proves the rotation of the Earth. Visitors can climb the Panthéon's lofty dome between April and October (it was the highest spot in Paris until the Eiffel Tower was erected in 1889) to see the city unfurl in a higgledy-piggledy sprawl of gray rooftops. It's a breathtaking sight, spreading all the way out past the Eiffel Tower to the high-rises of Paris' out-of-town business district, La Défense.

pl. du Panthéon, 5th arrond. www.paris-pantheon.fr. *©* **01-44-32-18-00.** Admission 11.50€ adults, free for children 17 and under; dome 3.50€ extra. Apr–Sept daily 10am–6:30pm; Oct–Mar daily 10am–6pm; dome Apr–Oct only. Métro: Cardinal Lemoine. RER: Luxembourg.

St-Etienne-du-Mont ★★ CHURCH   One of the city's prettiest churches, this gem is a joyous mix of late Gothic and Renaissance styles. The 17th-century facade combines Gothic tradition with a dash of classical Rome; inside, the 16th-century chancel sports a magnificent **rood screen** (an intricately carved partition separating the nave from the chancel) with decorations inspired by the Italian Renaissance. Bookended by twin spiraling marble staircases, this rood screen is the only one left in the city. The entire church has been cleaned, making it easy to appreciate its riches, which include 16th- and 17th-century stained glass. A pilgrimage site, the church was once part of an abbey dedicated to St-Geneviève (Paris' patron saint), and stones from the saint's original sarcophagus lie in an ornate shrine here. That's about all that is left of her—the saint's bones were burned during the Revolution, and her ashes were thrown in the Seine. The remains of two other great minds, Racine and Pascal, are buried here.

1 pl. St-Geneviève, 5th arrond. www.saintetiennedumont.fr. (C) **01-43-54-11-79.** Free admission. Tues–Fri 10am–noon and 4–7:30pm; Sat 10am–noon and 3–8pm; Sun 10:30am–12:30pm and 4–8pm. Métro: Cardinal Lemoine. RER: Luxembourg.

St-Germain-des-Prés & Luxembourg (6th Arrondissement)

In the 20th century, the St-Germain-des-Prés neighborhood became associated with writers like Jean-Paul Sartre, Simone de Beauvoir, Albert Camus, and the rest of the intellectual bohemian crowd that gathered at **Café de Flore** (p. 132) or **Les Deux Magots** (p. 134). But back in the 6th century, a mighty abbey was founded here that ruled over a big chunk of the Left Bank for almost 1,000 years. The French Revolution put a stop to that, and most of the original buildings were pulled down. You can still find remains of both epochs in this neighborhood, notably at the 10th-century church **St-Germain-des-Prés** and the surviving bookstores and publishing houses that surround it. After your tour, relax at the delightful **Jardin du Luxembourg** nearby.

Jardin du Luxembourg ★★★ GARDEN   Out of the many parks and gardens in Paris, this is my personal favorite. Rolling out like an Oriental carpet before the Italianate Palais du Luxembourg (the seat of the French Senate since 1958, not open to the public), this vast expanse of fountains, flowers, lush lawns, and shaded glens is the perfect setting for a leisurely stroll, a relaxed picnic, or a serious make-out session, depending on who you're with. At the center of everything is a fountain with a huge basin, where kids can sail toy wooden sailboats (3€ for 30 min.) and adults can sun themselves on the green metal chairs at the pond's edge. Sculptures abound: At every turn there is a god, goddess, artist, or monarch peering down at you from his or her pedestal—Vulcan, Venus, George Sand, or Anne de Bretagne, to name but a few. The most splendid waterworks is probably the **Medici Fountain** (most easily reached via the entrance at Place Paul Claudel behind the Odéon), draped with lithe Roman gods sculptured by Auguste Ottin and topped with the Medici coat of arms, in honor of the palace's first resident, Marie de Médicis.

In 1621, the Italian-born French queen, homesick for the Pitti Palace of her youth, bought up the grounds and existing buildings and had a Pitti-inspired palace built for herself as well as a smaller version of the sumptuous gardens. She relocated here in 1625, only to be banished in 1630 for taking the wrong side against powerful Cardinal Richelieu. The palace passed on to various royals until the Revolution, when it was turned into a prison. American writer

Palais du Luxembourg.

Thomas Paine was incarcerated there in 1793 after he fell out of favor with Robespierre; he narrowly escaped execution. On the plus side, the Revolutionaries increased the size of the garden and made it a public institution. The orchards of the neighboring charterhouse were annexed, the remnants of which can still be visited at the southwest corner of the gardens. There, visitors can see a horticulture school where pear trees have been trained into formal, geometric shapes, as well as beehives maintained by a local apiculture association. After the Revolution, the palace and grounds stayed in government hands up until today (the palace houses the French Senate), with the exception of the Orangerie, which now holds the **Musée du Luxembourg,** 19 rue de Vaugirard, 6th arrond. (www.museeduluxembourg.fr; ✆ **01-40-13-62-00;** admission and hours vary with exhibits; Métro: Odéon, RER: Luxembourg), which is only open during its excellent temporary exhibits.

Entry at pl. Edmond Rostand, pl. André Honnorat, rue Guynemer, or rue de Vaugirard, 6th arrond. www.senat.fr/visite/jardin. ✆**01-42-34-20-00.** Free entry to the park; charges for playgrounds, see box p. 189. Daily 8am–dusk. Métro: Odéon. RER: Luxembourg.

Monnaie de Paris ★ MUSEUM Unbeknownst to most (even many Parisians), not only does Paris have its very own working—and somewhat palatial—coin minting factory on the edge of the Seine in St-Germain-des-Près, but it also comes with a Michelin-starred restaurant and an ever-changing roster of cutting-edge contemporary art exhibitions. The former royal mint, a Republican mint since the Revolution, makes for a fascinating hour's visit, showcasing the history of France's coinage as well as the history of money in general and the industrial process behind it all. Collectors will revel in the rare coin displays: One interactive area contains an écu—France's currency until the Revolution—from the reign of Louis XVI (the story goes it was partly because of his recognizable profile on the coin—Louis had a rather large nose—that he was caught while trying to escape during the Revolution). Other areas let you glimpse into the factory and try your hand at pressing your own coin. The visit ends in the boutique, which brims with collector's coins and jewelry. Don't leave without looking at the contemporary art displays dotted around the building; they contrast beautifully with the factory's palace-like neoclassical architecture, which dates from 1775.

11 quai Conti, 6th arrond. www.monnaiedeparis.fr. ℂ **01-40-46-56-66.** Admission 12€ adults, free for children 18 and under. Tues–Sun 11am–6pm (until 9pm on Wed). Métro: Pont Neuf or Mabillon.

Musée National Eugène Delacroix ★ MUSEUM

Housed in what was once the painter's apartment and studio, this small museum is dedicated to Eugène Delacroix, one of the greatest artists of the Romantic period. Delacroix was old and sick when he moved here in 1857 to be closer to the church of St-Sulpice, where he was decorating a chapel. He managed to finish the paintings 3 years before his death here in 1863. "It takes great fortitude to be yourself," he once said, and he certainly had it: At his death, he left behind some 8,000 paintings, drawings, and pastels. Though none of his major works are in the museum, several smaller paintings decorate the walls, including the mysterious *Mary Magdalene in the Wilderness.* Furniture, mementos, and other personal items are displayed, including the artist's palette and paint box. The museum is on the exquisitely beautiful rue de Furstenberg, a small, leafy square. ***Note:*** You can buy a joint ticket for the Louvre (p. 144) here too for 17€, which is the price of the Louvre's ticket alone.

6 rue de Furstenberg, 6th arrond. www.musee-delacroix.fr. ℂ **01-44-41-86-50.** Admission 7€ adults, free for children 17 and under. Wed–Mon 9:30–11:30am and 1–5:30pm (1st Thurs of month until 9pm). Métro: St-Germain-des-Prés or Mabillon.

Musée Zadkine ★★ MUSEUM

You could easily miss the alleyway that leads to this tiny museum in the small but luminous house where Ossip Zadkine lived and worked from 1928 until his death in 1967. A contemporary and neighbor of artists such as Brancusi, Lipchitz, Modigliani, and Picasso, this Russian-born sculptor is closely associated with the Cubist movement; he was also influenced by the art of Greece and Africa. His sober, elegant sculptures combine abstract geometry with deep humanity. Dozens of examples of his best works, like a superb 2.7m (9-ft.) plaster sculpture of biblical Rebecca carrying a water pitcher, or a vaguely African head of a woman in limestone, are displayed in small, light-filled rooms. Be sure to visit the artist's workshop, tucked behind the tranquil garden. ***Note:*** Because of the museum's small size, during temporary exhibits you'll have to pay to enter even the permanent collection (which is usually free).

100 bis rue d'Assas, 6th arrond. www.zadkine.paris.fr. ℂ **01-55-42-77-20.** Free admission to permanent collections. Tues–Sun 10am–6pm. Métro: Notre-Dame des Champs or Vavin.

Frazzled parents take note: The Jardin du Luxembourg has loads of activities for kids who need to blow off steam. First off, swings and slides fill a revamped **playground** (2€ adults, 2.50€ children 11 and under). Then there are the wonderful wooden **sailboats** (3€/30 min.) to float in the main fountain, as well as an ancient **carousel** (2.50€, next to the playground) to ride. At the **marionette theater** (www.marionnettesduluxembourg.fr; 6.80€ each, parents and children; Wed, Sat, Sun, and school vacation days, shows usually start at 3:15pm and 4:30pm; Sat–Sun additional shows at 11am), you can see Guignol himself (the French version of Punch) in a variety of puppet shows aimed at ages 2 to 6.

St-Germain-des-Prés ★★ CHURCH   The origins of this church stretch back over a millennium. First established in 543 by King Childebert, who constructed a basilica and monastery on the site, it was built, destroyed, and rebuilt several times over the centuries. Nothing remains of the original buildings, but the bell tower dates from the 10th century and is one of the oldest in France. Most of the rest of the church was built in the 11th and 12th centuries and is Romanesque in style. The church and its abbey became a major center of learning and power during the Middle Ages, remaining a force to be reckoned with up until the eve of the French Revolution. Once the monarchy toppled, however, all hell broke loose: The abbey was destroyed, the famous library burned, and the church vandalized. Restored in the 19th century, the buildings have regained some of their former glory, though the complex is a fraction of its original size.

The first thing you'll notice on entering is that much of the interior is painted in a dazzling range of greens and golds—one of the few Parisian churches to retain a sense of its original decor. Several murals by 19th-century artist Hippolyte Flandrin fill the archways in the nave. The heart of King Jean Casimir of Poland is buried here, as are the ashes of the body of René Descartes (his skull is in the collections of the Musée de l'Homme). On the left as you exit, you can peek inside the **chapel of St-Symphorien,** where during the Revolution over 100 members of the clergy were imprisoned before being executed on the square in front of the church. The chapel was restored in the 1970s and decorated by contemporary artist Pierre Buraglio in 1992.

Classical music concerts are regularly held in the church (tickets and information are at www.fnactickets.com). On the last Sunday of the month, afternoon organ recitals are free.

3 pl. St-Germain-des-Prés, 6th arrond. www.eglise-sgp.org. © **01-55-42-81-10.** Free admission. Daily 8am–7:45pm. Métro: St-Germain-des-Prés.

St-Sulpice ★★ CHURCH   The majestic facade of this enormous edifice looms over an entire neighborhood. Construction started in the 17th century over the remains of a medieval church; it took over 100 years to build, and one of the towers was never finished. Inside, the cavernous interior seems to command silence; several important works of art are tucked into the church's chapels. The most famous are **three masterpieces by Eugène Delacroix:**

Jacob Wrestling with the Angel, Heliodorus Driven from the Temple, and *St-Michael Vanquishing the Devil* (on the right just after you enter the church). Jean-Baptiste Pigalle's statue of the *Virgin and Child* lights up the Chapelle de la Vierge at the farthermost point from the entrance. A bronze line runs north–south along the floor; this is part of a **gnomon,** an astronomical device set up in the 17th century to calculate the position of the sun in the sky. A small hole in one of the stained-glass windows creates a spot of light on the floor; every day at noon it hits the line in a different spot, climbing up to the top of an obelisk and lighting a gold disk at the winter equinox. Because of their size, churches were an ideal spot for this type of measurement, making for a rare collaboration between science and religion.

pl. St-Sulpice, 6th arrond. www.paroissesaintsulpice.paris. ⓒ **01-42-34-59-98.** Free admission. Daily 8am–7:45pm. Métro: St-Sulpice.

Eiffel Tower & Les Invalides (7th Arrondissement)

The Iron Lady towers above this stately neighborhood stuffed with embassies and ministries, where the very buildings seem to insist that you stand up straight and pay attention. You'll see lots of elegant black cars with smoked glass cruising the streets, as well as many a tourist eyeing the **Eiffel Tower** or the golden dome of **Les Invalides,** and scurrying in and out of some of the city's best museums, like the **Musée du Quai Branly, Musée d'Orsay,** and **Musée Rodin.**

Eiffel Tower ★★★ MONUMENT   In his wildest dreams, Gustave Eiffel probably never imagined that the tower he built for the 1889 World's Fair would become the ultimate symbol of Paris, and for many, of France. Originally slated for demolition after its first 20 years, the Eiffel Tower is one of the most visited sites in the nation. No fewer than 50 engineers and designers worked on the plans, which resulted in a remarkably solid structure that, despite its height (324m/1,063 ft., including the antenna) does not sway in the wind.

Although the engineers rejoiced, others howled. When the project for the tower was announced, a group of artists and writers, including Guy de Maupassant and Alexandre Dumas *fils,* published a manifesto that referred to it as an "odious column of bolted metal." Others were less diplomatic: Novelist Joris-Karl Huysmans called it a "hole-riddled suppository." Despite the objections, the tower was built—over 18,000 pieces of iron, held together with some 2.5 million rivets. In this low-tech era, building techniques involved a lot of elbow grease: The foundations, for example, were dug entirely by shovel, and the debris was hauled away in horse-drawn carts. Construction dragged on for 2 years, but finally, on March 31, 1889, Gustave Eiffel proudly led a group of dignitaries up the 1,665 steps to the top, where he unfurled the French flag for the inauguration.

Over 130 years later, the tower has become such an integral piece of the Parisian landscape that it's impossible to think of the city without it. Over time, even the artists came around—the tower's silhouette can be found in the paintings of Seurat, Bonnard, Duffy, Chagall, and especially those of Robert Delaunay, who devoted an entire series of canvases to the subject. It has also inspired a range of stunts, from Pierre Labric riding a bicycle down the stairs from the first level in 1923, to Philippe Petit walking a 700m-long (2,296-ft.) tightrope from the Palais de Chaillot to the tower during the centennial celebration in 1989. Eiffel performed his own "stunts" toward the end of his career, using the tower as a laboratory for scientific experiments. By convincing the authorities of the tower's usefulness in studying meteorology, aerodynamics, and other subjects, Eiffel saved it from being torn down.

The most dramatic view of the tower itself is from the wide esplanade at the Palais de Chaillot (Métro: Trocadéro) across the Seine. From there it's a short walk through the gardens and across the Pont d'Alma to the base. Though several elevators whisk visitors skyward, they do take time to come back down, so be prepared for a wait. The first floor has a restaurant and a bit of glass floor, so you can pretend you are walking on air. Personally, I think the view from the second level is the best; you're far enough up to see the entire city, yet close enough to clearly pick out the monuments. But if you are aching to get to the top, an airplanelike view awaits. The third level is, mercifully, enclosed, but thrill-seekers can climb up a few more stairs to the outside balcony (entirely protected with a grill). The base of the tower is surrounded by bulletproof glass walls as part of a plan to protect visitors from terror attacks. Don't be alarmed: It's precautionary and not the sign of imminent danger, and you'll still be able to walk underneath for free once you've passed the security checks—though build in at least 20 minutes of extra time for passing the check points. The construction of the wall marked the start of a major modernization plan to improve access to the tower in general and provide shelter for visitors in bad weather. Paris wouldn't be Paris without the tower, so the monument will remain open throughout the work, which will last until 2031. *Note:* For all access, you now need to book a time-stamped e-ticket in advance online so you can spend as little time as possible in lines.

Champ de Mars, 7th arrond. www.tour-eiffel.fr. ℂ **01-44-11-23-23.** Lift to 2nd floor 16.70€ adults, 8.40€ ages 12–24, 4.20€ ages 4–11; lift to 2nd and 3rd floors 25.10€ adults, 13.10€ ages 12–24, 6.60€ ages 4–11; stairs to 2nd floor 10.50€ adults, 5.20€ ages 12–24, 2.60€ ages 4–11; stairs to 2nd floor and lift to the top 19.90€ adults, 9.90€ ages 12–24, 5€ ages 4–11. Free admission children ages 3 and under. At time of writing, opening times for 2022 had not been confirmed, so check the website for details. Métro: Trocadéro or Bir Hakeim. RER: Champ de Mars–Tour Eiffel.

Get a Workout & a Bargain at the Eiffel Tower

No need to go to the gym after marching up the 704 steps that lead you to the first and second floors of the Eiffel Tower. Not only will you burn calories, but you'll save money: At 10.50€ for adults, 5.20€ ages 12 to 24, and 2.60€ ages 4 to 11, this is the least expensive way to visit. Extra perks include an up-close view of the amazing metal structure and avoiding the long lines for the elevator. If you do decide to go to the top, buy a combined stairs and lift ticket (19.90€ adults, 9.90€ ages 12–24, and 5€ ages 4–11); as an adult, it'll save you 6.20€ from the lift-only price.

Hôtel des Invalides/Napoleon's Tomb ★★ MUSEUM Military history rules at this grandiose complex, which houses a military museum, church, tomb, hospital, and military ministries, among other things. Over the entryway, LUDOVICUS MAGNUS is inscribed in huge letters, in homage to the builder of this vast edifice, otherwise known as Louis XIV. Determined to create a home for wounded soldiers, Louis commissioned architect Libéral Bruant to design a monumental structure with formal gardens on what was then the outskirts of the city. The first war veterans arrived in 1674—between 4,000 and 5,000 soldiers would eventually move in, creating a minicity with its own governor. An on-site hospital, constructed for the severely wounded, is still in service today.

As you cross the main gate, you'll find yourself in a huge courtyard (102×207m, 335×207 ft.), the *cour d'honneur,* which was once the site of military parades. At the far end on the second story is a statue of "The Little Corporal" (Napoleon I) that once stood on top of the column in Place Vendôme. The surrounding buildings house military administration offices and the **Musée de l'Armée,** one of the world's largest military museums, with a vast collection of objects testifying to humankind's capacity for self-destruction. The most impressive section is **Arms and Armor,** a panoply of 13th- to 17th-century weaponry. Viking swords, Burgundian battle axes, 14th-century blunderbusses, Balkan *khandjars,* Browning machine guns, engraved Renaissance serpentines, musketoons, grenadiers—if it can kill, it's enshrined here. A huge wing covers the exploits of everyone from **Louis XIV to Napoleon III;** another wing covers the two **World Wars.** Also on-site is the **Musée des Plans et Reliefs,** a somewhat dusty collection of scale models of fortresses and battlefields, and the **Musée de l'Ordre de la Libération,** which retraces the history of the Liberation (1940–45).

The **Eglise des Soldats** is actually the front half of the **Eglise du Dôme,** which was split in two when Napoleon's tomb was installed under the dome. The "Soldier's Church" is lovely and light-filled, decorated with magnificent chandeliers and a collection of flags of defeated enemies.

On the other side of the glass partition rests the Little Corporal himself. The **Tomb of Napoléon** lies under one of the most splendid domes in France. Designed by Hardouin-Mansart and constructed from 1679 to 1706, the interior soars 107m (351 ft.) up to a skylight, which illuminates a brilliantly colored cupola fresco by Charles de la Fosse. Ethereal light filters down to an opening in the center of the room, where you can look down on the huge porphyry sarcophagus that holds the Emperor's remains, encased in five successive coffins (one tin, one mahogany, two lead, and one ebony). Surrounding the sarcophagus are the tombs of two of Napoleon's brothers, his son, and several French military heroes. Don't blame the over-the-top setting on Napoleon; the decision to transfer his remains to Paris was made in 1840, almost 20 years after his death. Tens of thousands of people crowded the streets to pay their respects as the coffin was carried under the Arc de

Triomphe and down the Champs-Élysées to Les Invalides, where it waited another 20 years until the spectacular tomb was finished.

pl. des Invalides, 7th arrond. www.musee-armee.fr ✆ **01-44-42-37-72.** Admission to all the museums, the church, and Napoleon's Tomb 14€ adults, free for children 17 and under. Daily 10am–6pm (Tues until 9pm). Métro: Latour-Maubourg, Varenne, or Invalides. RER: Invalides.

Musée des Egouts de Paris ★ MUSEUM   *Note: At time of writing, the museum had closed for extensive renovations, with reopening set for 2022.* If you want to get a better idea of Jean Valjean's underground ordeal in "Les Misérables," take a trip through Paris' sewer museum. Though you won't actually get on a boat, you will be able to walk through a short stretch of the city's 2,400km (1,490 miles) of sewers (don't worry, you'll be on a raised sidewalk on the side of the, uh, water), which should give you a pretty good idea of the different types of passageways and equipment that exist in this underground domain. Interactive circuits of displays will explain the history of the city's water supply and waste disposal issues (this was no joke; for centuries, the lack of a proper sewage system helped spread diseases like the Black Plague), as well as technical aspects of this stinky world. Because it's underground and part of the working system, the museum closes when the Seine is high.

Pont de l'Alma, in front of 93 quai d'Orsay, 7th arrond. www.paris.fr. ✆ **01-53-68-27-81.** Admission 4.40€ adults, 3.60€ students and children 6–16, free for children 5 and under. Times may vary after reopening. May–Sept Sat–Wed 11am–6pm; Oct–Apr Sat–Wed 11am–5pm. Métro: Alma-Marceau. RER: Pont de l'Alma.

Musée d'Orsay ★★★ MUSEUM   What better setting for a world-class museum of 19th-century art than a beautiful example of Belle Epoque architecture? The magnificent Gare d'Orsay train station, built to coincide with the 1900 World's Fair, has been brilliantly transformed into an exposition space. The huge, airy central hall lets in lots of natural light, which has been artfully combined with artificial lighting to illuminate a collection of treasures that were once scattered among the Louvre and the Musée National d'Art Moderne collections.

The collection spans the years 1848 to 1914, a period that saw the birth of many artistic movements, such as the Barbizon School and Symbolism, but today it is best known for the emergence of Impressionism. Seeing the styles all together in one place makes it instantly obvious what a fertile time this was. All the epoch's superstars are here: Monet, Manet, Degas, Renoir, Cézanne, and Van Gogh.

The top floor is the home of the most famous Impressionist paintings, like Edouard Manet's masterpiece, *Le Déjeuner sur l'Herbe.* Though Manet's composition of bathers and friends picnicking on the grass draws freely from those of Italian Renaissance masters, the painting shocked its 19th-century audience, which was horrified to see a naked lady lunching with two fully clothed men. Manet got into trouble again with his magnificent *Olympia,* a seductive odalisque stretched out on a divan. There was nothing new about the subject; viewers were rattled by the unapologetic look in her eye—this is not an idealized nude, but a real woman, and a tough cookie, to boot.

Musée d'Orsay.

The middle level is devoted to the post-Impressionists with works by artists such as Gauguin, Seurat, Rousseau, and Van Gogh, like the latter's *Church at Auvers-sur-Oise*, an ominous version of the church in a small town north of Paris where he moved after spending time in an asylum in Provence. This was one of some 70 paintings he produced in the 2 months leading up to his suicide.

A few other standouts:

o **Renoir's *Dance at Le Moulin de la Galette, Montmartre*:** The dappled light and the movement of the crowd in this joyous painting are such that you wonder if it's not going to suddenly waltz out of its frame. The blurred brushstrokes that created this effect rankled contemporary critics.

o **Monet's *La Gare St-Lazare*:** Here is another train station when steam engines were still pulling in on a regular basis. The metallic roof of the station frames an almost abstract mix of clouds and smoke; rather than a description of machines and mechanics, this painting is a modern study of light and color.

o **Gauguin's *The White Horse*:** The horse isn't even really white, but you don't care when you gaze at Gauguin's Tahitian version of paradise. Not everyone was charmed by the artist's use of vibrant color: The pharmacist who commissioned the painting refused it because the horse was too green.

Sculptures and decorative arts are also on display here, including a remarkable collection of Art Nouveau furniture and objects. Photo fans will appreciate the fine examples of early photography, including Félix Nadar's portrait of Charles Baudelaire; there are also some interesting works by nonphotographers like Edward Degas and Emile Zola.

1 rue de la Légion d'Honneur, 7th arrond. www.musee-orsay.fr. ℂ **01-40-49-48-14.** Admission 16€ adults, 13€ ages 18–25, free for children 17 and under. Tues–Wed and Fri–Sun 9:30am–6pm; Thurs 9:30am–9:45pm. Métro: Solférino. RER: Musée d'Orsay.

Musée du Quai Branly—Jacques Chirac ★★★ MUSEUM   Just a few blocks from the Eiffel Tower, this museum's wildly contemporary design has forever changed the architectural landscape of this rigidly elegant neighborhood. Its enormous central structure floats on a series of pillars, under which lies a lush garden, which is separated from the noisy boulevard out front by a huge glass wall. Looking up from the garden level, the museum looks a little like the hull of a container ship, with its rust-colored body and oddly stacked "boxes" sticking out from its sides. However you feel about the outside, you cannot help but be impressed by the inside: The vast space is filled with exquisite examples of the traditional arts of Africa, the Pacific Islands, Asia, and the Americas. Designed by architect Jean Nouvel, it makes an ideal showcase for a category of artwork that has too often been relegated to the sidelines of the museum world.

This magnificent collection is displayed in a way that invites visitors to admire the skill and artistry that went into the creation of these diverse objects. Delicately carved headrests from Papua New Guinea in the form of birds and crocodiles vie for attention with intricately painted masks from Indonesia. There's a selection of giant wooden flutes from Papua New Guinea, "magic stones" from the island nation of Vanuatu, Australian aboriginal paintings, an extensive Asian art section, and an African collection that includes embroidered silks from Morocco, geometric marriage cloths from Mali, and wooden masks from the Ivory Coast. The Americas collection includes rare Nazca pottery and Inca textiles, as well as an intriguing assortment of North American works, such as Haitian voodoo objects, Sioux beaded tunics, and a huge totem pole from British Columbia, Canada. Though some documentation is translated in English, **audioguides** (5€) are a big help for non-French speakers.

37 quai Branly and 206 and 218 rue de Université, 7th arrond. www.quaibranly.fr. ℂ **01-56-61-70-00.** Admission 10€ adults, free for children 17 and under. Tues–Wed and Fri–Sun 10:30am–7pm; Thurs 10:30am–10pm. Métro: Alma-Marceau. RER: Pont d'Alma.

Musée Rodin ★★★ MUSEUM   Behind the Hôtel Biron, which houses the museum, is a formal garden with benches, fountains, and even a little cafe (no picnics allowed, unfortunately). Of course, it would be foolish not to go inside and drink in some of the 6,600 sculptures of this excellent collection (don't worry, not all are on display), but it would be equally silly not to take the time to admire the large bronzes in the garden, which include some of

Rodin's most famous works. Take, for example, *The Thinker.* Erected in front of the Panthéon in 1906 during an intense political crisis, Rodin's first public sculpture soon became a Socialist symbol and was quickly transferred to the Hôtel Biron by the authorities, under the pretense that it blocked pedestrian traffic. Today, specialists query whether the man is actually "thinking" or mourning. Rodin was an admirer of classical sculpture and the way the hand supports the chin is in line with how Ancient Greeks depicted grief. Other important sculptures in the garden include the *Burghers of Calais, Balzac,* and the *Gates of Hell,* a monumental composition that the sculptor worked on throughout his career.

Indoors, marble compositions prevail, although you will also see works in terra cotta, plaster, and bronze, as well as sketches and paintings on display. The most famous of the marble works is *The Kiss,* which was originally meant to appear in the *Gates of Hell.* In time, Rodin decided that the lovers were too happy for this grim composition, and he explored it as an independent work. The sculpture was inspired by the tragic story of Paolo and Francesca, in which a young woman falls in love with her husband's brother. Upon their first kiss, the husband discovers them and stabs them both. As usual with Rodin's works, the critics were shocked by the couple's overt sensuality, but not as shocked as they were by the large, impressionistic rendition of *Balzac,* exhibited at the same salon, which critic Georges Rodenbach described as "less a statue than a strange monolith, a thousand-year-old menhir." Hundreds of works are here, many of them legendary, so don't be surprised if after a while your vision starts to blur. That'll be your cue to head outside and enjoy the garden.

79 rue de Varenne, 7th arrond. www.musee-rodin.fr. © **01-44-18-61-10.** Admission 13€ adults, 9€ ages 18–25, free for children 17 and under. Tues–Sun 10am–6:30pm. Métro: Varenne or St-Francois-Xavier.

Montparnasse (14th & 15th Arrondissements)

Even though its heart was ripped out in the early 1970s, when the original 19th-century train station was torn down and the **Tour Montparnasse,** an ugly skyscraper, was erected, this neighborhood still retains a redolent whiff of its artistic past. Back in the day, artists such as Picasso, Modigliani, and Man Ray hung out in cafes like **Le Dôme, La Coupole, La Rotonde,** and **Le Sélect,** as did a "Lost Generation" of English-speaking writers like Hemingway, Fitzgerald, Faulkner, and James Joyce. Today the cafes are mostly filled with tourists, but the neighborhood still has quiet corners and even artists' studios. Amazingly, **La Ruche,** the legendary artists' studio from the Golden Years, is still standing (https://laruche-artistes.fr). And of course, if you don't want to look at the Tour Montparnasse you should take the lift to the 56th-floor observation deck and marvel at the 360-degree views of Paris (www.tourmontparnasse56.com; 15€ adults, 12.50€ ages 12 to 18, 8€ ages 4 to 11, free for children 3 and under), or sip a cocktail in its panoramic bar, Ciel de Paris (www.cieldeparis.com).

Cimetière du Montparnasse ★ CEMETERY   This quiet cemetery is the final resting place of many French celebrities. A map to the left of the main gateway will direct you to the gravesite of its most famous couple, Simone de Beauvoir and Jean-Paul Sartre. Others resting here include Samuel Beckett, Guy de Maupassant, Pierre Larousse (famous for his dictionary), Capt. Alfred Dreyfus, auto tycoon André Citroën, sculptors Ossip Zadkine and Constantin Brancusi, actress Jean Seberg, composer Camille Saint-Saëns, photographer Man Ray, poet Charles Baudelaire, and American intellectual and activist Susan Sontag, who was interred here in 2005. You can download a map on the municipal website (see just below).

3 bd. Edgar-Quinet, 14th arrond. www.paris.fr/equipements/cimetiere-du-montparnasse-4082. ℂ **01-44-10-86-50.** Mon–Fri 8am–6pm; Sat 8:30am–6pm; Sun 9am–6pm. Métro: Edgar-Quinet.

Le Musée du Général Leclerc de Hautclocque et de la Libération de Paris–Musée Jean Moulin ★★★ MUSEUM   The museum with the longest name in Paris opened in 2019 in time for the 75th anniversary of the Liberation of Paris, and is a must for anyone interested in World War II history. Housed in brand-new buildings at Denfert-Rochereau (including revamped 18th-century pavilions built by the neoclassicist architect Nicolas Le Doux), the museum retraces the history of the Résistance and the figures who helped liberate France—notably Général Leclerc de Hautclocque (who famously joined De Gaulle's government-in-exile in Britain and furthered the Allied cause in Africa) and Jean Moulin, the head of the Résistance. The museum leads you through wartime events, with displays of around 300 items, including official documents and rare film archives. Part of the visit takes you through the underground bunker where Colonel Rol-Tanguy planned the Liberation of Paris.

pl. Denfert-Rochereau, 14th arrond. www.museesleclercmoulin.paris.fr. ℂ **01-71-28-34-70.** Free admission except to temporary exhibitions. Tues–Sun 10am–6pm. Métro/ RER: Denfert-Rochereau.

Les Catacombes ★ CEMETERY/HISTORIC SITE   Definitely not for the faint of heart, the city's catacombs are filled with the remains of millions of Parisians whose bones line the narrow passages of this mazelike series of tunnels. In the 18th century, the Cimetière des Innocents, a centuries-old, overpacked cemetery near Les Halles, had become so foul and disease-ridden that it was finally declared a health hazard and closed. The bones of its occupants were transferred to this former quarry, and were later joined by those of other similarly pestilential Parisian cemeteries. In 1814, the quarry stopped accepting new lodgers, and the quarry inspector had a novel idea. Rather than leaving just a hodgepodge of random bones, he organized them in neat stacks and geometric designs, punctuating the 1.5km (1 mile) with sculptures and pithy sayings carved into the rock. The one at the entrance sets the tone: STOP—HERE IS THE EMPIRE OF DEATH. The visit will be fascinating for some, terrifying for others; not a good idea for claustrophobes or small children

Catacombes.

(there are 243 steps). The lighting is appropriately eerie, so you should bring a flashlight if you really want to see. Explanations are in English, French, and Spanish. It's cool down here (around 12°C/54°F) and damp, so a jacket or sweatshirt and rubber-soled shoes are indispensable. For security reasons, only a limited number of people are allowed to visit at a time. Buy an e-ticket with a time slot online—you'll still have to wait in line, but hopefully not for more than 10 minutes. Advance tickets cost 15€ more than same-day e-tickets, but if you hold out for a same-day ticket, there may not be any left.

1 av. du Colonel Henri Rol-Tanguy, 14th arrond. www.catacombes.paris.fr. © **01-43-22-47-63.** Admission 14€–29€ adults, 5€ ages 18–26, free for children 17 and under. Tues–Sun 9:45am–8:30pm (last entry 7:30pm). Métro and RER: Denfert-Rochereau.

Musée Bourdelle ★ MUSEUM   Recently renovated and expanded, this museum is a testament to the sculptor Antoine Bourdelle (1861–1929), whose work went far beyond the 10 years he spent as Rodin's assistant. A renowned teacher who influenced an entire generation of sculptors, including Alberto Giacometti and Aristide Maillol, Bourdelle was one of the pioneers of 20th-century monumental sculpture. Proud, muscular centaurs, gods, and goddesses stride across these rooms, as well as monuments to famous people. You can also visit the sculptor's studio. **Audioguides** in English (5€) are a big help here.

18 rue Antoine-Bourdelle, 15th arrond. www.bourdelle.paris.fr. © **01-49-54-73-73.** Free admission to the permanent collection. Tues–Sun 10am–6pm. Métro: Montparnasse-Bienvenüe.

ORGANIZED TOURS & CLASSES

If you've only got a couple of days and you just don't have the stamina to do the research, an organized tour can provide good background information on the city and help you get your bearings. Here are a few ideas for getting to know Paris in an easy and different way.

Boat Tours

The famed **Bateaux-Mouches** (www.bateaux-mouches.fr; ℂ **01-42-25-96-10**; Métro: Alma-Marceau) cruises leave from Pont de l'Alma on the Right Bank of the Seine, and last for a little over an hour. They tend to be touristy but can be a worthwhile way to enjoy the beauty of the Seine's sites. Tickets cost 14€ for adults, 6€ for kids 4 to 11, and are free for children 3 and under; the recorded commentary is in French, English, and up to three other languages. Brunch, lunch, and dinner cruises are also available (ranging 55€–139€).

On the other side of the river, in front of the Eiffel Tower, the **Bateaux Parisiens** (www.bateauxparisiens.com; ℂ **01-76-64-14-45**; Métro: Bir Hakeim, RER: Champ de Mars–Tour Eiffel) offers similar 1-hour tours (recorded commentary), but in smaller boats. Tickets cost 15€ for adults, 7€ children 3 to 12, and are free for children 2 and under. Bateaux Parisiens also runs a tour departing from Notre-Dame, but the service is less regular. Gourmet lunch and dinner cruises start at 69€ for lunch, and 99€ for dinner.

A little less touristy, **Vedettes du Pont Neuf** (www.vedettesdupontneuf.com; ℂ **01-46-33-98-38**; Métro: Pont Neuf) runs 1-hour cruises with live guides in French and English from the Square du Vert Galant at the tip of the Île de la Cité. Tickets cost 14€ for adults, 8€ children ages 4 to 12, and are free for children 3 and under; cheaper tickets can be bought online.

Canauxrama (www.canauxrama.com; ℂ **01-42-39-15-00**; Métro: Jaurés or Bastille) tours both the Seine and the picturesque Canal St-Martin. For the canal, boats leave from either the Bassin de la Villette or the Bassin de l'Arsenal (near the pl. de la Bastille); tickets cost 18€ and are free for children 4 and under. The cruise takes about 2½ hours. The first part, which runs through a tunnel under the Place de la Bastille, is eerie (in a fun way), and afterward you'll enjoy a lovely ride through locks and under pretty arched bridges. Tours daily from May to September; less frequent service the rest of the year.

Multi-Michelin-starred chef Alain Ducasse launched the city's first ever fine-dining tour on an electric boat in the Seine: **Ducasse sur Seine** (www.ducasse-seine.com; Métro: Trocadéro) is a 180-person vessel offering 90-minute cruises and contemporary seasonal cuisine. It's docked at Port Debilly on the Right Bank opposite the Eiffel Tower. Lunch and dinner cruises start at 95€ and 150€.

Marin d'Eau Douce, Bassin de la Villette, 37 quai de Seine, 19th arrond. (www.boating-paris-marindeaudouce.com; ℂ **09-70-71-40-60**; Métro:

Such websites as **GetYourGuide.com, Viator.com, ToursByLocals.com, TakeWalks.com,** and **Airbnb.com/ experiences** are undeniably convenient to use. In just a few minutes you can have advance reservations and/or tickets for tours, museums, historic sites, cooking classes, guided walks, and more. These sites also include reviews from recent customers; sometimes they'll offer discounts on high-volume products like bus and boat tours.

But there can be downsides to using them. Because these websites take a significant commission from these tour providers and attractions, sometimes the price charged will be higher than it would have been had you gone directly to the source. I recently purchased a cooking class in Paris for $85. At the class I learned that a fellow student had paid $135 to one of the above companies—for the same experience. The chef needed to make ends meet and so charged those who didn't book with her directly significantly more. She did so quietly—the web company she works with has a price guarantee—but her actions are not uncommon.

As well, many of these companies sell priority access for a bit extra, allowing their customers to get on the "reserve line" rather than the regular one. But before Covid-19, many travelers were reporting, especially at such sites as the Eiffel Tower, that so many folks were anteing up for VIP treatment that the "reserve line" moved just as slowly as the regular one. And post-pandemic, tourism may be so low (at least for a while) that you can get into attractions without big lines anyway. Just a small warning.

Stalingrad or Jaurès), has a fleet of electric self-guide vessels (for up to 5, 7, or 11 people) that don't require licenses, leaving you free to whoosh up and down the Canal de l'Ourcq to see little-known parts of the city. If you opt for the 1-hour cruise (40€–80€), you have to stick to the Bassin de la Villette, a 1km (.6-mile) lake-like stretch of water; the 2-hour (70€–140€), 3-hour (90€–190€), half-day (140€–230€), and full-day (200€–310€) routes let you zip along the canal past Parc de la Villette and out of Paris into Pantin, an up-and-coming area that has been (somewhat optimistically) coined the Brooklyn of Paris.

Bus Tours

Yes, they're touristy, and yes, Paris is easy to navigate without an organized bus tour, but hop-on-hop-off buses are worth considering if (1) you're in a hurry and want to see all the main sights in 1 or 2 days, and (2) you don't want to use the public transportation system. For the former, I suggest the **Big Bus Paris** company (www.bigbustours.com; ✆ **01-53-95-39-53;** 1-day adult ticket 39€, 2-day adult ticket 45€, 19€ children 4–12; prices cheaper online), which has just two routes, one stopping at 10 top sites (including the Eiffel Tower and Notre-Dame), and the other covering Montmartre. The key to these tours is not actually hopping on and off (although you could, of course), but staying on board to see everything in one sweep—in 2¼ hours for the main tour and in 1¼ hours for Montmartre—leaving you with plenty of time for serendipitous exploring of your own. To avoid using public transport, I suggest **TootBus** (www.tootbus.com; ✆ **01-42-66-56-56;** 1-day adult pass 39€, 2-day 45€, 19€ children 4–15), which has over 75 stops spread over four routes that run from around 9am to 5pm (and from 9pm in summer for night tours) just like normal buses. The advantage is that you will only be with like-minded visitors; the downside is that you may have a long wait between buses.

Whichever tour you choose, multilingual audioguides are provided (you can switch them off if you just want to look at the city), and both sell tickets that can be combined with a river cruise (see websites for details).

Cycling Tours

Fat Tire Bike Tours (www.fattiretours.com/paris; ✆ **01-82-88-80-96,** or in North America 866/614-6218; Métro: Dupleix) offers a 3½-hour day-tour of Paris by bike in English; adult tickets cost 34€, 32€ students and children ages 4 to 12. Kid-size bikes and toddler trailers are available, and the tour includes a break in a cafe in the Tuileries Gardens (where children can run around), so this is a good one to choose if you're traveling with your family. They also offer night tours and tours of Versailles and Monet's Garden in Giverny.

If you'd like to see Paris like a local, pick **Paris à Vélo,** 22 rue Alphonse Baudin, 11th arrond. (https://parisavelo.fr; ✆ **01-48-87-60-01;** Métro: Richard Lenoir). In addition to their "Heart of Paris" tour (which covers the Marais and the Louvre area), they offer two themed 3-hour bike tours—Unusual Paris and Paris Contrasts—both of which take you into areas tourists don't usually get to see. The first goes to the southern 13th and 14th arrondissements, home to cobbled lanes and artists' workshops; the second is to northern Paris, along the canals and on to futuristic Parc de la Villette. Tickets cost 35€ adults, 28€ ages 12 to 25, 20€ for children 11 and under. They also rent bikes. Tours are in French and English.

Bike About Tours (www.bikeabouttours.com; ✆ **06-18-80-84-92**) offers 3½-hour tours in small groups, led by friendly, knowledgeable, fluent-English speakers for 45€ per person (20€ children). All tours leave from Le Peleton Café (17 rue du Pont Louis-Philippe, 4th arrond.; www.facebook.com/lepelotoncafe) and cover all the main sights via the city's atmospheric back streets. They also include a pit stop in a Left Bank bakery (food not included) and a few quirky stop-offs, like at Jim Morrison's house and places where famous movies were shot. Bike rentals also available.

Walking Tours

Sight Seeker's Delight (www.sightseekersdelight.com; ✆ **07-63-07-09-68**) offers a range of walking tours in English, including Paris Along the Seine, Tickle Your Tastebuds, and Secrets of the Night. Tours last from 2½ to 4 hours and prices vary between 30€ and 99€ per person (half-price for ages 4–10, free for children 3 and under).

Paris Walks (www.paris-walks.com; ✆ **01-48-09-21-40**) organizes 2-hour walks of the city, based on either a theme or a neighborhood. Most of the walks cost 25€ for adults, 10€ ages 15–20, 8€ children 14 and under; special small-group themed tours (chocolate, the Louvre, fashion) range from 20€ to 40€ per adult. Reservations are only necessary for special tours.

Paris Greeters (https://greeters.paris) arranges free tours for one to six people with local volunteers. There's no catalog of specific tours; your walk is pretty much up to the greeter, who will choose a neighborhood. Register online and request a specific day and language; you'll then be contacted with the tour details.

Entrée to Black Paris (www.entreetoblackparis.com) runs a few good tours, from gourmet walks to art-themed visits (for around 25€ for adults and 15€ ages 20 and under). But where it really stands out is with its tours covering themes such as Black history around the Jardin du Luxembourg (scheduled roughly once a week) and Josephine Baker. These walks highlight the life and works of Black figures such as American authors Richard Wright and Chester Himes, and French writer Alexandre Dumas (famed for—among other works—*The Count of Montecristo* and *The Three Musketeers*), whose grandmother was an enslaved person of African descent. Tours usually last 2 hours.

Other Guided Tours

4 Roues Sous 1 Parapluie (www.4roues-sous-1parapluie.com; © **01-58-59-27-82**) offers chauffeur-driven themed rides around Paris in its colorful fleet of Citroën 2CV, the tiny, low-cost, and now classic French car that was jokingly referred to as "4 wheels under an umbrella." If there are three people in the car, prices start at 32€ per person for a 45-minute tour and 64€ per person for a 90-minute tour; the price of the car is the same, it's simply a question of how you divvy up the bill.

Paris and perfume also go hand in hand, but while most people can name perfume brands, few can actually accurately describe what they're smelling. Cue **Rendez-Vous Parfum** (www.rendezvousparfum.fr; © **06-35-53-40-47**), an olfactory tour led by Sophie Irles, who—as a perfume developer for major companies like Burberry and Lancel—is to perfume what a sommelier is to wine. The tour, which usually takes place in the Marais, teaches you about things like the groups of scent, how they interact, and the history of perfume, and of course, where to buy some to take home. It's a fascinating 2 hours and at 40€, money well spent.

Cooking Classes

Several cooking schools in Paris offer short-term or 1-day courses. The most famous is **Le Cordon Bleu** (www.cordonbleu.edu; © **01-85-65-15-00;** Métro: Vaugirard)—this is where Julia Child mastered the art of French cooking. Well-known for its professional cooking courses, it also offers short courses for lay food enthusiasts, with prices starting at 105€ for a 2-hour food and wine pairing demonstration and 120€ for macaron-making lessons. Classes are translated into English and fill up fast; reserve ahead.

At **Le Foodist** (www.lefoodist.com; ✆ **06-71-70-95-22**; Métro: Place Monge), over the course of several hours, students don't just master recipes—they learn techniques that they'll be able to use in numerous situations. Since this is delivered with brio and wit by owner Fred and his charming wife, Amanda, the classes are never dull. A range of options is offered, from croissant- and macaron-baking to wine tasting (99€–219€). The highlight, however, is the market visit and class, during which students accompany Fred through the lively Latin Quarter to an open-air market and sample scrumptious cheeses. After cooking together, everyone sits down to a delicious meal with wine.

Equally enjoyable are the cooking classes offered by **La Cuisine Paris** (www.lacuisineparis.com; ✆ **01-40-51-78-18**; Métro: Hôtel de Ville), a friendly school set up by a Franco-American team. It offers market tours and small classes by professional chefs in both French and English, including the popular French macaron class. Prices range from 99€ for 2 hours to 165€ for 5 hours.

Similarly, **Les Secrets Gourmands de Noémie** (www.lessecrets gourmandsdenoemie.com; ✆ **06-64-17-93-32**; Métro: La Fourche or Brochant) offers a range of individual and small-group classes, the most popular of which is the fabulous pastry class. All classes are taught in English by Noémie, who trained at the prestigious Le Nôtre cooking school. Prices start at 85€ for a 2½-hour class.

Language Classes

The **Alliance Française** (www.alliancefr.org; ✆ **01-42-84-90-00**) has been offering quality French language classes for over a century. Depending on how many hours and what kind of course you take, courses cost around 280€ per week for 1 to 4 weeks for spoken French; rates go down the more weeks you attend. There's also a 65€ joining fee.

ESPECIALLY FOR KIDS

Paris is not a particularly kid-friendly city, but it's not kid-unfriendly, either. For one, Parisians generally like kids, as long as they are not running wild. If you visit in the summer, in addition to the suggestions below, just about any age child (including grown-up ones) will have a blast at **Paris Plage** or along the reopened banks of the Seine, **Les Berges,** between Musée d'Orsay and Pont d'Alma, and the **Rives de Seine,** between Bastille and Tuileries (see box, below). Here are some attractions that children may enjoy:

Bois de Boulogne (p. 205)
Bois de Vincennes (p. 207)
Centre Pompidou (p. 155)
Château de Vincennes (p. 208)
Cité des Sciences et de l'Industrie (p. 176)
Les Dimanches au Galop (p. 48)

FOR TINY TOTS (0–5 YEARS OLD): Paris has many nice **playgrounds** with safe equipment. For precise locations, visit https://en.parisinfo.com (search "playground"), ask at your hotel, or just follow the strollers. The Jardin du Luxembourg (p. 186) has multiple activities and a large fountain where you can **rent wooden toy sailboats** (for around 3€) and push them around with a long stick. Most large gardens or parks in this book have a **merry-go-round;** visit www.offi.fr (search "manèges").

FOR THE MIDDLE YEARS (6–9 YEARS OLD): This is when it's time to turn to attractions like **Musée Grévin** (p. 153), the **Cité des Enfants** (p. 176), and the **Jardin d'Acclimatation** (see below), and if you are really desperate, there's always **Disneyland Paris** (p. 265). The **Parc Zoologique de Paris** (p. 174) is a good bet, as is another, smaller **zoo** at the Jardin des Plantes (the **Ménagerie,** p. 180). The revamped Les Halles district has an adventure playground, the **Jardin Nelson Mandela** (1 rue Pierre Lescot), with a trampoline and swings.

FOR THE TWEENS (10–13 YEARS OLD): At this age, the scale can tip both ways, between "not another museum!" and actually getting interested in some of the cultural offerings. A few museums are particularly suited to this age, like the **Musée des Arts et Metiers** (p. 160), the **Gaîté Lyrique** (p. 156), and, in particular, the **Cité des Sciences et de l'Industrie** (p. 176). **Boat** or **bike tours** (p. 199) also work for this crew, as does the **FlyView** (p. 152) virtual reality ride.

Jardin d'Acclimatation ★ AMUSEMENT PARK/GARDEN   You'll see plenty of grandmothers in designer coats at this elegant amusement park, which is adjacent to the swank suburb of Neuilly. There's a farm with some animals, but the main attractions here are the rides, which include bumper cars, merry-go-rounds, and small roller coasters. As the rides (*manèges*) quickly add up (you pay as you go), you may want to point your offspring in the direction of the huge playground, which includes an area where kids can run around under giant sprinklers in the hot weather. In the same area, you'll find a puppet theater (Wed, Sat–Sun, and school holidays 3 and 4pm) where the French puppet Guignol's adventures are presented free of charge. To reach the park from Porte Maillot, take the *Petit Train* (little train; ticket 3.50€) from Allée de Longchamp at the entrance to the Bois de Boulogne. If you have kids that rush around trying everything, buy a day passport (35€) for park entry and unlimited attractions.

Bois de Boulogne. www.jardindacclimatation.fr. ✆ **01-40-67-90-85.** Admission 6.50€ adults and children ages 3 and up, 3.20€ seniors, free for children 2 and under; attractions 3.50€/ticket, 39€ book of 15 tickets. Mon–Fri 11am–6pm; Sat–Sun and school holidays 10am–7pm. Métro: Sablons or Porte Maillot.

ACTIVE PARIS

"Working out" is now an important part of Parisian life, with gyms cropping up all over the place. The problem is that nearly all require an annual fee, so they're hard to access as a visitor. However, any enterprising sports enthusiast can easily find places to bike, in-line skate, or run.

Cycling

You can **rent a bike** by the hour in the **Bois de Vincennes** at Lac Daumesnil or Lac des Minimes and in the **Bois de Boulogne** (in front of the Jardin d'Acclimatation or next to the Lac Inferieur [lower lake]). If you are up to the challenge of Parisian traffic and want to cycle around the city, you can try **Vélib'** (the city's wildly popular self-service bike program) and other similar programs (p. 290). For longer-term rentals, try **Paris à Vélo** (https://paris avelo.fr) or **Bike About Tours** (www.bikeabouttours.com).

Ice Skating

Two **indoor ice-skating rinks** are open to the public: **Espace Glace** at the Espace Sportif Pailleron, 32 rue E. Pailleron, 19th arrond. (www.pailleron19. com; ✆ **01-40-40-27-70;** Métro: Bolivar), open year-round, and **Patinoire AccorHotels Arena,** 222 Quai de Bercy, 12th arrond. (www.accorhotelsarena. com/fr/arena/la-patinoire; ✆ **01-58-70-16-75;** Métro: Bercy), open September to May. The latter has DJ–hosted soirées until midnight Fridays and Saturdays. In addition, every year **outdoor rinks** are set up from December through February in public spaces; two of the best are found on the **Champs de Mars** park and at **Trocadéro,** where you can fill up on Eiffel Tower views as you glide. Both are free—you'll just have to pay a small fee for skate rental.

Parks

Bois de Boulogne ★★ PARK   In the 7th century, Dagobert, King of the Francs, used to go hunting in the woods that we now know as the Bois de Boulogne; it remained a hunting domain for the kings of France up until Louis

In a bid to make Paris more environmentally and visitor-friendly, portions of the Seine's banks have been turned into pedestrian- and bike-only stretches. The first part covers the area between the Musée d'Orsay to the Pont d'Alma (known as **Les Berges,** or "the embankments"), and since 2017, the quays between Bastille and the Tuileries Gardens have also been embellished with promenades, gardens, cultural spaces, cafes, sports facilities, and picnic areas along a stretch known as the **Rives de Seine.** This is great news for walkers, as it's now possible to stroll between Bastille and the Eiffel Tower (across bridges) without meeting a single car! You can also eat, drink, flirt at one of the bars, walk, or even take a tai chi class at various points along the route. You'll find kids activities here, too.

Another hugely successful riverside event is now into its second decade: **Paris Plage.** Every year from mid-July to mid-August, tons of sand is shipped in and dumped on the riverbanks to create a fun and funky "beach," complete with beach volleyball, tea dances, concerts, drink stands, and all sorts of excellent silliness. Success has been such that the beach can be found not only on the Voie Georges Pompidou (near the Hôtel de Ville, 4th arrond.) but also along edges of the Bassin de la Villette (19th arrond.), where you can rent electric boats, paddleboats, and canoes. The number of activities and events swells every season; for a complete rundown, visit the city's **Que Faire à Paris (What to Do in Paris)** website: https://que-faire.paris.fr/parisplages.

XVI, who finally opened it up to the public. Thick stands of trees, broken up by grassy knolls, manicured gardens, and even a lake or two plus several posh restaurants are tucked into this verdant spread. There is even a nice spot for tiny urbanites to unwind: The **Jardin d'Acclimatation** (see above), a large children's garden/amusement park, is a delight for kids of all ages.

Once Louis XVI was beheaded, and the Revolution got underway, the park was ravaged. It wasn't until Napoleon III decided to remodel the entire city in the mid-1800s that the Bois de Boulogne was attended to. Inspired by the English public parks that he had visited during his years of exile, the Emperor gave the command to rebuild the park. Over 400,000 trees were planted, and dozens of chalets, pavilions, snack stands, and restaurants were built. A network of roads and trails was laid down totaling 95km (59 miles). Here are a few of its most popular areas:

o The **Parc de Bagatelle** is a park-within-a-park, with a lush **garden,** a small **château** that hosts concerts in the summer (check listing magazines for details), and a **rose garden** with over 1,000 varieties. New varieties are introduced every year in June, during an international rose competition. The version of the garden you see today was designed by Forestier, a friend of Monet, who was inspired by Impressionism, which is evident in the artfully placed clusters of flowers and plants.

- The **Pré Catelan** is most famous for its elegant and extremely pricey restaurant, but there are plenty of other reasons to come here. This green enclave includes lush lawns, playgrounds, and flowerbeds, as well as the **Jardin Shakespeare,** which attempts to re-create settings from the Bard's plays. Here you'll find the heaths of Macbeth, the Forest of Arden, and the pond where Ophelia meets her watery death.
- The **Jardin d'Acclimatation** is an old-fashioned amusement park, with lots of grassy areas and nifty playgrounds (see above).

In addition to walking, in-line skating, and cycling (**bike rentals** at the edge of the Lac Inferieur and at the Jardin d'Acclimatation), you can **rent a boat** on the lake, **go fishing** in some of the ponds, or take in a horse race at the Longchamp and Auteuil hippodromes (www.france-galop.com). The spectacular **Fondation Louis Vuitton** (p. 163) is in the park, right next to the Jardin d'Acclimatation.

16th arrond. www.paris.fr. Métro: Porte d'Auteuil, Les Sablons, Porte Maillot, or Porte Dauphine.

Bois de Vincennes ★★ PARK

This park doesn't have as many gardens and restaurants as its western counterpart, but there is more of a sense of wilderness in this vast patch of greenery on the eastern end of Paris. Endless paths and alleys wind through woods and open fields; this is a great place for a long bike ride or a hike (though stick to the paths; people without homes have set up tents in some parts of the woods). Not that there are just trees here—if rambling isn't your game, there are plenty of other things to do as well. For starters, there is the **Parc Zoologique de Paris** (p. 174), a state-of-the-art zoo. Then there are the remains of a medieval castle, the **Château de Vincennes** (see below), and a large garden in the park, as well as theaters and a hippodrome for those who prefer to sit back and watch the action. In short, Bois de Vincennes has almost as many pleasures as the Bois de Boulogne, if not as much elegance.

Like the Bois de Boulogne, the Bois de Vincennes was once a royal hunting ground with a lodge built by Louis VII back in the 12th century. By the 13th century, it had grown into a castle, which Louis IX (St-Louis) became very fond of; it is said that he dispensed justice under one of the nearby oak trees. It wasn't until the 18th century, under Louis XV, that these woods were turned into a public park; unfortunately, after the Revolution, the army decided to use it as a training ground, and the castle became a prison (some of its more famous lodgers included the Marquis de Sade and the philosopher Denis Diderot). Needless to say, this did not do wonders for the landscaping. Finally, in the 19th century, Napoleon III made the park part of his urban renewal scheme, and it got the same thorough makeover as the Bois de Boulogne. Its troubles were not completely over, however. In 1944, the retreating German army left the château in ruins, but it has since been almost completely restored.

A few of the park's high points:

o The **Parc Zoologique de Paris** (aka the Paris Zoo; p. 174).

o The **Parc Floral:** Created in 1969, this modern mix of **flower beds, ponds, picnic areas,** and a fabulous **playground** is a very pleasant place to spend the afternoon, particularly between May and September when the open-air theater holds free music and theater performances. In July, the Paris Jazz Festival takes off for 3 weeks, and in most of August and September, the Festival Classique au Vert cooks up a great program of classical music. For the kids, **Guignol puppet shows** (http://guignolparcfloral.blogspot.com; 2.80€ adults and children) play most Wednesdays, Saturdays, and Sundays at 3 and 4pm, and daily during school holidays.

o The **Château de Vincennes:** It took 12 years to restore this former royal castle (the heart of France's monarchy until Louis XIV decided to move to Versailles in 1682), and the result—an ivory-colored compound with gracious, turreted ramparts—is truly beautiful. You can visit the imposing **castle keep,** a **Gothic chapel** with 16th-century stained-glass windows, and the multi-turreted **ramparts.** For the best views, opt for a guided tour of the keep's upper floors, usually closed to the public, though be prepared for a 250-step climb (av. de Paris, 12th arrond.; www.chateau-vincennes.fr; ✆ **01-48-08-31-20;** 9.50€ adults, free for children 17 and under; mid-Sept to mid-May daily 10am–5pm, mid-May to mid-Sept daily 10am–6pm; Métro: Château de Vincennes).

You can **rent bikes** in front of either of the two large lakes or on the esplanade by the château or **rent boats** for rowing around the lake. There are several **playgrounds,** as well as a **farm** (La Ferme de Paris), where children can watch cows being milked and (at the right time of year) sheep being shorn on weekends (daily during school holidays). You can also row boats and go on a pony ride. Thoroughbred racing fans can also check out the **Hippodrome Paris-Vincennes** (www.letrot.com).

Bois de Vincennes, 12th arrond. www.paris.fr. Free admission to main park. Metro: Porte Dorée or Château de Vincennes.

SHOPPING

Vuitton, Chanel, Baccarat—the names of famous French luxury brands roll around the tongue like rich chocolate. But while it's fun to window-shop at Cartier, few of us can actually afford to buy anything there. Guess what? Neither can most Parisians. And yet many manage to look terrifically put together. What's their secret?

Paris has always been the capital of *luxe*. As early as the 16th century, the city was known as the place to go for luxury goods. Over the centuries an entire industry grew up around the whims and whimsies of the French aristocracy. To keep up appearances, nobles spent outrageous amounts of money on sumptuous clothing, opulent homes, and lavish dinner parties for dozens of similarly well-heeled aristocrats. By the 18th century, thousands of merchants and artisans were working full-time to fill the voluminous orders of some 150 grand families, not to mention Louis XIV and his court in Versailles. It's no wonder that even today, the high and mighty, or just plain rich, come here for the best of the best.

Yet there is so much more shopping to explore than those big-name luxury stores around the Champs-Élysées. You'll discover boutiques by up-and-coming designers, lesser-known but fab chocolate stores, and wonderful home decoration shops that sell everything from kitchenware to antique knickknacks. Paris is shopaholic heaven, if you know where to go to find your *bonheur* (happiness).

SHOPPING BY AREA

In Paris, each neighborhood has its own personality, and each personality imposes itself on one or two main shopping streets. Aim for the areas with the highest concentration of your kind of store.

The Right Bank
LOUVRE & ÎLE DE LA CITÉ (1ST ARRONDISSEMENT)

The east side of this arrondissement includes the subterranean shopping mall **Forum des Halles** (covered by a *canopé*, a vast metal canopy covering shops like Lego), which is a short stroll from a major shopping strip on the **rue de Rivoli.** Both feature a wide range of affordable international clothing chains. Rue de Rivoli is also home to the revamped **La Samaritaine** department

Shopping Protocols

Depending upon the public health situation when you visit, you may or may not be required to wear a mask inside shops and show proof of Covid vaccination or a negative PCR test in order to enter. The rules change all the time, so for up-to-date information in English, check the French government website (www.gouvernement.fr/en/coronavirus-covid-19) and the Paris Tourist Office website (https://en.parisinfo.com/practical-paris/info/guides/info-disruption-paris).

store, which reopened (after being closed for 15 years) with much pomp and circumstance in 2021. And on rue Etienne Marcel is the spanking-new **Poste du Louvre,** a high-end shopping spot set in a 19th-century post office building. As you move west, the atmosphere shifts dramatically. **Rue St-Honoré** is lined with pricey, sophisticated stores, and prices go through the roof at **Place Vendôme,** which probably has the city's highest density of gemstones per square meter. Even if you are too shy to enter Chaumet or Boucheron, you can happily drool over the window displays.

OPÉRA & GRANDS BOULEVARDS (2ND & 9TH ARRONDISSEMENTS)

Boulevard Haussmann cuts through this neighborhood like a steamship's wake, drawing hordes of shoppers toward the city's two most famous department stores, **Galeries Lafayette** and **Printemps.** These two behemoths have spawned an entire neighborhood full of mass-market shops just north of the boulevard on **rue de Provence, rue de Mogador,** and **rue Caumartin.** To the south and east of the boulevard lies a maze of **19th-century covered shopping arcades** (see "Arcades," below), as well as a market street filled with enticing food stores, **rue de Montorgueil.** If you're still hungry, get your teeth into the glorious food shops along **rue des Martyrs** in trendy SoPi (South Pigalle, just below Montmartre in the 9th).

Passage Jouffroy.

arcades: 19TH-CENTURY SHOPPING MALLS

Paris is filled with covered arcades, primarily in the 2nd arrondissement. These lovely iron and glass galleries are 18th- and 19th-century antecedents of today's shopping malls—each one is lined with shops, eateries, and even the occasional hotel—and range in ambience from the up-and-coming to the already ultra-hip.

Built in 1825, the city's longest arcade, **Passage Choiseul**, 40 rue des Petits Champs, 2nd arrond. (Métro: Pyramides), runs from rue des Petits Champs to rue de Saint Augustin and shelters everything from bargain shoe shops to used book stores to art galleries. The **Passage des Panoramas**, 11 bd. Montmartre, 2nd arrond. (Métro: Grands Boulevards), intersects with several other short arcades (**Feydeau, Montmartre, Saint-Marc,** and **Variétés**), making an interesting warren of bookshops, collectors shops (stamps, coins, postcards, engravings), and increasingly, trendy restaurants, including **Coinstôt Vino** (p. 105). Across the street is the entrance to **Passage Jouffroy,** 10 bd. Montmartre, 9th arrond. (Métro: Grands Boulevards), lined with collectors shops featuring figurines, dollhouses,

and cinema memorabilia. Pricier gifts are to be found at **Passage Verdeau,** across the street from the back end of Jouffroy, 31 bis rue du Faubourg Montmartre, 9th arrond. (Métro: Grands Boulevards), a particularly atmospheric arcade with stores selling rare books, antique engravings, and vintage photos. If you're with kids, don't miss **Passage des Princes,** 3-5 bd. des Italiens, 2nd arrond. (Métro: Richelieu Drouot). The entire space houses **JouéClub Village** (p. 227), a behemoth kids store, brimming with games and toys.

Farther south, near the Palais Royal, is the chic **Galerie Vivienne,** 4 rue des Petits Champs, 2nd arrond. (www. galerie-vivienne.com; Métro: Bourse), a beautifully restored arcade with a mosaic tile floor and neoclassical arches. Stores here sell high-end clothes, handbags, textiles, and *objets d'art*. **Legrand Filles et Fils** (p. 226) has tons of fine bottles of wine, as well as a wine school and bistro. Toward Les Halles is the very stylish **Passage du Grand Cerf,** 10 rue Dussoubs, 2nd arrond. (Métro: Etienne Marcel), filled with flashy designer jewelry, clothing stores, and interior design agencies.

THE MARAIS (3RD & 4TH ARRONDISSEMENTS)

The success of the hip boutiques on the **rue des Francs-Bourgeois** has been such that trendy clothing stores have been cropping up on all the streets around it, even crowding out the kosher restaurants on **rue des Rosiers,** the historic Jewish quarter. Not as pricey as the luxury boutiques to the west, these stores have stylish duds at vaguely attainable prices (and they are open on Sunday, a rarity in this city). The streets around **rues de Bretagne** and **Charlot** in the northern Marais are a hotbed of independent French designers.

CHAMPS-ÉLYSÉES, TROCADÉRO & WESTERN PARIS (8TH, 16TH & 17TH ARRONDISSEMENTS)

Dozens of chic and designer boutiques dot the **rue du Faubourg St-Honoré,** but this shopping street pales in comparison to ultra-exclusive **avenue Montaigne.** Paris' most glamorous shopping street is lined with fancy shops, where you float from Dior to Chanel and everything in between. Teens, tourists,

Taxes, *Detaxe* & Refunds

Most items purchased in stores (aside from certain categories like food and tickets to performances) are subject to a 20% Value Added Tax (VAT), which is included in the price you pay (and not tacked on at the end like in the U.S.). The good news is that non–E.U. residents who are 16 and over and stay in France less than 6 months can get a refund of VAT (TVA in French) if they spend over 100€ in a single shop offering tax-free shopping (or at the same brand of shops) over a maximum of 3 days. Ask the retailer for a *bordereau de vente à l'exportation* (export sales invoice), which will have a bar code. Both you and the shopkeeper sign the slip, and you then choose how you will be reimbursed (credit on card, bank transfer, or cash). At the airport, before you check your luggage, scan the code in one of the "Pablo" terminals (if your airport doesn't have one, just go to the *"détaxe"* or customs counter). Once the form has been approved, head to the reimbursement counter to immediately claim your money. If Customs decides to check that you meet the refund conditions, make sure you can present your passport, travel ticket, and the purchases for which you want to be refunded. For more info, visit the **Paris Tourist Office** website (www.parisinfo.com), and under "Practical Paris" search for "Money," then "'Détaxe' tax refund and duty-free" for a rundown.

and other young things flock to the neighboring **Champs-Élysées** to crowd into hot mass-market flagships and a "concept" version of the **Galeries Lafayette** department store (p. 214). High-end food shops (Maille, Maison de la Truffe) live in the area around the **Madeleine,** as does Paris' first city-center IKEA.

MONTMARTRE (18TH ARRONDISSEMENT)

Small, fairly affordable design, fashion, jewelry, and gourmet food shops fill the winding streets around Montmartre's **Place des Abbesses.** Wander along **rue des Abbesses,** down **rue Houdon,** and up **rue des Martyrs** and discover hidden treasures. Part of **rue Lepic** is a fabulous foodie street, brimming with open shop fronts hawking roast chicken, fresh seafood, and wine. Lining the streets around rue d'Orsel, below the Sacré-Coeur Basilica, is a collection of fabric markets, the most famous of which, **Marché Saint Pierre,** has lent its name to the entire area.

RÉPUBLIQUE, BASTILLE & EASTERN PARIS (11TH & 12TH ARRONDISSEMENTS)

As **rue du Faubourg St-Antoine** heads east from the Place de la Bastille, you'll find a number of chain stores. The choices get more interesting in and around **rue de Charonne,** home to offbeat, youth-oriented clothing and goodies. A great place to window-shop is the **Viaduc des Arts,** along avenue Daumesnil: A collection of about 30 specialist craft stores occupies a series of vaulted arches under the **Promenade Plantée** (aka Coulée verte René-Dumont; p. 173).

BELLEVILLE, CANAL ST-MARTIN & LA VILLETTE (10TH, 19TH & 20TH ARRONDISSEMENTS)

TThe **Canal St-Martin** is a bastion of local bohemian charm, and you can find interesting shops along neighboring streets such as **rue de Marseille, rue Beaurepaire,** the **quai de Valmy,** and **quai de Jemmapes.** Belleville may not have trendy boutiques, but it's an interesting place to explore specialty shops from the city's various immigrant communities. Set in the Cité des Sciences museum building (p. 176), **Vill'Up** in Parc de la Villette is the latest modern mall to hit Paris (p. 216), offering around 40 boutiques as well as entertainment spots like **iFly** (www.iflyfrance.com), a free-falling experience in a transparent cylinder.

The Left Bank

LATIN QUARTER (5TH & 13TH ARRONDISSEMENTS)

Chain stores have taken over much of **boulevard St-Michel,** formerly known for its cafes and bookstores. Opposite Notre-Dame, **Shakespeare and Company** (p. 221) draws hordes to its higgledy-piggledy bookshelves, while food enthusiasts flock to the shops at the southern end of **rue Mouffetard. Chinatown** is also here, home to Pan-Asian stores including the famous **Tang Frères** supermarkets (www.tang-freres.fr).

ST-GERMAIN-DES-PRÉS & LUXEMBOURG (6TH ARRONDISSEMENT)

Even if it's technically in the 7th arrondissement, the shopping nerve center of this smart neighborhood is **Le Bon Marché,** the city's most stylish department store. Radiating eastward is a network of streets with oodles of delightful shops, ranging from bargain-oriented **rue St-Placide** to chain stores and shoe heaven on **rue de Rennes** to designer labels and cute boutiques on **rue St-Sulpice, rue du Cherche Midi,** and **rue du Vieux Colombier.** Down toward the Seine, **rue Bonaparte** and **rue Jacob** tempt with classy, if pricey, offerings; you can stop in at the hip **Taschen** (p. 221) bookstore just off **boulevard St-Germain** for gorgeous coffee-table books on pop culture, photography, and architecture.

EIFFEL TOWER & NEARBY (7TH ARRONDISSEMENT)

Most of this area is more focused on culture than shopping, but along its eastern edge, around the **rue du Bac** and **rue du Grenelle,** you'll find expensive designer shops and **Beaupassage** (p. 129), a chic, open-air food arcade. The market street of **rue Cler** also has dozens of food shops.

MONTPARNASSE & NEARBY (14TH & 15TH ARRONDISSEMENTS)

An ugly shopping center in the Tour Montparnasse complex is filled with the usual chain stores, but the more interesting shopping draw here is **rue Daguerre,** a lovely market street filled with food shops that is as cute as rue Cler but less famous (you'll hear a lot more French here). Farther south in the 15th, **rue de Commerce** buzzes with high-street shops and restaurants, and **Beaugrenelle** (p. 215) is a contemporary mall south of the Eiffel Tower, with curated French fashion brands, hip pop-up stores, and a reduced version of Galeries Lafayette.

DEPARTMENT STORES & MALLS

Les Grands Magasins

Known as the *grands magasins* ("big stores"), the great Parisian department stores were born in the late 19th century and have become landmarks. Over the last few years, the city has also adopted another shopping model: the mall. I've listed the best two here, but at the time of writing, the city's famous 24/7 post office building on rue Etienne Marcel was poised to reopen in 2022 as **La Poste du Louvre** (https://lapostedulouvre.fr), a chic spot mixing offices, apartments, high-end shops, eateries, a rooftop bar and a five-star hotel.

Galeries Lafayette ★★ This grandest of the *grands magasins* was a humble haberdasher shop when it opened in 1895. Success inspired architectural excess, like the sumptuous Belle Epoque dome under which fashionable goodies are displayed. Here you'll find everything from luxury labels to kids' stuff to stationery. A separate building is just for men (**Lafayette Homme**), and another across the street has housewares (**Lafayette Maison**) as well as a wine and gourmet shop/food court (**Lafayette Gourmet**). Another satellite opened in an Art Deco building on the Champs-Élysées (no. 60; www.galerieslafayettechampselysees.com; ✆ **01-83-65-61-00**) in 2019. This new branch is set up like a huge concept store, with over 600 hand-picked fashion labels and over 150 stylists ready to help you. Some clothes hang on "smart hangers" that tell you whether your size is in stock and send the info to the fitting rooms. 40 bd. Haussmann, 9th arrond. www.galerieslafayette.com. ✆ **01-42-82-34-56.** Métro: Chausée d'Antin-Lafayette.

La Samaritaine ★★ After almost 2 decades of renovations, the famous riverfront department store reopened in June 2021 to include a fashion concept store, the biggest beauty studio on the European continent (only Harrods in London has a bigger one), a spa, and even a luxury hotel (Cheval Blanc Paris; p. 54). To differentiate La Samaritaine from the city's other department stores, many brands by French creators are

Galeries Lafayette's stained-glass cupola is classified as a historic monument.

Shopping Hours

In general, shops are open from 9 or 10am to 7 or 8pm. Many larger stores and most department stores stay open late (that is, 9pm) one night during the week (called a *nocturne*), and most supermarkets are open until at least 8pm, often 9pm. Many shops close on Monday, and most close on Sunday, which is still considered a day of rest in this country. This is great for family get-togethers but hard on working shoppers, who have only Saturday to get to the stores. Don't shop on Saturday if you can avoid it; the crowds are annoying, to say the least. If you do want to shop on a Sunday, head to the **Marais,** one of the only areas where boutiques stay open, or the **Carousel du Louvre,** a chic shopping mall below the Louvre museum.

The French tradition of closing for lunch is quickly vanishing in Paris (although it is still very common elsewhere in France). However, smaller, family-run operations still sometimes close between 1 and 3pm.

Final note: Many shops close down completely for 2 or 3 weeks during July or August, when a mass vacation exodus empties out major portions of the city.

exclusive to the store—and if nothing else, its Art Nouveau and Art Deco interiors are more than worth checking out. 19 rue de la Monnaie, 1st arrond. www.dfs.com. ℂ **01-56-81-28-40.** Métro: Hôtel de Ville.

Le Bon Marché ★★★   Founded by an enterprising milliner in the mid-1800s, this was one of the world's first department stores. Despite its name (*bon marché* means "affordable"), this is one of the most expensive of Paris' *grands magasins*. It is also *very* stylish, with beautiful displays and fabulous clothes of every imaginable designer label, both upscale and mid-range. Right next door is its humongous designer supermarket, **La Grande Epicerie Rive Gauche** (p. 225). 24 rue de Sèvres, 7th arrond. www.24s.com. ℂ **01-44-39-80-00.** Métro: Sèvres–Babylone.

Printemps ★★   The glistening domes of this 19th-century building bring to mind a grand hotel on the French Riviera. *Printemps* means "spring," which is certainly eternal in this elegant store, split into five sections (women's, men's, housewares, beauty, and food). Four of the seven floors of women's fashion are devoted to designer labels. If you can't handle the crowds inside, you can always enjoy the famed *vitrines,* or **window displays,** which are usually creative and original. Better yet, ride to the top of Printemps Homme (menswear) and munch your way around the food court, where every item, from the vodka to the truffles, is French; the views over the city's rooftops are more than Instagrammable there, too. 64 bd. Haussmann, 9th arrond. www.printemps.com. ℂ **01-42-82-50-00.** Métro: Havre-Caumartin or St-Lazare.

Malls

Beaugrenelle ★★   Shopping lovers will enjoy perusing this mall's 120 boutiques and 20 restaurants in a contemporary structure close to the Eiffel Tower and the Seine. You'll find the usual international suspects (Zara,

H&M, etc.), plus, more interestingly, plenty of French and Parisian fashion brands and a Galeries Lafayette outpost. There's also a 10-screen movie theater. And it's open on Sundays. 12 rue Linois, 15th arrond. www.beaugrenelle-paris.com. ✆ **01-53-95-24-00.** Métro: Charles Michel or Bir-Hakeim.

Vill'Up ★   There's shopping galore, but this mall focuses on entertainment too, with iFLY, a transparent indoor skydiving tunnel (www.iflyfrance.com); a Pathé movie theater; and a laser and virtual reality adventure center. 30 av. Corentin Cariou, 19th arrond. https://villup.com. ✆ **01-49-70-83-30.** Métro: Porte de la Villette.

MARKETS: FOOD & FLEA
Food Markets

Marchés (open-air or covered markets) are small universes unto themselves where nothing substantial has changed for centuries. The fishmonger trumpeting the wonders of this morning's catch probably doesn't sound a whole lot different than his/her ancestor in the Middle Ages (although their dress has changed), and people no doubt assessed the goods in the stalls with the same pitiless stares that they do today. Certainly, the hygiene and organization have improved and there are no more jugglers or bear baiters to entertain the crowds, but the essence of the experience remains the same—a bustling, joyous chaos where you can buy fresh, honest food.

Even if you don't have access to cooking facilities, *marchés* are great places to pick up picnic goodies or just a mid-morning nosh; along with fruit and vegetable vendors, you'll find bakeries, *charcutiers* (sort of like a deli, but better), and other small stands selling homemade jams, honey, or desserts. Some of the covered markets have small cafes and restaurants—these are ideal for sitting down and soaking up the atmosphere.

A few marché rules: Unless you see evidence to the contrary, don't pick up your own fruits and vegetables with your hands. Wait until the vendor serves you and point. Also, don't be surprised if the line in front of the stand is an amorphous blob of people; this is the French way. Surprisingly, fistfights are rare; somehow everyone seems to be aware of who came before them, and if they aren't, no one seems to care.

Every arrondissement in the city has a *marché*. Below is a selective list of the best; you can find hours and locations of all on the municipal website (www.paris.fr/equipements/marches-alimentaires) in French only, or just ask at your hotel.

- **Le Food Market,** street food stalls along bd. de Belleville, 10th arrond. (one Thurs evening per month; www.lefoodmarket.fr; Métro: Ménilmontant or Couronnes)
- **Marché d'Aligre,** aka Marché Beauvau, with food and antiques; pl. d'Aligre, 12th arrond. (outdoor market Tues–Fri 7:30am–1:30pm, Sat–Sun 7:30am–2pm, covered market Tues–Sat 9am–1pm and 4–7:30pm, Sun 9am–1:30pm; Métro: Ledru Rollin or Gare de Lyon)
- **Marché Bastille,** bd. Richard Lenoir btw. rue Amelot and rue St-Sabin, 11th arrond. (Thurs and Sun 7am–2:30pm; Métro: Bastille)
- **Marché Batignolles,** organic; bd. Batignolles btw. rue de Rome and pl. Clichy, 17th arrond. (Sat 9am–3pm; Métro: Rome)
- **Marché Grenelle,** bd. Grenelle, btw. rue Lourmel and rue du Commerce, 15th arrond. (Wed and Sun 7am–2:30pm; Métro: Dupleix)
- **Marché Monge,** pl. Monge, 5th arrond. (Wed, Fri, and Sun 7am–2:30pm; Métro: Place Monge)
- **Marché Raspail,** bd. Raspail btw. rue de Cherche-Midi and rue de Rennes, 6th arrond. (Tues and Fri 7am–2:30pm, organic Sun 9am–3pm; Métro: Rennes)
- **Marché Saxe-Breteuil,** av. du Saxe near pl. de Breteuil, 7th arrond. (Thurs and Sat 7am–2:30pm; Métro: Ségur)

Antiques Fairs & Brocantes

You've probably heard of the famous *marché aux puces,* or **flea market,** at Clignancourt (see below), and if you're an inveterate browser, it's probably worth the visit. But the better deals are to be had at the *brocantes,* antiques or jumble sales, held periodically around the city. Though most of what you will find at these sales is sold by professional *brocanteurs* who scout estate sales and other insider sources, your selection will be much wider and the chances of finding a postwar ceramic pastis pitcher or heirloom lace curtains at affordable prices are much higher than at some of the more overpopulated flea markets. To find out where and when the *brocantes* are happening, a good site to try is http://quefaire.paris.fr/brocantes.

Flea Markets

Marché aux Puces de la Porte de Vanves ★★   This weekend event sprawls along two streets and is easily the best flea market in Paris—dealers swear by it. There's little in terms of formal antiques and furniture. It's better

Shopping for antiques at Marché aux Puces de Paris St-Ouen–Clignancourt.

for old linens, vintage Hermès scarves, toys, costume jewelry, perfume bottles, and bad art. Sadly, dealers tend to up the prices when they hear a foreign accent. Don't be shy; haggle them down. Get there early—the best stuff goes fast. av. Georges-Lafenestre, 14th arrond. www.pucesdevanves.fr. No phone. Sat–Sun 7am–2pm. Métro: Porte de Vanves.

Marché aux Puces de Paris St-Ouen–Clignancourt ★ Engulfing the Porte de Clignancourt area at the northern edge of the city, this claims to be the world's largest antiques market. Split into 15 specialty markets, the sprawling, trendy mini-city is visited by thousands of visitors. Although it was once a bargain-hunter's dream, prices now often rival those of regular antiques dealers. Still, hardcore browsers will get a kick wandering the alleyways of this Parisian medina and may turn up a treasure. ***Note:*** Beware of pickpockets. Also, to avoid the tatty markets surrounding Les Puces, get off at Métro Garibaldi. Porte de Clignancourt, 18th arrond. www.marcheauxpuces-saintouen.com. ✆ **01-40-11-77-36.** Fri 8am–noon, Sat 9am–6pm, Sun 10am–6pm, Mon 10am–5pm. Métro: Porte de Clignancourt or Garibaldi.

RECOMMENDED STORES
Antiques, Art & Collectibles

Drouot ★ This auction house sells a bit of everything, from fine and rare art to vintage and reproduction decorative objects, jewelry, and housewares. There are two sales centers: The main one, Drouot Richelieu, has been an institution since it opened in 1852, with 15 rooms dedicated to art. The other, by Montmartre (23 rue d'Oran, 18th arrond.), is the place to hunt for everyday collectibles and furniture. At Richelieu, artworks are usually displayed the day before the auction, whereas in Montmartre, they're displayed on the morning of the sale. Anyone can bid; just raise your hand or shout out a price. L'Hôtel Drouot, 9 rue du Drouot, 9th arrond. www.drouot.com. ⓒ **01-48-00-20-20.** Métro: Richelieu-Drouot.

59 Rivoli ★★★ Want some Parisian art to take home? This delightful and quirky artists' studio is a must. Every inch of it—from the frescoed ceilings to the graffiti-clad stairwell—is devoted to creation, with each room devoted to a different artist (there are 30 of them!). This means you can find everything from hand-engraved skateboards to sculpture. There are usually free concerts Saturday and Sunday evening (Sept–June). There's no other place quite like it in Paris. 59 rue de Rivoli, 1st arrond. www.59rivoli.org/homepage. No phone. Métro: Châtelet.

Village St-Paul ★★ When you pass through an archway on rue St-Paul, you come upon a lovely villagelike enclosure, the remnant of a centuries-old hamlet that was swallowed up by the city. Today, it's a village of antiques dealers and design shops, selling everything from old bistro chairs to vintage lingerie to Iranian kilim rugs. Check the website for the periodic antiques fairs. rue St-Paul, 4th arrond. www.levillagesaintpaul.com. No phone. Métro: St-Paul.

Beauty & Perfume

At the airport, you'll be assaulted with **duty-free shops** carrying loads of tax-free perfume; another colony of similar shops is near the Opéra, usually with lines of people waiting outside. But you will most likely get the same tax rebate no matter where you go (as long as you spend a minimum of 100€; see p. 212). If you're short on time, seek out one of two huge perfume and make-up chains: the ubiquitous **Marionnaud** (www.marionnaud.fr) and the user-friendly **Sephora** (www.sephora.fr). For something more original, try one of the shops listed below.

Detaille 1905 ★ Founded by the Countess of Presle in 1905, this hand-some, old-fashioned store offers its own elegant line of *eau de toilette* and other beauty products for both men and women, such as its signature *Baume Automobile,* developed by the Countess when she realized (even back then) what pollution can do to your skin. These unique products can only be purchased at the wood-paneled boutique or ordered by phone or online through the shop's website. 10 rue St-Lazare, 9th arrond. www.detaille.com. ⓒ **01-48-78-68-50.** Métro: Notre-Dame-de-Lorette.

The Different Company ★★ Indeed, something *is* different about this perfume company. This independent operation, founded in 2000, makes its own unique fragrances with mostly natural materials. Signature scents include Osmanthus, Sel de Vétiver, and Rose Poivrée. 10 rue Ferdinand Duval, 4th arrond. www.thedifferentcompany.com. ⓒ **01-42-78-19-34.** Métro: St-Paul.

Sylvia Beach: Mother of the Lost Generation

Born in Baltimore in 1887, **Sylvia Beach** fell in love with Paris early in life and moved there for good at the end of World War I. A few years later, with the encouragement of her companion, bookshop owner Adrienne Monier, Beach opened **Shakespeare and Company,** a bookstore and lending library specializing in English and American books. For the next 20 years, the shop at 8 rue Dupuytren served as an unofficial welcome center for American and English visitors, particularly literary ones, and specifically those who would later come to be known as members of **"The Lost Generation":** T. S. Eliot, Ezra Pound, F. Scott Fitzgerald, Gertrude Stein, and Ernest Hemingway. But the one who made the biggest impression, literally, was James Joyce. After his novel "Ulysses" was banned in both the U.S. and England and no publisher would touch the manuscript,

Beach courageously published it herself. In February 1922, after endless proofs and corrections by the author, the 1,000 copies arrived in the store and were all snapped up instantaneously. Later, the book became a modern classic, making a mint for its publisher, Random House. Beach never saw a penny but claimed that she didn't mind because she'd have done anything for Joyce and his art. In 1941, during the Nazi occupation of Paris, the contents of the entire bookstore "vanished" overnight (hidden in a vacant apartment in the same building) to avoid confiscation by the Nazis. The books were saved, but Beach spent 6 months in an internment camp. After the war, she returned to Paris, but the bookshop's doors never reopened. The store's memory lives on in its more recent incarnation at 37 rue de la Bûcherie (see Shakespeare and Company, above).

Editions de Parfums Fréderic Malle ★★ Master perfumer Fréderic Malle established this chic temple to the nose in 2000, and he now offers a superb range of original fragrances. In his Marais store, evocative-sounding aromas like Noir Epices and Lipstick Rose are displayed in ultramodern wooden structures that look like floating clouds. There are stores in three other locations: 140 av. Victor Hugo in the 16th arrondissement, 37 rue de Grenelle in the 7th, and 21 rue du Mont Thabor in the 1st. 13 rue des Francs Bourgeois, 4th arrond. www.fredericmalle.com. © **01-40-09-25-85.** Métro: St-Paul.

Books
ENGLISH BOOKSTORES

Paris' English-language bookshops tend to double as cultural meeting places. Those that have survived the ongoing bookshop crisis are good places to pick up English-language newsletters, chat in English, and attend readings (sometimes by famous authors).

The Abbey Bookshop ★ Canadians will be happy to find a cozy store that specializes in Canadian authors, as well as other English-language literature. You'll have to squeeze in between the piles of books, but this is a relaxed, welcoming place with good readings and events, including hikes in nearby forests. 29 rue de la Parcheminerie, 5th arrond. https://abbeybookshop. wordpress.com/about/. © **01-46-33-16-24.** Métro: St-Michel.

Galignani ★★★ The oldest English-language bookstore in Paris, this old-fashioned shop has thrived since 1810. Owned by the literary Galignani family, whose ancestor used one of the first printing presses back in 1520, the store is filled with a terrific range of both French and English books, with emphasis on French classics, modern fiction, sociology, and fine arts. 224 rue de Rivoli, 1st arrond. www.galignani.com. ✆ **01-42-60-76-07.** Métro: Tuileries.

San Francisco Book Company ★★ Centrally located, this shop has a few new books and an excellent stock of used books, including hardback classics, paperback airplane reading, and rare and out-of-print editions. 17 rue Monsieur Le Prince, 6th arrond. www.sfparis.com. ✆ **01-43-29-15-70.** Métro: Odéon.

Shakespeare and Company ★★ The venerable literary shrine is so popular with tourists that you may have to wait to get in because of the store's limited capacity. Run by George Whitman for some 60 years, it's helmed by his daughter, Sylvia, who was named after Sylvia Beach (she founded the original bookshop in 1919; see box below). Many legendary writers (Allen Ginsberg and Henry Miller, to name a couple) have stopped in over the decades for a cup of tea; many an aspiring author has camped out in one of the back rooms. Check the website for readings and events. A coffeeshop run by the same people behind **Bob's Juice Bar** (p. 114) is next door and serves wonderful lemon pie. 37 rue de la Bûcherie, 5th arrond. www.shakespeareandcompany.com. ✆ **01-43-25-40-93.** Métro/RER: St-Michel–Notre-Dame.

Sylvia Whitman, owner of Shakespeare and Company.

FRENCH & ENGLISH BOOKSTORES

Les Mots à la Bouche ★ It may have moved from the Marais, but this is still Paris' best-stocked gay bookstore. You can find French- and English-language books as well as gay-info magazines such as "Têtu." 37 rue St-Ambroise, 11th arrond. www.motsbouche.com. ✆ **01-42-78-88-30.** Métro: Rue St-Maur or St-Ambroise.

Taschen ★ This hip bookstore sells tomes in French and English about art, architecture, fashion, pop culture, and design, catering to those who love coffee-table books and beautiful pictures. The section at the back features framed photos from the books. 2 rue de Buci, 6th arrond. www.taschen.com. ℰ **01-40-51-79-22.** Métro: Odéon or Mabillon.

Clothing & Shoes

Antoine & Lili ★★   Hot pink is the signature color at this bohemian store for ladies, where the gaily painted walls are hung with colorful objects from around the world. Clothes are innovative yet wearable, and come in a range of bright colors. Paris has five branches (see website). 95 quai de Valmy, 10th arrond. www.antoineetlili.com. ℰ **01-40-37-41-55.** Métro: Jacques Bonsergent.

Balibaris ★★   Kick-started by a young Parisian fashion entrepreneur, this is where Parisian men go for cool, smart outfits that work just as well on a night out as in the office. You'll find classically cut pants and chinos, and denim and suede jackets, along with a spattering of cotton and leather bags. The city has 24 branches (including in Galeries Lafayette, p. 214, and Printemps, p. 215). 13 rue Vavin, 6th arrond. www.balibaris.com. ℰ **01-42-38-18-67.** Métro: Notre-Dame des Champs or Vavin.

French Trotters ★   This emporium is the flagship store for this temple of urban chic for men and women. While the original store (30 rue de Charonne, 11th arrond.) features both hot local French labels and the store's own brand of relaxed *branchitude* (hipness), this one sells all that plus housewares, books, and shoes. 128 rue Vieille du Temple, 3rd arrond. www.frenchtrotters.fr. ℰ **01-44-61-00-14.** Métro: St-Sébastien-Froissart or Files du Calvaire.

Kiliwatch ★   At this institution for fashion lovers who like to mix vintage garb with brand-new clothes, whole sections are dedicated to anything from the 1960s to the 1990s, as well as a host of hip French men's and women's brands you won't usually find back home. For pure women's vintage, visit Kiliwatch Collector (see below). 64 rue Tiquetonne, 2nd arrond. http://kiliwatch. paris. ℰ **01-42-21-17-37.** Métro: Etienne Marcel.

Zadig & Voltaire ★   I don't know what the philosopher would make of this trendy young French brand, but Voltaire might have appreciated its rock- 'n'-roll spirit. Look for perfectly distressed jeans, comfy cashmeres, biker boots, and more, for men, women, and children. Dozens of branches are open around Paris. 3 rue du Vieux Colombier, 6th arrond. www.zadig-et-voltaire.com. ℰ **01-45-48-39-37.** Métro: St-Sulpice.

CHILDREN'S CLOTHING

Botoù ★★   If you're looking for something funky for your children's feet, this is where to start. These cool and colorful shoes will make your kids look like they live in this fun and hip neighborhood (SoPi), with options from goldfish-print sneakers to chick-yellow ankle boots. 20 rue Milton, 9th arrond. https://botou.fr. ℰ **09-83-82-06-58.** Métro: Notre-Dame-de-Lorette.

L'Île aux Fées ★★   This boutique's exquisite dresses for little girls are all handmade in Madagascar (the owner's birthplace) and embroidered according to local techniques with pretty flowers and bows. You'll find gorgeous outfits for baby boys too—mostly 1920s-inspired sailor's outfits with puffy shorts and wide-collared tops. Prince Louis, eat your heart out! 66 rue Notre-Dame des Champs, 6th arrond. www.lileauxfees.com. ℂ **01-43-25-07-59.** Métro: Vavin.

Marie Puce ★★   You can dress everyone—from babies to teens—here. Marie offers easy elegance—especially for tots who need to dress up (at least a little) but can't stand frills. Much of the clothing here is 100% made in France. 60 rue du Cherche Midi, 6th arrond. www.mariepuce.com. ℂ **01-45-48-30-09.** Métro: Sèvres-Babylone or St-Placide.

LINGERIE

Judging from the number of lingerie stores in even the smallest French towns, it's safe to say that French women *love* underwear. And for good reason— French lingerie is exquisite and worth the splurge.

Fifi Chachnil ★★★   A boudoir-boutique tucked into a courtyard, this is where young French movie stars go to find retro-sexy-fun-posh underthings with a decidedly girly feel. Prices are steep, but the experience and the lingerie are unique. It has one other pink and fluffy boutique: 34 rue de Grenelle in the 7th. 68 rue Jean-Jacques Rousseau, in the courtyard, 1st arrond. www.fifichachnil.com. ℂ **01-42-21-19-93.** Métro/RER: Les Halles.

Saint-Germain des Slips ★★   The store is a Left Bank outpost of Le Slip Français, a quirky company (*slip* means "underpants") that makes every undergarment it sells—from men's boxer shorts to women's bras—in France. You can accessorize with bags and T-shirts to match your undies, too. See the website for more locations. 20 rue du Vieux Colombier, 6th arrond. www.leslipfrancais.fr. ℂ **01-45-38-90-56.** Métro: St-Sulpice.

VINTAGE CLOTHING

Some Parisian vintage shops sell designer clothing; others scour the U.S., U.K., and other European countries for the everyday retro garb they sell. Unless you aim for the designer category, it can be hit and miss. The Marais has several excellent vintage boutiques, so it's a good place to start.

Didier Ludot ★   An homage to the haute couture of yesteryear has fancy frocks created between 1900 and 1980. This swank boutique is more of an antiques shop than a clothing store. 24 galerie de Montpensier, in the arcades of the Palais Royal, 1st arrond. www.didierludot.fr. ℂ **01-42-96-06-56.** Métro: Palais-Royal–Musée du Louvre.

Free'p'Star ★   Vintage hunters will delight in terrific finds at this trendy store in the heart of the Marais, which specializes in funky fashions from yesteryear. Some of it is tatty, but real bargains can certainly be had. There are five branches, two of the best being 52 and 61 rue de la Verrerie, also in the 4th arrondissement. 20 rue de Rivoli, 4th arrond. www.freepstar.com. ℂ **01-42-77-63-43.** Métro: St-Paul.

Kiliwatch Collector ★★   Kiliwatch's (see above) hip Left Bank sister is a true vintage store, featuring everything from upcycled 1970s strapless dresses and leather satchels to '60s hats and '80s silk shirts. It carries bags and scarves, too. 46 rue St-André des Arts, 6th arrond. www.kiliwatchcollector.fr. © **09-62-65-61-36**. Métro: Mabillon. RER: St-Michel Notre-Dame.

Concept Stores

Trendiness oozes from the walls of all of Paris' concept stores—basically one-stop boutiques selling curated items by different designers and brands. Some have a cult following; most include a hip coffee shop for perusing your purchases post-splurge.

Empreintes ★★ French art and crafts take center stage in this glorious, four-story space that showcases handmade jewelry, tableware, furniture, lighting, and *objets d'art*. Prices start under 75€. A projection room shows arts and crafts–themed movies. 5 rue de Picardie, 3rd arrond. www.empreintes-paris.com. © **01-40-09-53-80**. Métro: Filles du Calvaire or Temple.

L'Exception ★★ This boutique in Les Halles is the sort you go to for cool ready-to-wear French designer clothes and come away with a pineapple-shaped light and a scented candle. The stationery's fun, with funky notebooks and must-have (if you're a hipster) hippo-shaped staplers. 24 rue Berger, 1st arrond. www.lexception.com. © **09-67-71-92-64**. Métro/RER: Châtelet or Les Halles.

Merci ★★ Set in a former factory on the edge of the Marais, Merci offers hand-picked designer brands mixed with vintage one-offs on the 2nd floor, with cool kitchenware in the basement. Jewelry, linen, and stationery are other favorites here. Sip coffee in one of the cafes. 111 bd. de Beaumarchais, 3rd arrond. www.merci-merci.com. © **01-42-77-00-33**. Métro: Filles du Calvaire.

Food & Drink
CHOCOLATE
A La Mère de Famille ★ Founded in 1761, this piece of Parisian history (rumor has it the original owner hid the mother superior of the nearby convent from revolutionaries during the Terror) has committed its soul to candies and chocolates à *l'ancienne*. You'll find classic chocolates as well as old-fashioned bonbons like *berlingots*, lemon drops, caramels, and jellied fruits. Eleven other locations are around the city. 35 rue du Faubourg Montmartre, 9th arrond. www.lameredefamille.com. © **01-47-70-83-69**. Métro: Grands Boulevards.

François Pralus ★★★ Pralus owns a cacao plantation in Madagascar, ensuring the extraordinary quality of every bean that goes into his chocolate, which comes in "crus" (vintages), rather like wine. Choose between 21 lip-smacking types, each wrapped in colorful paper like exquisite parcels. Be sure to try the *barre infernale*—melt-in-your-mouth bars of dark chocolate–encased praline. And the pink-dotted *Praluline* is the most delicious, buttery brioche you may ever taste. This is one of four boutiques in Paris. 35 rue Rambuteau, 4th arrond. www.chocolats-pralus.com. © **01-57-40-84-55**. Métro: Rambuteau.

Jean-Charles Rochoux ★★ Here is an opportunity to sample the delights of one of France's most artistic *chocolatiers*. Everything Rochoux makes—from the gemlike individual chocolates to the intricate chocolate sculptures and pots of chocolate spreads—is beautiful. Some sculptures are museum-worthy. 16 rue d'Assas, 6th arrond. www.jcrochoux.com. © **01-42-84-29-45.** Métro: St-Sulpice.

Patrick Roger ★★   Is that a life-size chocolate orangutan in the window? Oh yes, it is. Not only is Patrick Roger a master *chocolatier,* but he is also a sculptor who uses his medium (chocolate) to convey his message. One year he found inspiration in elephants, and in the past he's tackled subjects as challenging as a 4m-tall (13-ft.) chocolate version of Rodin's *Balzac.* He has seven Parisian shops (see website for locations). 108 bd. St-Germain, 6th arrond. www. patrickroger.com. © **01-43-28-38-42.** Métro: Odéon.

SPECIALTY GROCERIES

Comptoir des Abbayes ★★★   *Ora et labora* (pray and work) is the guiding rule for monks and nuns in France's many monasteries, who produce handmade, unique goodies to eat and drink, as well as traditional handicrafts. Usually, you'd need to trek into the mountains to buy their wares, but thanks to this boutique, you can nab a bottle of artisanal chartreuse, a jar of tomato jam, or handmade beeswax candles right in the middle of Paris. A specialty: herbal teas and remedies recommended by none other than Hildegarde von Bingen, the 12th-century German saint. 23 rue des Petits Champs, 1st arrond. https://comptoir-des-abbayes.com. © **01-42-96-11-24.** Métro: Pyramides.

La Grande Epicerie Rive Gauche ★★   Though its new decor feels more international than Parisian, this huge gourmet grocery mecca, an outgrowth of Le Bon Marché department store (p. 215), still stocks every gourmet substance you could possibly imagine, and many that you couldn't. Sculpted sugar cubes, designer mineral waters, truffle-balsamic vinegar, pink salt from the Himalayas—need we go on? It also has an excellent (if expensive) takeout department if you are looking for picnic items. A second address is at 80 rue de Passy in the 16th. 38 rue de Sèvres, 7th arrond. www.lagrandeepicerie.fr. © **01-44-39-81-00.** Métro: Sèvres-Babylone.

Maille ★   True, you can find Maille gourmet mustard all over the place, but you can only get it hand-pumped here in the official boutique. Pumped fresh into a stoneware pot and sealed with a cork, it has an altogether different taste, and it is delicious. Choose from mustard made with a dash of Chablis, Chardonnay, Sauternes, or splurge on Chablis with truffle bits. 6 pl. de la Madeleine, 8th arrond. www.maille.com. © **01-40-15-06-00.** Métro: Madeleine.

WINES

Wine in France is stunningly cheap. In Paris you can buy a bottle of something extremely pleasant for as little as 5€ or 6€. But before you start planning to stock your wine cellar back home, consider this sad truth: Most non–E.U. countries won't let you bring back much more than a bottle or two (p. 296). Wine stores abound, and even the humblest of them are generally staffed by knowledgeable wine-lovers who will be glad to help you find the perfect bottle to celebrate your Parisian adventure.

Cave des Abbesses ★ This small wine shop/wine bar has been serving residents of Montmartre since 1986. Not only will the staff help you muddle through excellent vintages, you can also sample a few while you're there and nibble on cheese and charcuterie (open until 10:30pm). 43 rue des Abbesses, 18th arrond. www.cavesbourdin.fr. ✆ **01-42-52-81-54.** Métro: Abbesses.

Legrand Filles et Fils ★★ More than just a wine store, this is a place where you can learn everything there is to know about the sacred grape. The store has a dedicated, well-informed staff and a huge stock of wines; hosts wine tastings and classes; and also sells books and paraphernalia. It's in the glamorous Galerie Vivienne (p. 211). 1 rue de la Banque, 2nd arrond. www.caves-legrand.com. ✆ **01-42-60-07-12.** Métro: Bourse.

Les Domaines Qui Montent ★★★ French wine-drinkers know that you'll get the best prices when you buy direct at a vineyard. In an attempt to make these prices available to urbanites, this association of some 150 wine producers offers a vast selection of *vins du producteur,* wines that come from small, independent vineyards where the emphasis is on quality and *terroir,* not quantity. Prices are very good, and if you come by at lunchtime you can open a bottle and eat a meal at their *table d'hôte* (16.90€ for two courses). They have five other locations across the city. 22 rue Cardinet, 17th arrond. www.les domainesquimontent.com. ✆ **01-42-27-63-96.** Métro: Courcelles or Wagram.

Gifts & Souvenirs

Arty Dandy ★★ Dedicated to selling French and European brands (especially when they're eco-friendly), this chic shop has a stock that might include sheepskin wine coolers (yes, sheepskin—by the brand Kywie), handmade ceramics and jewelry, funky clothes, and all sorts of accessories you never knew existed. There's another branch in the Marais at 43 rue de Turenne, 3rd arrond. 1 rue Furstemberg, 6th arrond. https://artydandyofficiel.com. ✆ **01-43-54-00-36.** Métro: Mabillon.

Fnac ★ A huge chain that sells a compelling combination of books, music, electronics, and tickets to shows and museums, Fnac (pronounced "fnack") has branches all over the city. This is an ideal spot to visit if you need something for your computer, smartphone, or camera. 136 rue de Rennes, 6th arrond. www.fnac.com. ✆ **08-25-02-00-20** (.20€/min). Métro: St-Placide.

Paris Est une Photo ★ Tucked in a delightful covered passage, this hybrid gallery-cum-boutique is the place to come for stunning Paris-themed photos. Some of them are old black and white; others are quirky and contemporary. Everything would look good on a wall at home. 55 passage Jouffroy, 9th arrond. https://photo.paris. ✆ **01-56-92-04-47.** Métro: Grands Boulevards.

Housewares, Kitchen & Decoration

E. Dehillerin ★★★ This venerable store near Les Halles is where the city's chefs come to buy their kitchen material. E. Dehillerin sells everything from copper pans and ergonomic zesters, to icing bags, fish-bone tweezers, whipped cream siphons, and plenty of other things you never knew you needed. Keep track of what you want to buy on a piece of paper, then pay at the till, where you'll be handed your order. Unlike elsewhere in Paris, prices are displayed without VAT, which is added when you pay. 18 and 20 rue Coquillère, 1st arrond. www.edehillerin.fr. ☎ **01-42-36-53-13.** Métro/RER: Les Halles.

La Maison Ivre ★★   Linens and beautiful handmade pottery from all over France, especially Provençal ceramics, are sold here, including ovenware, bowls, platters, plates, pitchers, mugs, and vases. The beautiful tea towels, placemats, and tablecloths here make great gifts and pack easily. 38 rue Jacob, 6th arrond. www.maison-ivre.com. ☎ **01-42-60-01-85.** Métro: St-Germain-des-Prés.

Jewelry & Accessories

Bijoux Blues ★★   Unique jewelry at reasonable prices handmade in an atelier in the Marais—who could ask for more? Made of Austrian and bohemian crystals, natural and semiprecious stones, pearls, and coral, the designs are fun and funky, yet elegant. Pieces can be custom-designed. 30 rue St-Paul, 4th arrond. www.bijouxblues.com. ☎ **01-48-04-00-64.** Métro: St-Paul.

Bijoux Burma ★   Pretend you are a princess with these excellent copies of the kind of spectacular pieces you could never afford. These famous, high-quality synthetic jewels, set in gold, silver, or vermeil, are some of the best fakes around. All five branches are strategically placed in the fanciest shopping neighborhoods. 50 rue François 1er, 8th arrond. www.bijouxburma.com. ☎ **01-47-23-70-93.** Métro: Franklin-D-Roosevelt.

WHITE bIRD ★★   If you are looking for a unique engagement ring or present for your sweetheart, this is a good bet. The low-key store offers a terrific selection of jewelry made by talented independent craftspeople and designers. A second store is at 7 bd. des Filles du Calvaire, and a third at 62 rue des Saint-Pères. 38 rue du Mont Thabor, 1st arrond. www.whitebirdjewellery.com. ☎ **01-58-62-25-86.** Métro: Concorde.

Toys & Games

JouéClub Village ★   As the village part of its name suggests, this toy store is huge, taking over the whole of Passage des Princes (p. 211). Separate shop entrances lead into different themed areas, covering everything from baby toys and teddy bears to Lego and dress-up clothes. It is full of every possible game, book, puzzle, or toy you could imagine. 3-5 bd. des Italiens, 2nd arrond. www.joueclub.fr. ☎ **01-53-45-41-41.** Métro: Richelieu Drouot.

Tikibou ★★   One of the oldest toy stores in Paris (founded in 1884), this human-size establishment is a marvelous example of the quintessential French toy store. Wooden toys, scale models, figurines, music boxes, musical instruments, dolls, board games, stuffed animals, costumes—in short, everything that delights and enchants and doesn't need batteries. A second store is at 33 bd. Edgar Quinet, close to the Montparnasse train station. 20 av. Félix Faure, 15th arrond. www.tikibou-jouets.com. ☎ **01-45-58-17-44.** Métro: Félix Faure.

ENTERTAINMENT & NIGHTLIFE

Paris blooms at night. Its magnificent monuments and buildings become even more beautiful when they're cloaked in their evening illuminations. The already glowing Eiffel Tower bursts out in twinkling lights for the first 5 minutes of every hour. Simply walking around town can be an excellent night out, but the city is also a treasure trove of rich nightlife offerings. Choose from bars and clubs from chic to shaggy, sublime theater and dance performances, top-class orchestras, and scores of cinemas and art-house movie theaters.

While Paris isn't a 24-hour town like some international capitals, and many neighborhoods may seem pretty quiet after sundown, you will still have plenty of places to go if you are ready for a night out. So, whether you're planning to hit the most happening clubs or are happy with a 4€ beer in a student bar in the Latin Quarter, here's how to find your way. Below is a biased selection of some of the better entertainment options, from drinking hot spots to sports venues.

GETTING TICKETS   Many hotels will help you get tickets, and most venues offer reservations online, some with apps to download your ticket onto your phone. Otherwise, one of the easiest ways to buy tickets is at **Fnac** (p. 226), the giant bookstore/music chain that has one of the most comprehensive box offices in the city (follow the signs to the "Billeterie"). You can also **order your tickets online** in English at www.fnactickets.com or **by phone** at ℭ **08-92-68-36-22** (.40€/min.). **Ticketmaster.fr** offers a similar service.

Discount hunters can stand in line at one of the city's three **half-price ticket booths,** all run by **Le Kiosque Théâtre** (www.kiosqueculture.com). One is in front of the Montparnasse train station, another on the west side of the Madeleine (facing 15 pl. de la Madeleine, exit rue Tronchet from the Madeleine Métro stop), and a third in Paris's main tourist office (Office de Tourisme et des Congrès de Paris; 29 rue de Rivoli, 4th arrond.). At time of writing, the entertainment world had just begun reopening after Covid-19, and the ticket booths' opening hours were up in the air; it's best to check the website. Plenty of ticket discounts can also be had at **BilletRéduc,** www.billetreduc.com (in French).

THEATER

Paris has dozens of theaters, most of which have something going on almost every night. The obvious catch here is, almost all of it is in French. But even if you can't spit out much more than *bonjour,* you have options, including an English-speaking box office service and a few English-language shows (see "Theater in English," below). Alternatively, you can opt for one of the many avant-garde offerings at theaters like Théâtre National de Chaillot or Théâtre de la Ville, where the shows combine dance, theater, and images, and don't really need translation.

Comédie-Française ★★ In 1680, Louis XIV announced the birth of a company of actors, chosen by himself, with the aim of "making theater productions more perfect." More than 300 years later, it is still considered by many the crème de la crème of the French theater scene. In addition to the gorgeous main theater (**Salle Richelieu**), the company presents its offerings in its two other theaters: the medium-size **Théâtre du Vieux Colombier,** 21 rue du Vieux Colombier, 6th arrond. (Métro: St-Sulpice or Sèvres–Babylone), and the smaller **Studio-Théâtre,** Galerie du Carrousel du Louvre, under the Pyramid, 99 rue de Rivoli, 1st arrond. (Métro: Palais Royal–Musée du Louvre). pl. Colette, 1st arrond. www.comedie-francaise.fr. ℓ **01-44-58-15-15.** Métro: Palais-Royal–Musée du Louvre.

Theater in English

English-language shows are rare, and comedians even more so, but a couple of long-standing gigs in town are worth a detour. One of the best stand-up performers is **Sebastien Marx** (https://sebmarx.com/en), though at time of writing, his gig, the **"New York Comedy Night,"** wasn't playing. This doesn't mean it won't come back, so check his website for up-to-date information. Another good show is **"How to Become a Parisian in One Hour"** (at Théâtre des Nouveautés; reservations at www.oliviergiraud.com), a one-person show written by Olivier Giraud, a Frenchman who spent several years in the U.S. For "theater" proper (so to speak), an excellent English-language box-office service is **Theatre in Paris** (www.theatreinparis.com), with tickets to multiple shows offering English supertitles.

Odéon, Théâtre de l'Europe ★ Less venerable and more modern, this grand theater presents both new plays and old classics, but even the classics usually get a modern twist. You can see lots of cutting-edge, contemporary pieces here, including several from other European countries (hence the moniker "Théâtre de l'Europe"). Foreign productions are supertitled, which can be a plus if you can read French. The Odéon's second space, **Ateliers Berthier,** 1 rue André Suarès, 17th arrond. (Métro: Porte de Clichy), presents smaller-scale productions, as well as theater for young actors. pl. de l'Odéon, 6th arrond. www.theatre-odeon.eu. ℂ **01-44-85-40-40.** Métro: Odéon.

8 LANDMARK MULTIUSE VENUES

La Seine Musicale ★★★ The latest major addition to the Parisian music scene resembles a futuristic cruise ship in the middle of the Seine. This architectural marvel sits on an island in the river next to the western suburb of Boulogne-Billancourt. The complex includes recording studios, restaurants, a garden, and two top-notch concert spaces: one dedicated to classical music, and the other for dance, pop music, musical comedies, and other cultural events. The magnificent classical music hall is encased in a huge, globe-shaped structure protected by an enormous photovoltaic sail that slowly rotates around the globe, screening it from the sun and producing solar energy. It's a bit of a trek to get here, but it will be a concert experience you won't soon forget. Ile de Seguin, Boulogne-Billancourt. www.laseinemusicale.com. ℂ **01-74-34-54-00.** Métro: Pont de Sèvres, then a 10-min. walk.

Stade de France ★★★ In the nearby suburb of Saint-Denis, this vast stadium is first and foremost for sports, hosting national and international soccer and rugby games. But it's also one of France's most prestigious concert venues, drawing megastars like Bruno Mars, Ed Sheeran, Beyoncé, and Jay-Z, and filling all 81,000 seats with screaming, dedicated fans. If you're with sports-mad kids, the daytime guided tours run by Cultival (some in English; www.cultival.fr) are worth the 90 minutes, taking you into the locker rooms and other places usually off-limits during matches (from 15€ adults, 10€ children 5–18, free for children 4 and under). www.stadefrance.com. ℂ **01-73-03-60-03.** Métro: Saint-Denis Porte de Paris. RER B: La Plaine Stade de France.

Finding Out What's On

Sortir à Paris (www.sortiraparis.com) lists everything from plays and festivals to concerts and movie screenings in English. If you can read French, two other websites to try are **l'Officiel des Spectacles** (www.offi.fr) and **Télérama** (www.telerama.fr). Or for the latest info about live music, try **Lylo** (www.lylo.fr), also in French. By the way, if you see a sign at a theater or on an events website that says *location,* that means "box office," not location. If you want to see a new movie, remember that Wednesday is France's release day.

Dance Performances

Paris is the nation's dance capital, and most of the country's best companies are based here, including the phenomenal **Ballet de l'Opéra National de Paris** (see "Opéra de Paris," below). Top French choreographers like Angelin Preljoçaj, Blanca Li, and José Montalvo have produced here, as well as other European stars like Sidi Larbi Cherkaoui and Mats Ek. Two of the biggest dance venues are **Théâtre National de Chaillot** and **Théâtre de la Ville** (see below). Dance is often grouped with classical music in magazine and website listings.

Théâtre de la Ville ★★ It's hard to say which lineup is the most impressive here: theater (new and recent authors), dance (modern dance companies, such as Anne Teresa De Keersmaeker and Lucinda Childs), or music (mostly young stars of the classical music scene). A lot of international productions stop by here on tour. There's also a separate World Music series. 2 pl. du Châtelet, 4th arrond. www.theatredelaville-paris.com. ☏ **01-42-74-22-77.** Métro: Châtelet.

Théâtre du Châtelet ★★ Specializing in all that is big and splashy, this lovely, freshly revamped 19th-century theater hosts visiting international orchestras, divas, and ballet companies, as well as revivals of musical-theater classics (usually in their original language). Previous biggies have included "Singing in the Rain" and "An American in Paris," created by the theater itself and winner of four Tony Awards. 1 pl. du Châtelet, 1st arrond. www.chatelet.com. ☏ **01-40-28-28-40.** Métro: Châtelet.

Théâtre National de Chaillot ★★ Dance and theater are on equal footing at this beautiful Art Deco theater in the Palais de Chaillot, where contemporary choreographers and theater directors share a jam-packed program. There is a lot of blurring of lines here between the two disciplines; dance programs often include video and text, and theater productions often incorporate the abstract. 1 pl. du Trocadéro, 16th arrond. www.theatre-chaillot.fr. ☏ **01-53-65-30-00.** Métro: Trocadéro.

OPERA & CLASSICAL MUSIC

Opéra Comique/Salle Favart ★★ For a lighter take on opera, try this architectural puff pastry filled with operettas. Created in 1714 for theatrical performances that included songs, the Opéra Comique endured several fires before finally settling down in a beautiful 19th-century theater with huge chandeliers. It's an excellent opportunity to enjoy both history and music in a splendid setting. Works by 19th-century composer Jacques Offenbach are nearly always on the program. 5 rue Favart, 2nd arrond. www.opera-comique.com. ☏ **01-70-23-01-31.** Métro: Richelieu–Drouot or Quatre-Septembre.

Opéra de Paris ★★★ This mighty operation includes both the **Palais Garnier,** pl. de l'Opéra, 9th arrond. (an attraction in itself; p. 154) and the

Heaven-Sent Music Venues: Concerts in Churches

Many of Paris' most beautiful churches and cathedrals, including St-Eustache and Sainte-Chapelle, host organ and other classical music concerts. Not only is the setting delightful, but the acoustics are generally otherworldly. While there is no central ticketing for these artistic houses of God, concerts are usually listed in the weekly-listings website l'Officiel des Spectacles (www.offi.fr), under concerts. Most churches print monthly music schedules, which they display near the entrance to the sanctuary (and sometimes post on their websites). Ticket prices are reasonable; sometimes concerts are free, and if they aren't, you likely won't pay more than 30€.

Opéra Bastille, pl. de la Bastille, 12th arrond., a slate-colored behemoth that has loomed over the Place de la Bastille since 1989. Not wanting to abandon the Palais Garnier, the company decided to split its energies between the two venues. In theory, more operas are performed at Bastille, which has more space and supposedly better acoustics. The Garnier, home of the **Ballet de l'Opèra National de Paris,** focuses more on dance, but you can see either at both. The opera program sticks pretty much to the classics (although productions can be cutting edge), while the ballet offerings are becoming more adventurous. Subtitles are often in English. www.operadeparis.fr. ⓒ **08-92-89-90-90** (.35€/min.); from outside France ⓒ 01-71-25-24-23.

Philharmonie de Paris ★★★ Hovering over La Villette like a visiting spaceship, this mega venue seats 2,400 spectators and serves as the home of the Orchestre de Paris. Yet another creation of über-architect Jean Nouvel (this time in partnership with Harold Marshall and with input from Yasuhisa Toyota), this silvery apparition also encompasses a music museum and other performance spaces in the adjacent **Cité de la Musique** building, as well as a nifty cafe and restaurant. In keeping with La Villette's policy of making culture accessible to all, the season includes symphonic and choral concerts, as well as performances for young people, families, and audiences that don't usually

The beautiful ceiling at the Palais Garnier, home of the Ballet de l'Opèra de Paris.

The Opéra Bastille was inaugurated in 1989 for the bicentennial of the Revolution.

find themselves in concert halls (though these book up fast). The Cité de la Musique complex offers a wide range of music options from classical to contemporary to jazz, and a good dose of the offbeat and unexpected. Highlights include young musicians and rising stars; small orchestras and chamber musicians also show up on the program. 221 av. Jean-Jaurès, 19th arrond. https://philharmoniedeparis.fr. ✆ **01-44-84-44-84.** Métro: Porte de Pantin.

CABARET & CHANSON

At the end of the 19th century, cabarets and music halls opened in Montmartre, frequented by oddballs and artists, as well as aristocrats, the bourgeoisie, and demimondaines looking for a good time. These nightclubs offered an offbeat reflection of the times: Singers like Aristide Bruand would sing about the life of the destitute, and sharp political satire would share the stage with cheeky dancing girls dancing that new step, the can-can. Those days are long gone. There is nothing particularly Parisian, or even French, about cabarets anymore. Today's audiences are more likely to arrive in tour buses than touring cars, and contemporary shows are more Vegas than Paris.

If music's your thing, try "chanson" instead—those peculiarly melody-challenged songs that Edith Piaf sang. If you don't understand the words, it can be hard to understand why so many French people get all misty-eyed when they listen to this music. But that's just it: With chanson, it's the words that count. Each song is a poem set to music; in fact, some lyrics are the works of famous French authors. Whether it's cabaret or chanson you're looking for, these places will tick your boxes, albeit with a large dose of cliché.

Les Trois Baudets ★★ You've heard it: the tremulous voice, the monotonous tunes, the intense sincerity of it all. Yes, that's chanson, and in recent years, a new generation of young singers/writers has been coming up with their own poetic versions of the trials and tribulations of life, and their heroes are not so much Piaf and Aznavour as Leonard Cohen and Bob Dylan. This place is the biggest venue for contemporary chanson these days. You can make a night of it, thanks to its bar/restaurant. 64 bd. de Clichy, 18th arrond. www.lestroisbaudets.com. ✆ **01-42-62-33-33.** Tickets 10€–25€. Métro: Pigalle or Blanche.

Lido de Paris ★ For a full-on glamour gala, head for the Lido. Headdresses and high heels are of such dimensions that the dancers can't do much dancing, but you're probably not coming here for prima ballerina turns. The latest show, "Paris Merveilles," conceived by Franco Dragone of Cirque du Soleil fame, includes 200kg (440 lb.) of feathers, 300 projectors, and of course, the famed Bluebell Girls. Unlike some of the other cabarets, the music is live here and the food is of a higher caliber. A few afternoon shows with lunch options are offered. 116 av. des Champs-Élysées, 8th arrond. www.lido.fr. ✆ **01-40-76-56-10.** Show only 75€–180€; afternoon show 55€–105€; afternoon show with lunch 150€; show with dinner 145€–450€. Métro: George V.

Moulin Rouge ★ When it opened in 1889, the Moulin Rouge was the talk of the town, and its huge dance floor, multiple mirrors, and floral garden inspired painters like Toulouse-Lautrec. In later decades, legendary French singers like Charles Trenet and Charles Aznavour regularly wowed the crowds. Times have changed. Today's Moulin Rouge, with its "Féerie" show, relies heavily on lip-syncing and prerecorded music, backed by dozens of be-feathered long-legged Doriss Girls. Be prepared for plenty of glitz and not a whole lot else. 82 bd. Clichy, pl. Blanche, 18th arrond. www.moulinrouge.fr. ✆ **01-53-09-82-82.** Show only 77€–245€; show with dinner 190€–420€. Métro: Blanche.

MOVIES

With over 400 movie screens and between 450 and 500 films on offer every week, Paris merits its title as cinephile capital of the world. The art house cinemas specialize in rare films, old classics, and independent works. You can find listings of both mainstream and art house theaters online at **Allocine** (www.allocine.fr). Many of the mainstream movies shown in the big chain movie theaters are dubbed in French (v.f., or *version française*). If you want to see a mainstream English-language film, make sure you find one in v.o. (*version orginale*); cinema companies **MK2** and **UGC** will nearly always be showing an English-language movie. Or check out **Lost in Frenchlation** (http://lostinfrenchlation.com), a film society that organizes three to four monthly screenings of French movies with English subtitles.

Some of the most famous art houses include **Le Champo, Reflet Medecis,** and **Ecoles Cinéma Club,** all in the Latin Quarter. The most scandalous is **Studio 28,** 10 rue Tholozé, 18th arrond. (www.cinema-studio28.fr; ✆ **01-46-06-36-07;** Métro: Blanche or Abbesses), where Luis Buñuel's polemical 1930 movie, "L'Age d'Or," was censored after only two showings here. One of the newest additions to the art house scene is the reborn **Louxor,** 170 bd. Magenta, 10th arrond. (www.cinemalouxor.fr; ℰ **01-44-63-96-96;** Métro: Barbès-Rochechouart), a gorgeous neo-Egyptian 1920s movie palace that had been abused and abandoned until the city took it over and restored it.

In addition to regular movie theaters, two giant **cinema archives** have their own theaters and programs. The first is the **Forum des Images,** Forum des Halles, Porte St-Eustache, 1st arrond. (www.forumdesimages.fr; ℰ **01-44-76-63-00;** Métro: Châtelet–Les Halles), which is funded by the City of Paris and has a bank of over 7,500 films, including thousands that feature Paris as either the subject or the setting. The other is the **Fondation Jérôme Seydoux-Pathé,** 75 av. des Gobelins, 13th arrond. (www.fondation-jeromeseydoux-pathe.com; ℰ **01-83-79-18-96;** Métro: Place d'Italie), which specializes in film history and regularly screens silent films accompanied by live pianists.

LIVE ROCK, JAZZ, ELECTRO & MORE

Paris has a wide range of places to hear live music, from tiny medieval basements to huge modern concert venues. Whatever your musical tastes, you are bound to enjoy your outing: Not only do many of the world's greatest musicians swing through the city on a regular basis, but you can't beat the walk to the nightclub/bar/theater with the lights of Paris twinkling in the background.

Live Music
JAZZ CLUBS

Paris has been a fan of jazz from its beginnings, and many legendary performers like Sidney Bechet and Kenny Clark made the city their home. Still a haven for jazz musicians and fans of all stripes, Paris boasts dozens of places to duck into and listen to a good set or two. Some of the best are listed here.

Baiser Salé ★★   On a street lined with famous jazz clubs, this one holds its own with a lineup that shows off jazz in all its diversity. Some of the biggest Franco-African jazz stars, like Richard Bona and Angelique Kidjo, got their start here, and the program still highlights the best in African, Caribbean, and Asian jazz, as well as French jazz. Regular jam sessions are on Sundays and Mondays. 58 rue des Lombards, 1st arrond. www.lebaisersale.com. ℰ **01-42-33-37-71.** Cover free–25€. Métro: Châtelet.

Caveau de la Huchette ★   This temple of swing has seen business boom since it was recreated in a short scene in the 2016 hit film "La La Land." Legends like Count Basie and Lionel Hampton once graced this basement club, and some excellent jazz musicians still play here. The first part of the evening (starting at 9pm) is usually for enjoying the music. After that, there's often swing and Lindy Hop until 2:30 or 4am. 5 rue de la Huchette, 5th arrond. www.caveaudelahuchette.fr. ℰ **01-43-26-65-05.** Sun–Thurs cover 13€; Fri–Sat 15€; students 24 and under 10€. Métro/RER: St-Michel.

Le Duc des Lombards ★★ This is one of the most renowned jazz clubs in Paris, where famous names come to play in a small, intimate space. That said, it's a relatively low-key place, and tickets aren't too hard to get—but good seats are (they are not numbered). Reserve your ticket in advance, then get here early if you want to sit up front. Light meals are served. Before the Covid-19 pandemic, the club hosted free jam sessions on Fridays and Saturdays after midnight. At time of writing, the sessions had been canceled, but they are set to return, so check the website for details. 42 rue des Lombards, 1st arrond. www.ducdeslombards.com. © **01-42-33-22-88.** Cover free–41€; dining options available. Métro: Châtelet.

Le Sunset/Le Sunside ★★ Yes, this is another famous jazz club on the rue des Lombards, but what sets this one off is its split personality. Le Sunset Jazz, created in 1983, is dedicated to electric jazz and international music, whereas Le Sunside, launched in 2001, is devoted to acoustic jazz for the most part. Some of the hottest names in French jazz appear here regularly (Jacky Terrasson and Didier Lockwood, to name a couple), along with a new crop of international stars like Kyle Eastwood. 60 rue des Lombards, 1st arrond. www.sunset-sunside.com. © **01-40-26-46-60.** Tickets free–35€. Métro: Châtelet.

New Morning ★★★ Big names and hot acts? Look no further. This place has terrific lineups, including virtuosos like bassist Avishai Cohen, pop-soul masters like Roy Ayers and Joan Armatrading, and a long list of fusion upstarts and world music stars. This relatively large club (the room holds 300) fills up quickly, and it's no wonder: This is one of the best jazz venues in town, but the top ticket price is only around 30€. 7 rue des Petites-Ecuries, 10th arrond. www.newmorning.com. No phone. Cover free–30€. Métro: Château-d'Eau.

CONCERT VENUES

Cabaret Sauvage ★★ Is it a cool club or a circus tent? The answer is not clear at this unusual space where you are just as likely to encounter Brazilian samba, electro funk, or trapeze artists. Blues bands from the Balkans and Vietnamese jazz musicians share the calendar with avant-garde circus acts and Algerian acrobats. Although this big-top cabaret is essentially a performance space with an accent on world music and dance, it also hosts themed dance parties, where you can boogie to jungle and techno, as well as *raï* (a kind of Algerian folk music), mambo, samba, and so forth. Parc de la Villette, entrance at 59 bd. MacDonald, 19th arrond. www.cabaretsauvage.com. © **01-42-09-03-09.** Métro: Porte de la Villette.

La Cigale ★★ This 19th-century music hall draws some of the biggest artists working in music today—playing everything from indie rock to hip-hop to jazz. Balcony seating is available for those who arrive early, and there's plenty of open floor space for those who want to dance. 120 bd. de Rochechouart, 18th arrond. www.lacigale.fr. © **01-49-25-89-99.** Métro: Pigalle or Anvers.

Le Petit Bain ★★ Small and intimate, this cool music boat floating on the Seine is a place to see emerging bands, mostly of the rock, pop, and electro

The New Morning club.

variety. There's a waterside restaurant and a rooftop bar for those who want to make a night of it. In summer, the fun spreads onto the riverbank, with dining and more music outside. 7 port de la Gare, 13th arrond. https://petitbain.org. No phone. Métro: Quai de la Gare or Bibliothèque François Mitterand.

Olympia ★★★ For French musicians, playing the Olympia is a little like reaching the golden heaven of the Greek gods. Legends like Georges Brassens, Edith Piaf, Louis Armstrong, and Aretha Franklin have all appeared at this cavernous hall, which draws French and international pop, rock, and jazz stars like Juliette Greco, Diana Krall, and Sting. 28 bd. des Capucines, 9th arrond. www.olympiahall.com. ✆ **08-92-68-33-68** (.40€/min.). Métro: Opéra or Madeleine.

MUSIC BARS

Whether you're into rock, pop, or electro, Paris has bars aplenty to choose from. Many have stages for live shows, while others are the realms of DJs big and small. In the 1990s Paris and Versailles were the hubs of a new sound, *La French Touch*, aka electronic music that drew inspiration from disco and added its own beats (often inspired by house music). The trend took the world by storm, creating groups and artists like Daft Punk, Saint Germain, Kavinsky (of the 2011 "Drive" movie fame), and Justice. While these groups are more likely to be headlining stadiums nowadays, Paris' music bar scene is still creative. Keep your eyes and ears open, and you might just hear the next big sound.

L'Alabama ★ Love heavy metal? This über-hip bar by Canal St-Martin belongs to Mikkey Dee, the legendary ex-Motörhead drummer (now with the

Scorpions), and has a rebellious air about it. Tattooed crowds flock to the bar for IPA and whiskey as a jukebox spins rock and metal classics well into the wee hours. 32 rue Albert Thomas, 10th arrond. www.facebook.com/AlabamaBarParis. No phone. Métro: Jacques Bonsergent.

Les Disquaires ★★ In party HQ (aka the Bastille area), this is the place to come early for the happy hour, then stay for the live jazz, soul, hip-hop, funk, and pop concerts. Once the show's over, it's DJ time until 2am (5am Fri and Sat). 4–6 rue des Taillandiers, 11th arrond. http://lesdisquaires.com. No phone. Métro: Bastille or Ledru Rollin.

Supersonic ★ In a cool industrial building at Bastille, this temple to the independent spirit is free and promotes unknown stars of tomorrow. Live bands play anything from garage and electro to post-punk and psych, and there's a specialist indie music record shop open on Friday, Saturday, and Sunday afternoons from 2 to 7pm. 9 rue Biscornet, 12th arrond. www.supersonic-club.fr. ℂ **01-46-28-12-90.** Métro: Bastille.

CATEGORY-DEFYING VENUES

An increasing number of venues are so multifunctional they defy any attempt to fit them under the usual headings. Sure, you can enjoy music and dance in these places, but you can also go to a screening, check out a poetry lounge, visit an art expo, happen in on a lecture/demonstration, and of course, eat, drink, and be merry. Many are all-day affairs, where the activities change as the sun goes down, while others are purely for night owls. With so many variables, checking the venue's program online is the best way to find out what's on during your stay.

Favela Chic ★★ It's always Rio at this Brazilian hot spot where patrons dance to bossa jazz, samba rap, and tropical electro into the wee hours of the night in the club. There are three other spaces too: a 1930s-inspired speakeasy serving some of the best mojitos in town; a pop-up gallery for art launches that morphs into a summer terrace; and a restaurant whipping up copious plates of Franco-Brazilian delights. 18 rue du Faubourg du Temple, 11th arrond. www.favela-chic.com. ℂ **01-40-21-38-14.** Métro: République.

La Bellevilloise ★★ This 19th-century building was the home of the city's first workers' cooperative, offering cultural activities and meeting spaces to the downtrodden. Today the structure has been transformed, but the mission is still a cultural one. Dedicated to "light, night, and creativity," the lofty space has been divvied up into art galleries, performance spaces, a concert hall, a club, and a restaurant with a lovely outdoor terrace where you can have a drink. The program ranges from film festivals to fashion shows, with a good dose of contemporary music. On Sundays, there's a popular brunch (reservations recommended) with live jazz and an all-you-can-eat buffet. 19–21 rue Boyer, 20th arrond. www.labellevilloise.com. ℂ **01-46-36-07-07.** Métro: Gambetta.

Live Rock, Jazz, Electro & More

ENTERTAINMENT & NIGHTLIFE

La Recyclerie ★★★ Describing itself as an "eco-responsible place of experimentation," this converted train station by Porte de Clignancourt and the St-Ouen flea market in northern Paris is part restaurant, part bar, part urban farm, and part furniture repair shop. Bees produce honey in rooftop hives, chickens lay eggs in open-air pens, and vegetables grow in lovingly tended patches. In nice weather, a suitably downscale-hip **bar and restaurant** sprawls out onto the former rail lines, where everyone from cool 20-somethings to families with kids tuck into weekly-changing menus that might include Lebanese mezes or handmade burgers. 83 bd. Ornano, 18th arrond. www.larecyclerie.com. ℂ **01-42-57-58-49.** Métro: Porte de Clignancourt.

Le Centquatre ★★★ What was once the municipal morgue is now a vast space dedicated to all things artistic and fun. You'll find food for both the soul and the stomach here: theater, dance, music, and visual arts, as well as a gourmet grocery, cafes, and restaurants. Along with concerts and dance parties for grown-ups are activities for families and little ones (musical events, art workshops, and so forth). If that's not enough, you can also shop in the Emmaüs shop (a charitable organization that sells wonderful used knickknacks and furniture) or browse the bookstore. 5 rue Curial, 19th arrond. www.104.fr. ℂ **01-53-35-50-00.** Métro: Riquet.

Machine du Moulin Rouge ★★ A heck of a lot hipper than its historic next-door neighbor (the Moulin Rouge, p. 234), this three-story multitasker has dance floors, concert space, and bars—basically, everything you need for a rollicking night out. The music-savvy crowds come for electronic everything: rock, funk, pop, dubstep, glitch, drum'n'bass, house—not to mention live music by rising stars. There's also a seasonal rooftop and a champagne bar that serves a popular brunch. 90 bd. de Clichy, 18th arrond. www.lamachinedumoulinrouge.com. ℂ **01-53-41-88-89.** Métro: Blanche.

THE BAR SCENE

For a city that does not seem to have a particularly feisty nightlife at first sight, Paris has an astounding assortment of bars. There are cafes galore, of course, but a cafe is not necessarily a bar. Though both serve alcoholic beverages, cafes offer a laid-back place to sip at any time of day or night, whereas anything that calls itself a bar usually has an edgier feel and gets going after dark. Bars, be they beer-, wine-, or cocktail-oriented, generally stay open until around 2am.

Bars & Cafes

Andy Wahloo ★★ After a decade or so of hosting the happening crowd in an ambience of North African kitsch, this ultra-cool bar has had a makeover—now it is sleek and sophisticated, with a decor that gives a nod to the 1950s. In keeping with the times, the bartenders outdo themselves working up clever cocktails. 69 rue des Gravilliers, 3rd arrond. www.andywahloo-bar.com. ℂ **01-42-71-20-38.** Métro: Arts et Métiers.

Café Charbon ★ A turn-of-the-20th-century beauty (it was once a dance hall), this cafe welcomes hordes of happy night owls under its arched ceilings. The door in the back leads to the nightclub, **Le Nouveau Casino** (http://nouveaucasino.fr), where live bands and DJs shake it up until the wee hours. You can come here any time of day for coffee, a drink, or a decent meal. 109 rue Oberkampf, 11th arrond. http://lecafecharbon.fr. *C* **01-43-57-55-13.** Métro: Parmentier or Ménilmontant.

La Palette ★ Cézanne, Picasso, and Braque once hung out in this old-world Left Bank bar, and you'll still find a spattering of artists, students, and gallery owners today. The front room's where the regulars prop themselves up; the beautiful back room is where the romantics go to sip wine amid original frescoes and old mirrors. 43 rue de Seine, 6th arrond. www.lapalette-paris.com. *C* **01-43-26-68-15.** Métro: St-Germain-des-Prés.

Lavomatic ★★ This fun joint can only be accessed by a hidden door inside a working laundromat. Once you find it (try the washing machine door in the corner opposite the entrance), you're in for a night of funky electro sound and regressive cocktails. Try the Nuage Rose (pink cloud), a gin drink with red-fruit syrup, lemon juice, hibiscus tonic, and mini marshmallows. To really fit in with the locals, bring your clothes for a spin in the washer while you have fun upstairs. Lavomatic opens at 6pm. 10 rue René Boulanger, 10th arrond. www.lavomatic.paris. No phone. Métro: République, Temple, or Jacques Bonsergent.

Le Perchoir ★★★ Take in a fabulous view of eastern Paris from this rooftop bar, which has been so successful it has spawned a passel of other high-altitude nightspots on top of buildings in the Marais, Buttes Chaumont, and even (in summer) on the roof of the Gare de l'Est (check website for all locations). Sip a cocktail on an outdoor sofa and gaze at Sacré-Coeur, or flirt at the tented bar; if you want to sit down, come early before the crowd arrives. 14 rue Crespin du Gast, 11th arrond. www.leperchoir.tv. *C* **01-48-06-18-48.** Métro: Ménilmontant.

Alfresco: Summer Terraces with a View

From May to October, Parisians head outdoors, sharpening their elbows to vie for the best rooftop, riverboat, and sidewalk terraces. And you should, too: Many spots offer some of the best views the city has to offer. For dreamy vistas onto Île-Saint-Louis, try **Les Maquereaux** river barge, Quai de l'Hôtel de Ville, Parc Rives de Seine, 4th arrond. (www.lesmaquereaux.com; *C* **01-73-78-36-41**; Métro: Hôtel-de-Ville), where those in the know sit on the tree-shaded quayside to indulge in crisp rosé and oysters. Or for sweeping views over the city's rooftops and the Eiffel Tower, hit **Moncoeur Belleville,** 1 rue des Envierges, 20th arrond. (*C* **01-43-66-38-54**; Métro: Pyrénées), which sits on a hill above Parc de Belleville. It's particularly good on Bastille Day (July 14), when you can see the fireworks exploding all over the city (arrive early to claim your spot).

With its frescoes in the back room, La Palette is a magnet for art students.

Wine Bars

Wine fans can lose their heads in this city, not because they drink too much but because Paris has so many tempting wine bars to choose from. Not only can you sample all sorts of delightful fruits of the vine at a *bar à vin,* but you can also usually nibble something salty and delicious (generally cheese or charcuterie) to complement what's in the glass.

G.A.G. ★ The initials G.A.G. stand for *Gras, Alcool, Gluten* (fat, alcohol, and gluten), which pretty much sums up what this hybrid little spot at the end of an old-world passage has to offer. The fat part refers to the meat (beautiful, succulent platters of duck and ham) that soaks up the natural wines, the "alcohol," (from *petits* French producers), while the gluten is all about the leavened bread, made from ancient varieties of wheat. Pop by for a drink or a meal. The food is as good as the wine. 3 rue Palestro, 2nd arrond. ⓒ **01-42-86-01-26.** Métro: Etienne Marcel.

La Cave à Michel ★★ Wear comfy shoes, as this long, narrow bar in gritty Belleville is standing-only—which is part of the fun. Snag a spot at the bar and watch the locals kiss cheeks as they greet each other and chat over the impressive collection of natural wines (mostly French and Italian) and some of the best tasting plates in northern Paris (think marinated sea bass ceviche, black pig ham, and beef tataki, all excellently prepared). For a fabulous sit-down meal, the next-door neo-bistro, Le Galopin, is run by the same crew. 36 rue Ste-Marthe, 10th arrond. www.facebook.com/lacaveamichel. ⓒ **01-42-45-94-47.** Métro: Belleville.

La Vache dans les Vignes ★★   It's all about that magic duo cheese and wine at this hip neighborhood spot along the Canal St-Martin. Just choose your wine, then sit back and let the staff pair it with one of their in-house matured cheeses (their crumbly Mimolette is a winner). Fancy a picnic along the canal? Buy everything to take out. 46 quai de Jemmapes, 17th arrond. www.facebook.com/lavachedanslesvignes. © **01-77-10-88-36.** Métro: République or Goncourt.

Le Baron Rouge ★★   This neighborhood institution spills out on a corner that it shares with the sprawling Marché d'Aligre. It has only a few tables, so most people stand at the counter or outside, glass in hand, especially during market hours. Huge vats of wine are stacked up inside, and you can fill up if you bring a bottle. In season, platters of oysters accompany your wine; otherwise, the menu is limited to cheese and charcuterie. It's a little rough and tumble getting in your drink order at the bar, but that's half the fun. 1 rue Théophile Roussel, 12th arrond. © **01-43-43-14-32.** Métro: Ledru-Rollin.

Cocktail Bars

Over the last few years, Paris has become a mixology powerhouse, with fabulous cocktail bars opening in all sorts of places across town, from speakeasies hidden behind unmarked doors to tapas joints where cocktails steal the show from the wine. Hotel bars are some of the loveliest spots for cocktails too, especially the palaces where each drink (albeit expensive—around 26€) comes with free nibbles (p. 63). Elsewhere, expect to pay between 10€ and 15€.

Le Baron Rouge.

Candelaria ★★ Concealed at the back of a Mexican taqueria, this place kick-started the speakeasy trend in 2011, and it's still one of the best. The bar is tiny, so reserve ahead, then sip delights like Las Ciguapas (gin, rum, violet, and citrus jam) in intimate, candlelit surrounds. When the munchies set in, the tacos out front are scrumptious. 52 rue Saintonge, 3rd arrond. www.quixotic-projects.com. ✆ **01-42-77-98-37.** Métro: St-Sébastien-Froissart.

Experimental Cocktail Club ★★★ A sophisticated place to spot stars, this bar is known for its gourmet cocktails and has the feel of a neo-baroque speakeasy. Live DJs play on weekends, though the music is never cranked up to a wild party level. Things stay cool and refined as you sip delightful house creations like Bees Kiss (rum, pepper, and honey) and Experience No. 1 (vodka, elderberry, lemon, and basil). 37 rue St-Sauveur, 2nd arrond. www.experimentalgroup.com. ✆ **01-45-08-88-09.** Métro: Sentier.

Harry's Bar ★★ It may be filled with expats, but there's something truly Parisian about Harry's. Probably because its history is so intrinsically linked to the city: Hemingway drank here, Gershwin composed much of "An American in Paris" here, and the Bloody Mary was allegedly created here in 1921. If you're here after 10pm, head straight to the basement piano bar for music. 5 rue Danou, 2nd arrond. https://harrysbar.fr. ✆ **01-42-61-71-14.** Métro: Opéra or Quatre-Septembre.

Le Mary Celeste ★★ Though it's not a cocktail bar per se—the wine, oysters, and excellent small plates shout out "restaurant"—the drinks at this coveted Marais address are wonderfully mixed and slide down easy with or without the food. The Rain Dog (whiskey, fern syrup, mint, and lemon) goes wonderfully with the oysters, which—incidentally—sometimes get their own happy hour between 5 and 7pm, when they cost around 1€ each. 1 rue Commines, 3rd arrond. www.quixotic-projects.com. ✆ **01-42-77-98-37.** Métro: St-Sébastien–Froissart.

Moonshiner ★ Another speakeasy-style joint, this one is hidden at the back of a small, red-fronted pizzeria (Pizza da Vito). Nibble on pies laden with Parma ham and spicy sausage, then step through the fridge door into an Art Deco boudoir where vintage jazz plays as you sip wonderful, offbeat creations like the Numéro 7: rum, Cachaca Paraty (Brazilian whiskey), cucumber juice, yogurt, honey syrup, and lime. 5 rue Sedaine, 11th arrond. https://moonshinerbar.fr. ✆ **09-50-73-12-99.** Métro: Bréguet-Sabin.

Beer Bars

The French are famous for their wine, but they've always loved their beer. King Charlemagne granted monks the monopoly of its production as far back as the 9th century, and in the 1800s, Paris had over sixty breweries. Though two World Wars took the fizz out of the industry (and Stella Artois became the cafe staple), dozens of microbreweries have recently opened to rekindle the city's love of ale. Parisian craft brews tend to have telling names like La Parisienne and Parisis, and are often served (like wine) with cold meats and cheese.

BAPBAP ★★ Set in an enormous Eiffel-style metal structure, this boutique-cum-brewery is a chill place to try craft beers like Canopée (an organic IPA with a grapefruit tang) and the signature Originale, a pale ale with notes of caramel. If you want to see where your drink was made, book one of the brewery tours (15€), which involves yet more tasting opportunities. 79 rue St-Maur, 11th arrond. www.bapbap.paris. ✆ **01-77-17-52-97.** Métro: Rue St-Maur.

Outland Bar ★★ This spacious "American-style" brew pub offers 12 artisanal beers on tap, eight of which hail from the terrific Outland brewery in a nearby suburb. The low-key atmosphere includes hanging sausages and hams, sliced and served along with other tapas-esque fare to accompany beers with names like "Clearly Hoppy" and "Shameless." 6 rue Emile Lepeu, 11th arrond. www.outland-beer.com. ✆ **01-46-59-04-28.** Métro: Charonne.

Paname Brewing Company ★★ A 19th-century warehouse overlooking the Bassin de la Villette canal holds this hip joint. Six beers are brewed on-site, from the refreshing, amber-hued Barge du Canal to the Bête Noire (aka "Black Beast"), a delicious dark ale with a licorice/caramel finish. Soak it all up with international street food along the lines of pizza and burgers. 41 bis quai de la Loire, 19th arrond. www.panamebrewingcompany.com. ✆ **01-40-36-43-55.** Métro: Laumière or Ourcq.

THE GAY & LESBIAN SCENE

Paris has a vibrant gay nightlife scene, primarily centered around the Marais. Gay dance clubs come and go so fast that even the magazines devoted to them, like **Qweek** (www.qweek.fr), have a hard time keeping up. **Têtu** magazine (www.tetu.com), sold at most newsstands, has special nightlife inserts for gay bars and clubs. Both publications are in French.

Bonjour Madame ★ A new spot for dining, drinking "margayritas," debating, and attending concerts and exhibitions, this isn't a lesbian bar per se, but it has a definite feminist slant and a desire to welcome the LGBTQ community. To find out what's on, check out the Facebook page www.facebook.com/bonjourmadame/paris11. 40 rue de Montreuil, 11th arrond. ✆ **09-83-51-61-33.** Métro: Faidherbe-Chaligny or Rue des Boulets.

La Champmeslé ★ This low-key and colorful dive bar is one of the Marais' stalwart lesbian hangouts. The nights tend to start off quietly, but don't be fooled: Several potent mojitos later, and there's dancing on the bar and loud music until 4am. 4 rue Chabanais, 2nd arrond. www.lachampmesle.fr. ✆ **01-42-96-85-20.** Métro: Pyramides.

Les Souffleurs ★★★ The challenge is finding this cozy bar, tucked into a corner of the Marais. Known for its relaxing ambience, there's an open-minded ethos here that makes it a favorite nightspot. Though the clientele is mostly young and masculine, women and trans people are welcome. On weekends, the energy level cranks up with DJs and dance parties. 7 rue de la Verrerie, 4th arrond. www.facebook.com/lessouffleursofficiel. No phone. Métro: Hôtel de Ville.

Open Café ★   Relaxed and diverse, this cafe-bar has a busy sidewalk terrace that is usually full both day and night. Everyone from humble tourists to sharp-looking businessmen to TV stars hangs out here. Happy hour is long, from 6 to 10pm. 17 rue des Archives, 4th arrond. www.opencafe.fr. No phone. Métro: Hôtel-de-Ville.

Raidd Bar ★   This wild, trendy place offers hunky bartenders, a spacious dance floor, go-go dancers, and male strippers who take it all off under an open shower. On weekends you might have to get past the *selectionneur* at the door who decides who's cool enough to enter. 23 rue du Temple, 4th arrond. www.facebook.com/LERAIDDPARIS. ✆ **01-53-01-00-00.** Métro: Hôtel-de-Ville or Rambuteau.

SPECTATOR SPORTS

For inveterate sports fans who need a good dose of athletic adrenaline, Paris can supply an ample fix. The French go crazy for soccer, rugby, tennis, and horse racing, among other sports.

Horse Racing

Race information is available in newspapers like **L'Equipe,** sold at Paris kiosks, and online at www.france-galop.com (in English).

    The epicenter of Paris horse racing is the **Hippodrome de Longchamp,** in the Bois de Boulogne, 16 arrond. (www.parislongchamp.com; ✆ **01-44-30-75-00;** RER or Métro: Porte Maillot, and then a free shuttle bus on race days; otherwise, bus 244 to the Les Moulins–Camping stop). Established in 1855 during the autocratic and pleasure-loving reign of Napoleon III, it's the most prestigious track, boasts the greatest number of promising thoroughbreds, and awards the largest purse in France. The most important event at Longchamp is the **Qatar Prix de l'Arc de Triomphe** in early October. Sports aside, it's also the venue for some of the city's biggest music festivals.

    Another racing venue is the **Hippodrome d'Auteuil,** also in the Bois de Boulogne (✆ **01-40-71-47-47;** Métro: Porte Auteuil), known for its steeplechases and obstacle courses. On Sundays in April and May, both venues host **Les Dimanches au Galop,** day-long racing fiestas that include races by both professionals and amateurs, shows, games, and of course, pony rides, all free of charge. Visit www.evenements.france-galop.com for details (and see p. 48). Also see **Hippodrome de Vincennes** (p. 207), famed for its harness racing.

Soccer (Football)

Known throughout France as *le football,* or just *le foot,* soccer is one of France's most popular national sports. The Paris team is **Paris Saint-Germain,** also known as **PSG.** They play their home matches at the **Parc des Princes,** 24 rue du Commandant Guilbaud, 16 arrond. (www.psg.fr; Métro: Porte de St-Cloud), a stadium with a capacity of almost 49,000 spectators. The season runs September to May; tickets start at 12€ and go through the roof. *Note:* A very small but nasty segment of PSG fans can get violent at games, particularly when the match is against a rival team like Marseille. National games, played at the **Stade de France** (p. 230) in the nearby suburb of Saint-Denis are generally much calmer.

Tennis

France's version of Wimbledon, the **French Open** (or as it's known here, **Roland Garros;** www.rolandgarros.com) takes place over 2 weeks between late May and early June in the Roland Garros Stadium in the 16th arrondissement (Métro: Porte d'Auteuil). Tickets should be purchased online well in advance for this world-scale tennis event.

DAY TRIPS FROM PARIS

P arisians generally feel that their capital is the center of the universe. They may be correct, if only geographically speaking. Paris is at the heart of a vast, new-fangled region known as the *Métropole du Grand Paris* (or Greater Paris)—an eclectic sprawl of 131 municipalities that is inhabited by 12 million people and dotted with wonderful cultural and historic treasures. You'll find everything from majestic palaces to picturesque artistic villages, and all are only a short train ride from the city center.

If you've never been there, your first choice should probably be the château and gardens of **Versailles.** They're close by, easily accessible by train, and truly not to be missed. **Chartres** (though just outside Grand Paris) would be my second choice, for its breathtaking Gothic cathedral, its winding streets, and its half-timbered houses, which will give you a taste of something completely different from Paris. After that, it's a toss-up. If castles are your game, **Fontainebleau** should be high on your list. Fans of Claude Monet love exploring the gardens at **Giverny** (in Normandy), and families with kids in tow tend to pick **Disneyland Paris.** All of these sites are reachable by train from Paris; train tickets do not require reservations and can be bought the day you travel.

VERSAILLES ★★★

21km (13 miles) SW of Paris, 71km (44 miles) NE of Chartres

The grandeur of the Château of Versailles is hard to imagine until you are standing in front of it. Immediately, you start to get an idea of the power (and ego) of the man who was behind it, King Louis XIV. One of the largest castles in Europe, it is also forever associated with another, less fortunate king, Louis XVI, and his wife, Queen Marie Antoinette, who were both forced to flee when the French Revolution arrived at their sumptuous doorstep. The palace's extraordinary gardens, designed by the legendary landscape architect André Le Nôtre, are worth the visit on their own.

Don't feel you have to see everything. For many, a visit to the palace is enough culture, and a nice, relaxing stroll/picnic/nap in the park is a great way to finish off the day. To escape the hordes

Some places covered in this chapter may require advance booking with a time slot for entry. You could also be asked to wear a mask or show proof of Covid vaccination or a negative PCR test in order to get in. Information changes regularly, so stay up-to-date by checking the individual website for each sight, along with the French government website (www.gouvernement.fr/en/coronavirus-covid-19) and the Paris Tourist Office site (https://en.parisinfo.com/practical-paris/info/guides/info-disruption-paris).

(and they're intense at Versailles), my favorite spot is Marie Antoinette's Estate, where—hidden from the palace—you'll get a more bucolic taste of life during the Ancien Régime, thanks to the quaint garden, the pretty Trianons (mini-palaces), hamlet, and other small buildings. You won't be alone, but you won't be elbow-to-elbow with crowds either.

Essentials

GETTING THERE   Take the **RER C** (www.transilien.com; about 30–40 min. from the Champs de Mars; Pont d'Alma, Invalides, St-Michel, or Musée d'Orsay stations) to **Versailles-Château–Rive Gauche.** Make sure the final destination for your train is Versailles-Château–Rive Gauche and *not* Versailles Chantier. The latter runs in the opposite direction, touring all around Paris before arriving at Versailles, which will add an hour or so to your journey. Assuming you've taken the right train, it's about a 5-minute walk from the Versailles–Rive Gauche train station to the château—don't worry, you can't miss it. Versailles has a second station, **Versailles–Rive Droite,** accessed from Gare St-Lazare station in Paris (4.45€ one-way). This is a great option if you plan to picnic in the palace grounds, as you'll go down rue du Maréchal Foch, past a U Express supermarket (no. 45) and **Marché Notre-Dame** (daily 7am–7pm; outdoor stalls in the center of the square Tues, Fri, and Sun 9am–2pm), the town's main market, where you can fill up on French delights. Glass is permitted in the park, so don't feel you have to skimp on wine!

Unless you have a **Paris Visite** or other pass that includes zones 1 to 5 (p. 288), you'll need to buy a special ticket for the RER C (one-way fare 3.65€ adults, 1.80€ children 4–10, free for children 3 and under); a regular Métro ticket will not suffice. You can buy a ticket from any Métro or RER station; the fare includes a free transfer on the Métro.

VISITOR INFORMATION   Château de Versailles: www.chateau versailles.fr; (C) **01-30-83-78-00. Palace:** Apr–Oct Tues–Sun 9am–6:30pm; Nov–Mar Tues–Sun 9am–5:30pm. **Marie Antoinette's Estate:** Tues–Sun noon–5:30. **Garden and park:** Apr–Oct daily 7am–8:30pm; Nov–Mar daily 8am–6pm. **Versailles Tourist Office:** 2 bis av. de Paris; www.versailles-tourisme.com; (C) **01-39-24-88-88.**

Métropole du Grand Paris

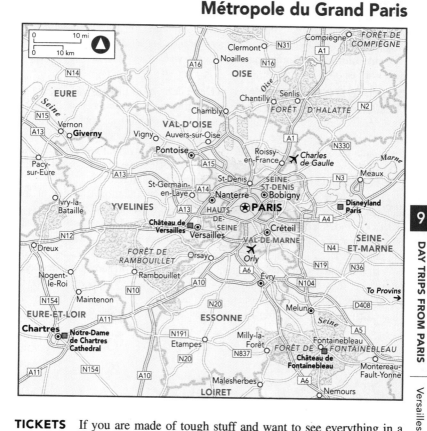

TICKETS If you are made of tough stuff and want to see everything in a day, you can buy the all-inclusive 1- or 2-day **Château Passeport,** which grants you access to the main château, the gardens, the Trianon palaces, Marie Antoinette's Estate, and the temporary exhibitions (1 day Nov–Mar 20€ adults, Apr–Oct including Les Grandes Eaux Musicales 27€ adults; 2 days Nov–Mar 25€, Apr–Oct 30€; free for children 17 and under). If you'd like to make an overnight of it (and it's worth doing as Versailles is such a lovely city), consider the **2-day Passport.** If you have limited time and energy, you can buy a **ticket to just the Palace** (18€, free for children 17 and under) or **just the Trianons and Marie Antoinette's Estate** (12€).

Important note: You will probably have to reserve a time slot for your visit. This should be done online when you purchase your ticket. The good news is that visitor numbers are limited, so you shouldn't have to wait in a long line whatever time you choose.

EVENING SHOWS Spectacular **fountain night shows** are held from mid-June to mid-September (28€ adults, 24€ ages 6–17), where you stroll around the gardens and enjoy illuminated fountains, music, and fireworks.

Big names in classical music, theater, and dance fill the stage at the magnificent **Opéra Royal** in the palace; reserve well in advance and expect royal ticket prices (45€–140€).

DAYTIME SHOWS From April to October on most Fridays and Tuesdays, **"Les Grandes Eaux Musicales"** (depending on your ticket, this could be included; otherwise 8.50€ adults, 8€ ages 6–17) play throughout the gardens closest to the castle. This consists of baroque music playing as a backdrop to the fountains. While it's pleasant, you won't miss anything essential if your ticket does not offer you entrance to this part of the gardens (the rest of the park is accessible from side entrances and is free of charge).

Tickets: You can purchase tickets to all shows mentioned above at the château, at www.chateauversailles-spectacles.fr (© **01-30-83-78-89**).

Les Grandes Ecuries: The **Académie Equestre de Versailles** (www.bartabas.fr) is housed in the **royal stables,** a palatial edifice immediately opposite the château. Both the school and its shows are directed by Bartabas, whose equestrian theater company, Zingaro, has garnered world fame. On weekend afternoons (Sat 6pm; Sun 5pm; 16€–28€), you can watch their "equestrian ballet" in full swing. You can also buy a combined 2-day passport with the show included for 52€. After the shows, visitors can tour the stables.

The entrance to Versailles.

Versailles

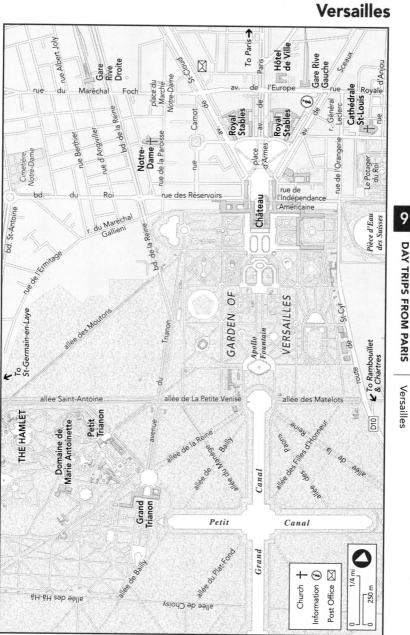

Fancy a night in the palace? You're in luck. As of summer 2021, you can sleep like the Sun King at Versailles' new Airelles Château de Versailles, Le Grand Contrôle hotel, set in three palatial 17th-century buildings on the château's grounds. Each of the 14 rooms costs a pretty packet (from 1,500€/night), but boy, are they special: busy French country–style decor with bold patterns, chandeliers, antique furniture, palatial bathrooms, and views over the Orangerie (the royal citrus grove). Food-wise, expect French classics with a modern twist, courtesy of celebrated French chef Alain Ducasse. There's also a sumptuous spa by Valmont (famed for their cellular cosmetics). The most exciting part, perhaps, is that guests get daily private after-hours tours of the palace, so you can walk its endless gilded chambers and really get a feel for what royal life would have been like without the crowds. www. airelles.com/en; 🕿 **01-85-36-05-50.**

9 The Château of Versailles

Back in the 17th century, after having been badly burned by a nasty uprising called Le Fronde, Louis XIV decided to move his court from Paris to Versailles, a safe distance from the intrigues of the capital. He also decided to have the court move in with him, so he could keep a close eye on them and nip any new plots or conspiracies in the bud. This required a new abode that was not only big enough to house his court (anywhere from 3,000 to 10,000 people would be palace guests on any given day), but also one that would be grand enough to let the world know who was in charge.

A château was already on the site when Louis came to town; his father, Louis XIII, had built a small castle, "a hunting lodge," there in 1623. This humble dwelling simply would not do for the so-called "Sun King," who brought in a flotilla of architects, artists, and gardeners to enlarge the castle and give it a new look. In 1668, the king's architect, Louis Le Vau, began work on the enormous "envelope," which literally wrapped the old castle in a second building. From the front, you can see the remnants of the old castle; the buildings that surround the recessed central courtyard (called the **Marble Court**) are what's left of that structure.

Meanwhile, famous garden designer André Le Nôtre was carving formal gardens and a huge park out of what had been marshy countryside. Thousands of trees were planted, and harmonious geometric designs were achieved with flower beds, hedges, canals, and pebbled pathways dotted with sculptures and fountains.

Construction, which involved as many as 36,000 workers, ground on for years; in 1682 Louis XIV and his court moved in, but construction went on right through the rest of his reign and into that of Louis XV. Louis XVI and his wife, Marie Antoinette, made few changes, but history made a gigantic one for them: On October 6, 1789, an angry mob of hungry Parisians marched on the palace, and the royal couple was eventually forced to return to Paris. Versailles would never again be a royal residence.

The Hall of Mirrors in Versailles Palace.

The palace was ransacked during the Revolution, and in the years after, it fell far from its original state of grace. Napoleon and Louis XVIII did what they could to bring the sleeping giant back, but by the early 1800s, during the reign of Louis-Philippe, the castle was slated for demolition. This forward-thinking king decided to invest his own money to save Versailles, and in 1837 the vast structure was made into a national museum. Precious furniture and art objects were retrieved or re-created; paintings, wall decorations, and ceilings were restored. Restoration is ongoing, but even if a few areas are closed, the place is so huge that you can still tour yourself into a 17th-century stupor.

TOURING THE PALACE

The rooms in the "envelope," or the newer part of the building, were designed to impress, which they do. They include the **Grand Apartments,** used primarily for ceremonial events (a daily occurrence), the **Queen's Apartments,** and the **Galerie des Glaces.** These, along with the **King's Apartments** and the **Chapel,** are must-sees. If you have the fortitude, you can take a **guided visit** to the royal family's private apartments (an additional 10€; some in English) to get a more intimate look at castle life.

Each room in the **Grand Apartments ★★★** is dedicated to a different planet (that circles around the sun, as in the Sun King), and each has a fabulous ceiling fresco depicting the god or goddess associated with said heavenly sphere. The first and probably the most staggering, painting-wise, is in the **Salon d'Hercule ★★**. It holds an enormous canvas by Paolo Veronese,

Christ at Supper with Simon, as well as a divinity-bedecked ceiling by François Lemoyne that portrays Hercules being welcomed by the gods of Olympus. At 480 sq. m (5,166 sq. ft.), it is one of the largest paintings in France. The **Salon d'Apollon ★**, not surprisingly, was the Sun King's throne room.

The ornate **Salon de Guerre ★** and **Salon de Paix ★** bookend the most famous room, the **Galerie des Glaces (the Hall of Mirrors) ★★★**. Louis XIV commanded his painter-in-chief, Charles Le Brun, to paint the 12m-high (40-ft.) ceiling of this 73m-long (240-ft.) gallery with representations of his accomplishments. This masterwork is illuminated by light from the 17 windows that overlook the garden, which are matched on the opposite wall by 17 mirrored panels. Add to that a few enormous crystal chandeliers, and the effect is dazzling. This splendid setting was where, in 1919, World War I officially ended with the signing of the Treaty of Versailles.

The **Queen's Apartments ★★** include a gorgeous bedroom with silk hangings printed with lilacs and peacock feathers. It looks exactly as it did in 1789, when the queen, Marie Antoinette, was forced to flee revolutionary mobs through a secret door (barely visible in the wall near her bed). The **King's Apartments ★★★** are even more splendiferous, though in a very different style: Here the ceilings have been left blank white, which brings out the elaborate white and gold decoration on the walls. The **King's Bedroom ★★★**, hung from top to bottom with gold brocade, is fitted with a banister that separated the king from the 100 or so people who would watch him wake up in the morning.

The **Chapel ★★★**, a masterpiece of light and harmony by Jules Hardouin Mansart, is where the kings attended mass. This lofty space (the ceiling is more than 25m/82 ft. high) reflects both Gothic and baroque styles.

TOURING THE DOMAINE DE MARIE ANTOINETTE

Northwest of the Apollo Fountain lies the **Domaine de Marie Antoinette ★★★** (if you don't have a Château passport, you'll need a separate ticket to get in). It was here that the young queen sought refuge from the strict protocol and infighting at the castle. Her husband gave her the **Petit Trianon ★★**, a small manor that Louis XV used for his trysts, which she transformed into a stylish haven. When the queen had finished decorating the manor in the latest fashions, she set to work creating an entire world around it, including a splendid **English garden ★**, several lovely pavilions, a jewel-like **theater ★★**, and even a small **hamlet ★**, complete with a working farm and a dairy, where she and her friends would play cards and gossip, or take a stroll in the "country." Although the **Grand Trianon ★** is not linked to the story of Marie Antoinette, it is worth a brief visit. Built by Louis XIV as a retreat for himself and his family, this small palace consists of two large wings connected by an open columned terrace that has a delightful garden **view ★**. The furniture and decor date mostly from the Napoleonic era. Throughout the 20th century it was used for official state receptions and for notable guests such as John and Jackie Kennedy, General de Gaulle, and Queen Elizabeth II.

TOURING THE GARDENS & PARK

The entire 800-hectare (2,000-acre) park is laid out according to a precise symmetrical plan. From the terrace behind the castle is an astounding **view ★★★** that runs past two parterres, down a central lawn (the Tapis Vert), down the **Grand Canal ★★**, and seemingly on into infinity. Le Nôtre's masterpiece is the ultimate example of French-style gardens: geometric, logical, and in perfect harmony—a reflection of the divine order of the cosmos. Given that the Sun King was the star of this particular cosmos, a solar theme is reflected in the statues and fountains along the main axis of the perspective; the most magnificent of these is the **Apollo Fountain ★★★**, where the sun god emerges from the waves at dawn on his chariot. On the sides of the main axis, near the castle, are a set of six groves, or **bosquets ★**, leafy mini-gardens hidden by walls of shrubbery; some were used as small outdoor ballrooms for festivities, others for intimate rendezvous out of reach of the prying eyes of the court. Today, you can **picnic, bicycle** (bikes can be rented next to the restaurant La Flottille; 21€/day, plus shorter time options), rent a *petit véhicule* (golf cart) next to the bike area (from 36€/hr; only for visitors 25 and over with a driver's license), or even **row a boat** (from 14€/30 min.). The hop-on-hop-off **Little Train** stops at several spots around the garden (8.50€ adults, 6.50€ children 13–18, free for children 12 and under).

CHARTRES ★★★

97km (58 miles) SW of Paris, 76km (47 miles) NW of Orléans

You'll spot it long before you see the actual town: the spire of the cathedral of Chartres rising above a sea of wheat fields. This stunning edifice and its inspiring stained-glass windows are easy to tour, and you'll still have time to wander through the narrow streets of the ancient (and beautiful) town.

Essentials

GETTING THERE   From Paris' Gare Montparnasse, **trains** run directly to Chartres, taking about 1 hour. Tickets cost 18.40€ one-way; for more information and reservations, see www.oui.sncf or call ⓒ **36-35**. If **driving,** take A10/A11 southwest and follow signs to Le Mans and Chartres. (The Chartres exit is marked.)

VISITOR INFORMATION   The **Office de Tourisme** is in the Maison du Saumon, 8 rue de la Poissonerie (www.chartres-tourisme.com; ⓒ **02-37-18-26-26**).

Exploring the Cathedral

This magnificent UNESCO-protected Gothic cathedral, with its carved portals and three-tiered flying buttresses, would be a stunning sight even without its legendary **stained-glass windows**—though the world would be a drearier place. These ancient glass panels are truly glorious: A kaleidoscope of colors so deep, so rich, and so bright, it's hard to believe they are some 700 years old.

Meant as teaching devices more than artwork, the windows functioned as a sort of enormous cartoon, telling the story of Christ through pictures to a mostly illiterate populace. From the church's beginnings, pilgrims came to see a piece of cloth that believers say was worn by the Virgin Mary during Christ's birth. The **relic** is still here, but these days it's a different sort of pilgrim who is drawn to Chartres: More than 1.5 million tourists come here every year to admire the magnificent edifice.

A Romanesque church stood on this spot until 1194, when a fire burnt it virtually to the ground. All that remained were the towers, the Royal Portal, and a few remnants of stained glass. The locals were so horrified that they sprang into action; in a matter of only 3 decades a new cathedral was erected, which accounts for its remarkably unified Gothic architecture. This was one of the first churches to use buttresses as a building support, allowing the architect (whose name has been lost) to build its walls at twice the height of the standard Romanesque cathedrals and make space for its famous windows. The new cathedral was dedicated in 1260 and has survived the centuries with relatively little damage. The French Revolution somehow spared the cathedral. During World War I and World War II, the precious windows were dismounted piece by piece and stored in a safe place in the countryside.

Before you enter the church, take in the **facade ★★**, a remarkable assemblage of religious art and architecture. The base of the two towers dates from the early 12th century (before the fire). The tower to your right (the **Old Tower,** or South Tower) is topped by its original sober Romanesque spire; that

The *Assumption of the Virgin* in Chartres Cathedral.

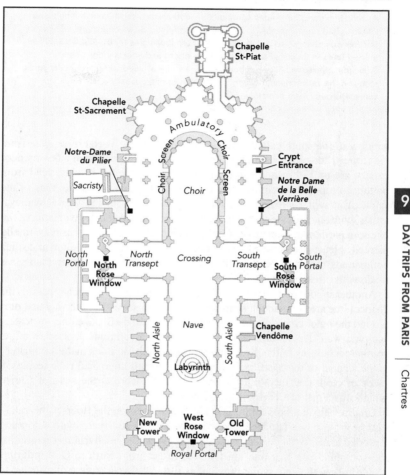

on your left (**New Tower,** or North Tower) was blessed with an elaborate Gothic spire by Jehan de Beauce in the early 1500s, when the original burned down. Below is the **Royal Portal ★★★**, a masterpiece of Romanesque art. Swarming with kings, queens, prophets, and priests, this sculpted entryway tells the story of the life of Christ. The rigid bodies of the figures contrast with their lifelike faces; it is said that Rodin spent hours here contemplating this stonework spectacle.

Once you're inside the cathedral, the radiant colors of the **stained-glass windows ★★★**, which shine down from all sides, pierce the dim interior. Three windows on the west side of the building, as well as the beautiful rose

At time of writing, all guided tours of Chartres had been canceled indefinitely. But this may change, so do ask about guided tours in English. For more than 3 decades, Malcolm Miller has been studying the cathedral and giving **tours.** His rare blend of scholarship, enthusiasm, and humor will help you understand and appreciate what you are looking at (© **02-37-28-15-58** for prices and information). You may also be allowed to rent an **audioguide** (in English; usually 6.50€).

window to the south called **Notre Dame de la Belle Verière ★**, date from the earlier 12th-century structure; the rest, with the exception of a few modern panels, are of 13th-century origins. The scenes depicted in glass read from bottom to top and recount stories from the Bible as well as the lives of the saints. You will soon find yourself wondering how in the world medieval artists, with such low-tech materials, managed to create such vivid colors. The blues, in particular, seem to be divinely inspired. In fact, scientists have finally pierced at least part of the mystery: The blue was made with sodium and silica compounds that made the color stand up to the centuries better than glass made with other colors.

Another indoor marvel is the **chancel enclosure ★★★**, which separates the chancel (the area behind the altar) from the ambulatory (the walkway that runs around the outer chapels). Started in 1514 by Jehan de Beauce, this intricately sculpted wall depicts dozens of saints and other religious superstars in yet another recounting of the lives of the Virgin and Christ. Back in the ambulatory is the Chapel of the Martyrs, where the cathedral's cherished **relic** resides: a piece of cloth that the Virgin Mary supposedly wore at the birth of Christ, which was a gift of Charles the Bald in 876.

Chartres also harbors a rare **labyrinth ★**, traced on the floor of the cathedral near the nave. The large circle is divided into four parts with a winding path that leads to the center. In the Middle Ages, these labyrinths represented the symbolic path that one must follow to get from earth to God; pilgrims would follow the path while praying, as if they were making a pilgrimage to Jerusalem. *Note:* The cathedral asks that visitors not talk or wander around during mass, which is generally held in the late morning and early evening. You are welcome to sit in on services, of course.

16 Cloître Notre-Dame. www.cathedrale-chartres.org. © **02-37-21-75-02.** Cathedral free admission. Mon–Fri 10am–1pm and 3–6:45pm, Sat–Sun 8:30am–6:45pm.

Exploring the Old Town

Give yourself a little time to explore the medieval cobbled streets of the **Vieux Quartier (Old Town) ★★**. The narrow lanes near the cathedral have some gabled houses, including the colorful facades of **rue Chantault,** one of which

9

Chartres | **DAY TRIPS FROM PARIS**

is 8 centuries old. Seek out **rue du Bourg,** where you'll find the famous **Salmon House** (which houses the tourist office) and some lovely sculptures (including a certain fish). In the lower town, you can stroll along the picturesque **Eure River** with its stone bridges and ancient washhouses. If you go on a Saturday or Wednesday morning, a covered farmers market takes over **Place Billard** (until 1pm), the perfect place to grab some supplies for a casual picnic in the park behind the cathedral or along the river. Between April and December, also look out for **Chartres en Lumières,** a fabulous sound-and-light show (www.chartresenlumieres.com; free; daily dusk–1am), which turns the cathedral's facade into a beautiful, rippling screen of color.

Centre International du Vitrail ★ Get the stained-glass backstory at this international center devoted to the glory of this luminous art form. The permanent collection focuses on Renaissance stained glass, while the temporary shows highlight contemporary works. The center also offers workshops, classes, and training for both professionals and amateurs.

5 rue du Cardinal Pie. www.centre-vitrail.org. © **02-37-21-65-72.** Admission 7€ adults, 5.50€ students and children 14–18, free for children 13 and under. Daily 2–5:45pm.

Musée des Beaux-Arts de Chartres ★ Housed in an impressive former episcopal palace, this museum of fine arts boasts a collection covering the 16th to 20th centuries, including the work of masters such as Zurbarán, Watteau, and Soutine.

29 Cloître Notre-Dame. © **02-37-90-45-80.** Free admission. May–Oct Thurs 10am–12:30pm and 2–8pm, Wed and Fri–Sat 10am–12:30pm and 2–6pm, Sun 2–6pm; the rest of the year, until 5pm.

GIVERNY ★★

74km (46 miles) NW of Paris

For this trip, a lot depends on the weather. If you luck out and the sun is shining, it's worth the schlep by train or car to bask in the glory of this stunning garden, which bears the artistic stamp of its genius creator, Claude Monet. The painter and his family moved to this tiny town in 1883, and Monet liked it so much he spent the rest of his life here, painting views of the dreamlike garden that he created out of the grassy slope behind his house. Today, the **Fondation Claude Monet** (see details below) is open to the public April to October, and for a fee, you too can wander about the brilliant flower beds, lush bowers, and water-lily ponds that inspired this Impressionist master (though you will not be alone). After the garden, sample the bucolic joys of the village, which manages to stay charming despite the seasonal tourist infestation. You can also take in one of the excellent temporary exhibits at the **Musée des Impressionismes** (see below). On the other hand, if it is raining or truly dreary out, you'll be better off staying in Paris and getting your Monet fix at the **Musée Marmottan Monet** (p. 167) and/or visiting the water lilies at the **Orangerie** (p. 144).

Essentials

GETTING THERE **Trains** (SNCF; for schedules, visit www.oui.sncf) leave every hour or two from the Gare St-Lazare train station to Vernon, the closest stop to Giverny, which is about 7km (4 1/2 miles) away. The trip takes between 50 minutes and just over an hour (depending on the train), and costs between 9€ and 24€ (depending on your ticket). From Vernon, you can either take a shuttle bus (10€ round-trip) or rent a bike at the station (L'Arrivé de Giverny; ✆ **02-32-21-16-01;** 17€/day) and pedal there on the marked bike path.

If you're **driving,** take the Autoroute A14 to the A13 toward Rouen. Take exit 16 for Vernon and follow the D181 across the Seine into the town. From Vernon, take the D5 to Giverny. Expect it to take about an hour from Paris; try to avoid weekends.

TICKETS Advance online reservations are not mandatory at the Fondation Claude Monet, but they're highly recommended. Numbers are limited, so this way you're sure to get in. It's a long way to travel if you can't visit. You can buy your tickets online at the Fondation Claude Monet site (see below), at a Fnac ticket office, or on the Fnac site (in English, www.fnactickets.com). Tickets are 12€ for adults (2€ more via Fnac), 7.50€ for ages 7 to 18 and students, and free for children 6 and under.

Exploring Giverny: the Fondation Claude Monet

When you enter this kingdom of color, you'll quickly realize that Monet wasn't just a brilliant painter, he was also a gifted gardener. His dual talents complemented each other completely; by the end of his life, the garden was just as much a work of art as the paintings, or perhaps they *were* the paintings. If you have visited the Orangerie in Paris and seen Monet's magical *Nympheas,* or water lilies, spread across huge canvases in two oval-shaped rooms, in a way you have already visited this garden; they were painted here, with the aim of faithfully re-creating the feeling you would have if you were looking at the same flowers at Giverny.

The first and closest garden to the house is the **Clos Normand ★★**, an ostensibly French-style garden that is a glorious riot of color depending on the

---

Where to See Impressionist Paintings in Giverny

While you won't see any original paintings at the Fondation Claude Monet, you will see plenty of Impressionist art at the **Musée des Impressionismes,** 99 rue Claude Monet (www.mdig.fr; ✆ **02-32-51-94-65;** 9€ adults, free for children 17 and under; May–mid-Nov and late Dec–early Jan daily 10am–6pm, mid-Nov–mid-Dec and early Jan–mid-Jan Fri–Sun 10am–6pm; advance online reservation required). Housed in a sleek modern building with yet another lovely garden, this airy museum offers temporary exhibits that explore the movement, both in France and abroad.

Monet's house in Giverny.

season. Gladioli, larkspur, phlox, daisies, and asters, among other flowers, clamor for your attention; irises brighten the small lawn. In the midst of it all is **Monet's house** ★, where you can admire his **Japanese print collection.**

The painter's most famous works, the endless water-lily series, were born in the **Water Garden** ★★★, farther down the slope. Here, Monet's intention was to build a garden that resembled those in the Japanese prints he collected, including a **Japanese bridge** ★ that figures prominently in several of his canvases. Today the garden looks much as it did when Monet was immortalizing it. Willows weep quietly into the ponds; heather, ferns, azaleas, and rhododendrons carpet the banks; and frogs croak among the water lilies. This garden was a sanctuary for the painter, who came here to explore one of his favorite subjects: the interplay of water and light.

This is an extremely popular outing for both individuals and tour groups, so your best bet is to come on a slow day like Monday or Wednesday, and/or to arrive at the opening or after 3pm, when the groups have left. You can't picnic in the gardens, but the museum has a cafe or you can lunch at the **Restaurant Baudy** in the village, an old inn where many an Impressionist used to stay when they visited Claude (81 rue Claude Monet; www.restaurantbaudy.com; ✆ **02-32-21-10-03**).

84 rue Claude Monet. www.fondation-monet.com. ✆ **02-32-51-28-21.** Admission 12€ adults, 7.50€ students and ages 7–18, free for children 6 and under. Apr–Oct daily 9:30am–6pm. Closed Nov–Mar.

FONTAINEBLEAU ★★★

60km (37 miles) S of Paris, 74km (46 miles) NE of Orléans

Napoleon called it "the house of the centuries; the true home of kings," and he had a point: Fontainebleau was a royal residence for over 700 years. Elegant and dignified, this grand château of 1,500 rooms carries the architectural imprint of many a monarch. Dense forest and verdant countryside surround the château, making a day here a relaxing green interlude to your Parisian trip.

GETTING THERE   **Trains** to Fontainebleau leave from the Gare de Lyon (schedules and info at www.transilien.com). The 40-minute trip costs 8.85€ for adults and 5.10€ for children 4 to 10 one-way. Get off at Fontainebleau–Avon and take the local bus (line 1), direction Lilas, to the Château stop; the fare is 2€ one-way; you can also use a regular Métro ticket. The frequent buses are timed to meet the train from Paris. If you're **driving,** take A6 south from Paris, exit Fontainebleau.

VISITOR INFORMATION   The **Office de Tourisme** is at 4 bis place de la République (www.fontainebleau-tourisme.com; ✆ **01-60-74-99-99**) in the town center.

Exploring Fontainebleau

Though kings were already living here by the 12th century (Philippe August and Saint Louis both spent a good deal of time at the castle), it was during the Renaissance that Fontainebleau really took on its regal allure. In 1528, inveterate castle-builder King François I decided to completely rebuild

The Gallery of François I at Fontainebleau.

Fontainebleau and make it into a palace that would rival the marvels of Rome. He tore down everything but the core of the medieval castle and hired an army of architects and artisans to construct a new one around it. He also brought in two renowned Italian artists, Il Rosso and Primaticcio, to decorate his new home. Their style of work came to be known as the School of Fontainebleau, which was characterized by the use of stucco (moldings and picture frames) and frescoes that depicted various allegories and myths. This school was highly influenced by the Mannerist style of Michelangelo, Raphael, and Parmigianino.

François I was also an art collector: His vast accumulation of Renaissance treasures included Da Vinci's *Mona Lisa* and *The Virgin of the Rock,* both of which once hung here. After François' death his descendants continued work on the castle, but it wasn't until the 17th century and the arrival of Henri IV on the scene that there were any major transformations. Henri added several wings and a courtyard (the **Cour des Offices ★★**), and made major changes to the decor, inviting a new clutch of artists, who established a second School of Fontainebleau. This time, the artists were of French and Flemish origin (Ambrose Dubois, Martin Fréminet, and others) and used oil paint and canvas instead of frescoes. Louis XV and Louis XVI found the palace to their liking and added their own decorative flourishes. Napoleon was also very fond of this palace and made a lasting imprint on the castle's interior. No doubt, Fontainebleau made an imprint on the Emperor as well: On April 20, 1814, he abdicated here, before being sent off to exile on the island of Elba.

TOURING THE CHÂTEAU

Most of what you'll want to see (and what is described below) is in the **Grands Appartements.** The **Petits Appartements,** a series of rooms that were Napoleon's private residence, can only be seen on a guided tour and require an extra ticket—though they're worth the effort if you have time.

Your first encounter with the château will take place in the **Cour du Cheval Blanc ★★★** at the entrance to the palace. It was in this grand square, which is surrounded by wings of the castle on three sides, that Napoleon said adieu to his faithful imperial guards. "Continue to serve France," he pleaded. "Her welfare was my only concern." The main building before you dates from François I's era; the sumptuous **horseshoe staircase ★★** was added by Henri II. On the left as you enter is the **Chapelle de la Trinité ★**. When he was 7, Louis XIII climbed up the scaffolding to watch Martin Fréminet, his art instructor, paint the glorious ceiling. This is where Louis XV married Polish princess Marie Leczinska and where the future Napoleon III was baptized. Linking the chapel with the royal apartments is the **Gallery of François I ★★★**, a stunning example of Renaissance art and decoration. Overseen by Il Rossi, a team of highly skilled artists covered the walls with exceptional frescoes, moldings, and *boisseries* (carved woodwork). The paintings, which are full of mythological figures, pay tribute to the glory of the monarchy and the wisdom of the king's rule. Throughout the gallery (and elsewhere in the castle) you will see the salamander, François' official symbol.

The Fontainebleau Forest is riddled with *sentiers* (hiking trails) made by French kings and their entourages who hunted here. In 1842, a forest-loving veteran of Napoleon's army, Claude François Denecourt, created the first official public walking trails, some 150km (93 miles) of pathways called the *sentiers bleus*. A "Guide des Sentiers" is available at the tourist information center (see above). Bike paths also cut through the forest. You can rent bikes at **A La Petite Reine,** 14 rue de la Paroisse, in the center of town, a few blocks from the château (www.alapetitereine.com; ℰ **01-60-74-57-57**). The cost of a bike is 8€ per hour and 15€ for a full day. You'll also find route suggestions on the website.

The other major must-see is the **Salle de Bal ★★★**. This 30m-long (98-ft.) ballroom is a feast of light and color; the frescoes by Primaticcio and Nicolo dell'Abate have been completely restored, and their rich hues radiate as if they were painted yesterday. Huge windows let in light; the monumental fireplace at the far end was designed by 16th-century architect Philibert Delorme.

The **Royal Apartments ★★** have been decorated and redecorated by successive monarchs. Louis XIII was born in the **Salon Louis XIII ★**, a fact that is symbolized in the ceiling mural showing Love riding a dolphin. Though several different queens slept in the **Chambre de l'Impératrice ★★**, its current setup reflects the epoch of Empress Joséphine (Napoleon's first wife). The sumptuous bed, crowned in gilded walnut and covered in embroidered silk, was made for Marie Antoinette in 1787. The queen would never see it; the Revolution exploded before she could arrange a visit to the château. Napoleon transformed the Kings' bedroom into the **Salle du Trône ★**, or Throne Room. Since several centuries of kings, from Henri IV to Louis XVI, slept here, the decor is a mashup of styles: The throne is Empire, the folding chairs are Louis XVI, and the ceiling murals date from the 17th and 18th centuries.

You can learn more about the Emperor at the **Musée Napoléon 1er ★**, in the Louis XV wing, where you'll see historic memorabilia and artwork relating to his reign.

Separate from the Musée Napoléon, and at the price of an additional ticket for a guided tour (16€ combined with entry to the main château), you can visit the **Petits Appartements ★★**, which date from Louis XV but were redecorated in Empire style for Napoleon and his Empress (first Joséphine, then Marie-Louise).

TOURING THE GARDENS

The lush and quiet **Garden of Diane ★**, on the castle's north side, was created during the time of François I and centers around a statue of the goddess surrounded by four dogs. The **English Garden ★**, complete with an artificial stream and lush groves of tall trees, was added by Napoleon. The vast **Carp Pond ★**, which extends directly from the south side of the **Cour de la Fontaine,** has a small island in the center with a small pavilion for the royal residents. Surrounding the gardens and park is **Fontainebleau Forest ★★**, which, if you have the time, is worth the visit (see box, below).

pl. du Général-de-Gaulle, 77300 Fontainebleau. www.chateaudefontainebleau.fr. ✆ **01-60-71-50-70.** Grands Appartements & Musée Napoléon 1er 13€ adults, 11€ students 18–25, free for children 17 and under. Apr–Sept Wed–Mon 9:30am–6pm; Oct–Mar Wed–Mon 9:30am–5pm.

DISNEYLAND PARIS ★

41km (25 miles) E of Paris

It might not be particularly French, but there's no denying that this is a fun place to visit. You have two parks here to choose from: **Disneyland Paris** and **Walt Disney Studios.** Disney has announced a 2€-billion makeover for the park, with the addition of three themed lands in Walt Disney Studios (between 2021 and 2025), based on Marvel, "Star Wars," and "Frozen." As a result, some rides might be closed during your visit. Also, bear in mind that since Covid-19, the park has scrapped the popular free line-jumping voucher known as the **FastPass,** replacing it with the **Disney Premier Access** scheme, whereby you have to fork out more money for the privilege of fast-track lines (8€ to 15€ depending on the attraction's popularity). Some shows may also have been canceled. For up-to-date information, check www. disneylandparis.com on the day of your visit.

Essentials

GETTING THERE By far the easiest way to get to the parks from central Paris is by **RER A** (RATP; www.ratp.fr; 45 min.; 7.60€ adults, 3.80€ children 4–10 one-way). Get on at any of its downtown stations and take it all the way to its terminus at Marne-la-Vallée–Chessy (just make sure that this is the terminus—the RER A has multiple destinations). When you get out, you'll be a 5-minute walk from the entrance. By **car,** head east on the A4 and take the Parcs Disney exit. By train, from outside Paris, you could arrive by **TGV** (the

---

The World's First Marvel Hotel

If you want to stay at the parks, you could do a lot worse than booking a night at the spanking-new Disney's Hotel New York – The Art of Marvel. It's currently the only Marvel hotel on the planet, which makes it a must if your brood's into the franchise. It brims with stuff to geek out on, including museum-worthy artwork from the films and comics, Iron Man suits, Captain America's shield, and a superhero photo station where you can have a pic with Spider-man. Budding wee artists can also head to the Marvel Design Studio to learn to draw their favorite superheroes. Room decor is subtle—lots of beige and some reds—with yet more Marvel artworks on the walls. Check prices when you book; they vary according to the ticket/hotel packages available on the dates you choose.

If Disney's re-created medieval towns were real, they would undoubtedly look like Provins. Bridging the Greater Paris and Champagne regions, this quaint, fairy tale–like settlement of half-timbered houses, medieval ramparts, spooky underground passages, and cobbled streets was once the Count of Champagne's capital, famed across medieval France for its *foires*, or fairs. Today it's just over an hour from Paris (by train from Gare de l'Est; www.transilien.com; from 11.35€) and Disneyland Paris (by bus no. 50; 2€), and is a great place for a family-themed day out, with falconry and jousting shows, and pleasant strolls along age-old streets lined with UNESCO-protected medieval buildings like the vaulted Grange aux Dîmes and the Tour César, a 12th-century dungeon. For more information, visit the tourist website www.provins.net.

French railway's high-speed train); see www.oui.sncf. From Paris' Roissy-Charles de Gaulle (CDG) and Orly airports, you could also catch the **Magic Shuttle** (http://magicalshuttle.co.uk; 23€ adults, 10€ children 3–10, free for children 2 and under), a direct shuttle to the parks and Disney hotels.

VISITOR INFORMATION **Disneyland Paris Guest Relations Office,** in City Hall on Main Street U.S.A. (www.disneylandparis.com; ✆ **08-25-30-05-00**). For general regional tourist information, visit the **Point Information Tourisme** between the train station and Disney Village (www.visitparisregion.com; ✆ **01-60-43-33-33**).

TICKETS Admission varies depending on the season. In peak season, a 1-day, 1-park ticket (for either the main park or Walt Disney Studios) costs about 68€ adults, 51€ children 3 to 11, and free for children 2 and under; a 2-day park-hopper ticket is roughly 169€ adults, 156€ kids; and a 3-day park-hopper ticket is around 211€ adults, 195€ kids. Special offers can include transportation to and from Paris; check the website.

HOURS Hours vary throughout the year, but most frequently they are daily 10am to 7:30pm. Check the website for exact hours during your stay.

Exploring Disney

This giant resort comprises two parks: the classic **Disneyland,** complete with "It's a Small World" and Star Wars Hyperspace Mountain, and **Walt Disney Studios,** which (in addition to the new lands under construction) has thrill rides and exhibits themed around Disney animation techniques and films. Yes, there's also a golf course, a spa, tennis courts, and **Disney Village** here, with its boutiques, restaurants, disco, and IMAX theater. But for the purposes of this guide, I'll just stick with the parks.

DISNEYLAND PARK

Isn't it comforting that some things never change? Here you are in France, and yet there are Frontierland, Adventureland, and Fantasyland, just the way you remember them back home. Okay, not exactly. For one thing, everyone's speaking French. And Bulgarian, Hindi, and Farsi; and the fries are called "frites." When you enter the park, you'll step right into **Main Street U.S.A,** that utopian rendition of early-20th-century America, complete with horse-drawn buggies and barbershop quartets. Here you'll find the **information center** as well as a train that leaves from Main Street Station. The train, which does a circuit around the park, will whisk you off to **Frontierland,** where you'll find Big Thunder Mountain, Phantom Manor, the **Thunder Mesa** paddle-wheel steam-

Walt Disney Studios Park.

boat, and the Lucky Nugget saloon. Next is a chug through **Adventureland,** with old favorites like the Swiss Family Robinson treehouse and the Pirates of the Caribbean. Onward toward **Fantasyland,** with Sleeping Beauty's Castle (Le Château de Belle au Bois Dormant), whizzing teacups, flying Dumbos, and "It's a Small World." Last stop: **Discoveryland,** home of Star Wars Hyperspace Mountain and Autopia. Parades course down Main Street every afternoon, and around closing time there's a spectacular light and fountain show.

WALT DISNEY STUDIOS PARK

Walt Disney Studios makes a decent alternative for older kids who have already done Disney and are up for something different. Along with films and parades, the park offers an introduction to the wonders of moviemaking at **Disney Animation Studios** and puts on special effects and stunt shows. Fun rides here include **Ratatouille: A Recipe for Adventure,** a 4D ride where you get a rat's-eye view of the restaurant kitchen in the movie of the same name. Smaller visitors can try the **Toy Soldiers Parachute Drop** or the brand-new Cars ROAD TRIP ride, where they can speed along Route 66 on the lookout for popular characters like Mater and Lightning McQueen.

WALKING TOURS OF PARIS

P aris is a walking city. You simply won't be able to fully appreciate the flavor of the place if you don't stroll through the streets and absorb the sights, sounds, and even smells that make up its sensory identity. A mere city block can encompass several centuries' worth of history. Below are tours of two of the city's best areas for ambling about.

WALKING TOUR 1: MONTMARTRE

START:	**Place des Abbesses (Métro: Abbesses).**
FINISH:	**Sacré-Coeur (Métro: Abbesses).**
TIME:	**About 1½ hours.**
BEST TIME:	**Weekdays, when stores are open and the crowds are smaller.**
WORST TIME:	**Weekends, when the area around Sacré-Coeur looks like the Métro at rush hour.**

Montmartre has become forever linked with a certain mythic image of Paris: quaint cobblestoned streets, accordion serenades, and the Sacré-Coeur hovering in the background. Or maybe it's the Moulin Rouge and can-can girls whooping it up on the Place Blanche. Although the area just around Sacré-Coeur is probably the most tourist-clogged in the capital and the Moulin Rouge is a tour-bus trap, the Butte (as it's called) still has its own magic and it's not hard to find. Though legendary artists like Picasso and Utrillo are gone, new ones have taken their place, and they aren't the ones hawking portraits in the Place du Tertre. In fact, within a couple blocks of the mobs on the *place* are quiet cobbled streets lined with lovely vine-trimmed houses and punctuated by cute cafes and shops.

---

1 Place des Abbesses

The first thing you'll notice when you are coming out of the Métro is the exit itself: This lovely Art Nouveau confection of smoked glass and metal is one of two surviving Métro entrances by Hector Guimard with a glass roof (the other is at

Montmartre Walking Tour

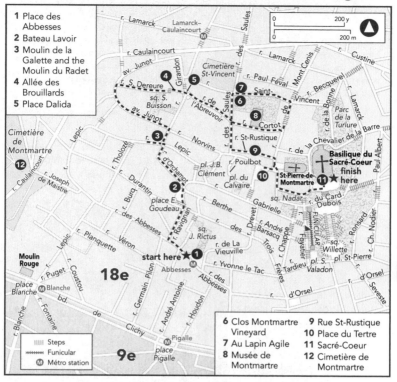

1 Place des Abbesses
2 Bateau Lavoir
3 Moulin de la Galette and the Moulin du Radet
4 Allée des Brouillards
5 Place Dalida

6 Clos Montmartre Vineyard
7 Au Lapin Agile
8 Musée de Montmartre

9 Rue St-Rustique
10 Place du Tertre
11 Sacré-Coeur
12 Cimetière de Montmartre

Porte Dauphine in the 16th arrond.). Now, look around the leafy plaza. Back in 1134, King Louis *Le Gros* (the Fat, otherwise known as Louis VI) founded an abbey up here, and this square is named after the various abbesses who ran it. As most of them came from wealthy, aristocratic families, they did not fare well during the French Revolution. In 1794, the 43rd abbess, Louise de Montmorency-Laval, who was 71 years old and both blind and deaf, was guillotined, and the abbey was pillaged. Her crime? She was found guilty of "blindly and deafly plotting against the Revolution."

Walk west on rue des Abbesses to rue Ravignan, where you will make a right uphill. At the top of the street is Place Emile Goudeau. At no. 11 bis–no. 13 is the:

2 Bateau Lavoir

This building started out as a piano factory but later was home to a virtual hall of fame of artists, actors, and poets, who stayed here when they were all young and struggling. In 1889, this odd edifice—constructed on

The actual distance on the walk described below is not long, but the terrain will make it seem a lot longer. Montmartre is up on a high hill (*butte*) overlooking the city, so be prepared for some steep ups and downs. Visitors with reduced mobility (or who are simply tired) might replace parts of this walk with **bus line 40** (the former Montmartrobus) that makes a wide circuit of the Butte. The bus, which costs a regular Métro ticket, leaves Place Pigalle every 12 to 15 minutes. For information and a map, visit www.ratp.fr.

different levels to accommodate the steep slope it was built on—was divided into artists' studios. By 1904, a young man named Pablo Picasso was living and working here, as well as Kees Van Dongen, Juan Gris, and Amadeo Modigliani, not to mention the poets Max Jacob and Guillaume Apollinaire, among others. It was here that Picasso painted *Les Demoiselles d'Avignon* (even though he was nowhere near Provence), a painting that signaled the birth of Cubism. Unfortunately, this fertile artistic breeding ground, which was dubbed the **Bateau Lavoir,** or the Floating Laundry, by Jacob, burned down in 1970. All that's left of the original structure is one facade on the small plaza. The rest was rebuilt in 1978 and today still houses a few artists' studios, though none are open to the public.

Abbesses Métro entrance.

Turn left on tiny rue d'Orchampt, a quiet cobbled street, which curves up to an intersection with rue Lepic. Take a short detour left down rue Lepic to the:

3 Moulin de la Galette & Moulin du Radet

More than 30 windmills once dotted Montmartre's vineyard-covered slopes. Here are the last two that still exist: the **Moulin du Radet,** which is now a swank restaurant called the Moulin de la Galette, and—somewhat confusingly—the "real" **Moulin de la Galette,** of Renoir painting fame, located down the street at no. 75, also known as the Moulin Blute-Fin. Whatever its name, this old mill, which was owned by the same family of millers since the 17th century, was a witness to tragedy. In 1814, it had the misfortune of being attacked by a garrison of Cossacks, who were in town because the Allies (Germany, Prussia, and Russia, among a host of others) had come to Paris to stop French attacks on the rest of Europe and put Napoleon in his place. The miller tried valiantly to defend his property but ended up hacked to pieces and nailed to the blades of his windmill. Years later, the miller's son turned the farm into an outdoor music hall, the famous Moulin de la Galette depicted in a legendary painting by Renoir (you can see the painting at the Musée d'Orsay; p. 193). Other painters who frequented these bucolic dance parties included Toulouse-Lautrec, Van Gogh, and Utrillo. Today you won't get to dance here—the mill is private property and a prim little sign outside informs you that it is under electronic surveillance and protected by radar and guard dogs.

Return to rue Giradon and turn left, then left again on av. Junot, walking past some of Montmartre's most elegant homes. Follow av. Junot as it curves to the right, making a sharp right on rue Simon Dereure. The street ends at Place Casadesus; climb the stairs to the footpath called:

4 Allée des Brouillards

This tranquil path leads past a number of massive houses, set back in large gardens, most of which are at least partially shielded from prying eyes by tall fences. The largest garden surrounds a white country manor known as the **Château des Brouillards,** or Fog Castle. Built in 1772 for a lawyer in the Parisian Parliament, this romantic dwelling most likely got its name from the mist that crept up from a nearby spring when the water contacted the cold morning air (real fog is a rare thing up here). Gérard de Nerval lived here in 1854, and surely this was the ideal writer's haven for this quintessential Romantic-era poet. Painter Pierre-Auguste Renoir lived and worked in one of the houses behind the château; his son, filmmaker Jean Renoir, was born there.

Continue down the path to its end, at:

5 Place Dalida

This small crossroads is graced with a bust of one of Montmartre's most beloved residents, Yolanda Gigliotti, aka Dalida. This Egyptian-born singer, of Italian ancestry, was one of France's biggest stars, recording hundreds of hits and winning 70 gold records. The blonde bombshell moved to the Butte in 1962, where she lived out the rest of her stormy life in a four-story mansion that her fans dubbed "Sleeping Beauty's Castle." After a series of unfortunate love affairs, two of which ended with her partners' suicides, she took her own life in 1987. Her **statue** looks out on one of the most prototypical views of Montmartre, down rue de l'Abreuvoir: a cobbled lane leading up a hill with Sacré-Coeur in the background.

Walk up rue de l'Abreuvoir and turn left on rue des Saules:

6 Clos Montmartre Vineyard

As you make your way down rue des Saules, you will notice an unlikely vineyard on the right-hand side of the street. This is in fact the last of Montmartre's vineyards; for centuries, vineyards covered the Butte. Back in the 16th century, wine-making was the primary industry in the area—though nobody ever bragged about the high quality of the product,

Bronze bust of Dalida.

which was mainly known for its diuretic virtues. A ditty about Montmartre wine went thus: "The wine of Montmartre—whoever drinks a pint, pisses a quarte." By the way, in those days, a "quarte" equaled 67 liters (70 quarts). Whatever its merits, this tiny vineyard still produces. The harvest is celebrated with a raucous street party every year (p. 51), and rare bottles of Clos Montmartre are auctioned off with the proceeds benefitting local public projects.

Continue down rue des Saules to the intersection with rue St-Vincent:

7 Au Lapin Agile

The story goes that a certain André Gill, a habitué of this rowdy corner cabaret—which was then called the Cabaret des Assassins—painted a sign for the place showing a rabbit (*lapin*) jumping out of a stockpot. The cabaret became known as the Lapin à Gill (Gill's rabbit), which in time mutated into Au Lapin Agile (the Agile Rabbit). The singer Aristide Bruant (immortalized in a poster by Toulouse-Lautrec) bought the inn in 1902 and asked Frédé, a local guitar legend, to run it. Under Frédé's guidance, the cabaret thrived, and the best and the brightest of the Montmartre scene were drawn to its doors, including Picasso, Verlaine, Renoir, Utrillo, and Apollinaire. Not everyone who came was a fan of modern art, however. The writer Roland Dorgelès had had enough of "Picasso's band" from the Bateau Lavoir and decided to play a trick on them: He tied a paintbrush to the end of Frédé's donkey, Lolo, and let him slop paint over a canvas. Dorgelès then entered the painting, which he titled *And the Sun Set Over the Adriatic*, in the Salon des Indépendants, a major art show in Paris. The critics loved it—until they found out who really painted it, and a scandal ensued. Today Au Lapin Agile is still a cabaret, though a much calmer one, showcasing traditional French chanson (p. 233). The shows are heavy on nostalgia and cheesy sing-alongs, but they can be good, kitschy fun when you're in the mood.

Turn right on rue St-Vincent, then right on rue Mont Cenis. Climb the stairs and turn right on rue Cortot:

8 Musée de Montmartre

At 12 rue Cortot lies the peaceful **Musée de Montmartre – Jardins Renoir** (p. 172), which offers an overview of neighborhood history and is housed in the former residence of Rosimond, a famous 17th-century actor who was in Molière's troupe. In another century, Renoir painted here (this is where he created the *Bal du Moulin de la Galette*), as did Utrillo, who lived here with his mother, the model and painter Suzanne Valadon, and her lover André Utter. The gardens make for some wonderful down time, with views over the vineyards and the northern side of the city. At the seasonal cafe, chairs are sprawled out toward the lawns on hot days, and young kids can run around safely (just watch out for the pond).

Au Lapin Agile.

When it comes to strolling through historic cemeteries (a favorite Parisian pastime and a surprisingly lovely way to spend a peaceful hour), the Cimetière du Père-Lachaise in the 20th arrondissement steals the show with the graves of legends such as Jim Morrison, Oscar Wilde, and Edith Piaf. But overlook **Montmartre's cemetery** at the foot of the Butte and you'll miss more than just a tranquil stroll. This is where the tombs of famous artists such as Edgar Degas, ballet dancer Vaslav Nijinsky, and the New Wave movie director François Truffaut lie along higgledy-piggledy alleys (alongside not-so-famous greats, including Adolphe Sax, the inventor of the saxophone). It's like walking through history, and a great spot for some downtime on a sunny day. Tag it onto the end of your tour by heading back to Place des Abbesses and following rue des Abbesses westward. When it turns into rue Lepic, take rue Joseph Maistre on the left, and turn left again onto rue Caulaincourt. As you walk over the bridge, look for the staircase down to avenue Rachel on the left; the entrance is on your left.

Continue to the end of rue Cortot and turn left on rue des Saules; walk up to rue St-Rustique and turn left:

9 Rue St-Rustique

By now you'll have noticed the crowds thickening and a change in the atmosphere toward the Disneyesque. Trinket shops appear on every corner, and "artists" badger you to draw your portrait. Dive quickly into rue St-Rustique, a narrow channel of calm. Not only does the noise die down, but you'll be rewarded with an excellent photo op of the bulblike tops of Sacré-Coeur sprouting above the end of the street. This is one of the oldest streets in Montmartre, with a medieval-style gutter in its center and no sidewalks.

Walk to the end of rue St-Rustique and turn right. On your right is the entrance to:

10 Place du Tertre

Now there's no avoiding it: the most tourist-drenched, mob-swamped spot in Paris. A quick walk down the hill toward the Place des Abbesses will lead you to plenty of nice restaurants and cafes. You will probably be approached by people begging to do your portrait—these "artists" may do nice caricatures, but if you think you're looking at the next Picasso, you're kidding yourself.

Duck back out of Place du Tertre and continue down rue du Mont Cenis until it curls around to the left and becomes rue Azaïs. Keep walking until you're in front of:

11 Basilique du Sacré-Coeur

After you've looked up at the gleaming white basilica and its odd, pseudo-Byzantine domes, turn around and admire the stunning view from the esplanade, or parvis, in front of the church; on a clear day you can see as far as 50km (31 miles). No matter how many people are standing around snapping pictures, it just won't ruin the beauty of this sight. Though you won't be able to see the Eiffel Tower (it's too far over on the right, though you can see it if you walk to the corner of rues Azaïs and Saint-Eleuthère just below), you will take in a majestic panorama that includes the Pompidou Center, St-Eustache, the Opéra, and the Louvre, not to mention distant hills and vales beyond the city. What you are mainly looking at here is eastern Paris, the more plebian side—an entirely appropriate view from this historically working-class, low-rent neighborhood. The view actually gets better as you walk down to the bottom-most level of the esplanade; from here you can also take in the lovely gardens below, which had a starring role in the ultimate Montmartre movie, "Amélie," by Jean-Pierre Jeunet (2001). Also see p. 171.

WALKING TOUR 2: **THE MARAIS**

START:	**Village St-Paul (23–27 rue St-Paul; Métro: St-Paul).**
FINISH:	**Place des Vosges.**
TIME:	**1½ hours, not including time spent in shops, restaurants, or museums.**
BEST TIME:	**During the week, when the streets are full of life, and Sundays, when unlike other parts of the city, many shops and restaurants are open.**
WORST TIME:	**Saturdays, when shoppers flood most of the neighborhood and the Jewish quarter completely shuts down.**

The Marais is one of the few areas that Baron Haussmann largely ignored when he was tearing up the rest of the city in the 19th century; for that reason, it still retains a medieval feel. Though very few buildings actually date from the Middle Ages, this warren of narrow streets and picturesque squares is layered with a rich history, which is apparent in the pleasing hodgepodge of architectural styles. The neighborhood's glory days date from the 16th and 17th centuries, when anyone who was anyone simply had to build a mansion or a palace here. Though the area fell from grace in the 18th and 19th centuries, many of the grand *hôtels particuliers* (private mansions) were reborn as museums and public archives when the neighborhood was restored in the latter half of the 20th century. Today, the Marais is a fascinating mix of hip gentrification and the remnants of a working-class neighborhood. It is at once the center of the city's gay life, as well as the historic Jewish quarter, even if a much larger Jewish community lives in the 19th arrondissement. Some of the city's best museums and boutiques are in the Marais, so you could easily spend an entire day here.

1 Village St-Paul

Many centuries ago, a small hamlet sat on this spot when the area was still mostly marshland (*marais* means "swamp"). While the neighborhood has transformed many times since, a small reminder of this village lives on, hidden behind an ordinary row of buildings on rue St-Paul. Pass through the entryway and you'll come into a kind of large interior courtyard that dates from the 14th century, when it was part of the gardens of Charles V's royal residence. At one point the houses and buildings built over and around the gardens were slated for demolition; a neighborhood committee saved them, and in the 1970s the village was restored and turned into a sort of antiques center, with stores and art galleries (see www.levillagesaintpaul.com and "Shopping," p. 219). The village hosts seasonal *déballages,* or outdoor arts and antiques fairs. Today the commercial emphasis has shifted from antiques to design.

Exit the village on rue des Jardins St-Paul. On one side of this street is a playground that runs along a huge stone wall, the:

2 Rampart of Philippe Auguste

Before you is the best-preserved stretch of the city walls built by Philippe Auguste, King of France. Before leaving town on a crusade in 1190, Philippe decided the time had come to beef up security. The result was a mighty rampart that defined what were then the city limits. The wall in front of you once ran in a semicircle from the Seine, up to around rue Etienne Marcel, and curved over to protect the Louvre and back down to the Seine (a similar semicircle was built 20 years later on the Left Bank). Aside from this stretch, only small fragments can be found here and there on both banks, so you'll have to imagine the rest; you'll also have to imagine the towers and the six massive portals that once were the only land access into the city.

Remnant of the 12th-century walls of Philippe Auguste.

The Marais Walking Tour

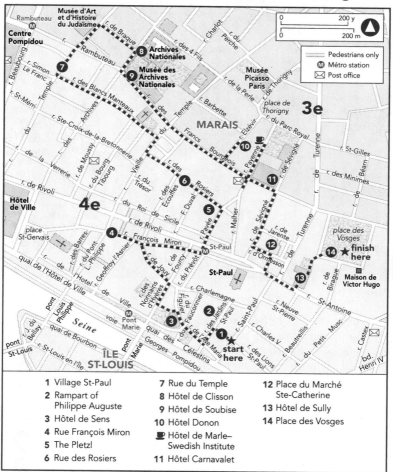

1 Village St-Paul
2 Rampart of Philippe Auguste
3 Hôtel de Sens
4 Rue François Miron
5 The Pletzl
6 Rue des Rosiers
7 Rue du Temple
8 Hôtel de Clisson
9 Hôtel de Soubise
10 Hôtel Donon
🐚 Hôtel de Marle–Swedish Institute
11 Hôtel Carnavalet
12 Place du Marché Ste-Catherine
13 Hôtel de Sully
14 Place des Vosges

Turn left down rue des Jardins St-Paul and right on rue de l'Avé Maria. Just where it branches off to the right on rue du Figuier is:

3 Hôtel de Sens
Built between 1475 and 1519, this splendid fortress/mansion is a rare example of medieval urban architecture. When Paris came under the jurisdiction of the Bishop of Sens back in the 15th century, he promptly built himself a suitably fabulous home in the city. Later, Henri IV briefly used it to house his strong-minded wife, Queen Margot, whose many love affairs were causing him ceaseless headaches. The bishops stopped

Hôtel de Sens.

coming to the Hôtel de Sens altogether in 1622, preferring to rent it out. By the time the city bought it in 1911, it was in a pitiful state; the building's restoration—which started in 1929—wouldn't be completed until 1961. The Hôtel now houses the **Bibliothèque Forney,** a library dedicated to the decorative arts. Take a minute to admire the turrets and towers in the courtyard (visible from the street).

Follow the side of the building down rue du Figuier and turn left onto the path that leads around to the back of the Hôtel and its pretty French gardens. The path leads to rue des Nonnains d'Hyères, where you'll turn right, then walk left on rue de Jouy to where it intersects with:

4 Rue François Miron

Walk left down rue François Miron to the corner of rue Cloche Perce. You will notice two multistoried half-timbered houses: the **Maison à l'Enseigne du Faucheur** (no. 11) and the **Maison à l'Enseigne du Mouton** (no. 13). Pre-Haussmann, houses like these were once all over the city; now they are extremely rare. These two date from the 14th century, though after 1607 the crisscrossed wood facades of all such houses were covered with a layer of plaster in accordance with a law that aimed to reduce the risk of fire. When these houses were restored in the 1960s, the plaster was removed and the wood was once again revealed.

Double back and continue down rue François Miron until it ends at the St-Paul Métro station. Cross the rue de Rivoli and continue left up rue Pavée to:

5 The Pletzl

You are now entering the city's oldest Jewish quarter, once called the *Pletzl* ("little place" in Yiddish), where there has been a Jewish presence since the 13th century. This community swelled and shrank over the centuries, in line with various edicts and expulsions, but the largest influx was in the 1880s, when tens of thousands of Eastern European Jews, fleeing poverty and persecution back home, settled in France. The Pletzl was hit hard during the infamous roundups of 1942, when police came and emptied apartment buildings and even schools of their Jewish occupants and sent them off to Nazi concentration camps. Though the neighborhood is slowly being eaten up by the area's advancing gentrification, and chic shops pop up next to kosher butchers, a small and fairly traditional community still lives here. At no. 10 is the unusual **Synagogue de la rue Pavée,** designed by Hector Guimard, the Art Nouveau master who created the famous Métro entrances. This is the only existing religious edifice by Guimard, whose wife was Jewish (they fled to the U.S. during World War II). In 1940, on Yom Kippur, the Germans dynamited the synagogue; it was eventually restored and is now a national monument (open for religious services only).

Continue up rue Pavée to where it crosses:

6 Rue des Rosiers

Rumor has it that this street got its name from the rose bushes that once lined its edges, back in the days when it ran along the exterior of the city walls. Up until recently, it was the main artery of the Jewish quarter; today, all that's left are a few kosher restaurants and a bookstore or two. Great falafel can still be found here (**L'As du Fallafel;** p. 100); if you happen to be in the area around lunchtime, you might get handed a free sample from one of the competing restaurants.

Turn left on rue des Rosiers and continue to the end, where you'll turn right on rue Vieille du Temple. You are now in the thick of the trendier (and gay) part of the neighborhood, which is filled with fun restaurants and boutiques. Take the first left at rue des Blancs Manteaux and follow this pretty street all the way to where it ends at:

7 Rue du Temple

By the time you hit this street you'll notice that the neighborhood has changed from trendy to workaday; rue du Temple is lined with jewelry and clothing wholesalers. But this street—which back in medieval times led to the stalwart fortress of the Knights Templar—also harbors some lovely examples of 17th-century *hôtels particuliers* (private mansions). Turn right and walk to no. 71, the **Hôtel de St-Aignan,** otherwise known as the **Musée d'Art et d'Histoire du Judaïsme** (p. 159). This exercise in 17th-century grandeur includes a sneaky architectural trick: One of the three facades facing the courtyard, which seems to be the front of an enormous building, is really just a facade. Despite the presence of carefully curtained windows, on the other side of the wall is merely another wall, yet another chunk of Philippe Auguste's ramparts.

Continue up to rue de Braque and turn right. Walk to the end where the street intersects with rue des Archives. Across the street is the:

8 Hôtel de Clisson

The vaulted archway is what is left of the **Hôtel de Clisson,** a magnificent mansion that was built in 1380 and for centuries housed some of the grandest of the grand, including dukes of Guise, who hung out there for 135 years. Well, it may have been good enough for them, but by 1700, when François de Rohan, the Prince of Soubise, got his hands on it, he decided the time had come for a change (see below).

Turn right and walk down rue des Archives to rue des Francs Bourgeois and turn left. First thing you'll see on your left is the sumptuous gateway to the:

9 Hôtel de Soubise

The enormous *cour d'honneur,* a huge horseshoe-shaped courtyard, is edged with open galleries holding 56 pairs of double columns. These lead to a largely 17th-century palace, which now holds the National Archives. This jaw-dropping sight was the creation of architect Pierre Alexis Delamair, who was hired by the Prince of Soubise to build on to the courtyard and overhaul the building. Later the prince's son, the future Cardinal de Rohan, asked Delamair to build him his own palace next

Hôtel de Soubise.

door, the adjoining **Hôtel de Rohan-Strasbourg** (more archives are stashed here, not open to the public). A part of the Hôtel de Soubise houses the **Musée des Archives Nationale** (60 rue des Francs-Bourgeois, 3rd arrond.; www.archives-nationales.culture.gouv.fr; ☏ **01-40-27-60-96;** admission to permanent collection 5€, free for visitors 25 and under; Mon and Wed–Fri 10am–5:30pm, Sat–Sun 2–5:30pm), which displays tantalizing items from the vast National Archives, as well as temporary exhibitions. You can also visit the **apartments of the Prince and Princess of Soubise.** Though just a few rooms, they retain the opulent decor of the period and give a sense of how the other half lived in the 18th century. And in 2021, the Hôtel de Rohan unveiled sumptuous decor taken from the former **Chancellerie d'Orléans,** a palatial 18th-century mansion that was demolished in the early 20th century.

Continue down rue des Francs Bourgeois and window-shop (or just plain shop) in the stylish boutiques that line this street. Turn left onto rue Elzevir, and head to the:

10 Hôtel Donon

This sumptuous 16th-century mansion houses the **Musée Cognacq-Jay** (p. 158), a small but fabulous and free museum dedicated to 18th-century art. Originally built in 1575, the *hôtel* got its name from its first owner, Médéric de Donon, Controller General of the Royal Estates. By the early 20th century, the building had (like many other Marais mansions) become commercial premises. Fortunately, it was acquired by the City of Paris in 1974 and restored to its former glory. Architecturally, the building is typical of other 16th-century Marais *hôtels*—symmetrical design, with wings set around a rectangular courtyard—but it stands out for its stonework, which is much less ornate than that of other grand mansions in the Marais.

Go back and turn left back onto rue des Francs Bourgeois, then left again to the intersection with rue Payenne for a short detour, about half a block down:

Take a Break 🍽

The Hôtel de Marle, the home of the **Institut Suédois,** Swedish Institute (11 rue Payenne, 3rd arrond.; https://paris.si.se; ☏ **01-44-78-80-11;** Tues–Sun noon–6pm), has a lovely **cafe** with tables in the courtyard in the summer. Nibble a vanilla-scented *kanelbulle* while you take in the exterior of this 16th-century mansion, which at one point was the home of Yolande de Polastron, a close friend of Marie Antoinette. If you still need a rest, sprawl out on a bench in the Square Georges Cain, a small, leafy park just across the street.

Walk back down rue Payenne, turn left onto rue des Francs Bourgeois, then left again onto rue Sévigné to:

11 Hôtel Carnavalet

If you're interested in learning about the history of Paris, the newly revamped **Musée Carnavalet** (p. 157) is a must. Not only does it cover thousands of years of the city's past, but it also has beautiful gardens, from which you can admire the exterior of this magnificent Renaissance mansion. Originally built in 1548, the *hôtel* got its name from its second owner, the widow of a Breton nobleman named François Kernevenoy, whose surname no one could pronounce. The mangled Parisian pronunciation, "Carnavalet," stuck. In 1660, a new owner gave François Mansart the job of enlarging and modernizing his lodgings: The result was so pleasing that in 1677, Madame de Sévigné, famed letter-writer and woman of the world, rented the building and lived there until her death. There are superb sculptures in the garden courtyards, including a **bronze statue of Louis XIV** in the **Cour d'Honneur.**

Follow rue de Sevigné south, then turn left onto rue d'Ormesson to:

12 Place du Marché Ste-Catherine

The name speaks to the open-air market that once stood here; today, this shaded plaza remains a lovely oasis of green and quiet in this busy neighborhood. Thankfully, no cars are allowed on the square, and the cafes on its edges all have outdoor seating in nice weather.

Continue to rue St-Antoine and turn left without crossing the street to no. 62:

13 Hôtel de Sully

The most splendiferous of the many splendiferous mansions in the Marais, the **Hôtel de Sully** was built by a rich 17th-century businessman, a certain Mesme-Gallet. While his version was quite sumptuous, the mansion really came to life when it was bought by the Duc de Sully, who hired architect François Le Vau to give it a makeover. After his death, the palacelike edifice was sold, divided, and built upon—like so many mansions in the Marais. Using the original plans and contemporary drawings and etchings, the building was completely restored in the 1970s to Le Vau's version; you can now stroll through the courtyard and admire the sculpted exterior in its virtually pristine state. Though the building is closed to the public, you can traipse through the front courtyard to a second one with a peaceful **garden** filled with sparrows.

Go through the archway in the back of the garden to the:

14 Place des Vosges

Officially inaugurated in 1612, this exquisite **Renaissance square,** bordered by 36 virtually identical stone and brick town houses, was the idea of King Henri IV, who unfortunately didn't live to see it finished. After a stroll under the arcades, which run below the town houses, take a seat on a bench in the square and admire the tall trees and elegant symmetry of the landscaping, as well as the huge **statue** in the middle of Louis XIII astride his horse. The square has seen a number of illustrious tenants over the centuries: Madame de Sévigné was born at no. 1 bis, the 19th-century actress Rachel lived at no. 9, and poet Théophile Gautier and novelist Alphonse Daudet both lived at no. 10. The most famous inhabitant, no doubt, was writer Victor Hugo, who lived at no. 6 from 1832 to 1848; his house is now the free-to-visit **Maison de Victor Hugo** (p. 157).

PLANNING YOUR TRIP TO PARIS

N ot all roads lead to Paris, but getting there is a pretty straightforward affair. Once you arrive, you'll need to know how to get around and how to take care of practical matters. Below I supply all the nitty-gritty details you need to have a comfortable, safe, and affordable stay in Paris.

GETTING THERE

By Plane

Paris has two international airports: **Aéroport d'Orly,** 18km (11 miles) south of the city (mostly European flights), and **Aéroport Roissy-Charles-de-Gaulle** (**CDG;** mostly long-haul carriers), 30km (19 miles) northeast. The contact information for both airports is www.parisaeroport.fr; ✆ **00-33-1-70-36-39-50** from abroad, and ✆ **39-50** from France (.35€/min.). Before you fly, check this website for up-to-date airport information.

If you are taking Ryanair or another discount airline to **Beauvais airport** (see below), be advised that that airport is about 80km (50 miles) from Paris.

ROISSY-CHARLES-DE-GAULLE (CDG) AIRPORT CDG has three terminals that are some distance from one another. A free train called the **CDGVAL** connects all three to the two train stations.

The quickest way into central Paris from the airport is the fast **RER B** (www.ratp.fr) suburban trains, which leave every 10 to 15 minutes between roughly 4:50am and 11:50pm. It takes about 40 minutes to get to Paris, and RER B stops at several central Métro stations, including Châtelet-Les-Halles and Saint-Michel–Notre-Dame. A single ticket, which can be bought at the machines in the stations at the terminals, costs 11.40€ adults, 7.40€ children ages 4–10, free for children 3 and under.

The **Roissybus** (www.ratp.fr; ✆ **34-24**) departs every 20 minutes from the airport daily from 6am to 12:30am and costs 12€ for the 70-minute ride. The bus leaves you in the center of Paris, at the corner of rue Scribe and rue Auber, near the Opéra.

Like much of the world, France went into a full lockdown to defeat Covid-19 in March 2020 and has been taking cautious measures toward public safety ever since. The terms "mask wearing," "social distancing," and "vaccination certificates," the latter also known as the Health Pass or E.U. Digital Covid Certificate (see box p. 285), have all become a regular part of our vocabulary, and may or may not still be relevant by the time you travel. The rules are changing all the time, according to the number of Covid-19 cases. So what was in place at time of writing will almost certainly have evolved by the time you read this guide or begin your travels—including requirements for entering France and reentering the United States. During your trip, you may be required to wear a mask in indoor public places, show proof of Covid vaccination, have a health pass or a negative PCR test, follow social distancing in lines and shops, or even (in the worst-case scenario) quarantine. The only way for you to stay on top of things is to check the following official websites:

U.S. Embassy & Consulates in France: https://fr.usembassy.gov/covid-19-information for up-to-date traveler information during the pandemic, including E.U. Digital Covid Certificate (Health Pass) information, entry information for France, and information for reentry into the United States after your trip.

French government website: www.gouvernement.fr/en/coronavirus-covid-19

Paris Tourist Office website: https://en.parisinfo.com/practical-paris/info/guides/info-disruption-paris

European Commission E.U. Digital Covid Certificate: https://ec.europa.eu/info/live-work-travel-eu/coronavirus-response/safe-covid-19-vaccines-europeans/eu-digital-covid-certificate_en

The **taxi** rate from Roissy into the city is around 53€ to the Right Bank and 58€ to the Left Bank, not including supplements (1€/item of luggage, 20% extra 5pm–10am and Sun and bank holidays). Taxi stands are outside each airport terminal. If you're approached by anyone offering you a taxi, please politely turn them down. Alternatively, Uber functions in France and costs 45€ to 55€ in an UberX car (www.uber.com; also see p. 293) depending on traffic and distance. Prices increase when demand is high.

ORLY (ORY) AIRPORT   Orly has two terminals: Orly Sud and Orly Ouest. To get to the center of Paris, take the 8-minute monorail **OrlyVal** to the RER station "Antony" to get **RER B** into the center. Combined travel time is about 40 minutes. Trains run between 5:30am and 11:30pm; the one-way fare for the OrlyVal plus the RER B is 13.25€ adults, 6.60€ children ages 4 to 10, free for children 3 and under.

The **Orlybus** (www.ratp.fr), which leaves every 15 minutes between 5am and 12:30am, links the airport with Place Denfert-Rochereau, a 30-minute trip that costs 8.70€ for both adults and children.

A **taxi** from Orly to central Paris costs around 32€ for a Left Bank destination, and 37€ for the Right Bank, not including supplements (1€/item of luggage, and 20% extra 5pm–10am and Sun and bank holidays). Uber costs around 32€ to 37€ in an UberX car (www.uber.com; also see p. 293). Prices increase during high demand.

BEAUVAIS (BVA) AIRPORT Beauvais airport (www.aeroportparis beauvais.com; ✆ **08-92-68-20-66**; .45€/min.) is around 80km (50 miles) from Paris and is served by budget airlines such as Ryanair and Wizz Air. Buses leave about 20 minutes after each flight has landed and, depending on the traffic, take about 1 hour and 15 minutes to get to Porte Maillot on the western edge of Paris. To return to Beauvais, you need to be at the bus station at least 3 hours before the departure of your flight. A one-way ticket costs 15.90€ (29€ return ticket) if you purchase it online in advance.

By Train

One of best ways to get around France and Europe is by train. The French railway agency, the **SNCF (Société Nationale des Chemins de Fer Français;** www.oui.sncf), has a vast network that connects most major cities and quite a few smaller towns, though you will often have to pass through Paris to get from one place to another. The cheapest tickets are sold online at www.ouigo. com, which is part of Oui SNCF, but the on-board service (which usually includes a buffet car or trolley service, and lets you travel with as many bags as you need) is different. On Ouigo trains no food or drink is sold (bring your own or starve), and as with low-cost airlines, you are allowed one item of size-restricted hand luggage, plus a shoulder bag. Any extra/larger items are charged at 5€ each way upon reservation. If you are caught with more luggage than you reserved, you will be asked to pay 20€ extra per bag as you go through the ticket gate (aka the cattle-herd gate, as people line up untidily as they wait their turn). As a result, travelers must arrive 30 minutes before departure. This is especially necessary at Gare Montparnasse, where Ouigo trains leave from platforms in the Hall Vaugirard, which is a good 10-minute walk from the main station.

If you're traveling with kids 3 and under, in this post-Covid era they are no longer allowed to sit on your knees and travel for free. You must pay a small

E.U. Digital Covid Certificate

As we go to press, member states of the European Union, including France, are issuing vaccination certificates known as the E.U. Digital Covid Certificate, a pass proving your vaccination status (fully vaccinated, negative PCR test, or fully recovered). The pass has a customized, scannable QR code that can be downloaded on smartphones or printed. A mobile app, TousAntiCovid, can be used to store a pass. This pass may be required for entry into the country and even for entry into public spaces. Though designed for E.U. citizens, the scheme is also open to Americans (and citizens of other countries too). For regularly updated information about how American visitors can obtain the certificate, please check the U.S. Embassy & Consulates in France website: https://fr.usembassy.gov/covid-19-information.

fee for their seat (between 5€ and 8€), but they have the same bag allowance as you.

With a standard (non-discounted) Oui SNCF ticket, you can carry as much luggage as you need, and it is recommended that you arrive 15 minutes in advance.

The SNCF connects to railways in neighboring countries, including the U.K. The **Eurostar** (www.eurostar.com), which passes under the channel for 20 minutes, will get you from Paris' Gare du Nord to St. Pancras Station, London, in just 2¼ hours. If London is your destination, know that even though the regular ticket price can be high (around 200€ one-way!), scads of discounts are available (from as little as around 40€ one-way) on the website, especially if you purchase in advance and/or are flexible about times. Brussels is only 1 hour and 15 minutes away on the high-speed **Thalys** (www.thalys.com) train, and tickets range anywhere from 25€ to 145€ depending on what deal you get. Visit the site for high-speed trains to Brussels, Amsterdam, and Cologne. For rail passes that you can use throughout Europe, visit **Rail Europe** (www.raileurope.com).

Paris has seven major train stations: **Gare d'Austerlitz** (13th arrond.), **Gare de Lyon** (12th arrond.), **Gare de Bercy** (12th arrond.), **Gare Montparnasse** (14th arrond.), **Gare St-Lazare** (8th arrond.), **Gare de l'Est** (10th arrond.), and **Gare du Nord** (10th arrond.). Stations can be reached by bus or Métro. *Warning:* As in many cities, stations and surrounding areas can be seedy and are frequented by pickpockets. Be alert, especially at night.

By Bus

Cheapest of all, and the most time-consuming, is the bus. For travel within Europe, contact **Eurolines** (www.eurolines.com), a consortium of dozens of different bus lines with routes that span the continent (Lisbon to Prague, anyone?). Most long-haul buses arrive at the **Eurolines France** station on the eastern edge of the city (23 av. du Général-de-Gaulle, Bagnolet; Métro: Gallieni).

By Car

I wouldn't recommend driving in Paris to my worst enemy, but renting a car and driving around France can be a lovely way to see the country. All of the major car-rental companies have offices here, though you'll often get better deals if you reserve before you leave home. **AutoEurope** (www.autoeurope.com) is an excellent source for discounted rentals. Even better may be **Auto-Slash.com,** which applies discount codes to rentals from all of the major multinational firms; this can mean big savings. It also monitors prices, so if a rate drops, it re-books you automatically. You pay for the rental at the counter, not in advance. Also check out **Avis** (www.avis.com), **Hertz** (www.hertz.com), and **Europcar** (www.europcar.com).

Before you step on the gas, at the very least, try to get a list of international road signs; your car rental agency should have one. Driving in France is not substantially different from driving in most English-speaking countries (although British travelers will have to get used to driving on the "wrong" side of the road). However, you'll have to contend with French drivers, who tend to zoom around with what the more timid among us would call reckless abandon (particularly look out for motorcyclists, who can be daredevils). Truthfully, since the installation of radar a few years ago, drivers have become much more well-behaved; you, too, should pay attention to speed limits or risk a steep fine. The two biggest driving differences: *priorité à droite,* which means priority is always given to vehicles approaching from the right at intersections, unless otherwise indicated; and the fondness for **roundabouts** (traffic circles). Rule number one regarding the latter: The person entering the roundabout does *not* have priority. Rule number two: Look at the sign posted *before* the roundabout that indicates which exit goes in what direction so that you'll be prepared when it's time to get off. The good news is that if you miss your turnoff, you can just circle around until you figure out where it is. In Paris, certain large roundabouts, like Place Charles de Gaulle at the top of the Champs-Élysées, don't have marked lanes, so it can seem like a free-for-all. The key here is not to hesitate, and to look around you at all times.

GETTING AROUND

Finding an Address

The river Seine divides Paris into the **Rive Droite (Right Bank)** to the north and the **Rive Gauche (Left Bank)** to the south. You can figure out which is which if you face west. (Figuring out which way is west is another problem.) Paris is divided into 20 municipal districts called **arrondissements,** which spiral out clockwise starting with the 1st, which is the geographical center of the city. It's not easy to figure out without a map or an app, so I strongly suggest that you invest in a booklet called *Paris Pratique par Arrondissement,* which has a bus and metro map for each arrondissement. You can buy one for about 5€ in most *Presse*—newspaper—stands and at Fnac stores (p. 226), or on Amazon.com beforehand for considerably more. The only thing is that at time of writing, the current edition is old, so the Vélib' stand info is not up-to-date. The city layout won't have changed, though. Or there are, of course, dozens of good map apps for Paris if you prefer—though Wi-Fi doesn't always work as well as it should in public spaces, and it's near impossible to get 3G, 4G, or 5G coverage on the Métro.

By Public Transport

For everything you ever wanted to know about the city's public transport, visit the **RATP** (www.ratp.fr; ✆ **34-24**). Paris and its suburbs are divided into five travel zones, but you'll probably only be concerned with zones 1 and 2, which cover the city itself.

RATP tickets are valid on the Métro, bus, tram, and RER. You can buy tickets at the window (if you are lucky—ticket booths are an endangered species) or from machines at most Métro entrances. The machines take coins and chip-enabled credit cards only. If you don't have one of those, you can also buy tickets from some cafes that have a TABAC sign outside—though the number of them selling tickets is diminishing too. A **single ticket** costs 1.90€ and a *carnet* of 10 tickets costs 16.90€. Children 4 to 9 years old pay half-price; kids 3 and under ride free. A special transit pass for tourists called **Paris Visite** offers unlimited travel in certain zones on buses, Métro, and RER, and discounts on some attractions, but aside from the ease of having an unlimited pass to jump on and off buses and Métros, its usefulness is limited. Remember, Paris is a relatively small city, and you'll probably end up walking a lot. In the end, a cheaper *carnet* of 10 tickets does the trick just fine. Not only that, unlike a pass, a *carnet* can be shared with your fellow travelers. Next, there is the cost (high): A 1-day adult pass for zones 1 to 3 costs 12€, a 2-day pass 19.50€, a 3-day pass 26.65€, and a 5-day pass 38.35€. It is also possible to buy even more expensive passes for zones 1 to 5, which will get you to both Versailles and the airport.

However, if a transit pass is what you are after, other less expensive options serve the same purpose, even if they don't include Paris Visite's minimal attractions discounts. First is the slightly cheaper 1-day **Mobilis** ticket, which offers unlimited travel in zones 1 up to 5; a pass for zones 1 and 2 costs 7.50€. If you're staying for a week or longer and will be doing a lot of buzzing around, it may be worth getting the **Navigo,** a swipe card that you can buy on the RATP app (www.ratp.fr/apps/bonjour-ratp) and at certain Métro or train stations for 5€. You must provide a passport photo, but once you have the card, it offers unlimited travel in the relevant zones. The weekly tariff (which runs Mon–Sun) for zones 1 to 5 is 22.80€. That includes going to and from the airports (except OrlyVal) and transport for day trips such as Versailles or Fontainebleau, so it could quickly pay off. If your trip fits into a Monday-to-Sunday schedule, this 7-day card is substantially cheaper than a 5-day Paris Visite card.

BY MÉTRO (SUBWAY)

The city's first Métro, or subway, was at the apex of high tech at its inauguration on July 19, 1900, and over a century later, it still functions very well. The lack of cleanliness and wheelchair/stroller access are its greatest downfalls and somewhat embarrassing for the city that will be hosting the 2024 Paralympics. A big push to render the city more accessible is underway, however, so don't be surprised to find some stations closed between certain hours. Another problem is not technical, but political: Subway workers are fond of strikes (*grèves*) and periodically instigate slowdowns or complete shutdowns of a few lines. Usually, strikes are merely annoying and most of the time your route will not be affected, though your trip might take a little longer than normal. If you see the euphemism "Movement Social" on the TV monitor as you enter the station, read the message carefully to see if your line is involved (low groans and cursing by ticket holders are also good indicators of strike activity).

Strikes aside, the Métro is usually efficient and civilized, especially if you avoid rush hour (7:30–9:30am and 6–8pm). It's generally safe at night, and you don't need to worry about taking it at 3am because you can't. Alas, when people dolefully talk about "The Last Métro," they're usually not discussing a movie by François Truffaut. Instead, they're referring to a fact of Parisian life: Your evening out must be carefully timed so that you can run to the station before the trains shut down between midnight and 1am. To ease your pain, the transit authority added an extra hour on weekends, so now the Métro closes around 2am on Friday, Saturday, and pre-holiday evenings. The suburban trains (the RER, see below) close down around the same time (without the weekend bonus hour).

A map is essential (pick one up at any ticket window or take a look at the one on the inside back cover of this book); for a good app, download the one by the RATP (www.ratp.fr/apps/bonjour-ratp) or Île-de-France Mobilités (www.iledefrance-mobilites.fr), which cover the whole Paris region. The key is to know both the number of the line and its final destination. If you are on the no. 1 line (direction La Défense) and you want to transfer at the enormous Châtelet station to get to St-Michel, at Châtelet you'll need to doggedly follow the signs to the no. 4, direction Mairie de Montrouge.

BY RER

Your only underground express choice is the **RER** (pronounced "ehr-euh-ehr"), the suburban trains that dash through the city making limited stops. The down sides are (a) they don't run as often as the Métro, (b) they're a lot less pleasant, and (c) they're hard to figure out since they run on a different track system and the same lines can have multiple final destinations. *Important:* Make sure to hold on to your ticket because you'll need it to get out of the turnstile on the way out. To check your destinations, check the departure boards (or screens) on the quays: The stops served by the next train are either listed or lit up.

BY BUS

Thanks to a network of dedicated bus lanes, buses can be an efficient way to get around town, and you'll get a scenic tour to boot. The majority start running around 6am and stop anywhere from 9:30pm to midnight; service is reduced on Sundays and holidays. You can use Métro tickets on the buses, or you can buy tickets directly from the driver (2€). Alas, you can't reuse a ticket you've used on the Métro on the bus. You can, however, reuse the same ticket you've used on the bus on a tram (and vice versa) within a 90-minute limit. Tickets need to be validated in the machine next to the driver's cabin.

Inside the bus, the next stop is usually written on an electronic panel on the ceiling of the bus. Press the red button when you want to get off.

After the bus and Métro services stop running, head for the **Noctilien** night bus (www.transilien.com/en/page-deplacements/plans-noctilien). The 36 lines crisscross the city and head out to the suburbs every 30 minutes or so from 12:30 to 5:30am, at which time the usual bus and Métro services start up again. Tickets cost the same as for the regular bus (see above).

BY TRAM

Over the past few years, Paris has added 11 new tramway lines, with extensions and new lines in progress. These tramways connect Paris with its suburbs; within Paris they run along the outer circle of boulevards that trace the city limits. Tickets are the same price as the Métro.

On Two Wheels
BY BICYCLE

With around 1,000km (620 miles) of bike lanes, Paris has become a veritable cyclists' city—aided, undoubtedly by the hugely successful **Vélib'** (vel-*LEEB*) self-serve bike rental scheme launched in 2007 (the name comes from *vélo*, meaning "bicycle," and *liberté*, meaning "freedom"). Vélib' is still going strong, and now also includes electric bikes so you can get around even faster.

For Vélib', you have several subscription options (online or from the machine at over 1,000 bike stands): Buy a single journey ticket for 3€, for a 45-minute journey on either a pedal bike or an electric bike; get a 1-day pass for 5€ (pedal bike) or 10€ (electric), which gives you the right to as many 30-minute (45-minute for electric) rides as you'd like for 24 hours; and purchase the 3-day pass for 20€ (pedal or electric). If you want to go over 30 minutes, you pay 1€ for your extra 30 minutes on a pedal bike, and 2€ for the 45 minutes on an electric bike. The bikes are fitted with a V-Box, a computer system set between the handlebars, which enables you to lock and unlock the bikes. It also lets you leave your bike in an otherwise full station; follow the instructions and park it top-to-tail with another bike. The English version of the website (www.velib-metropole.fr) explains how everything works; the assistance phone number is *©* **01-76-49-12-34.** The one big catch is that to use the machines you must have a credit or debit card with a chip in it (at time of writing, you couldn't use phone pay apps like Apple Pay). This can be a problem for North American tourists, so I advise either getting a TravelEx "cash passport" with money on it (www.travelex.com), or even easier, buy your subscription ahead of time online (make sure you have your secret code to punch in on the stand). Helmets are not provided, so if you're feeling queasy about launching into traffic, bring one along. *Note:* Cyclists no longer always have the right to ride in the bus lanes; check for road signs. *One more tip:* Download the Vélib' app on your phone, so you don't waste precious time looking for a place to check in or check out.

If you don't want to self-serve, you can still rent a bike from **Paris à Vélo!,** 22 rue Alphonse Baudin (https://parisavelo.fr; *©* **01-48-87-60-01;** Métro: St-Sébastien-Froissart or Richard Lenoir). Rentals for a regular bicycle cost 13€ for half a day and 16€ for a full day, but they do require a safety deposit of at least 250€, depending on the type of bike you rent. If you're feeling extra lazy, electric bikes are available from 33€ for half a day and 40€ for a full day.

BY TROTTINETTE

The recent advent of the self-serve electric scooter (*trottinette*) has Parisians whooshing along the sidewalks at high speed (up to 25km [15 miles]/hr.), often two to a scooter. Watch out! And, if you can't beat 'em, join 'em—though avoid the sidewalk (it's not officially allowed) and opt for a cycle lane or the road instead. Unlike the Vélib' bike system (see above), scooter rentals are "free floating," which means there are no official parking stations. Parking on the sidewalk is no longer allowed, however, so there are designated scooter parking places on most roads; you find the nearest

---

Transit Price Check

With so many new options, deciding on how to get around can be brain busting. If price is your only criteria, here's a quick comparison based on a 30- or 45-minute ride:

Vélib': 3€
Métro: 1.90€
Vélib' electric: 3€
Electric scooter (standing): 7.50€
Scooter (electric moped): 4€–8.70€

---

available scooter via a geo-localization system. No matter which company you choose, expect to pay around 1€ for the rental fee, then .25€/minute as you ride (which equates to 7.50€ for 30 mins.). Here are the five main ones: **Bird** (www.bird.co), **Lime** (www.li.me), **Bolt** (https://bolt.eu/en), **Wind** (www.wind.co), and **Tier** (https://www.tier.app). *Note:* Helmets are not provided, though they are recommended, and you're not authorized to ride on the road.

BY E-SCOOTER

In a similar line to *trottinette* scooters, e-scooters (self-serve, two-wheeled, moped-style electric scooters) are all the rage right now, and people 18 and over can use them on the road (not in bike lanes or on the sidewalk). The main company is **Cityscoot** (www.cityscoot.eu), costing .39€/min (that's 11.70€ for 30 min.). If you were born before 1988, you don't need a driver's license to use an e-scooter; if you were born after 1988, you must have either a valid E.U. driving license or a license that was issued in your own country and translated into French by an accredited translator (plan well ahead and check with your embassy; the translation process can be costly and time-consuming). *Note:* Helmets are provided (with disposable helmet liners), but bring your own gloves, which must be worn.

One Word About Driving in Paris

Don't. Even if you are a Formula 1 racecar driver with years of experience, you'll be alternately outraged and infuriated by the aggressive tactics of your fellow drivers and the inevitable *bouchons* (literally, a bottle stopper or cork), or jams, that tie up traffic and turn a simple jaunt into a harrowing nightmare. To make matters worse, it's easy to believe that the street and direction signs were cunningly placed by a sadistic madman who gets kicks out of watching hapless drivers take wrong turns.

Your troubles are not over once you get to your destination, because then you will have to park, which is a whole other trauma. Spots are elusive, to say the least, and you'll probably find yourself touring the neighborhood for at least 20 minutes until you find one. By then you'll have figured out why it is that Parisians park on pedestrian crossings: Often, there's nowhere else to park.

One final hurdle: feeding the **parking meter.** All parking is *payant*—that is, you must pay (Mon–Sat 9am–8pm). And you can't use coins in the *horodateur* (parking meter) anymore—you must either pay with a chip-enabled credit card or via the PaybyPhone app (www.paybyphone.fr). If you pay by card at the parking meter, you'll get a print-out ticket that you must put on your dashboard. If you pay via the app, you don't have to do anything except state where you are parked; the traffic police have a device linked to the app and can see that you've paid from the car's license plate. Paris is a polluted city, so the city is trying to reduce traffic, largely with dissuasive parking prices. Today in the most central arrondissements (1 to 11), parking costs 6€ for the first hour, then increases incrementally to a whopping 75€ for 6 hours; in the outer arrondissements (12 to 20), it's 4€ per hour, up to 50€ for 6 hours. What's more, you can't stay in the same spot for more than 6 hours—and fines have increased to 75€ in zones 1 to 11, and 52.50€ in zones 12 to 20. Mercifully, on Sundays and from 8pm to 9am the rest of the week, all street parking is free. If you are not up to the challenge, try one of the many **underground parking lots,** indicated by a sign with a white "P" on a blue background; parking in one of these is between 2.60€ and 4€ per hour, or between 25€ and 35€ for 24 hours.

If, despite this rant, you still feel compelled to rent a car and drive around the city, or are forced to do so due to extenuating circumstances, at the very least get your hands on a basic explanation of international street signs (this should be available at your car-rental agency) and a good street map or app. Taxi drivers nowadays use the app Waze (www.waze.com), which works like a GPS using real-time traffic info to guide you to your destination using the fastest, least traffic-clogged route. Finally, try to keep your cool, because no matter how sure you are that you are following the rules of the road, at some point, someone in another car will curse you. Good luck—you're going to need it.

By Boat

The **Batobus** (www.batobus.com; ℰ **08-25-05-01-01;** .15€/min.) is a fleet of boats that operates along the Seine, stopping at 9 points of interest, including the Eiffel Tower, the Musée d'Orsay, the Louvre, Notre-Dame, and the Hôtel de Ville. Much like the hop-on-hop-off buses (see "Bus Tours," p. 200), these boats are more about sightseeing and less about getting quickly from place to place, though they will get you up and down the Seine. Unlike the Bateaux-Mouches (p. 199), the Batobus has the advantage of not providing cheesy, recorded commentary. The only fare option is a day pass valid for either 1 or 2 days, each allowing as many entrances and exits as you want. At time of writing, the 1- and 2-day passes cost the same: 19€ for adults and 9€ for children 3 to 15, though this may change as tourism increases. Boats operate daily from around 10am; boats come by every 25 to 40 minutes, depending on the season. Last call is anywhere from 5pm during the week in the winter to 9:30pm in the summer; see the website for exact intervals and closing hours.

By Taxi

Much to the disdain of regular taxi drivers (and as in most big cities), **Uber** (www.uber.com) has changed the taxi landscape. Just download the smartphone app and enter your credit-card details. Once you're logged on, you enter your location and your destination. No cash changes hands, and the cost of your journey is pre-calculated according to its "real" distance, so you're not penalized if you have to make a detour. While you wait, the screen shows the whereabouts of your ride in real time, as well as the car's number plate, the driver's name, and his/her photo. When traveling abroad (especially if you're a woman), it's reassuring to know who will be driving your Uber, and for central Paris, you rarely have to wait more than 5 minutes for an Uber to arrive.

That said, Uber's controversial presence in France kick-started the launch of several competing apps: **LeCab** (https://lecab.fr), **Bolt** (https://bolt.eu), and **Heetch** (www.heetch.com) all provide ridesharing services in English, and sometimes at a lower price. If you're an Uber hater, try one of the above instead. Heetch is particularly good for traveling between Paris and the suburbs, including the airports.

To hail a cab from the street, try for those with a full green or white light (red light or a single white bulb means they're taken), or look for a taxi stand, which resembles a bus stop and usually sports a blue TAXI sign. It's often easier to call a cab than to hail one: **Taxi G7** (www.taxisg7.fr; 𝄐 **36-07;** .45€/min.) is the main company. It also now has an app similar to those of ridesharing services in that you can pay without cash changing hands, which can be reassuring for travelers.

Calculating taxi fares is a complicated business. When you get in, the meter should read 2.60€. Then, the basic rates for Paris *intramuros* range from 1.06€ to 1.61€ per kilometer, depending on the day of the week and the hour. The minimum fare is 7.30€; if you have more than three people in your party, you'll be charged an extra 3€ too. You'll also be charged 1€ for each suitcase you put in the trunk. The saving grace here is that the distances are usually not huge, and barring excessive traffic, your average crosstown fare should fall between 15€ and 25€ for two without baggage. Tipping is not obligatory, but rounding up or a .50€ to 1€ tip is customary.

On Foot

If you have the time and the energy, the best mode of transport in this small and walkable city is your own two feet. You can cross the center of town (say from the Place St-Michel to Les Halles) in about 20 minutes. This is the best way to see and experience the city and take in all the little details that make it so wonderful.

Area Codes The country code for France is 33, and the area code for Paris is 01.

Business Hours

Opening hours in Paris are erratic. Most museums close 1 day a week (usually Mon or Tues) and some national holidays. Museum hours tend to be from 9:30am to 6pm, and some museums (like the Louvre, p. 144) have late-night openings. Generally, **offices** are open Monday to Friday from 9am to 6pm, but don't count on it—always call first. **Banks** tend to be open from 9am to 5pm Monday to Friday, but some branches are open on Saturday instead of Monday. **Large stores** are open from around 10am to 7 or 8pm. Some **small stores** still have a lunch break that can last for up to 2 hours, from 1 to 3pm, but this is becoming increasingly rare. Most shops, except those in the Marais or on the Champs-Élysées, are closed on Sunday. Restaurants are typically closed on Sunday evenings and/or Mondays, and many businesses across the city are closed for two weeks in August.

Cell Phones The three letters that define much of the world's wireless capabilities are **GSM** (Global System for Mobile Communications), a big, seamless network that makes for easy cross-border mobile phone use throughout Europe and dozens of other countries worldwide. You can use your mobile phone in France provided it is GSM and 3G, 4G, or 5G; just confirm this with your operator before you leave.

Using your phone abroad can be expensive, and you usually have to pay to receive calls, so it's a good idea to get your phone "unlocked" before you leave. Then you can buy a SIM card from one of the three main French providers: **Bouygues Télécom** (www.bouy guestelecom.fr), **Orange** (www.orange.fr), or **SFR** (www.sfr.fr). A temporary SIM card (*carte prepayée*) costs anywhere from 5€ to 40€, depending on the number of minutes bundled with it. Alternatively, if your phone isn't unlocked, you could buy a cheap mobile phone in Paris. To top up your phone credit, buy a prepaid card (*carte prépayée*) from *tabacs*, supermarkets, and mobile phone outlets. Prices range from 5€ to 100€.

A final strategy? Use Skype, FaceTime, or WhatsApp for phone calls. Make sure you have the app before you get to Europe and then use it whenever you have a signal for free or ridiculously inexpensive (Skype) phone calls.

Customs What you can bring into France: Citizens of E.U. countries can bring in any amount of goods as long as the goods are intended for their personal use and not for resale. Non–E.U. citizens are entitled to 200 cigarettes, 100 small cigars, 50 cigars, or 250g of tobacco duty-free. You can also bring in 4 liters of non-sparkling wine, 16 liters of beer, 2 liters of alcoholic beverages less than 22% alcohol, and 1 liter of spirits more than 22% alcohol. (Also see the box "What You Can Take Out of France," p. 296.)

Dentists & Doctors

Doctors are listed in the **Pages Jaunes** (French equivalent of the Yellow Pages; www.pagesjaunes.fr) under "Médecins." Online, type "medecin" in the left-hand search box and Paris in the right-hand one; names (and even photos) will appear. The standard fee for a consultation with a general practitioner (*médecin generaliste*) is 25€. **SOS Médecins** (📞 **36-24**, .15€/min., and 📞 **01-47-07-77-77;** www.sosmedecins.fr) makes house calls that cost around 90€ to 130€ (prices quoted are for people without French social security). Find a list of English-speaking dentists and doctors in Paris on the U.S. Embassy website: https://fr.usembassy.gov. You can also reach U.S. Citizens Services by phone at 📞 **01-43-12-22-22.** See also "Emergencies" and "Health," below.

Drinking Laws

Supermarkets, grocery stores, and cafes sell alcoholic beverages. The legal drinking age is 18. Wine and liquor are sold every day of the week, year-round. Cafes generally open around 7am and serve until closing (between midnight and 2am). Bars and nightclubs usually stay open until 2am (sometimes 5am), but they must stop serving alcohol 1½ hours before closing. You can drink in public, but you cannot be drunk in public.

The law regarding drunk driving is tough. A motorist is considered legally intoxicated if his or her blood-alcohol content exceeds .05%. If it is between .05% and .08%, the driver faces a fine of 750€. Over .08% and it could cost 4,500€ or up to 2 years in jail.

Electricity Electricity in France runs on 220 volts AC (60 cycles); the U.S. runs on 120 volts AC. Adapters for plugs (Type E is most useful in France) or transformers are needed to fit sockets; you can buy these in branches of Fnac (p. 226). You can also buy them at many electronics stores before your trip. Check if your appliance can handle 220 volts; fortunately many today are dual voltage. If your appliance isn't, though, you risk frying it. In such cases, use a transformer. If the appliance is dual voltage, you need only an adapter so you can plug into a socket.

Embassies & Consulates If you have a passport, immigration, legal, or other problem, contact your consulate.

Many require you to fill in an online form to explain your situation. Otherwise, call before you go—they often keep odd hours and observe both French and home-country holidays.

The Embassy of **Australia,** 4 rue Jean-Rey, 15e (https://france.embassy.gov.au; ℂ **01-40-59-33-00;** Métro: Bir Hakeim), is open Monday to Friday 9am to 5pm except public holidays. The Consular section is open Monday to Friday from 9am to noon and 2 to 4pm.

The Embassy of **Canada,** 130 rue du Faubourg Saint-Honoré, 8e (www.canada international.gc.ca/france; ℂ **01-44-43-29-02;** Métro: Franklin-D-Roosevelt or Alma-Marceau), is open Monday to Friday 9am to noon.

The Embassy of **Ireland,** 12 av. Foch, entrance 4 rue Rude, 16e (www.dfa.ie/irish-embassy/france; ℂ **01-44-17-67-00;** Métro: Argentine), is open Monday to Friday 9:30am to 5:30pm; consular and passport services 9:30am to noon.

The Embassy of **New Zealand,** 103 rue de Grenelle, 7e (www.mfat.govt.nz/france; ℂ **01-45-01-43-43;** Métro: Solferino), is open Monday 10:30am to 1pm and 2 to 5pm; Tuesday to Friday 9am to 1pm and 2 to 5pm.

The Embassy of the **United Kingdom,** 35 rue du Faubourg St-Honoré, 8e (www.gov.uk/world/france; ℂ **01-44-51-31-00;** Métro: Concorde or Madeleine), is open Monday to Friday

9:30am to 1pm and 2:30 to 5pm.

The Embassy of the **United States,** 2 av. Gabriel, 8e (https://fr.usembassy.gov; ℂ **01-43-12-22-22;** Métro: Concorde), is open Monday to Friday 9am to 6pm. Appointment required for passport and other services; you can schedule online on the website.

Emergencies In an emergency, call ℂ **112,** or the fire brigade (*Sapeurs-Pompiers;* ℂ **18**), who are trained to deal with all kinds of medical emergencies, not just fires. For a medical emergency and/or ambulance, call ℂ **15.** For the police, call ℂ **17.**

Etiquette & Customs Parisians like pleasantries and take manners seriously: Say *bonjour, madame/monsieur,* when entering an establishment and *au revoir* when you depart. Always say *pardon* when you accidentally bump into someone. With strangers, people who are older than you, and professional contacts, use *vous* rather than *tu* (*vous* is the polite form of the pronoun "you").

Health For travel abroad, non–E.U. nationals should consider buying medical travel insurance. For U.S. citizens, Medicare and Medicaid do not provide coverage for medical costs incurred abroad, so check what medical services your health insurance covers before leaving home. That said, medical costs are a fraction of what they are in

Australian Citizens The **Australian Customs Service** (www.abf.gov.au/entering-and-leaving-australia/duty-free; ℰ **131-881** in Australia, or 612/6196-0196 from abroad) has complete customs information on its website. The duty-free allowance in Australia is A$900 or, for those 17 and younger, A$450. Those 18 and over can bring home up to 2.25 liters of alcoholic beverages.

Canadian Citizens For a clear summary of Canadian rules, visit the **Canada Border Services Agency** (www.cbsa-asfc. gc.ca; ℰ **800/461-9999** in Canada, or 204/983-3500 from abroad). Canada allows its citizens a C$800 exemption. You can also bring back up to 1.5 liters of wine, 1.14 liters of other alcoholic beverage, or up to 8.5 liters of beer.

New Zealand Citizens The answers to most questions regarding customs can be found on the website of the **New Zealand Customs Service** under "duty and allowances" (www.customs.govt.nz; ℰ **0800/428-786**, or +64-9/927-8036 from outside New Zealand). The duty-free allowance for New Zealand is NZ$700. You are allowed to bring back 4.5 liters of wine or beer, and not more

than 3 bottles of spirits (each bottle not exceeding 1.125 liters).

U.K. Citizens Post-Brexit, there are now limits on what you can bring back to the country from France: You can bring 42 liters of beer, 18 liters of non-sparkling wine, 4 liters of spirits over 22% alcohol by volume or 9 liters of alcohol up to 22%. For information, contact **HM Revenue Customs** (www.gov.uk/bringing-goods-into-uk-personal-use/arriving-in-Great-Britain; ℰ +44/300-200-3700).

U.S. Citizens For specifics on what you can bring back and the corresponding fees, click on "Know Before You Go" at **www.cbp.gov**. Or, contact the **U.S. Customs & Border Protection (CBP;** ℰ **877/227-5511** in the U.S., or 202/325-8000 from outside the U.S.). Returning U.S. citizens who have been away for 48 hours or more are allowed to bring back, once every 31 days, $800 worth of merchandise duty-free. Included in your allowance is 1 duty-free liter of alcoholic beverage; after that, it depends what state you live in, so check with your state customs office for amounts.

the U.S. (for example, a visit to a GP costs 25€), so you may even decide to do a little medical tourism (be sure to bring your prescriptions). U.K. nationals need a U.K. Global Health Insurance Card (GHIC) or a **European Health Insurance Card (EHIC)** to receive free or reduced-cost medical care during a visit to a European Union (E.U.) country, Iceland, Liechtenstein, Norway, or Switzerland (go to www.nhs.uk, then type GHIC into the search box).

If you suffer from a chronic illness, consult your doctor before your departure. Pack prescription medications in your carry-on luggage and carry them in their original containers, with pharmacy labels—otherwise they won't make it through airport security. Carry the generic name of prescription medicines, in case a local pharmacist is unfamiliar with the brand name.

For further tips on travel and health concerns, and a list of local English-speaking

doctors, contact the **International Association for Medical Assistance to Travelers (IAMAT;** www. iamat.org; ℰ **716/754-4883** in the U.S., or 416/652-0137 in Canada). You can also consult a list of English-speaking dentists and doctors in Paris at the U.S. Citizen Services page on the U.S. embassy website (https://fr.usembassy.gov). See also "Dentists & Doctors," "Emergencies,"

"Hospitals," and "Pharmacies" in this section.

Hospitals Most Parisian hospitals have 24-hr. emergency rooms, and some have a specialty (Hôpitals Necker and Trousseau are two of the best children's hospitals in France, for example). For addresses and information on all Paris public hospitals, visit www.aphp.fr.

Two private hospitals in nearby suburbs have English-speaking staff and operate 24 hours a day (and cost much more than the public ones): the **American Hospital of Paris,** 63 bd. Victor Hugo, 92200 Neuilly-sur-Seine (www.american-hospital.org;
☏ **01-46-41-25-25;** Métro: Pont de Levallois; 15-min. walk from station; bus: 43, 82, 93, 163, 164, and 174); and the **Hôpital Franco-Britannique,** 3 rue Barbès or 4 rue Kleber, Levallois (www.hopitalfranco britannique.org/en; ☏ **01-47-59-59-59;** Métro: Anatole-France).

Hotlines S.O.S. Help is a hotline for English-speaking callers in crisis (www.sos-helpline.org; ☏ **01-46-21-46-46;** daily 3–11pm).

Internet & Wi-Fi Many Parisian hotels and cafes have Internet access, and Wi-Fi (pronounced *wee-fee* here) is increasingly common in public spaces.

Cybercafes are few and far between nowadays, but the huge **Milk** location in Les Halles is reliably open 24/7 (www.milklub.com).

LGBTQ Travelers
France is known for being a particularly tolerant country when it comes to gay and lesbian people, which made the acrimonious blather surrounding the legalization of same-sex marriage in 2013 all the more upsetting. "Gay Paree" boasts a large gay population, and had an openly gay mayor, Bertrand Delanoë, for over a decade. The center of gay and lesbian life is in the Marais. The annual Gay Pride March usually takes place on the last Sunday in June (p. 49). Information and resources can be found in Paris' largest, best-stocked gay bookstore, **Les Mots à la Bouche,** 37 rue Saint-Ambroise, 11th arrond. (www.motsbouche.com; ☏ **01-42-78-88-30;** Métro: Rue Saint-Maur), which carries publications in both French and English. To find listings and events, try **Qweek** (www.qweek.fr), a website focused on Paris.

Lost & Found If you lose an important belonging, contact the police's **Bureau des Objets Trouvés,** 36 rue des Morillons, 15 arrond. (https://objetstrouves prefecturedepolice.

franceobjetstrouves.fr/en). If you left something on the bus, Métro, or RER, consult www.ratp.fr/en and search for "lost and found," or if that doesn't work (the RATP's website has flaws), type "RATP lost & found" in your standard search engine. If your object is found (including on the RATP network), the police bureau will contact you by SMS.

Mail Every arrondissement has a post office (**La Poste;** www.laposte.fr; ☏ **36-31**). Most are open Monday to Friday 9am to 7pm, Saturday 9am to 1pm; the Louvre post office (16 rue Etienne Marcel; Métro: Louvre-Rivoli) is open Monday to Saturday 8am to 10pm and Sunday 10am to 10pm. Stamps are also sold in *tabacs* (tobacconists).

Money & Costs
Frommer's lists exact prices in the local currency. The currency conversions quoted below were correct at press time. However, rates fluctuate, so before departing consult a currency exchange website such as www.oanda.com or www. xe.com to check up-to-the-minute rates.

ATMs are widely available in Paris, but if you're venturing into rural France, it's always good to have cash in your pocket. Be sure you know your personal

THE VALUE OF THE EURO VS. OTHER POPULAR CURRENCIES

Euro (€)	US$	C$	UK£	A$	NZ$
1	1.17	1.48	0.86	1.61	1.67

identification number (PIN) and daily withdrawal limit before you depart. Many banks impose a fee when you withdraw money abroad, and that fee can be higher for international transactions than for domestic ones. In addition, the bank from which you withdraw cash may charge its own fee. For currency exchanges, always use a bank (you'll get a better exchange rate that way).

Visa is the most common credit card in France, but with the exception of American Express, which is sometimes refused, international credit cards are widely accepted. Foreign credit cards, particularly those without an embedded chip, do not always work in machines. At time of writing, many shops allow you to flash your card (without inputting the pin number) up to 50€. Payments from mobile phone apps are also increasingly accepted. Check for hidden fees when using your card abroad—some bank charges can be up to 3% of the purchase price. Some family-run shops, restaurants, and bars don't accept credit or debit cards; check in advance and have cash on hand.

Travelers' checks are no longer accepted.

Passports Citizens of New Zealand, Australia, Canada, the U.K., and the United States need a valid passport to enter France. The passport is valid for a stay of 90 days. All children must have their own passports.

Allow plenty of time before your trip to apply for a passport; at time of writing, processing in the U.S., for example, was taking up to 18 weeks. (Check https://travel.state. gov for the most updated information.) Keep in mind that if you need a passport in a hurry, you'll pay a higher processing fee.

Pharmacies You'll spot French *pharmacies* by looking for the green neon cross above the door. If your local pharmacy is closed, there should be a sign on the door indicating the nearest one open. Pharmacists give basic medical advice and can take your blood pressure. *Parapharmacies* sell medical products and toiletries, but they don't dispense prescriptions. Pharmacies open 24/7 include: **Pharmacie Européene,** 6 pl. de Clichy (✆ **01-48-74-65-18;** Métro: Place de Clichy); and **Citypharma,** 86 bd. Soult (✆ **01-43-43-13-68;** Métro/Tram: Porte de Vincennes). **Pharmacie du Drugstore des Champs-Élysées,** 133 av. des Champs-Élysées (✆ **01-47-20-39-25;** Métro/RER: Charles de Gaulle–Etoile) is open until 2am. See also "Emergencies" and "Health," above.

Police In an emergency, call ✆ **17** for the police, or ✆ **112,** the European Union–wide toll-free emergency number. The Préfecture de Police has stations all over Paris. To find the nearest one, call ✆ **17.** See also "Emergencies," above.

Safety In general, Paris is a safe city and it is safe to use the Métro late at night. However, certain Métro stations (and the areas around them) are best avoided at night: Châtelet-Les Halles, Gare du Nord, Barbès Rochechouart, and Strasbourg St-Denis. The RER can get scary late at night; try to find alternative transport to and from the airport (such as buses or taxis) late at night or early in the morning.

The most common crime problem in Paris is pickpockets. They prey on tourists around popular attractions such as the Louvre, the Eiffel Tower, the Champs-Élysées, Notre-Dame, St-Michel, Centre Pompidou, Versailles, and Sacré-Coeur, in the major department stores, and on the Métro. Take precautions and be vigilant at all times: Don't take more money with you than necessary, keep your passport in a concealed pouch (if you must carry it), and ensure that your bag is firmly closed at all times. Also, around the major sites it is quite common to be approached by a young Roma girl or boy and asked if you speak English. It's best to avoid these situations, and any incident that might occur, by shaking your head and walking away.

In cafes, bars, and restaurants, it's best not to leave your bag under the table or on the back of your chair. Keep it between your legs

Taxi from the airport to downtown Paris (Orly or CDG)	32.00–58.00
Métro ticket	1.90
Double room, expensive	350.00–800.00
Double room, moderate	150.00–350.00
Double room, inexpensive	85.00–150.00
Three-course dinner for one without wine	28.00–35.00
Glass of beer, 25cl	3.50–6.00
Espresso	1.00–3.00
Admission to most museums	10.00–17.00

or on your lap to avoid it being stolen. Never leave valuables in a car.

In times of heightened security concerns, the government mobilizes police and armed forces, so don't be surprised to see soldiers strolling around transport hubs and carrying automatic weapons. Also see "Terrorism," below.

Paris is a cosmopolitan city and most nonwhite travelers won't experience any problems, outside of some unpleasant stares. Although there is a significant level of discrimination against West and North African immigrants, harassment of African-American and Asian tourists is exceedingly rare. **S.O.S. Racisme,** 51 av. de Flandre, 19th arrond. (www. sos-racisme.org; © **01-40-35-36-55**), offers legal advice to victims of prejudice and will even intervene to help with the police.

Female travelers should not expect any more hassle than in other major cities, and the same precautions apply. French men tend to stare a lot, but it's generally harmless. Avoid walking around the less safe neighborhoods (Barbès Rochechouart, Strasbourg St-Denis, Châtelet-Les-Halles) alone at night and never get into an unmarked taxi. If you are approached in the street or on the Métro, it's best to avoid entering into conversation and walk away. If you feel threatened, enter the nearest cafe or bar.

Senior Travel Many discounts are available to men and women over 60. Although they often seem to apply only to residents of E.U. countries, discounts can be had by announcing at the ticket window of a museum or monument that you are 60 years old or more. You may not receive a discount, but it doesn't

hurt to ask. "Senior," incidentally, is pronounced *seenyore* in France. Senior citizens do not get a discount for traveling on public transport in Paris, but the national trains do offer them. Check www.oui.sncf for details.

Smoking Smoking is now banned inside all public places, including cafes, restaurants, bars, and nightclubs; it is still rife on cafe terraces, however.

Student Travel Student discounts are less common in France than in other countries, simply because young people 26 and under are usually offered reduced rates and even free entry to some museums and attractions. Some discounts only apply to residents of E.U. countries, who will need to prove this with a passport, ID card, or driver's license, but if you're not from the E.U. it's worth carrying an ID to prove your age and announcing it when buying tickets. SNCF offers 25% off for under-26-year-olds traveling on national trains (www.oui.sncf).

Taxes As a member of the European Union, France routinely imposes a value-added tax (VAT in English; *TVA* in French) on most goods. The standard VAT is 20% and is already included in virtually all prices for consumer goods and services (you'll know for sure when you see TTC, which means *toutes taxes comprises*, "all taxes included"). If you're over 16 and not an E.U. resident, you can get a VAT refund if you're spending less than 6 months in France and you purchase goods worth at least 100€ over a maximum of 3 days, at a retailer offering tax-free shopping (*vente en détaxe*) in the same brand or group of brands. Give them your passport and ask for a *bordereau de vente à l'exportation* (export sales invoice), which must have a barcode. Both you and the shopkeeper sign the slip, and you choose how you want to be reimbursed (credit on card, bank transfer, or cash). Once you get to the airport, scan the code in one of the "Pablo" terminals (if your airport doesn't have one, just go to the "detaxe" counter). Once the form has been approved, head to the reimbursement counter to immediately claim your refund. If all of this is too confusing, visit the French customs website, www.douane.gouv.fr/fiche/eligibility-vat-refunds, or

search for "duty free" at the tourist office: www.parisinfo.com.

Telephones France no longer has public telephone booths. If you want to pay for a call from a phone that is not your own, you can still use a prepaid card with a code. Called a *carte téléphonique à code*, or a *carte prépayé*, they are sold at newsstands, smoke shops, or cafes where you see a TABAC sign. This is not always the cheapest or most practical way to make a call, so it may make more sense to investigate mobile phone options (see "Cell Phones," above).

The country code for France is 33. To make a local or long-distance call within France, dial the 10-digit number of the person or place you're calling. Mobile numbers begin with 06 or 07. Numbers beginning with 0 800, 0 805, and 0 809 are free in France; most other numbers beginning with 8 are not. Many public service numbers are now four digits, and some are toll-free.

To make international calls from Paris, first dial 00 and then the country code (U.S. and Canada 1, U.K. 44, Ireland 353, Australia 61, New Zealand 64). Next dial the area code and number. For example, if you want to call the British Embassy in Washington, D.C., you would dial ✆ **001 202/588-6500.**

Terrorism France has reinforced its domestic security measures following the terror attacks of 2015

and 2017. But don't let the fear of terrorism dissuade you from traveling here. Just be vigilant and follow the advice of the local authorities. When you enter a new place, familiarize yourself with the emergency exits. If you see something untoward or notice an abandoned bag or package on public transport, get off the train/bus/tram or move away, and alert either a member of staff or the **police** (✆ **17** or 112). Elsewhere, if you see anything suspicious, call the police or go to the nearest police station. In the unlikely event that you find yourself in danger, the words to remember are "escape, hide, alert." Move away from the danger, help others to move away, and alert the people around you. If you need to hide, turn off both the ring and vibration mode on your telephone. If you see security forces, do not run toward them or make sudden movements, and keep your hands up or open.

Time France is on **Central European Time,** which is 1 hour ahead of Greenwich Mean Time. French daylight saving time lasts from the last Sunday in March to the last Sunday in October. France uses the 24-hr. clock. So 13h is 1pm, 14h15 is 2:15pm, and so on.

Tipping By law, all bills in cafes, bars, and restaurants say *service compris*, which means the service charge is included. Waiters are paid a living wage and do not expect tips. However, they certainly won't mind if you leave one, and if you are planning on frequenting a certain cafe, it's a good investment to leave 1 or 2€ after a meal. Taxi drivers usually appreciate a 5 to 10% tip, or for the fare to be rounded up to the next euro. The French give their hairdressers a tip of about 15%, and if you go to the theater, you're expected to tip the usher 1€ or 2€.

Toilets Paris is full of gray-colored street-toilet kiosks, which are a little daunting to the uninitiated, but free, and are automatically washed and disinfected after each use (though still smelly). If you're in dire need, you can duck into a cafe or brasserie to use the toilet but expect to make a small purchase (coffee standing at the bar will do) if you do so. If you're pregnant or with small children and ask, the cafe workers will usually let you use the facilities for free.

Travelers with Disabilities While the city still won't win any prizes for accessibility (tortuous sidewalks, few ramps at public facilities, endless stairways in Métro stations), slow and steady progress is being made (though not enough in my eyes, and certainly in the run-up to the 2024 Olympics and Paralympics). However, there are over 60 wheelchair-accessible bus lines and several RER stations; in addition, all stations on Métro line 14 are accessible. Access to all tram lines is flush with the ground, though you might have to navigate a curb to get to the station. To find the closest accessible stations, maps, and more, visit www.iledefrance-mobilites.fr/en/the-network/easy-access-transports or call ✆ **09-70-81-83-85** (in French). Many museums are now accessible; visit their websites for details. Several art museums even offer tactile visits for people who are visually impaired. Many hotels with three or more stars (under the French national rating system, not ours) have at least one wheelchair-accessible room. Hotels that are particularly sensitive to the subject may bear the "Tourisme & Handicaps" label. The **Paris Tourist Office** (www.parisinfo.com) has a good listing of accessible hotels on its site, as well as plenty of other info and links for travelers with disabilities. Click on the English flag, then search for "Disability." One other good resource is Sage Traveling (www.sagetraveling.com/paris-accessible-travel), which organizes wheelchair-accessible tours and offers a gold-mine of tips for navigating the city. Bear in mind that if you drive in Paris and have a disabled display card, you can park for free and for an unlimited amount of time in any parking space.

Visas E.U. nationals don't need a visa to enter France. Nor do U.S., British, Canadian, Australian, New Zealand, or South African citizens for trips of up to 3 months. If non–E.U. citizens wish to stay longer than 3 months, they must apply to a French embassy or consulate for a long-term visa. During 2022, however, U.S. nationals coming to some countries in the E.U. will require authorization through a system similar to the U.S.'s ESTA. Europe's version is the "European Travel Information and Authorization System," or ETIAS for short, and is available online. For more information and updates on the system's implementation, see the website www.schengenvisainfo.com/etias.

Visitor Information The **Office du Tourisme et des Congrès,** 29 rue de Rivoli, 1er (www.parisinfo.com), is open Monday to Saturday 10am to 6pm. Several other offices are around Paris: **Gare du Nord,** 18 rue de Dunkerque, 10 arrond. (Mon–Sat 9am–5pm except major holidays); and **Carousel du Louvre,** 99 rue de Rivoli, 4 arrond. (Wed–Mon 11am–7pm; Tues noon–6pm).

Water Drinking water is safe, if not particularly tasty. To order tap water in a restaurant, ask for *une carafe d'eau.* Drinking fountains—like the iconic, green Wallace fountains—are dotted all about the city, and you'll find drinking water taps in almost every park. Paris even has fizzy water fountains in certain green spaces (like the Jardin de Reuilly), designed to persuade people to ditch polluting plastic bottles and fill up from taps instead.

USEFUL TERMS & PHRASES

12

I t is often amazing how a word or two of halting French will change your hosts' disposition in their home country. At the very least, try to learn a few numbers, basic greetings, and—above all—the life-raft phrase, *Parlez-vous anglais?* (Do you speak English?). Many Parisians speak passable English and will use it liberally if you demonstrate the basic courtesy of greeting them in their language. *Bonne chance!*

BASIC VOCABULARY
THE BASIC COURTESIES

English	French	Pronunciation
Yes/No	Oui/Non	**Wee/Noh**
Okay	D'accord	**Dah-core**
Please	S'il vous plaît	**Seel voo play**
Thank you	Merci	**Mair-see**
You're welcome	De rien	**Duh ree-ehn**
Hello (during daylight)	Bonjour	**Bohn-jhoor**
Good evening	Bonsoir	**Bohn-swahr**
Goodbye	Au revoir	**O ruh-vwahr**
What's your name?	Comment vous appellez-vous?	**Kuh-mahn voo za-pell-ay-voo?**
My name is	Je m'appelle	**Jhuh ma-pell**
How are you?	Comment allez-vous?	**Kuh-mahn tahl-ay-voo?**
So-so	Comme ci, comme ça	**Kum-see, kum-sah**
I'm sorry/excuse me	Pardon	**Pahr-dohn**

GETTING AROUND & STREET SMARTS

English	French	Pronunciation
Do you speak English?	Parlez-vous anglais?	**Par-lay-voo ahn-glay?**
I don't speak French	Je ne parle pas français	**Jhuh ne parl pah frahn-say**
I don't understand	Je ne comprends pas	**Jhuh ne kohm-prahn pah**
Could you speak more loudly/more slowly?	Pouvez-vous parler plus fort/plus lentement?	**Poo-vay voo par-lay ploo for/ploo lan-te-ment?**
What is it?	Qu'est-ce que c'est?	**Kess kuh say?**
What time is it?	Qu'elle heure est-il?	**Kel uhr eh-teel?**

English	French	Pronunciation
What?	Quoi?	**Kwah?**
How? or What did you say?	Comment?	**Ko-mahn?**
When?	Quand?	**Kahn?**
Where is?	Où est?	**Ooh eh?**
Who?	Qui?	**Kee?**
Why?	Pourquoi?	**Poor-kwah?**
here/there	ici/là	**ee-see/lah**
left/right	à gauche/à droite	**a gohsh/a drwaht**
straight ahead	tout droit	**too drwah**
Fill the tank (of a car)	Le plein, s'il vous plaît	**Luh plen, seel-voo-play please**
I want to get off at	Je voudrais descendre à	**Jhe voo-dray day-sen drah-ah**
airport	aéroport	**air-o-por**
bank	banque	**bahnk**
bridge	pont	**pohn**
bus station	gare routière	**gar roo-tee-air**
bus stop	arrêt de bus	**ah-ray duh boohs**
by means of a car	en voiture	**ahn vwa-tur**
cashier	caisse	**kess**
cathedral	cathédrale	**ka-tay-dral**
church	église	**ay-gleez**
driver's license	permis de conduire	**per-mee deh con-dweer**
elevator	ascenseur	**ah-sahn-seuhr**
entrance (to a port building or a city)	porte	**port**
exit (from a building or a freeway)	sortie	**sor-tee**
gasoline	carburant/essence	**car-bur-ahn/eh-sahns**
hospital	hôpital	**oh-pee-tahl**
luggage storage	consigne	**kohn-seen-yuh**
museum	musée	**mu-zay**
no smoking	défense de fumer	**day-fahns de fu-may**
one-day pass	ticket journalier	**tee-kay jhoor-nall-ee-ay**
one-way ticket	aller simple	**ah-lay sam-pluh**
police	police	**po-leece**
round-trip ticket	aller-retour	**ah-lay re-toor**
store	magasin	**ma-ga-zehn**
street	rue	**roo**
ticket	billet	**bee-yay**
toilets	les toilettes/les WC	**lay twa-lets/les vay-say**
I'd like	Je voudrais	**Jhe voo-dray**
a room	une chambre	**ewn shahm-bruh**
the key	la clé (la clef)	**la clay**

NECESSITIES

English	French	Pronunciation
How much does it cost?	C'est combien?/ Ça coûte combien?	**Say comb-bee-*ehn*?/ Sah coot comb-bee-*ehn*?**
That's expensive	C'est cher/chère	**Say share**
Do you take credit cards?	Est-ce que vous acceptez les cartes de credit?	**Es-kuh voo zaksep-*tay* lay kart duh creh-*dee*?**
I'd like to buy	Je voudrais acheter	**Jhe voo-dray ahsh-*tay***
aspirin	aspirines	**ahs-peer-*een***
condoms	préservatifs	**pray-ser-va-*teef***
a gift	un cadeau	**uh kah-*doe***
a hat	un chapeau	**uh shah-*poh***
a map of the city	un plan de ville	**uh plahn de *veel***
a newspaper	un journal	**uh zhoor-*nahl***
a postcard	une carte postale	**ewn carte pos-*tahl***
a road map	une carte routière	**ewn cart roo-tee-*air***
some soap	du savon	**dew sah-*vohn***
a stamp	un timbre	**uh *tam*-bruh**

NUMBERS & ORDINALS

English	French	Pronunciation
zero	zéro	**zare-oh**
one	un	**oon**
two	deux	**duh**
three	trois	**twah**
four	quatre	**kaht-*ruh***
five	cinq	**sank**
six	six	**seess**
seven	sept	**set**
eight	huit	**wheat**
nine	neuf	**noof**
ten	dix	**deess**
eleven	onze	**ohnz**
twelve	douze	**dooz**
thirteen	treize	**trehz**
fourteen	quatorze	**kah-*torz***
fifteen	quinze	**kanz**
sixteen	seize	**sez**
seventeen	dix-sept	**deez-*set***
eighteen	dix-huit	**deez-*wheat***
nineteen	dix-neuf	**deez-*noof***
twenty	vingt	**vehn**
thirty	trente	**trahnt**
forty	quarante	**ka-*rahnt***
fifty	cinquante	**sang-*kahnt***

English	French	Pronunciation
one hundred	cent	**sahn**
one thousand	mille	**meel**
first	premier	***preh*-mee-ay**
second	deuxième	***duhz*-zee-em**
third	troisième	***twa*-zee-em**
fourth	quatrième	***kaht*-ree-em**
fifth	cinquième	***sank*-ee-em**
sixth	sixième	***sees*-ee-em**
seventh	septième	***set*-ee-em**
eighth	huitième	***wheat*-ee-em**
ninth	neuvième	***neuv*-ee-em**
tenth	dixième	***dees*-ee-em**

THE CALENDAR, DAYS & SEASONS

English	French	Pronunciation
January	Janvier	***jhan*-vee-ay**
February	Février	***feh*-vree-ay**
March	Mars	**marce**
April	Avril	**a-*vreel***
May	Mai	**meh**
June	Juin	**jhwehn**
July	Juillet	***jhwee*-ay**
August	Août	**oot**
September	Septembre	**sep-*tahm*-bruh**
October	Octobre	**ok-*toh*-bruh**
November	Novembre	**no-*vahm*-bruh**
December	Decembre	**day-*sahm*-bruh**
Sunday	Dimanche	**dee-*mahnsh***
Monday	Lundi	***luhn*-dee**
Tuesday	Mardi	***mahr*-dee**
Wednesday	Mercredi	***mair*-kruh-dee**
Thursday	Jeudi	***jheu*-dee**
Friday	Vendredi	***vawn*-druh-dee**
Saturday	Samedi	***sahm*-dee**
yesterday	hier	**ee-*air***
today	aujourd'hui	**o-jhord-*dwee***
this morning/this afternoon	ce matin/cet après-midi	**suh ma-*tan*/set ah-preh-mee-*dee***
tonight	ce soir	**suh *swahr***
tomorrow	demain	**de-*man***
summer	été	**aytt-*ay***
fall	automne	**aw-*tonne***
winter	hiver	**iv-*erre***
spring	printemps	**prehn-*tawm***

BASIC MENU TERMS

Note: No need to get intimidated when ordering in French. Simply preface the French-language menu item with the phrase *"Je voudrais"* (jhe voo-*dray*), which means, "I would like. . . ." *Bon appétit!*

MEATS

English	French	Pronunciation
beef	boeuf	**buhf**
beef stew	pot au feu	**poht o *fhe***
chicken	poulet	***poo*-lay**
dumplings of chicken, veal, or fish (often pike)	quenelles	**ke-*nelle***
duck breast	magret de canard	**maa-*gray* duh can-*ar***
preserved duck	confit de canard	**con-*fee* duh can-*ar***
fattened goose or duck liver	foie gras	**fwah grah**
ham	jambon	**jham-bohn**
kidneys	rognons	**row-nyon**
leg of lamb	gigot d'agneau	***jhi*-goh dahnyoh**
lamb	agneau	**lahn-*nyo***
lamb chop	cotelette d'agneau	**koh-te-*let* dahn-*nyo***
liver	foie	**fwah**
pork	porc	**pohr**
potted and shredded pork	rillettes de porc	**ree-yet duh pohr**
rabbit	lapin	**lah-*pan***
dried sausage	saucisson	**soh-see-*sohn***
snails	escargots	**ess-car-*goh***
steak	bifteck	**beef-*tek***
steak with pepper sauce	steak au poivre	**stake o *pwah*-vruh**
sweetbreads	ris de veau	**day ree duh voh**
veal	veau	***voh***
veal stew with white sauce	blanquette de veau	**blahn-*ket* duh voh**

FISH/SEAFOOD

English	French	Pronunciation
fish	poisson	**pwoss-*ohn***
herring	hareng	**ahr-*rahn***
lobster	homard	**oh-*mahr***
monkfish	lotte	**loht**
mussels	moules	***moohl***
oysters	huîtres	**hoo-*ee*-truhs**
pike	brochet	**broh-*chay***
sea bass	bar	**bar**

English	French	Pronunciation
sea bream	dorade	dor-*ahde*
shrimp	crevettes	kreh-*vette*
smoked salmon	saumon fumé	soh-*mohn* fu-*may*
trout	truite	tru-eet
tuna	thon	tohn

SIDES/APPETIZERS

English	French	Pronunciation
bread	pain	pan
butter	beurre	bhuhr
fries	frites	freet
green beans	haricots verts	*ah*-ri-co ver
rice	riz	ree
salad	salade	sa-*lahd*
vegetables	légumes	lay-*goom*

BEVERAGES

English	French	Pronunciation
beer	bière	bee-*aire*
coffee (espresso)	café	ka-*fay*
coffee (decaf)	décaféiné/déca	day-kah-fay-*nay*/day-ca
coffee (with milk)	café crème/café au lait	ka-*fay* krem/ka-*fay* o-*lay*
coffee (long, with hot water)	allongé	al-on-djhay
milk	lait	*lay*
orange juice	jus d'orange	zhoo dor-*ahnjhe*
soda	soda	so-*da*
tap water	eau du robinet	oh doo rob-in-*ay*
tea	thé	*tay*
tea (herbal)	tisane	tee-*zahn*
tea (w/lemon)	thé au citron	tay o see-*tran*
water	eau	oh
wine (red)	vin rouge	vhin *rooj*
wine (white)	vin blanc	vhin *blahn*

SPICES/CONDIMENTS

English	French	Pronunciation
mayonnaise	mayonnaise	may-o-*nayse*
mustard	moutarde	moo-*tard*
olive oil	huile d'olive	weele dol-*eeve*
pepper	poivre	*pwah*-vruh
salt	sel	*sel*
sugar	sucre	*sook*-ruh
vinegar	vinaigre	vin-*aigre*

Index

See also Accommodations and Restaurant indexes, below.

General Index

Restaurants

Map List

315

Photo Credits

p. i: © lexan / Shutterstock.com; p. ii: © Mapics; p. iii: © V_E; p. iv: © Efired / Shutterstock.com; p. v, top: © MarKord / Shutterstock.com; p. v, bottom: © Dennis Jarvis; p. vi, top: Courtesy of Marin d'Eau Douce; p. vi, middle: © Christian Mueller / Shutterstock.com; p. vi, bottom: © Vinicius Pinheiro; p. vii, top left: © Beckstet; p. vii, top right: © Edward Haylan / Shutterstock.com; p. vii, bottom: © Kiev.Victor / Shutterstock.com; p. viii, top: Courtesy of Hotel Chopin; p. viii, bottom left: © HUANG Zheng / Shutterstock.com; p. viii, bottom right: © Joe deSousa; p. ix, top: © meunierd / Shutterstock.com; p. ix, bottom left: Courtesy of Angelina/ A.Rinuccini; p. ix, bottom right: © NaughtyNut / Shutterstock.com; p. x, top left: © Coup d'Oreille; p. x, top right: © f11photo / Shutterstock.com; p. x, bottom: © steve estvanik / Shutterstock.com; p. xi, top: Courtesy of Big Mamma/ Inside Closet; p. xi, middle: © Songquan Deng / Shutterstock.com; p. xi, bottom: © Lauren Elisabeth / Shutterstock.com; p. xii, top: © Petr Kovalenkov / Shutterstock.com; p. xii, bottom: © Nikonaft / Shutterstock.com; p. xiii, top left: © Daderot; p. xiii, top right: © maziarz / Shutterstock.com; p. xiii, bottom left: © Heracles Kritikos / Shutterstock.com; p. xiii, bottom right: © VDB Photos / Shutterstock.com; p. xiv, top left: © Shadowgate / Shutterstock.com; p. xiv, top right: © Page Light Studios / Shutterstock.com; p. xiv, bottom left: © aliaksei kruhlenia / Shutterstock.com; p. xiv, bottom right: © Allen.G / Shutterstock.com; p. xv, top: © Takashi Images / Shutterstock.com; p. xv, bottom left: © jorisvo / Shutterstock.com; p. xv, bottom right: © Luciano Guelfi; p. xvi, top: © Mistervlad; p. xvi, middle: © Valdiney Pimenta; p. xvi, bottom: © Pack-Shot / Shutterstock.com; p. 2: © kavalenkava ; p. 3: © Paris Tourist Office - Photographer: Amélie Dupont ; p. 4: © 2p2play / Shutterstock.com; p. 5: © Petr Kovalenkov / Shutterstock.com; p. 6: © Sean Heatley / Shutterstock.com; p. 7: © Christian Bertrand / Shutterstock.com; p. 9: © javarman / Shutterstock.com; p. 14: © Andrey Yurlov; p. 16: © Nadiia_foto / Shutterstock.com; p. 19: © Nadiia_foto / Shutterstock.com; p. 21: © meunierd / Shutterstock.com; p. 24: © Kiev.Victor / Shutterstock.com; p. 30: © VDB Photos / Shutterstock.com; p. 31: © Sean X Liu; p. 35: © Kiev.Victor / Shutterstock.com; p. 36: © Heracles Kritikos / Shutterstock.com; p. 38: © bensliman hassan; p. 41: © Kiev.Victor / Shutterstock.com; p. 42: © maziarz / Shutterstock.com; p. 45: © Christian Mueller / Shutterstock.com; p. 60: Courtesy of Pavillon de la Reine/ David Grimbert; p. 61: Courtesy of Hotel Caron de Beaumarchais/ Gilles TRILLARD; p. 66: Courtesy of Hôtel Particulier/ Jefferson Lellouche; p. 68: Courtesy of Terrase/ Christophe Bielsa; p. 71: Courtesy of Hotel de la Porte Doree/ DAVID-EMMANUEL COHEN; p. 72: Courtesy of Generator Hostel/Nikolas Koenig; p. 78: Courtesy of Hôtel des Grandes Ecoles; p. 79: Courtesy of Relais St. Germain; p. 85: Courtesy of L'Apostrophe ; p. 94: Courtesy of Bocuse; p. 101: Courtesy of Le Grand Restaurant/ Khanh Renaud; p. 112: Courtesy of Ground Control/ GEORGES SAILLARD; p. 115: Courtesy of Hôtel du Nord/ Valérie Manikowski; p. 116: Courtesy of Rosa Bonheur / Pascal Montary; p. 118: © Petr Kovalenkov / Shutterstock.com; p. 131: © Page Light Studios / Shutterstock.com; p. 134: © Irina Kzan / Shutterstock.com; p. 143: © Marina99; p. 146: © Nadiia_foto / Shutterstock.com; p. 154: © Gilmanshin / Shutterstock.com; p. 156: © Malcangi Valentina / Shutterstock.com; p. 159: © Vincent Anderlucci; p. 161: © Claude Valette; p. 171: © Vincent Anderlucci; p. 179: © Markel Redondo; p. 184: © Curtis MacNewton; p. 187: © Paulo Valdivieso; p. 194: © Yann Caradec; p. 198: © Netfalls Remy Musser; p. 210: © gurezende / Shutterstock.com; p. 214: © VanderWolf Images / Shutterstock.com; p. 218: © Stefano Ember / Shutterstock.com; p. 221: © craigfinlay; p. 232: © mary416; p. 233: © Katchooo; p. 237: © Philippe Agnifili; p. 241: © Elisabeth Blanchet; p. 242: © Gideon; p. 250: © Gilmanshin / Shutterstock.com; p. 253: © V_E / Shutterstock.com; p. 256: © Dutourdumonde Photography / Shutterstock.com; p. 261: © RossHelen / Shutterstock.com; p. 262: © Yuri Turkov / Shutterstock.com; p. 267: © Ozgur Gonen / Shutterstock.com; p. 270: © cdrin / Shutterstock.com; p. 272: © Birute Vijeikiene / Shutterstock.com; p. 273: © Kiev.Victor / Shutterstock.com; p. 276: © EQRoy / Shutterstock.com; p. 278: © Kiev.Victor / Shutterstock.com; p. 280: © daryl_mitchell.

Frommer's EasyGuide to Paris, 8th Edition

Published by

FROMMER MEDIA LLC

Copyright © 2022 by Frommer Media LLC. All rights reserved. No part of this publication may be repro-
duced, stored in a retrieval system, or transmitted in any form or by any means, electronic, mechanical,
photocopying, recording, scanning or otherwise, except as permitted under Sections 107 or 108 of the
1976 United States Copyright Act, without the prior written permission of the Publisher. Requests to the
Publisher for permission should be addressed to support@frommermedia.com.

Frommer's is a registered trademark of Arthur Frommer. Frommer Media LLC is not associated with any
product or vendor mentioned in this book.

ISBN 978-1-62887-523-2 (paper), 978-1-62887-524-9 (e-book)

Editorial Director: Pauline Frommer
Editor: Linda Cabasin
Production Editor: Cheryl Lenser
Cartographer: Liz Puhl
Photo Editor: Meghan Lamb
Indexer: Cheryl Lenser
Cover Design: Dave Riedy

Front cover photo © shishic / iStockphoto
Back cover photo © Shutterstock / Olesya Kuznetsova

For information on our other products or services, see www.frommers.com.

FrommerMedia LLC also publishes its books in a variety of electronic formats. Some content that appears
in print may not be available in electronic formats.

Manufactured in the United States of America

5 4 3 2 1

ABOUT THE AUTHOR

British-born **Anna E. Brooke** moved to Paris in 2000 and hasn't looked back since. She is now a full-fledged bohemian, juggling life between freelance travel writing, songwriting, and authoring children's books. She has written seven guides for Frommer's and is the Paris expert for the UK's best-selling *Sunday Times Travel*.

ABOUT THE FROMMER TRAVEL GUIDES

For most of the past 50 years, Frommer's has been the leading series of travel guides in North America, accounting for as many as 24% of all guidebooks sold. I think I know why.

Though we hope our books are entertaining, we nevertheless deal with travel in a serious fashion. Our guidebooks have never looked on such journeys as a mere recreation, but as a far more important human function, a time of learning and introspection, an essential part of a civilized life. We stress the culture, lifestyle, history, and beliefs of the destinations we cover, and urge our readers to seek out people and new ideas as the chief rewards of travel.

We have never shied from controversy. We have, from the beginning, encouraged our authors to be intensely judgmental, critical—both pro and con—in their comments, and wholly independent. Our only clients are our readers, and we have triggered the ire of countless prominent sorts, from a tourist newspaper we called "practically worthless" (it unsuccessfully sued us) to the many rip-offs we've condemned.

And because we believe that travel should be available to everyone regardless of their incomes, we have always been cost-conscious at every level of expenditure. Though we have broadened our recommendations beyond the budget category, we insist that every lodging we include be sensibly priced. We use every form of media to assist our readers, and are particularly proud of our feisty daily website, the award-winning Frommers.com.

I have high hopes for the future of Frommer's. May these guidebooks, in all the years ahead, continue to reflect the joy of travel and the freedom that travel represents. May they always pursue a cost-conscious path, so that people of all incomes can enjoy the rewards of travel. And may they create, for both the traveler and the persons among whom we travel, a community of friends, where all human beings live in harmony and peace.

Arthur Frommer